The Scent of Scandal

The Florida History and Culture Series

UNIVERSITY PRESS OF FLORIDA

Florida A&M University, Tallahassee
Florida Atlantic University, Boca Raton
Florida Gulf Coast University, Ft. Myers
Florida International University, Miami
Florida State University, Tallahassee
New College of Florida, Sarasota
University of Central Florida, Orlando
University of Florida, Gainesville
University of North Florida, Jacksonville
University of South Florida, Tampa
University of West Florida, Pensacola

The greatest orchid discovery in a century traveled from Moyobamba, Peru, to Sarasota, Florida—and then plunged its admirers into the criminal justice system.

Illustration by Dan Morris.

CRAIG PITTMAN

THE
SCENT OF
SCANDAL

Greed, Betrayal, and the
World's Most Beautiful Orchid

*Foreword by Raymond Arsenault
and Gary R. Mormino*

UNIVERSITY PRESS OF FLORIDA

Gainesville/Tallahassee/Tampa/Boca Raton
Pensacola/Orlando/Miami/Jacksonville/Ft. Myers/Sarasota

Copyright 2012 by Craig Pittman
All rights reserved
Printed in the United States of America on acid-free, recycled paper

17 16 15 14 13 12   6 5 4 3 2 1

A record of cataloging-in-publication data is available
from the Library of Congress.
ISBN 978-0-8130-3974-9

The University Press of Florida is the scholarly publishing agency for the State
University System of Florida, comprising Florida A&M University, Florida
Atlantic University, Florida Gulf Coast University, Florida International
University, Florida State University, New College of Florida, University of
Central Florida, University of Florida, University of North Florida, University of
South Florida, and University of West Florida.

University Press of Florida
15 Northwest 15th Street
Gainesville, FL 32611-2079
http://www.upf.com

For Mom—

Does this make up for all those times that

I accidentally mowed over your flowerbed?

It was the founding father of Chinese thought, Confucius
. . . who first celebrated the orchid for its special qualities,
and awarded it primacy in the pantheon of plants. What
particularly attracted him was its gently insinuating perfume.
Understated yet pervasive, its fragrance symbolized for
him the virtuous and wise, who make their presence and
superiority felt while never seeking to oppress others.

Luigi Berliocchi, *The Orchid in Lore and Legend*

As dead flies give perfume a bad smell, so a little folly
outweighs wisdom and honor.

Ecclesiastes 10:1

Contents

Foreword

The Scent of Scandal: Greed, Betrayal, and the World's Most Beautiful Orchid is the latest volume in a series devoted to the study of Florida History and Culture. During the past half century, the burgeoning population and increased national and international visibility of Florida have sparked a great deal of popular interest in the state's past, present, and future. As the favorite destination of countless tourists and as the new home for millions of retirees and transplants, modern Florida has become a demographic, political, and cultural bellwether. Florida has also emerged as a popular subject and setting for scholars and writers. The Florida History and Culture Series provides an attractive and accessible format for Florida-related books. From killer hurricanes to disputed elections, from tales of the Everglades to profiles of Sunbelt cities, the topics covered by the more than forty books published so far represent a broad spectrum of regional history and culture.

The University Press of Florida is committed to the creation of an eclectic but carefully crafted set of books that will provide the field of Florida studies with a new focus and that will encourage Florida researchers and writers to consider the broader implications and context of their work. The series includes standard academic monographs as well as works of synthesis, memoirs, and anthologies. And while the series features books of historical interest, authors researching Florida's environment, politics, literature, and popular or material culture are encouraged to submit their manuscripts as well. Each book offers a distinct personality and voice, but the ultimate goal of the series is to foster a sense of community and collaboration among Florida scholars.

In *The Scent of Scandal*, Craig Pittman confirms the old adage that truth is sometimes stranger than fiction. One of Florida's most respected environmental writers and the author of two previous books published in the Florida History and Culture Series, Pittman applies his considerable skills as an investigative reporter to a complicated saga of greed, betrayal, and criminality. No garden-variety tale, this story takes us from tropical rain forests to federal courtrooms, introducing an extraordinary cast of characters along the way.

At the center of it all is "the world's most beautiful orchid," pursued or protected by adventurers, orchid growers, botany professors, federal prosecutors, investigators, and government bureaucrats. Thanks to Pittman's careful scrutiny and eloquent exposition, the evolving and sometimes bizarre relationships among these characters emerge from the shadows of the Sunshine State, casting light on the economics and psychology of the commodification of nature. Truth, beauty, and the human condition—all rooted in Florida's fertile soil, now revealingly turned over by a master storyteller.

Raymond Arsenault and Gary R. Mormino
Series Editors

Cast of Characters

Chuck Acker, a Wisconsin orchid dealer

John Atwood, an orchid expert from Vermont

John Beckner, Selby Gardens' orchid curator

Libby Besse, an accidental orchid discoverer

Eric Christenson, an orchid taxonomy expert

Jim Clarkson, an American Orchid Society judge

Elinor Colbourn, a federal prosecutor

Peter Croezen, a Canadian orchid expert

Stig Dalström, Selby's orchid illustrator

Glen Decker, a New York orchid entrepreneur

Calaway Dodson, Selby's first executive director

Barbara Ellison, a photographer married to Michael Kovach

Shawn Farr, a chief operating officer

Joel Fedder, a Selby board member

Jack Fernandez, a Tampa defense attorney

Roddy Gabel, the federal government's top orchid expert

Ted Green, a Hawaiian orchid grower

Robert Hearn, a Tampa defense attorney

Wesley Higgins, Selby's director of systematics

Bruce Holst, the editor of *Selbyana*

Mary Holt, a U.S. Fish and Wildlife Service investigator

Dave Hunt, a Texas orchid grower

Mark Johnson, an American Orchid Society judge from Florida

Harold Koopowitz, a professor and editor of *Orchid Digest*

Michael Kovach, a Virginia orchid collector

Caren Lobo, a bookseller and Selby board member

Meg Lowman, Selby's popular executive director

Carl Luer, an ex-surgeon and founder of Selby Gardens

Harry Luther, the world's foremost bromeliad expert

Alfredo Manrique, a Peruvian orchid grower

Faustino Medina, the proprietor of a roadside flower stand

Stephen Merryday, a federal judge

Angela Mirro, a botanical illustrator

Chady Moore, Lee Moore's wife

Lee Moore, the man known as "The Adventurer"

George Norris, a Texas orchid broker who types in ALL CAPS

Robert Rivas, Meg Lowman's attorney

Dr. Isaias Rolando, a Peruvian orchid collector

Bob Scully, Selby Gardens' board chairman

Manuel Arias Silva, a Peruvian teacher-turned-orchidist

Manolo Arias Silva, his son

Marni Turkel, a California orchid hobbyist

Karol Villena, Renato Villena's daughter and salesperson

Renato Villena, a Peruvian nursery proprietor

The Scent of Scandal

Prologue

The Choice of Snakes

If, when you finish it, you think the mystery has
been solved, all I have to say is you don't know
a mystery when you see one.

Rex Stout, *Black Orchids*

The bride glided across the lawn, her lacy white dress billowing like a sail. A sea breeze ruffled her red hair and stirred the leaves of the nearby banyan tree. Sunlight danced across Sarasota Bay, making the water glitter like distant diamonds.

The string quartet struck up *Pachelbel's Canon*—not the usual music cue—so some of us guests sitting in the neat rows of folding chairs were slow to catch on. Then we noticed the awestruck look on the groom's face and stood, catching our breath at the loveliness of the scene.

Decades later, long after the marriage that began in those moments had ended in divorce, my wife and I compared our memories of that golden day when our friends tied the knot. We agreed that it had been the perfect outdoor wedding, primarily because it had taken place in such a perfect setting, the Marie Selby Botanical Gardens in Sarasota.

But as Adam and Eve could testify, even the most perfect garden is likely to have a snake in it somewhere.

That perfect Selby Gardens wedding is far from a unique experience. Brides from all over the Sarasota region searching for a distinctive place to wed are drawn like a magnet to its 9 ½ acres of well-tended waterfront, about an hour south of Tampa. Selby offers not only a lush landscape for the ceremony, but also an elegant mansion for the reception afterward.

"The wedding is all about theater," a Selby employee explained once. "That's what the garden is—it's a theater."

This was not just any old playhouse, either. Selby Gardens has long been one of Sarasota's prime tourist attractions, ranking alongside the house of circus magnate John Ringling, the aquaria at the Mote Marine Laboratory, and, of course, the sugar-white beaches. Selby draws some 130,000 visitors a year. They come to gaze in amazement at its bromeliads, its Venus flytraps, and, especially, Selby's vast orchid collection, marveling at the vivid colors and fantastic shapes.

Orchids have always been Selby's specialty. Selby's staff of experts has been renowned among orchid fanciers worldwide for their ability to identify and classify orchids. When its Orchid Identification Center opened in 1976, it was the first in the nation.

But the most important orchid in Selby Gardens' history is not on view anywhere. It's the one that made headlines around the country. The one that cost the gardens hundreds of thousands of dollars in donations and created intense internal turmoil. The one that led to search warrants, a grand jury investigation, even criminal charges.

The one that blossomed into a scandal so big that it damaged Selby's carefully tended reputation.

Over the past twenty-five years, as a reporter for the *Sarasota Herald-Tribune* and then for the *St. Petersburg Times,* I have written my share of stories about Selby Gardens. A scientific institution that also functions as a tourist attraction and a wedding chapel will always make for good copy.

I can't claim to be an expert on orchids—I have trouble keeping a front-porch tub of Home Depot annuals alive—but I know a hot story when I see one. In 2002, when the Selby scandal broke, I was fortunate enough to be allowed to cover the unfolding drama for the *Times,* Florida's largest newspaper. Later I wrote a long piece about the case for *Sarasota* magazine. In reporting those stories, I interviewed many of the principals, read the documents, witnessed the courtroom denouement.

Floridians are accustomed to political scandals, business scandals, even sex scandals. But a scientific scandal? A floral scandal in the Land of Flowers? That was something new—and not just for Florida. Selby's involvement made this case unique in the annals of American justice.

As I delved into this story more deeply, I realized that orchid fans resemble baseball fans, nearly as besotted with talking and writing about their pastime as they are by the pastime itself. They produce books, magazines, newsletters, and reams and reams of Internet chatter. The only thing missing is a box score.

Every orchid person I contacted talked to me freely about their experiences and opinions, often at great length. Many shared documents and photos with me, along with their own theories about what everything meant. By comparison, the law enforcement sources I contacted mostly refused to talk at all. They also dragged their feet about turning over files I requested under the Freedom of Information Act.

When I began writing this book, I thought I already knew the story pretty well. But as I dug into the details, I saw new twists and turns. At one point, someone I interviewed told me that I really didn't know much at all. I had to admit that the more people I interviewed, the more I felt as if I were watching a performance of *Rashomon* in a hall of mirrors.

Everyone I talked to agreed that there was a snake in the garden at Selby, but they couldn't agree on what it was. There were quite a few to choose from: Greed? Lust for fame? Jealousy? Ambition? Hubris? Or could it be mere bureaucratic meanness, a senseless devotion to nonsensical rules?

Adding to the intrigue, of course, was that the flower at the heart of the legal struggle was so big and breathtaking. Its bloom was as big as a man's hand. Its vivid colors changed shades as the flower aged. And that shape! It looked like someone had grafted a pelican's beak onto a vintage DeLorean with its gull-wing doors open wide.

But the hardest question of all was: How could so much trouble stem from a flower? Selby's orchid experts hailed it as the most astounding discovery in a century. They were so enthralled by the flower's beauty that they failed to anticipate the legal consequences of their actions.

"What we weren't aware of was how we could get caught up in this web," a soft-spoken Selby orchid expert named John Atwood told me after armed investigators showed up at his rural farmhouse. "It was a shock."

But rival orchid expert Eric Christenson, a longtime critic of Selby, scoffed at any claims of innocent intentions gone awry.

"These people are idiots," he said. "Everyone involved knew it was illegal."

1

The Most Beautiful Party in Town

I never before realized that the story of a
botanical garden . . . could read as if it were
the drama of a pulp crime novel.

Margaret "Meg" Lowman, *It's a Jungle Up There*

As the party swirled around her, Meg Lowman had no idea how much peril she was about to face. She believed she had climbed to the pinnacle of success.

Actually, she was standing on a precipice.

The soiree Lowman was presiding over on this warm spring evening, the annual Orchid Ball, had a reputation as Sarasota's biggest black-tie event. The local newspaper's society columnist had dubbed it "the most beautiful party in Sarasota." It was also Selby Gardens' biggest fund-raiser. The staff worked on it for months, figuring out how to feed and entertain hundreds of wealthy and well-connected people, coaxing them to pull out their wallets.

Since it was an outdoor event, intended to showcase the gardens as well as put the attendees in a giving mood, the weather conditions had to be dry. Sometimes it had been cold enough to prompt the women to get their furs out of storage. Sometimes it had been so hot that no one wanted to dance or even move around. But always, for nineteen years, the ball had remained precipitation-free. It became something of a joke among the employees: "Marie Selby would *never* let it rain on the Orchid Ball!"

But on the ball's twentieth anniversary in 2001, the ghost let them down. Just as the guests arrived, the skies opened up and rain fell in cold sheets.

The Selby staff, many of them clad in kimonos in keeping with the theme of "Under an Asian Moon," splashed through the mud to set up tents over the tables.

In 2002, though, the ghost of Marie Selby was apparently back on the job. The *Sarasota Herald-Tribune's* society columnist later declared that the 2002 Orchid Ball was "a perfect no-rain 'Rendezvous in Rio' right here in our own exotic backyard. . . . A capacity crowd filled a tent flushed with every color in the spectrum that produced a fiesta atmosphere throughout . . . with ribbons, banners, flags, and Carmen Miranda–type mannequins."

More than four hundred people showed up for the shindig, handing their keys to the valet out front, walking through the stately mansion that served as the reception area, then emerging from the back door to stroll along the torch-lit path past the koi ponds to the main party area. Defying the humidity, women in sparkling gowns twirled on the checkerboard dance floor. Paunchy men in tuxedos knocked back cocktails under the giant banyan tree. Real estate moguls and mortgage-rate gamblers rubbed shoulders with theater angels and gallery geeks. Everyone munched on conch fritters, nut-encrusted sea bass, and Brazilian-style beef. It was the quintessential society soiree in a town rich enough and artsy enough to support its own opera company and annual film festival, a town so diverse that it provided a muse for both cynical noir grandmaster John D. MacDonald and silly comedic genius Pee-Wee Herman.

The one anomaly in this scene was Lowman herself. She wasn't one of the tanned-and-toned trophy wives. She wasn't one of the elderly widows who bankrolled causes around town. Nor was she a go-getter Chamber of Commerce type with power pearls and a gym membership. Although orchids galore decorated the tables, the most exotic flower of the night had to be Lowman.

At forty-eight years old, she wore her straight blond hair in an easy-care style that framed her oval face. She had a prominent chin, a flat nose, and a lean and muscular frame. Although she wore an elegant gown, she would have been more comfortable in filthy khakis and muddy boots. Her eyes were the giveaway. They were bright blue, filled with curiosity and an impish sense of humor. Behind them, though, lay a steely determination to overcome whatever challenge she faced.

Lowman was actually the biggest celebrity at the party. She was one of the pioneers in her field, the study of life in the world's jungle canopies—a field that, until she came along, had been dominated by men. She had written a memoir called *Life in the Treetops: Adventures of a Woman in Field Biology*, about trying to juggle her duties as a mom while pursuing her research.

At Selby Gardens, Meg Lowman emphasized forest canopy research and conservation—to the consternation of orchid enthusiasts. Photo courtesy of the *St. Petersburg Times*.

When Yale University Press published it in 1999, the book earned a front-page rave in the *New York Times'* Sunday book section. The reviewer called it "a funny, unassuming, and deeply idiosyncratic chronicle of her trials and triumphs."

As she made plain in her book, Lowman was a resourceful woman who was as comfortable living outside civilization as she was living in it. As a child in upstate New York, she packed her bedroom with birds' nests, bugs, rocks, and shells she had found. In the fifth grade, her wildflower collection earned her second place in a state science fair, and her course was set. She went on to earn a master's degree in Scotland, then traveled alone to Australia in the 1970s to study for her Ph.D. There she launched her first treetop studies in its tropical forests. To prepare for scaling the trees, she solicited advice from cave explorers on the proper rigging for her climbs. She sewed her first harness out of seatbelt webbing.

Her biggest scientific challenge, she wrote in her book, was the 200-foot-tall gympie-gympie, also known as the "giant stinging tree." Its leaves and twigs are covered with fine, hollow hairs that contain a powerful poison. Every time she climbed one to study its insects, no matter what precautions she took, she would always come away with her hands covered in red inflammations. Over time, Lowman wrote, she got used to the fiery stings. However, when she showed up one day to find the ground around the trees covered in highly venomous Australian brown snakes, she tiptoed away and picked a new study area that appeared to be snakeless.

She was willing to make sacrifices for her science, even sacrifices of an intensely personal nature. At one point her research led her to spend two weeks in a Cameroon jungle living with three dozen male researchers and a score of local pygmy tribesmen. The researchers "slept in hammocks, butt to butt, 40 people in a row," she told a reporter later. When she went to take a shower, that's when all the men decided it was time to climb on the roof and work on the pipes. She stuck it out anyway.

In Australia she married a sheep rancher and had two children, whom she toted along on her forest expeditions, scrambling down to the ground to nurse them and then climbing back into the treetops again. But she repeatedly failed in her efforts to reconcile her scientific pursuits with the Aussie ideal of a subservient housewife. Her father-in-law, in particular, couldn't understand why she didn't make it her top priority to have a hot meal waiting on the table when her man walked in the door. Ultimately the couple divorced.

In short, Lowman had plenty of experience in dealing with any hazard, from pygmies and piranhas to male chauvinist pigs. She was probably the only person at the Orchid Ball who had ever eaten crickets as hors d'oeuvres, not to mention the only mother there whose sons had adopted a pet tarantula. Very little could faze her—she thought.

In 1992, after she had spent a stint teaching at Williams College, Selby Gardens hired her as conservation director. Lowman didn't know anyone in Florida, and the job description gave little detail as to her duties. She took the job because she could use the position to further her rain forest research. She could also use it as a convenient place to roost while converting her personal journals into her first book. As an added benefit, Sarasota offered a good school system for her two boys.

Lowman's two worlds collided seven years later. She had just returned from grubbing around in the tropical mud of Queensland for two weeks, studying seedlings as part of a long-term project on rain forest biodiversity. Thanks to the glowing reviews of *Life in the Treetops*, she flew straight from Australia to Los Angeles to meet with Hollywood agents who were interested in turning her life story into a movie.

Lowman was soaking all the jungle crud off in a bubble bath at the Beverly Hills Wilshire Hotel when the phone rang. The call came from Sarasota. Selby's trustee board wanted to promote her to executive director.

Lowman hesitated. She hadn't planned to stay at Selby longer than five years, and she was already going on seven. But she had met a new love, a gray-bearded divorce attorney from St. Petersburg named Michael Brown, who was six years her senior.

Brown first encountered Lowman on a blind date. It wasn't your usual dinner-and-a-movie outing. She took him to Selby Gardens, and they climbed a tree. Brown became so entranced by her that he accompanied her on a trip to the Peruvian rain forest. They had a magical time, listening to jaguars howling at 2:00 a.m. He got along well with her sons, too. So he moved his practice to Sarasota, and they wed.

Still, Lowman had figured on leaving Selby and returning to teaching while continuing her research. Taking this promotion would mean cutting back on her scientific studies and taking on more administrative duties. Worse, she had no experience running a botanical garden. In fact, she had never run anything bigger than a sheep ranch. It sounded like a recipe for disaster.

She explained to the search committee that her degree was in botany, not business. They said they were fine with that. They promised to hire a chief operating officer to handle Selby's day-to-day operations. What they didn't mention was that they had run advertisements for an executive director in the *Wall Street Journal* and horticultural publications and were discouraged by the quality of applicants. Then someone on the board came up with the idea of promoting their resident celebrity scientist. What the board members told her they wanted was "a CEO with scientific credibility who could articulate a botanical mission to donors," Lowman wrote later.

Wooing the donors turned out to be a major part of the job—and a major downfall of her predecessor, she was told by the board members. He was a scientist, too. Like Lowman, he had never run a botanical garden before taking over Selby.

In his five years at Selby, Lowman's predecessor "had experienced personality conflicts with donors, his budget had been in the red, [and] deferred maintenance was at a critical stage," Lowman was told by the board. How critical? The roof of the administration building leaked badly, and a family of raccoons had moved into the third floor.

So when he left, the board decided their new leader was someone already on the fifty-member staff, someone who had made a splash in the book-publishing world and might even become a darling of Hollywood. Stories about and reviews of *Life in the Treetops* mentioned Selby, showing she could really put the place on the map. She had already been featured in a children's book and profiled in a *National Geographic* television special. The woman was a guaranteed publicity generator. Surely, they thought, that would lead to more grants and donations.

Lowman concluded that what the board really had in mind was a CEO who could serve as "a cheerleader for plants." So she took the job—and, as with the jungle flora and fauna she studied, Lowman figured out how to adapt to this new world she now inhabited.

She gave up swinging in the trees to give speeches to the Rotary Club. She hired Selby's first marketing director to think of ways to promote the place. She hired a development director to line up more donations and grants. She dedicated herself to something she called "friend-raising"—making personal connections with people who were in a position to hand over big sums of cash to Selby.

She took a management course at Duke University and signed up for a program created by the Florida Chamber of Commerce called Leadership Florida, where up-and-coming business executives and civic activists met state officials and industry leaders and studied the Big Issues. Most of the other classmates in Leadership Florida were pro-business Republicans whose politics didn't jibe with her more liberal leanings. She struck up a friendship with the other big liberal in the class, a frizzy-haired lawyer from Tallahassee named Robert Rivas. He had a sardonic sense of humor and sat on the board of the state chapter of the American Civil Liberties Union. The contacts she made in Leadership Florida would turn out to be important ones for her future—though not in the way she expected.

By 2002, the veteran tree climber had become skilled as a social climber. Her face became the face of Selby, the two synonymous in the public mind. With her in charge, each Orchid Ball became like a gift to the community's leaders, a magical evening to show them how special Selby was—if they kept the dollars flowing.

Now, as she greeted all the guests at the rain-free Orchid Ball, Lowman could reflect on three years of what seemed to her to be spectacular success.

Thanks to increased donations and grants, the gardens' budget was back in the black. It would finish its fiscal year showing revenue of more than $3.4 million and a profit of $400,000. Given the economic turmoil that had plagued the nation following the 9/11 terrorist attacks the previous fall, this seemed to her like a major victory. She had boosted the paying membership numbers by nearly 50 percent in the past three years. The number of private events such as weddings that paid to use the gardens' facilities had increased to the point that it was yielding $20,000 more in profit than it had in 1999. Clearly this garden was growing.

Lowman wasn't just focused on Selby's future, either. She had taken steps to renew a connection to Selby's historic past by inviting Carlyle "Carl" Luer to rejoin the board of trustees. Luer, a retired doctor in his eighties, had been one of Selby's original board members when it first opened but he had quit during a dispute twenty years before. At Lowman's request, he readily agreed to return to the garden he loved so much.

There were other marks of success that gave her a sense of a job well done. Lowman was in heavy demand as a speaker, not just around Sarasota but throughout the country. Wherever she went, she talked about that unknown world in the treetops and how important canopy science was to saving the rain forest—and burnished Selby's gleaming reputation as a scientific institution, of course.

During the Orchid Ball, the newspaper's society columnist asked Lowman for a quote about the party. Lowman replied that when she first arrived in Sarasota in 1992, she regarded science as the sole answer to the world's ecological problems.

"But I now realize that through events such as this, and the fantastic volunteers here at Selby, there are other ways to spread our conservation message," Lowman said over the clatter of glasses and silverware.

Still, there were intimations of the trouble that was brewing, hints that flickered around the edges of this perfect party like the shadows cast by the tiki torches.

Lowman felt like she was pouring her heart and soul into the job, all day, every day. Before, when Lowman spent days on end in the jungle, she could take her kids with her. Now she spent so much time working—both in the office and out promoting Selby—that she started missing family events. She missed a parent-teacher conference here, a sailing regatta there—precious moments of family time lost to the grind of the job.

Not everything was rosy at work, either. Some Selby staffers weren't thrilled with the changes she had made. They complained that she frequently told employees what they wanted to hear and then went her own way. They grumbled about how her pursuit of dollars had boosted the number of visitors lined up for admission each day, which would probably lead to idiot tourists trampling some of the gardens' plants. They regarded her as disorganized and flighty, changing direction frequently or failing to give them any in the first place. They were convinced that the only cause she was truly interested in promoting was Meg Lowman, not Selby Gardens. Inevitably, gossip spread that Lowman's efforts to woo some male donors led to wooing of a more physical kind.

The people most skeptical about Lowman's changes were her fellow scientists, all of them men. They had chafed under her supervision when she served as conservation director because they thought she focused on her own pursuits at the expense of the work in their fields.

They were no happier that she now ran the whole garden, especially when she came up with a new mission statement for the institution. The mission statement made no mention of Selby's traditional focus on their specialties. Instead it embraced a broader vision about ecology and conservation. Some Selby employees resigned in protest when she was promoted, allowing her to replace them with her own picks.

Since 1992, the scientists had primarily worked in a converted one-story house at 711 South Palm Avenue, a block away from the main garden at 811 South Palm. To get from the house, built in the 1950s, to the main part of the garden wasn't easy. It required crossing the four lanes of traffic on U.S. 41, one of the two main highways through Sarasota. The scientists tended to stay on their side unless they had some reason to visit the greenhouses that were part of the main garden. The physical separation led to them thinking of their work as completely unrelated to the tourism and wedding-related garden activities.

The other staffers referred to the scientists' building simply as "7-11." Lowman privately dubbed it "the Far Side," not just because of its location. The name also referred to Gary Larson's comic strip, which frequently featured gags about goofy scientists performing odd experiments in beaker-filled laboratories.

Inside 711 Palm Avenue, past the parquet floor at the entrance, lay a rabbit warren of cubicles and computers. Some scientists studied bromeliads, nothing else. Some glued pressed plant specimens to acid-free paper and filed them away in row after row of cabinets. Back in what should have been the garage was Selby's vast "spirit collection"—racks of glass jars containing thousands of plants pickled in a 70 percent alcohol solution.

At the heart of 7-11 were the rooms containing the Orchid Identification Center, or OIC for short. For the past two years the head of the OIC had been Wesley Higgins, although technically his title was "director of systematics." Higgins was a plainspoken, baggy-eyed man with a penchant for Hawaiian shirts. He sported a handlebar mustache that would have made him the envy of any barbershop quartet. Sometimes he was invited to the Orchid Ball to help schmooze donors, but not the 2002 one. That was fine with him. He preferred to spend the evening at home with his wife.

Higgins had a background that was different from any other Selby scientist: he had spent twenty-six years in the Coast Guard, rising to the rank of master chief petty officer. He spent most of that time in avionics repair. But orchids had been his hobby for more than three decades, and he frequently served as a judge at orchid shows. When he retired from the Coast Guard in 1993, Higgins decided to turn his hobby into his vocation. He earned a doctorate in horticulture. Then, in 2000, Lowman hired him to run the OIC. He had worked hard to get to this, his dream job. He had no idea what a nightmare it would soon become.

To Lowman, the guys over on the Far Side, and particularly at the OIC, were so focused on their special interests that they failed to appreciate the need to support the whole garden. When Lowman's new marketing director tried to enlist their help in promoting the garden, they grumbled and were reluctant to cooperate. She found orchid fans like Higgins particularly baffling. Orchid people were united in the passion they felt about their flowers, yet their world was riven by bitter rivalries she barely understood. She believed scientists should work together to find consensus. Surely all the schisms among the orchid worshippers couldn't be good for long-term scientific progress.

Actually Lowman didn't see much of her scientific staff. She was so busy promoting Selby that she was frequently absent from Selby's grounds, giving talks or participating in conferences. However, despite its promise to Lowman in 1999, the board had never gotten around to hiring a chief operating officer to run the day-to-day operations. That meant that if Lowman didn't handle a problem, it didn't get handled.

Into this leadership vacuum stepped the new chairman of the Selby board, Robert M. "Bob" Scully Jr. He was, as it happened, one of those orchid men whom Lowman didn't understand.

Scully, a tall and slender man with a head of wavy hair, maintained a neatly trimmed mustache that wouldn't have looked out of place on a fussbudget floorwalker in a 1940s screwball comedy. However, the mustache was the only frivolous thing about him. Scully had the confident manner of someone who knows what he knows and is convinced of his own correctness. Anyone who dared to challenge him would be pinned down with an unnerving blue-eyed stare. He did not suffer fools, gladly or any other way.

With his height and his bearing, Scully cut an imposing figure wherever he went, including at the Orchid Ball—although he would admit some time later, "I don't fancy myself a party boy." The society columnist noted in her write-up about the party that Scully had been present, granting him a rare bit of bold-faced notoriety, but she couldn't squeeze a quote out of him. The

Bob Scully had spent years running his own orchid business and did not think much of the way Lowman was running Selby Gardens. Photo courtesy of Bob Scully.

columnist grumbled later that she knew everyone of consequence in Sarasota—but she didn't know Scully at all.

Scully, who was closing in on sixty, was far more comfortable working with plants than with people. He had virtually grown up in a greenhouse. In 1945 his father, Robert Scully Sr., had partnered with a Florida surgeon to launch a small orchid-growing operation on a 10-acre site west of Miami International Airport. By the time Scully's father died in 1986, it was the largest orchid business in the Southeast. Jones & Scully shipped flowers all over the world. The elder Scully concocted colorful hybrids to boost sales, and also helped devise the judging system for international orchid competitions.

The younger Scully started working for his dad "as a tow-headed youth," he recalled. After he earned a master's degree in horticulture, he came home to take over the family business in 1977. He tried to grow the business even more by creating the industry's first mass-marketing program, selling hybrids, seedlings, and clones through nationwide garden centers. His aim, he said, was to take the mystique out of orchid growing "so that the average guy on the street will finally perceive that this product is affordable to him, as well as to the affluent." He also tried going beyond orchids by offering floral pieces of all kinds for use in the growing field of interior decoration.

Scully would have kept on running the family business in Miami if not for two things. In the mid-1990s, he used Benlate, a common fungicide made by DuPont, on his plants. But as he and thousands of farmers soon learned, some formulas of Benlate were poisonous not just to pests but also to their plants. Scully lost millions of dollars' worth of orchid stock, some of them flowers that had been grown by his family for decades. Then, just as he was recovering from that blow, along came an even bigger one. Hurricane Andrew swept through South Florida in 1992, flattening the brand-new greenhouses Scully had built when he moved the business to the Redland area south of Miami.

Scully and his wife, Sue, tried moving to Georgia. They found Savannah dominated by people obsessed with golf, a pastime neither of them enjoyed. So they moved again, this time settling in Sarasota in 1997.

When word got around that Scully was in Sarasota, he got a call from a mild-mannered, soft-spoken scientist named John Atwood. The shy and awkward Atwood had run Selby's Orchid Identification Center for nearly twenty years before resigning to move back to Vermont and care for his ailing mother.

Like Scully, Atwood's fascination with orchids began when he was just a boy. His grandmother had grown orchids on their farm in Vermont, and he became so enchanted by the flowers that he sold his bicycle to buy one from a catalogue for ten dollars—a lot of money for an orchid in 1959. In college, Atwood aimed first for a career in music, but then decided he didn't like the career prospects: marching band director or church organist. So he switched to botany, earned a doctorate at Florida State, and became a world-renowned expert in a particular type of orchid, which happened to be the type that his grandmother grew. They were known as slipper orchids because the lip of the flower forms a pouch that resembles a woman's shoe.

"They're almost animal," Atwood said once. "They are statuesque; they have a personality."

Atwood still worked part-time at the OIC, and he was sure someone with Scully's expertise could help improve Selby Gardens. He believed volunteering at Selby would give Scully a way to continue working with orchids without taking on all the headaches of running a big business.

Atwood did a superb sales job. After lunch with him, Scully joined the platoon of volunteers who helped keep Selby running.

But soon Scully clashed with Lowman's predecessor as executive director. Scully had devoted himself to fixing up the old greenhouses that had been built back when Selby first opened. He would show up in the late afternoon as the staff was packing up to head home. He would toil late into the shadowy hours rearranging benches and, in his view, lining up everything to make it easier to spot and treat plant diseases, pick up trash, and generally make the place function more efficiently, just the way he would have at Jones & Scully.

Scully was proud of his work. One day, with the permission of the scientist in charge of the greenhouses, Scully led a small group of Selby board members on a tour to show them what he'd done and what still needed doing.

The director, already on thin ice with the board, didn't like that. The director sent Scully a letter admonishing him for giving the tour. The letter also mentioned rumors that Scully wanted to take over as executive director. Worst of all was a complaint filed against Scully by one of the female staff members, accusing him of sexual harassment with "comments or discussions of a personal nature." There were also complaints that other employees and volunteers found him "autocratic," the letter said, because "you act like you're the boss." As a result of the complaints, the director told Scully he could no longer set foot in the greenhouses without prior approval from the staff.

The director subsequently sent Scully a card apologizing for his "insensitive" letter, and the harassment allegation was ruled unfounded. It turned out that all Scully had done was advise a woman who appeared to be coming down with the flu that she should take Vitamin C "until your pee runs golden."

So after Lowman took charge of Selby, she sent Scully a letter apologizing for the way he had been treated. She invited him to come back to the garden, just as she had invited Carl Luer back. Scully took a seat on Selby's board, and then, in the fall of 2001, he was elected chairman.

Scully was different from the other board members, though. It wasn't just that the other board members found him to be abrupt and socially stiff. Most of them had lived in the area for years and worked in real estate or banking. Through their abundant personal relationships and business contacts, they could tap any number of people for contributions to Selby.

Not Scully. He was still new in town and had no contacts outside the orchid business.

Everyone praised Scully's knowledge of orchids. He frequently was asked to judge at various orchid shows, which meant that he landed in the middle of what he called "orchid politics." He also ran a small consulting business called Tiger Orchids, which occasionally required him to visit his clients' greenhouses to advise them on problems. Except for those duties, though, he wasn't busy at all.

That meant he had the time to spend at Selby that Lowman did not. Wherever he went, he noticed problems she hadn't taken care of—sprinkler systems that didn't work right, fungus growing in a greenhouse. He grew irritated at Lowman's absences, even as complaints grew about Scully's own brusque manner, both with the employees and with potential donors.

Lowman, for her part, found Scully as prickly as any gympie-gympie. But she figured that, as with the Aussie trees, she would either find a way to work with him or around him.

Scully, she soon discovered, was particularly attentive to the needs and desires of the OIC scientists. Some of them were orchid-show judges too, such as his friends Atwood and Higgins. In fact, Scully expected to see one or two of them in May at the big Redland International Orchid Show, the biggest orchid show in the country, where he would be one of the judges. For him the Redland show would be something of a homecoming, too, a chance to chat with old friends and colleagues and hear about all the new orchid varieties that had been developed.

None of them—not Scully, and not the OIC scientists—were fans of how Lowman kept selling the idea of big-picture rain forest ecology as Selby's primary mission. To them, Selby Gardens' real reason for existence was to cater to orchidophiles like themselves. Lowman dismissed the idea, but they were right—and her failure to appreciate it would lead to her facing the biggest challenge of her career.

If Lowman had only asked Carl Luer, the old doctor who had once led Selby's board, he could have set her straight. He knew the whole story. He knew it because he was the one who really got Selby Gardens started—not Marie Selby. She was only his patient.

2

The Garden of Earthly Delights

[Susan] Orlean looks at a book called *The Native Orchids of Florida*. She comes to a photo of the ghost orchid glowing white on the page.... A line of text catches her eye: "Should one be lucky enough to see a flower all else will seem eclipsed."

Charlie Kaufman, screenplay for the film *Adaptation*

Among the first visitors to what is now Sarasota were fishermen from Cuba and Mexico, looking for a big catch. They had come to the right place. In the 1800s, so many fish swam in Sarasota Bay that "they came in immense schools, more than a mile long and hundreds of yards wide—so dense it seemed as though a person could walk on them," a historian later wrote.

That piscatorial abundance is also what attracted an Ohio businessman named Bill Selby to the area near the dawn of the twentieth century. In 1909, he brought along his new bride, Marie. They had been married just a year. They arrived that winter on a houseboat, reeling in fish left and right before moving on to a new harbor.

The close quarters might have strained other marriages, but not theirs. Outwardly they displayed very different personalities. Bill Selby was a rough-and-ready type who stood six foot-plus and weighed more than two hundred pounds. He was always chewing on an unlit cigar. People who knew him around Sarasota—or thought they did—regarded him as nothing but a hillbilly in his cowboy boots and old clothes. Marie, on the other hand, was a refined, demure lady who had attended a music conservatory and trained to be a concert pianist.

With Bill by her side, though, Marie Selby would tackle any adventure. When the couple read that the competitors in the first cross-country auto race had covered the whole continent in six days, they decided to see if they could do better. They did, beating the winner's time—and in the process made Marie Selby the first woman in American history to cross the country by car.

Bill and Marie Selby took a liking to Florida. Bill bought 3,000 acres in Manatee County for cattle ranching and put some horses out there—a pair of Morgans and a pair of Tennessee Walkers—just for his wife. She tried to go riding every day.

Finally, in 1927, the couple built a two-story house on 7 acres of laurels and banyans where Hudson Bayou flows into Sarasota Bay. It was supposed to be just temporary quarters while they designed a far grander home, but after a while they dropped those plans. The smaller home suited the childless couple just fine. Marie directed the landscaping herself, laying out elaborate flowered borders that bloomed along the roadway to the tip of their peninsula. The centerpiece of the design was a large rose garden, one she was always reluctant to leave untended when they went on trips.

When Marie went downtown to shop, she'd wear her riding outfit—blue jeans and a plaid shirt—or a plain dress and a floppy straw hat. Few people knew how incredibly wealthy the Selbys were. Bill Selby owned an Oklahoma oil company that eventually merged with one from Texas and became Texaco. He also had interests in Standard Oil and invested in Colorado mining, making millions. If they had wanted, Bill and Marie Selby could have hobnobbed with the other rich folks in Sarasota. There were, surprisingly, quite a few of them.

Early on, the queen of Sarasota was also the bejeweled empress of Chicago society, imperious Bertha Palmer. The widow of hotelier Potter Palmer, owner of the famous Palmer House, she pioneered the introduction of impressionist painting to American audiences and backed Jane Addams's Hull House, among other do-gooder causes. She didn't tolerate disrespect. Once, a visiting Spanish princess declined her hospitality, dubbing her "an innkeeper's wife." Mrs. Palmer retorted that the princess was merely a "bibulous representative of a degenerate monarch."

One day Bertha Palmer spotted an ad in a Chicago paper about land available in Sarasota. Her late husband had advised her to invest in real estate, so she promptly trekked down to the town of 840 people and bought up thousands of acres all around it. She built a grand home called "The Oaks," where paintings by Monet and Degas hung on the walls and she dressed for dinner in Paris gowns. Other family members soon built homes nearby, and other Chicagoans followed suit. When she died in 1918, she had built up the $8 million left by her husband into an estate worth $20 million, and Sarasota now boasted both a yacht club and a movie theater—rare amenities for a Florida town in those days.

In the meantime, another kind of art lover had joined Sarasota's social whirl. Circus magnate John Ringling arrived in 1911 and soon persuaded his brother Charles to buy adjoining property. Ringling spent millions acquiring overwrought Middle Ages masterworks, then built a $1 million home to put them in. His wife helped design the waterfront mansion: 36,000 square feet with forty-one rooms and fifteen bathrooms. He dubbed it Ca d'Zan ("House of John" in Venetian dialect). It looked like nothing else in Sarasota. The historian David Nolan described it as "something along the lines of the Doge's Palace topped with the tower from Madison Square Garden. . . . Only a man steeped in the circus aesthetic could have called it home."

While Bertha Palmer had big plans for the city's future, it was Ringling who really put Sarasota on the map. He began developing land on nearby islands and built a causeway—with a yacht canal, of course—to connect them to the mainland. He made Sarasota the winter home of his circus troupe, then persuaded John J. McGraw to bring the New York Giants down for spring training in 1924. McGraw wound up building his own $75,000 home there and developing a subdivision called Pennant Park. McGraw's success attracted Col. Jacob Ruppert, owner of the New York Yankees, who launched his own development plans, and then Ty Cobb's younger brother showed up to cash in on the baseball bonanza, too. Sarasota's boundaries, once set at a miniscule 2 square miles, now expanded to encompass 69 square miles.

But Bill and Marie Selby wanted nothing to do with the Palmers, Ringlings, McGraws, Rupperts, or Cobb the younger. Bill would bicycle down to Badger's Drug Store to sip coffee and chat with the other regulars. Then he'd head over to Mike Roth's Cigar Stand for more chitchat. His wife's only interest besides riding was her garden club. At night, instead of throwing parties or attending society dinners, they would stay home. Bill Selby would read while his wife played the piano. That was entertainment enough for them.

When Bill Selby died of leukemia in 1956, he left an estate of $10 million. Half went to his wife and half to the William and Marie Selby Foundation, a charitable trust the couple had set up primarily to provide scholarships for young people who wanted to undertake scientific or medical research. But after her husband died, Marie Selby took the foundation in a different direction. She wanted to help the handicapped and the poor. She helped the YMCA get a new pool and the hospital a new laboratory. She matched a grant from the foundation to help launch New College, a free-form four-year

Marie Selby just wanted her garden club to have a place
to meet after she died. She loved roses, not orchids.
Photo courtesy of Sarasota County Historical Division.

university. She quietly donated her own money to hundreds of causes, never asking for recognition, helping the city but staying in the shadows.

While the Palmers and Ringlings strove to build up Sarasota, Marie Selby wished it would stay the same. When a developer began building a high-rise condominium on Bird Key, ruining her view from that side of the property, she planted a large stand of trees so she didn't have to look at the concrete intruder.

As she grew older, Marie Selby withdrew even more from society. But as her thoughts turned to her own impending death, she would be determined that the one association she had maintained for decades was remembered in her will. When she died in 1971 at age eighty-five, she specified that she wanted her friends at the garden club to still have a place to gather.

"She left the home and $2 million for it to be maintained as a botanical garden," recalled Luer, her surgeon and neighbor.

All she wanted was to keep the place the way it was, with all her pretty landscaping, a spot of loveliness in the midst of all the rampant development around her. But the language in her will left a lot of wiggle room for how the executor would carry out her wishes. The will said the "botanical garden and park" should be developed "in such esthetic and utilitarian manner as Trustee may determine, from time to time, and shall be made available for enjoyment to the general public on such days and during such hours . . . and pursuant to such rules and regulations as the Trustees may determine from time to time."

Luer, a dapper man with a sharp face, his fringe of hair going gray, was a well-known figure around Sarasota. He was as likely to pop up in the society column as at the hospital. His patient list included the town's wealthy and well-to-do, including the world's most famous clown, Emmett Kelly. Luer was good friends with the head trustee of the Selby Foundation, who was also the chairman of the city's biggest bank. Luer pushed his friend to make Marie Selby's home a true botanical garden, a place dedicated to science.

"I twisted his arm," Luer said. "She wanted a meeting place for her garden club, and we made it into a botanical garden."

What Luer wanted the new botanical garden to focus its attention on was not roses but orchids. He had a passion for orchids. It began, as almost all stories about orchid collectors do, with a single plant.

In 1957, someone showed Luer and his wife a *Polyrrhiza lindenii* in bloom. They were fascinated by it—a leafless green plant, "the flower of which resembles the ghoulish ghost of a frog leaping in mid-air," he wrote later. They were even more astounded to learn that this particular plant was a native of Florida. They decided to track one down in the wild and photograph it.

Finding a ghost orchid—for that's what it was—took them to the Fakahatchee Strand, a heavily cut-over cypress swamp where "tracks of bear, panther, and otter may be seen in the mud," and the deeper water offered a hiding place for alligators and cottonmouth moccasins. But in those deep sloughs stood virgin groves of pop ash and custard-apple, "festooned with their treasures of epiphytic ferns, bromeliads, and orchids," Luer wrote.

At last, they spied their quarry: "While wading knee deep in swamp water, the thrill of chancing upon a plant in flower will never be forgotten. . . . Down low on the trunk the familiar spidery network of rambling green roots will not be hard to find. Should one be lucky enough to see a flower, all else will seem eclipsed. There, caught hovering in mid-air, will be a fantastic, fairy-like ghost, frozen in flight."

Finding that first orchid led to a search for others, then to a determination to track down and photograph every type of native orchid in Florida. That led, in turn, to Luer writing a groundbreaking book on the subject, called *The*

Carl Luer was such an orchid fanatic that he gave up his lucrative medical practice to start Marie Selby Botanical Gardens. Photo courtesy of Stig Dalström.

Native Orchids of Florida (the same book that Susan Orlean would consult twenty years later while writing *The Orchid Thief*, which became the basis for the film *Adaptation)*. Luer's large tome, illustrated with his vivid color photos and alliterative prose, would be published in 1972. He was already working on an even more ambitious companion volume, *The Native Orchids of North America.*

Luer had become so enamored of the idea of creating a garden devoted to orchids in his hometown that he was even willing to make the ultimate sacrifice for it. He was willing to give up his high-profile medical practice. Other doctors might find that odd, but not other orchid people. They're the ones who put the "cult" in "horticulture."

Invariably, when someone who is not enamored of orchids talks about an orchid lover like Luer, the word "obsession" is invoked, and not just for alliterative purposes.

While most orchid fanciers are content with the selection available from the garden department at Home Depot, a few are willing to spend thousands of dollars on a single plant. Sometimes their enthusiasm shades into even stronger emotions. In *Orchid Fever: A Horticultural Tale of Love, Lust, and Lunacy*, Eric Hansen recounts how a dispute between two orchid growers ended with one man beating the other senseless in his greenhouse. Hansen noted that in another case from California, two growers "had settled an argument . . . with a two-foot length of water pipe and a burst of gunfire. One man had died."

The more time he spent with orchid people, Hansen wrote, the more tales he heard of "midnight greenhouse break-ins with chainsaws . . . thefts of award-winning plants from orchid shows, government sting operations, orchid licking, fraud, murder, and money."

The historian Luigi Berliocchi, in his book *The Orchid in Lore and Legend*, explained the flowers' allure this way: "They have a magic whose secret will always elude us, a blend of witchcraft and romance, that sets them apart, above all other plants—a sorcery that conjures up our deepest passions, from idolatrous worship through the pure spirituality of aesthetic veneration to fear, revulsion, and mindless hatred."

Writers have struggled for years to explain why orchids drive otherwise rational people to such irrational extremes. Many have linked the passion to the flowers' sensual form. They say the pouty-lipped petals, tumescent blooms, and intoxicating scents cloud the judgment of otherwise sensible people.

Even the name says sex—but not because of the flowers. The word "orchid" comes from *orchis*, Greek for "testicle," because that's what the roots of European orchids resemble. For the same reason, they were once called "dogstones" and "sweet bollocks."

Because of this scrotal resemblance, for thousands of years orchids have been rumored to hold aphrodisiac properties. They were the Rx for sexual healing in Greece and China. The myth of the orchid's supposedly Viagra-like powers persisted in England for so long that, in 1640, John Parkinson complained in his *Theatrum Botanicum* that "our pharmacists are wont to adjudge every sort of orchid root an aphrodisiac."

Even in the nineteenth century, the name "orchid" remained so associated with sex that the famed English thinker John Ruskin tried in vain to get it changed to something less lascivious. In *Swann's Way*, Marcel Proust has his protagonist make a pretense of arranging the *Cattleya* orchids in his lady love's bodice as a first step toward caressing and kissing her. Soon the couple would employ the name for that species of orchid as a synonym for making love, until "the metaphor 'do a *Cattleya*'" became "a simple verb which they would employ without thinking of its original meaning when they wished to refer to the act of physical possession."

Although the sublimated-sex explanation may be entertaining in a *Beavis and Butthead* way, it cannot account for orchids' broad appeal to both cerebral interests and aesthetic senses. Their beauty can be astonishing, and their variety is downright dizzying. The family Orchidaceae contains 25,000 to 30,000 different species, more than any other type of plant. Add in the 100,000 or so types of hybrids and you can see why no collector could ever find a reason to grow bored.

The variations are tied to the diverse ways the plants spread their pollen, usually by tricking insects into serving as carriers. Take, for instance, the subfamily of lady slipper orchids—the type that John Atwood had made his specialty—that are so called because the flowers are shaped like a shoe.

The nectar in slipper orchids attracts certain insects—sometimes bees, sometimes flies—that buzz in through the flower's large opening. Once inside, they can't back out. Instead they slip down deeper in the slipper until they find two holes in the back that offer an exit, like climbing out a window. To get to those holes, though, the insects must first squeeze past the pollen receptor, where they leave behind any pollen deposited on them by other plants, and are brushed with a fresh load from the flower they're trying to escape. The dimensions of the holes that they must climb through to leave the slipper orchid exactly match the size of the insects now carrying its pollen on to other slippers to fertilize them.

Some people see that precision as the hand of God. They contend it's proof that there's an intelligent design to the universe, one so complex that it's beyond human comprehension.

For Charles Darwin, on the other hand, all the oh-so-precise match-ups among the orchid family showed that his evolutionary theory was spot-on. His follow-up book to 1859's *The Origin of the Species* was *On the Various Contrivances by Which British and Foreign Orchids are Fertilised by Insects*, published in 1862. In it, he not only documented the pollination methods of orchids found growing in the English countryside, but also speculated about how tropical orchids he had studied might trick insects into helping with fertilization, based on their shape and structure. He opened the second book by apologizing for not including "this little treatise" in his first one, explaining that it had become "inconveniently large" and thus had to be published separately. His "little treatise" on orchids runs more than 350 pages.

Inevitably, anyone who writes about orchid obsession invokes a famous quote from an otherwise obscure 1939 book, *The Orchid-Hunters*. It's the memoir of a couple of naïve city boys from New Jersey who thought they could make a killing in the orchid trade. In the book, they say they braved trees that put people to sleep and moths whose sting drives men insane, all in an effort to snatch 6,000 orchids from the South American jungles and bring them back to the United States to sell.

"When a man falls in love with orchids, he'll do anything to possess the one he wants," one of the hunters, Norman McDonald, wrote after the trip ended. "It's like chasing a green-eyed woman or taking cocaine; it's a sort of madness." Of course, for McDonald, it was also a source of income. Despite the dangers encountered on his first trip, by the time the book came out, he was back in the jungle hunting for more orchids.

In recent years, orchids have become more than a botanical fixation. They're also a $44 billion-a-year industry worldwide, making them the most lucrative flower business around. Orchid sales generate more than $23 million in Florida alone.

That's just the legal side of the business. On the illegal side, no one knows how much money black-market orchids are worth, but it's enough to prompt thieves to make off with some of the more valuable plants. In 1975, someone swiped two valuable orchids from a display at an orchid show in the Virgin Islands. In 2002, a thief broke into the Miami home of an orchid collector and made off with orchids worth an estimated $8,750—plants likely sold to other collectors.

Among some orchidophiles, there is a drive to own the best, the most exotic, the rarest orchids in the world, even if it means breaking the law.

"It is an extremely important thing, if you're an orchid person, to own some of the very, very finest," a California orchid dealer told the *Los Angeles Times* in 1995. "And if you can get a plant that nobody in the world has but you, you have done something that has put you way above everybody else."

Back in 1971, though, the orchid world consisted of only a loose affiliation of wealthy hobbyists like Luer. The doctor had financed his own expeditions, both around Florida and overseas, to search out new species. He knew that one thing he and all his fellow orchidophiles needed was some scientific expertise to help them out—say, a place where orchid experts could sort out one variety of orchid from another that might appear similar. An orchid identification center, if you will.

At Luer's behest, the Selby trustees brought in five botanists from the University of Florida to aid in planning the layout of the new institution.

Meanwhile, Luer set to work luring his pick for executive director away from a nice, safe university job.

With his wavy silver hair and Clark Gable mustache, Calaway "Cal" Dodson looked more like a stage magician than a scientist. All he needed was a cape and a wand. He had a mellifluous baritone and a quick wit, too, just right for a nice line of stage patter while pulling a rabbit out of his hat.

Actually, Dodson came from a long line of California farmers, and if not for a stint in the army and the education offered by the GI Bill, he might have ended up following the family plow. His agricultural background led him to take classes in botany, and after reading Darwin's book he became fascinated by orchids.

He made a name for himself as a grad student by discovering that some orchids in a particular species had far fewer chromosomes—ten—than others in the same species that had twenty-four. Later, in Ecuador, he earned his doctorate by tracing back a stand of natural hybrids found in the wild to their parent plants. He also met his wife, Piedad, there, and they had two children.

Dodson was considered an expert on how orchids pollinate, and had once spent a whole year in Peru studying how a certain type of bee pollinated the orchids there. His scholarly writings on the subject included a book, *Orchid Flowers: Their Pollination and Evolution*, published in 1966. He wound up teaching at the University of Miami as well as serving as the orchid curator for Fairchild Tropical Botanic Garden in Miami. When Luer finished his own book, he asked Dodson to vet it for accuracy. The professor found the surgeon's book to be outstanding. They became friends.

One day Luer took his friend out to the Everglades to see a rare orchid he had found. On the way, he pitched him what Dodson later called "a crazy idea." Luer asked Dodson if he'd be interested in becoming director of a new botanical garden in Sarasota.

"That sounds like one of the cruelest jokes I've ever heard," Dodson replied. "Botanical gardens are ineffective. Most don't amount to anything. Unless there's a large pool of oil located underneath them or it's in Saudi Arabia, they never have enough money."

Luer persisted, but Dodson brushed him off. He had a good, solid job at the University of Miami, and someday his kids would get a free college education there. How could some botanical garden that existed only in Luer's mind ever top that?

Luer was not deterred. Sometime later, he flew down to Ecuador to visit Dodson while the professor was doing some fieldwork. Luer brought along the banker who headed up the Selby Foundation. They told Dodson they were there to recruit him to head up the new botanical garden.

Calaway Dodson and his wife, Piedad, left Ecuador behind to move into the rundown Selby home and launch the botanical garden. Photo courtesy of Calaway Dodson.

"I said, 'Thanks, kiddies, but no thanks,'" Dodson recalled years later. "They said, 'What's your salary?' I said, 'Oh, about $16,000.' And they said, 'We'll offer to double it—for a start.'"

Astonished, Dodson accepted. Selby Gardens had its executive director.

Despite his strong interest in orchids, Dodson insisted from the outset that Selby Gardens would have a broader focus than just one family. He said it would study all the plants that grow on trees and take their moisture from the air. As a class, these are known as epiphytes, and include such plants as bromeliads.

"We've avoided calling it an orchid garden—the term would degrade it," Dodson told the *Sarasota Herald-Tribune* in 1973. "We want to study the whole picture of why plants grow on trees. No other garden in the world is devoted to epiphytes."

Dodson, his wife, two sons, and a pair of college interns moved into Marie Selby's house. They brought along a menagerie of animals as well: dogs, cats, tropical birds, even a few snakes. The house had been vacant for two years, so it smelled of mildew and there were a few bullet holes in the door, evidence the trustees had done a poor job of protecting it from vandals.

Over the next two years, prior to the gardens' official opening in 1975, Dodson and Luer worked hard at converting this rundown property into a world-class scientific institution. Their tasks ranged from hiring a raft of Ph.D.s to battling city officials over where visitors could park. They built big greenhouses, and Dodson brought in his own orchid collection as a starter. They also ripped out the trees Marie Selby had planted to block the view of Bird Key. They needed that view for the gardens' visitors.

At Dodson's insistence, they built a walkway through the grounds that was wide enough for three people to walk abreast. Most garden walkways were only big enough for two. Dodson felt strongly that a wider path would make this garden a more attractive place for strolling visitors.

In those early days, the place bustled with activity. Grad students from Florida State—including Atwood—drove down from Tallahassee to marvel at the growing collection of epiphytes and the brand-new greenhouses that had been built to house them.

"There were lots of samples to study, both in the herbarium and in the living collection," recalled Atwood. Upon completing his Ph.D. in 1982, he returned and began his twenty-year stint as the head of Selby's OIC.

Atwood was not alone in finding in Selby a long-term home. One of his coworkers took that literally.

Harry Luther was a shy, bearish man who had grown up in St. Petersburg back when the city still offered woods in which a boy could wander. As a teenager he had become fascinated by bromeliads and joined the local bromeliad collectors' society, learning everything he could about them. He took some college courses on botany but didn't graduate. Instead he came home and took a job at a plant warehouse, but he didn't like it.

Then he heard Selby was looking for someone to take charge of its bromeliad collection. Luther convinced Dodson to hire him, despite his youth and lack of a degree. It would turn out to be a good decision: Over the next twenty years, on expeditions to mountains and jungles across the globe, Luther would discover some sixty new species of bromeliads in the wild. He became known as the world's foremost expert on bromeliads.

He would also let his red hair and beard grow as long and unruly as a clump of jungle vines. Luther loved Selby so much he moved into an apartment on the grounds and lived there for years. But he was so shy, Dodson said, that it became a problem. People would mistake the big bearded giant's reticence for an insult. Dodson would have to step in and smooth the ruffled feathers.

Another gifted amateur who made a name for herself at Selby had no trouble speaking her mind. A year after Selby opened, some Selby employees visited the home of one of Luer's medical colleagues, Dr. Byron Besse, to see his backyard collection of palms and cycads. It turned out the doctor's wife, Libby Besse, was actually the keeper of the collection. She had kept meticulous notes about their cultivation and growth.

Impressed, Dodson recruited the slender, silver-haired woman as a volunteer. Her note-taking skills led to her becoming the keeper of Selby's plant records. She oversaw its ever-expanding herbarium, where dried specimens were mounted on stiff paper and filed away for future reference like cards in an old-fashioned library catalogue.

However, Dodson soon found her somewhat difficult to deal with. She came from a moneyed family in Philadelphia and was accustomed to getting her way, he said. Whenever he wanted to fire her or anyone else, Luer would talk him out of it, and he'd be stuck with the employee. However, being stuck with Libby Besse turned out to be a blessing.

"She had learned that she could use her money to put together trips for the younger staff members—what's the term these days? Cougar? There was certainly a touch of that involved," Dodson recalled. "Every trip she'd take about two young men along."

One such Besse field trip—what Dodson called "take the kiddies out in the woods"—yielded a huge boon for the fledgling garden. In July 1981, Besse took a young male Selby employee and six Miami plant hobbyists and headed for Peru.

Driving a truck along a twisting mountain road between Tarapota and Yurimaguas, they spotted a particularly attractive strap-leaf *anthurium* growing high in a tree. The group stopped the truck and began poking at the plant with a pole, trying to knock it down to add to their collection.

Meanwhile, the doctor's wife wandered off for a stroll near a wet stone cliff. As she walked, she glanced up and saw a striking coral-colored flower. She knew it was an orchid. She also knew it wasn't like any orchid she had ever seen before. She pulled herself up through a tangle of briars and was just able to hang out over the top ledge of the cliff and push a couple of the flowers off with a stick. The Selby employee climbed up to help. They snapped a few pictures and then put one specimen, with flowers still attached, into a bottle of alcohol to preserve it.

"Collecting the plants was easy," Mrs. Besse said later. "It took only a few minutes. But we spent an entire aggravating day in Iquitos getting its proper export permits."

Upon Libby Besse's return to Selby Gardens, Dodson said, "she came into

my office one day and said, 'What is this?'" When he looked at the dull specimen in alcohol, he wasn't impressed. But when he saw her color slides of the
crimson flower, Dodson realized she had made an electrifying discovery: a
brand-new species of tropical slipper orchid, one sure to set the collecting
world ablaze.

Seeing the look on Dodson's face, Besse said later, "was really my best
moment."

Up until then, everyone considered slippers to be fairly bland compared
to other orchids. Their flowers were mostly soft greens and browns. What
the doctor's wife had discovered in the Peruvian jungle was a plant that bore
stunning scarlet flowers. This was more than a scientific coup. The flower's
striking color meant it would be commercially valuable as well. Orchid
growers would immediately see how it could revolutionize the range of hybrid possibilities within the slipper family.

Dodson called in Selby's staff illustrator. He told her to drop whatever
she was doing and get to work drawing this new plant, pronto. Then he sat
down with the scientist in charge of the OIC, and they wrote a description,
officially naming the plant for its discoverer, *Phragmipedium besseae*. They
rushed it and the drawing over to the American Orchid Society's headquarters in Delray Beach for publication in its newsletter, which would make the
name officially valid.

When word got out about the discovery, *Phragmipedium* pandemonium
broke out among orchid-collectors. Everyone had to have one of Libby
Besse's namesake flowers.

"Although we knew there were not too many of them, vast quantities—
truckloads—came in from Peru into the United States and Great Britain,"
Dodson said. "It caused quite a storm."

Collectors quickly stripped the Peruvian site bare, but Dodson himself
later discovered big fields of the same flower growing on a cliff in Ecuador.

When Selby auctioned off three of Besse's flowers in 1982, they sold for
$1,700 each. Two went to commercial growers in Ohio and California. The
third was a retirement gift for the Smithsonian Institution's orchid curator.
He promised to take good care of it—in his own greenhouse.

Selby's scientific celebrity began attracting fans, including a Swedish civil
engineer named Stig Dalström. Fascinated by orchids and already adept at

drawing, Dalström sent Dodson a letter claiming to be a "field orchidist" with a "specialty in botanical illustration."

When Dodson wrote back to ask for samples of his artwork, Dalström had to take a crash course in that type of art so his lie wouldn't be exposed.

With his blond hair, blue eyes, and cocksure manner, Dalström resembled the cool Russian secret agent in *The Man from U.N.C.L.E.* Actually, he was a man who was ready to cry uncle. He wanted to escape Sweden, to flee what looked to him to be a dull and dreary future. This offer from Dodson seemed like his hole in the back of the orchid.

"Botanical art . . . seemed to be the only way, aside from prostitution, to make a living wherever you are," he explained years later.

He flew to Miami and took a bus to Sarasota, where he became a freelance botanical illustrator who frequently worked for Selby on contract. As a result, he could travel the world searching for new species. In the next twenty-five years, Dalström would discover several new species of mistletoe and bromeliads, and about twenty species of orchids.

From Dr. Luer's perspective, Dalström arrived near the end of Selby's golden age. His friend Cal Dodson, while an excellent scientist, turned out to be a poor money manager. By 1981, the gardens' budget ran as red as a *Phragmipedium besseae* blossom. The debt totaled $200,000. Local suppliers had cut off Selby's credit, and the greenhouse cooling system was on the verge of collapse. Dodson resigned as executive director, instead taking the title of research director.

His replacement, a retired army general, managed to turn the finances around. But the general believed Selby should be treated more as a tourist attraction than a research institution. At one point, Dodson recalled, the general commanded the staff to empty out one of the greenhouses so it could be converted into a meeting room they could rent out.

Dodson tried to warn his old friend about the general: "I said, 'Carl, that guy is a son of a bitch.'" For the longest time, he said, Luer didn't listen.

One day in November 1983, the mild-mannered Atwood stopped by Luer's office. The New Englander regarded Luer and Dodson as giants in their field, men who prized intellect over passion, so he was stunned at what he saw. When Atwood asked Luer a simple question, "he choked up a bit, holding back tears, and his voice broke."

The next day Atwood found out the reason for Luer's rare emotional display: The doctor had resigned from the board of the institution he had founded. He did it because the general had fired Dodson.

"I was dismayed to discover that his solution to the problem of financial support was to cut back severely on the research side while emphasizing the commercial plant production aspects," Dodson told the *Herald-Tribune* at the time. "I was concerned by his obvious failure to understand the nature of a botanical garden."

Dodson headed back to Ecuador to study tropical orchids for the Missouri Botanical Garden. He sometimes went back to visit friends at Selby such as Atwood, but he never worked for the place again.

Over the next twenty years, Harry Luther, Stig Dalström, John Atwood, and other scientists continued exploring new territories, searching for new species. They did so even though the gardens' own board members often didn't seem to appreciate their hard work, Dalström said.

"Comments were like, 'We don't give a damn about what you do,'" Dalström said. "It became clear to me that the research department depended on the support from a bunch of clowns that had no clue what their own organization really was all about, and was working on."

In fact, by May 2002, Meg Lowman had begun talking about pushing the OIC in a new direction, looking for ways to boost its income and also cut its expenses. Her first proposed cut: Get rid of their contract scientist, Atwood. Alarmed at losing Atwood's expertise on slipper orchids, the mustachioed Wesley Higgins sought help from his fellow orchid judge Bob Scully.

"I am concerned about the future of the orchid program at Selby Gardens when the executive director talks about reducing our orchid scientists and having OIC turn a profit," Higgins warned Scully. "Scientific programs will never be money producers. We capitalize on these programs through a world-class reputation, not in dollars. The public perception is that Selby is orchids."

Even as Lowman was looking for a way to cut the OIC's budget, Dalström thought he saw a way to turn things around.

"The way out of this was to get some great and earthshaking publicity," he said.

And the best way to garner publicity, Dalström figured, would be for someone connected to Selby Gardens to find the next *Phragmipedium besseae*, the next species that would shake the orchid world. In short, like the fishermen who first settled Sarasota, they needed a big catch.

But searching for something no one has discovered before carries with it certain risks—risks of injury, sickness, and death, of course, but also risks of running afoul of the authorities. For an adventurous few, though, that's part of what makes it such a kick. Just ask the man who's known as The Adventurer.

3

The Adventurer

Adventure and excitement will follow me the rest of
my life. . . . It is in my blood to explore it all.

Lee Moore, quoted in *The Orchid Thief*

The most popular book about orchids is Susan Orlean's *The Orchid Thief*. It concerns an attempt by a Florida man named John Laroche, aided by some Seminole Indians, to steal a ghost orchid—like the one that Carl Luer fell in love with—from Fakahatchee Strand State Park. Published in 1998, the book became a *New York Times* best seller, and the basis for the movie *Adaptation*. The movie starred Chris Cooper, who won an Oscar, as Laroche, and Meryl Streep as Orlean.

A lot of orchid people hate this book.

They complain that it's chock full of errors about their favorite flower— for instance, giving the number of species as sixty thousand when the correct number is, at best, half that. When some of them noticed that the book's acknowledgments page says Ned Nash of the American Orchid Society helped check the text for accuracy, Nash was bombarded with complaints. But he said Orlean never asked him to check anything.

The most vivid character in Orlean's book—one who is unaccountably absent from the movie—is not Laroche or Orlean. It's Lee Moore, the one character that Orlean got just about right.

If you saw Moore in the grocery store or a restaurant, you might think he ran the local head shop or played in a Grateful Dead tribute band. He's tall but a bit stooped. He has long silver hair that he wears in a ponytail, a neatly trimmed gray beard, and the parchment-like skin of a man who's spent lots of time outdoors. But if you were to ask Moore for his business card, he might smile slyly as he handed it to you, knowing in advance the reaction it will get. It says, "Lee Moore—The Adventurer."

This is no idle boast. Since the late 1950s, Moore has been traipsing around in South American jungles, living by his wits, digging up and hawking whatever treasures he could find. He boasts of avoiding death nine times. He has, on occasion, tangled with the law.

In *The Orchid Thief*, Orlean quotes Moore's wife, Chady, as saying: "We were on the Ten Most Wanted List in Mexico! We were always smuggling something. . . . We had more going on, more situations than Indiana Jones! Oh my God!"

But if you call Moore an orchid smuggler—as Orlean did in her book—he will correct you. He never smuggled orchids, he says. He used the orchids to hide what he was *really* smuggling.

Moore was born in Georgia, then spent some time growing up in Chevy Chase, Maryland. His father oversaw civilian airports during the Eisenhower administration until he became embroiled in a classic Florida scandal. Miami airport officials gave him "a complete electric kitchen—including stove, refrigerator, automatic dishwasher, sink, and hot water heater," the *Miami News* reported in 1954. In exchange, the paper reported, Phillips Moore made sure the Miami airport got $5 million in federal aid. He later sold the refurbished Maryland home for double what he paid for it, and took a new job running the Miami airport to which he had steered so much federal money.

For the young Moore, his family's move to Miami would prove to be life-changing. Growing up on the edge of the Everglades sparked a lifelong fascination with nature.

"Every weekend we were out in the Everglades with a flashlight, looking for snakes, while everybody else was going to school dances and basketball games," he recalled.

Sometimes, out in the marsh, he'd find peculiar-looking flowers growing on the trees. Fascinated, he would cut them down and bring them back home to hang in his father's backyard avocado trees. That's how he began learning about orchids.

He spent a year in forestry school, then reluctantly joined the construction company his father owned. In 1961, Lee and his then-wife, Deedee, decided to go camping through Mexico and Central America. To pay for their trip, they collected orchids along the way. As they came to a town, they would package up the flowers they had found and ship them to a friend in the States.

When they got back to Miami, "I had a giant orchid sale and sold 400 of them for $1.50 each," Moore told the *Miami News* in 1965. At that point, Moore admitted, he didn't know what he'd found, just that they were pretty. He sold the unidentified flowers to anyone who wanted one.

Thanks to that trip, Moore was hooked. No more construction work for him. He started learning about how to identify orchids and other plants. He formed a partnership with a tropical fish collector, and the pair headed down to Peru to gather both fish and flowers. Some of the plants Moore found in the jungle he couldn't identify, so he shipped a few to experts at the Smithsonian and other scientific institutions. Many of them had never been named. He had discovered a new species.

"That is when I realized the jungle held untold numbers of undiscovered plants," Moore told the paper. "It turned into a challenge I couldn't resist."

He and his wife started a mail-order plant business. When Moore was drafted into the army, she kept it running until he could return. After he mustered out, Moore borrowed $3,000 from various plant nurseries, promising to pay them back in orchids. Then he headed back to the jungle again—and straight into a disaster.

For this trip, he decided to work with one of his childhood snake-hunting buddies. The buddy planned to fly a cargo plane down to Peru to collect snake venom. Moore loaded supplies onto the plane to build a nursery in Iquito, Peru, and also entrusted his buddy with his customer list and his dog, Buck. Then Moore and his wife took a commercial flight down.

When they landed in Lima, they learned that the cargo plane had crashed in the jungle. Buck somehow survived. Moore's buddy did not.

But Moore stuck with his plan. Paying off his creditors in orchids from the Peruvian jungle took him a year and a half. By the time the *Miami News* caught up with him, Moore had a thriving mail-order business going again. A photo of Moore from this era shows a lean and darkly handsome rogue, a lock of hair drooping over his forehead as if he were Robert Mitchum's rakish younger brother.

Moore had built a nursery on 2 acres of land, and he hired a pair of skinny Peruvian teenagers to help him scout the jungle for plants to sell. Peru, Moore had learned, was a virgin landscape just ripe for the picking—if you had the stamina to go where the rarest plants grew.

"The men follow the 2,000-mile-long Amazon and explore its tributaries," the paper reported. "Moore spots with binoculars, and when a rare plant is sighted the men cut their way to the tree with a machete. They use jungle vines to climb the trees, often 200 feet tall. During the six weeks they are out, the men set up shelters along the way to leave the plants that they have cut, then pick them up on a raft on the way back."

One of his most dramatic discoveries was an orchid with a curving, hand-sized yellow flower with red splashes near its wavy rim. The new species, which he first found in the Amazonian jungle in 1958, bears his name: *Cattleya mooreana.*

These were the days when Moore first began building his swashbuckling reputation. Actually, though, some of his discoveries resulted more from luck than daring.

One day while scouting for plants along a logging road, Moore's Volkswagen van got stuck in some muddy ruts. He got out to push the van free, but all his straining and struggling couldn't budge it. Finally, covered in sweat, he collapsed under a tree to cool off. He looked up and spotted, hanging above him, the largest staghorn fern species ever seen. The species had been first described by an English explorer in the 1800s and never seen since.

Moore knew immediately what a big find this would be. A group of spear-carrying Indians happened to pass by just then, Moore said. They helped him get his van unstuck and then he persuaded one of them to also climb the tree and cut down the fern for him.

Moore's discoveries began attracting attention in the scientific world. His nickname, "The Adventurer," had started out as joshing from older botanists who didn't think much of him, Moore said, but he embraced it. As the number of plants bearing his name grew, the joshing stopped.

Soon his little nursery attracted a visitor. Cal Dodson, at that point still a university professor, came calling. He had a Fulbright fellowship to teach at the university in Iquitos for a year, and between his duties there, Dodson would stop by Moore's nursery to study how certain bees pollinated the orchids in the greenhouse.

"He'd be out there early in the morning with his camera, ready to photograph those bees," Moore said.

The two orchid fanciers became friends, although Dodson says he had no illusions about Moore.

"Eventually I discovered that the best way to deal with Lee was to lend him money," Dodson said years later. "Give him enough so he can't pay it back comfortably, and you wouldn't hear from him."

Moore's friendship with Dodson later led to him traveling to Sarasota from time to time to visit Selby Gardens. If Moore found an orchid or a bromeliad he thought might be an unidentified species, he figured Selby's staff would be the best ones to identify it. As a result, over the years, he got

Lee Moore earned his nickname "The Adventurer" while tracking down new plant species and lost pre-Columbian treasures in the jungles of South America. Photo courtesy of Lee Moore.

to know not just Dodson but most of the other Selby scientists, including John Atwood and Stig Dalström.

Initially Moore could ship his orchids out of Peru without much, if any, paperwork. Back then there weren't a lot of laws governing how plants were transported from one country to the other. There was no such thing as orchid smuggling because the export and import of orchids were free of regulation.

However, Moore then discovered a far more lucrative product he could harvest from the jungle: archaeological artifacts. He continued shipping orchids out of the jungle, but now his mail-order business had a dual purpose.

"I used to smuggle out pre-Columbian art in my orchid boxes," he explained. Beneath the beautiful flowers would be hidden gold and silver jewelry, vases, and other remnants of ancient Peruvian civilizations, bound for buyers in the United States and other countries.

Taking the artifacts out of Peru was against the law in Peru, but at that point importing them into the United States was not against U.S. law, Moore said. As a result, he had little trouble with U.S. Customs officials. Still, he had to be careful—landing planes in cow pastures, dodging the Latin American authorities. He got so good at it, he says, that he once smuggled an entire temple wall out of Mexico.

When another plane crash wiped out his orchid stock—which, he says, led to his mother reading his premature obituary in the *Miami Herald*—

Moore decided to let his plant business go so he could focus exclusively on pre-Columbian art.

"I was considered one of the five top pre-Columbian art dealers in the world, with contributions to the most famous of private collections and museums around the world," he wrote in an e-mail to one of his critics.

By this time, Moore had divorced his first wife and fallen for a gamine brunette he'd seen walking up a street in Lima one day. She looked like a Latina Audrey Hepburn, slender and chic, but with an inner fire. He didn't know it at the time, but she had already been divorced twice. She had grown up amid wealth and privilege. Her father had been one of his region's biggest ranchers, but after he died the land was lost in a military coup.

At first she just called Moore "the gringo," but in a matter of months they got married, and so far they have stuck together for three decades. She turned out to be as adventurous as he was, ready for anything. At one point in his smuggling career, Moore said, he had a particularly close call: "The authorities caught onto me and I had to run out of there before they put me in jail."

"Who ran faster?" asked Chady Moore, a note of pride throbbing in her voice. Now she walks with a cane, but back then she had moves a whole army couldn't match.

They sold the Iquitos nursery and used the money to search for more antiquities.

"We used to fly out in this airplane and look for lost cities," he recalled. "We'd see pieces of a temple sticking out [of the jungle] and then go out and cut our way in to the place. Then we'd stay out there for weeks" digging out the most valuable artifacts to sell.

Their investment brought a staggering profit. Moore says he had his own plane, two Lincoln Continentals, and a fancy house. He told the *Miami News* in 1973 that he enjoyed a six-figure income. The paper described him as "an urbane, polished adventurer, equally at home in luxurious museums and galleries and in the humid, dangerous jungles of Yucatan and Peru."

Moore saw nothing wrong with what some critics might term looting. He boasted that he was saving artifacts for museums to study and display that they would otherwise miss.

"As dealers we are preserving these objects and making them available for the world to appreciate," Moore told a reporter in 1984. "I think the artifacts belong to the world, not just the country whose ancestors conquered the ancient civilizations."

However, the United States soon signed a treaty that did make Moore's activities illegal. Now, to his consternation, U.S. Customs officials began confiscating his shipments, costing him tens of thousands of dollars each time he failed to deliver to his customers.

Finally Moore gave up and went back to the plant business, back to hacking his way through the jungle to find that one undiscovered flower no one had ever seen before, as orchid-hunters have done for two centuries.

England ruled the seven seas in the 1800s, when sailing vessels returning from South American and Asian ports would bring back spices, sugar, lumber, and occasionally a flower so exotic that it caused a sensation.

Gardeners clamored for these "tropical parasites," and then inevitably killed them because they didn't know how to grow them. They would notch a cut in a tree and tie the orchid in the notch with twine, figuring it would draw its nourishment from the flowing sap.

Even once they figured out that that was wrong, they were still killing their new acquisitions as fast as they arrived. Because the plants came from a tropical clime, the European growers believed the orchids needed suffocating heat and moisture—even if its original jungle habitat happened to be amid the clouds high in the Andes Mountains. If a flower bloomed once before wilting, the growers counted it a huge success. Then they would demand their sources send more orchids to replace the ones that shriveled up. Often they wanted as many as they could get their hands on, which led to the collectors stripping the jungle of every orchid they could dig up. One brought back forty-five thousand plants.

The English passion for orchids dates to 1818, when a naturalist named William Swainson made what was then the most astounding orchid discovery of the age—although he didn't realize it. He shipped a package home to England from Rio de Janeiro using some native plants as packing material to make sure nothing was damaged. When the crate arrived, the recipient, William Cattley, decided the packing material was more valuable than anything else Swainson had sent back. From it, he coaxed out a mauve flower five inches across, with a trumpet-like lip and a yellow throat. Named for its discoverer, *Cattleya labiata* caused a sensation among Victorian horticulturists, who dispatched collectors to jungles around the world to search for other hidden beauties.

The orchid frenzy that followed required the services of scores of collectors willing to brave any hardship in search of new plants. Many were "ill-equipped both in knowledge of their destination and supplies," a historian later wrote. "Many of them were never heard of again."

The best orchid hunters were daring, persistent, resourceful, imaginative, and often downright sneaky. Thomas Lobb didn't even trust his own employers, sending them wildly misleading information about where he found orchids in Asia so no rival collectors could ever take his place. Karl Theodor Hartweg, who spent seven years scouring Mexico for orchids, made his most spectacular discovery after he noticed a gorgeous bloom in the hat of a Quichole Indian and then tracked down the original plant it came from. George Ure Skinner, while exploring Guatemala, dreamed two nights in a row about a beautiful new orchid, then figured out where in the mountains it would be growing. He was delighted to discover his dream flower was in bloom, even though finding it "cost me all my clothes and shoes—being literally torn to shreds by climbing over precipices and rocks and spending two days in the woods."

They were men who could bear any hardship as long as there were never-before-seen orchids at the end of it. As Joseph Hooker searched the Indian jungles for plants, he was tormented by insect pests galore. Hooker wrote that he was bitten repeatedly by sand flies of a type he termed "an insatiable bloodsucker," while leeches "got into my hair, hung on my eyelids and crawled up my legs and down my back. I repeatedly took upwards of a hundred from my legs." Sundown brought no respite, he wrote, because "large and small moths, cockchafers, glow-worms, and cockroaches made my tent a Noah's ark by night . . . together with winged ants, May-flies, flying earwigs, and many beetles."

Worst of all, though, was a "loathsome tick" so horribly invasive and painful to remove that Hooker wrote: "A more odious insect it has never been my misfortune to encounter. . . . The very writing about them makes the flesh creep." Undaunted, he plowed on, discovering the *Dendrobium hookerianum* among other species. He then explored uncharted areas of Africa and North America before returning to England to take charge of the Royal Botanical Garden. Despite all the leeches and ticks, he lived to be ninety-four.

The all-time king of the orchid hunters has to be Benedict Roezl, a big, self-possessed Czech with a hook for a hand. He collected orchids from California to Patagonia, often traveling alone on foot or on horseback. He sent back eight hundred species previously unknown to science, and single-handedly (so to speak) stripped much of the Central American jungle bare. In 1869, Roezl sent an English nursery ten thousand orchids collected from Panama and Colombia.

As a lone traveler, Roezl became a frequent target for bandits. Once, robbers attacked him and were about to kill him. They opened his bag and discovered it held nothing but plants. Convinced he was mad, they let him live—it was considered bad luck to kill the insane. They fled, making the sign of the cross.

Roezl lived to be sixty-two and died in his own bed. He was such a well-respected figure that the kaiser himself attended his funeral. Prague put up a statue in his memory.

The risks faced by orchid hunters are somewhat different in modern times. In 2000, English orchid hunter Thomas Hart Dyke was kidnapped by Marxist guerrillas in Colombia. They held him and a companion hostage for nine months before freeing him.

"I thought we were going to die but it was worth it," he said after his release. "When you see orchids flowering they are extraordinary. Seeing something like a slipper orchid bloom can make you feel faint."

He then expressed a strong desire to go back into the jungle for a new search, explaining, "My whole life revolves around orchids." Instead, he wound up the star of a reality television show—the modern equivalent of a statue in Prague.

Without the orchid hunters risking life and limb, the science behind orchids would have lagged considerably. In many cases, their rewards were small: a bit of spending cash and taxonomic immortality.

Yet that form of immortality can be very appealing. It was, after all, what drove Lee Moore to return to the jungle year after year, plane crash or no plane crash.

Then, too, he had fallen in love with Peru just as he had fallen for Chady. Beyond the cities lay a rough country, a wild frontier where, as the saying goes, "Everything is difficult, but anything is possible." Moore said that's the very reason why he decided to live there: "It was plain and simple for the adventure of it."

Gringos had been hunting beautiful flowers in Peru since 1778, when Spain's King Carlos III had sent botanical expeditions to the Andes. In 1830, one of Victorian England's biggest orchid dealers assigned two of its top orchid hunters to Peru exclusively, under orders to hunt for new species.

Although some things had changed since the 1830s, a foreign-born orchid hunter living in Peru still had to keep his wits about him to stay alive—in fact, so did the Peruvians. The land of the Incas, once hailed by Spanish explorers as offering the richest bounty in the world, was now being torn apart.

Orchids weren't the only natural resource to be exploited. There were forests full of fine mahogany that rich people wanted for their furniture and fine homes. And then there were the coca leaves that the natives chewed.

By the 1980s, the whole country was under assault by cocaine gangs and Shining Path guerrillas, not to mention the military forces trying to shut down the first two. All three seemed bent on killing anyone who strayed into their path. In 2003, a presidential truth commission reported that during the last two decades of the twentieth century, the military and the Communist guerrillas killed an estimated twenty-nine thousand Peruvians, most of them dark-skinned peasants in villages scattered through the Andes. Seeking justice for even the worst transgression was often futile because corruption was rampant. Eventually even the president himself was convicted on corruption charges.

For someone like Moore, what offset the danger was the fact that Peru featured an astonishing array of plant life. It grew everywhere, from the tropical rain forest to the Andean plains and mountainsides. The peak of the globe's plant diversity, according to scientist E. O. Wilson, can be found in the combined flora of Colombia, Ecuador, and Peru, where an estimated forty thousand species grow on 2 percent of the world's land surface. Because the growing conditions vary—not just between jungle and mountain but even between ridges on the same mountain—small populations of each species are the rule. The plants tend to evolve quickly and then go extinct just as quickly—especially when new roads or ranches wipe out their habitat.

In the early 1990s, Moore and his wife bought 27 acres for a new nursery outside Moyobamba, a valley town well off the usual tourist track, about halfway between the steamy Amazon and the frozen Andes. The humid air gives visitors to Moyobamba the feeling that it was just carved out of the jungle. Actually it has been a city since 1540. The name Moyobamba means "circular plain" because the city sits on a flat spot overlooking the muddy Rio Mayo, where riverboats still ply the turbulent current. There are caves and waterfalls galore for the adventurous, but that's not what attracted The Adventurer.

Moyobamba is known as "the Orchid City" because in the cloud forest that still surrounds it are more than 2,500 recorded species of orchid and an untold number of unrecorded ones. Visitors are greeted at the entrance to the town by a gigantic statue of a *Cattleya* in bloom. Every fall, the city celebrates the Semana de la Orquides, or Orchid Festival.

"It's one of the richest areas for orchids in all of Peru," Moore said.

The Moores kept their overhead low by bringing in materials to build the

Peruvian nursery, rather than paying South American prices they believed to be exorbitant. On the Florida end, they didn't build or rent any commercial space in Miami, knowing how expensive that would be. Instead, they would ship their Peruvian orchids to their quiet apartment in a Miami suburb known as Kendall.

"I put them in my bedroom and in my living room," Moore said. "I sit and box them up and mail them out from my living room."

To mark their new beginning, he and Chady named their new orchid business Vivero Nuevo Destino—New Destiny Nursery. Yet the same old things kept happening to him.

In 1991, he attempted to import into the United States one of his namesake orchids, a *Cattleya mooreana*. Remarkably, the plant bore a seedpod. It marked the first time anyone had ever seen one of the flowers with as many as 2 million seeds.

"It took thirty-plus years to find this plant," Moore told the *Miami Herald*. If those seeds had been planted, "the plant would no longer have been rare."

He shipped it out of Peru with 1,500 more common orchids, a shipment he later figured was worth $60,000 in advance sales. But customs officials, believing he was smuggling orchids, seized the shipment.

Moore swore all the plants had been grown in a nursery, making them legal to import into the United States. His permits showed they all came from Vivero Agro-Oriente, a Moyobamba nursery run by a man named Renato Villena. Moore insisted Villena had provided him with all the proper Peruvian export permits. But that's not the way the U.S. Department of Agriculture perceived it.

"In looking over the plants, our experts determined that they were wild collected, not nursery-grown, so the certificate was invalid," a USDA spokeswoman told the paper.

The mislabeling of wild orchids is, in fact, a popular dodge among the Moyobamba orchid dealers, Moore said years later. Most of the nurseries in the Orchid City don't really know how to grow the orchids in their greenhouses, he explained. They find it far easier to pay the poorer residents of the area to go into the jungle around the city to bring back what they need, then label the flowers as if they had been grown in a greenhouse.

Moore was incensed at being accused of smuggling orchids. He took the federal government to court to force it to return his plants. In the end, he said, he both won and lost. He got the orchids back, but by then they were dead, and his seedpod lost.

The outcome had a certain ironic justice, however. Nearly two decades later, he conceded that the USDA had him dead to rights. His permits from Vivero Agro-Oriente were bogus. He said he fought against the accusation just because the government had made him mad.

"I said, 'Some little asshole in the federal government wants to put a feather in his cap at my expense,'" Moore recalled. "So the government said they were wild-collected—which they were."

Since then, Moore says, he has always been on the up and up, and he's had no further trouble with the USDA over his shipments of orchids and bromeliads.

Despite his problems with the government, Moore's past made him something of a rock star to certain orchid fanciers, and he knew it. He is prone to say, "I am an icon," or "They call me an icon."

In 2001, while flying back to Miami from Peru, Moore found himself in conversation with a tall, skinny man sitting in the seat next to him. Moore's seatmate had long brown hair pulled back in a ponytail, glasses, and a mouth like a mail slot. He said he, too, collected orchids. He had a nursery in Virginia and was looking to stock it with some of the jungle's beauties. His name: James Michael Kovach, pronounced KO-vack. He preferred to be called Michael—not James, not Jim, not Jimmy.

A friendship blossomed. Kovach simply couldn't get enough of the man for whom the *Cattleya mooreana*, *Catasetum moorei*, and *Scuticaria mooreana* are named.

"He told me once, 'Lee, you're famous because you've got a lot of plants named for you. I wish I could have a plant named for me,'" Moore recalled.

Soon Kovach would get his chance—and it would change his life, and the lives of dozens of other people, in ways he could never have anticipated.

"Oh, the cost of fame," Moore chuckled.

4

The Carpenter

With some individuals it is difficult to decide whether
orchids were the fulfillment or the curse of a lifetime,
whether there was a mission with a guiding principle or an
ill-starred passion that would exact the highest price.

Luigi Berliocchi, *The Orchid in Lore and Legend*

The town where Michael Kovach lived was built on looking for the big payoff, the discovery that would put you on Easy Street for the rest of your life. It's even part of the name: Goldvein.

About 15 miles from the state capital of Richmond, Goldvein sits atop Virginia's 200-mile-long gold belt. Early settlers panned for gold in the rivers. But then, in the early 1800s, they began digging mines, searching for the veins that would lead them to the mother lode. Eventually Fauquier County, where Goldvein is located, became home to about eighteen gold mines. The most famous, the Franklin, had shafts that went 300 feet deep. From 1825 to the Civil War, miners working the Franklin found more than $1 million worth of gold. The Franklin had its own lumber mill, too, which produced the boards used to build the miners' bunkhouses, their dining hall, a pay office, and ties for the railroad that carried the gold to the bank.

As with all gold mines, though, this one eventually played out and the miners moved on. Now it's the site of a mining museum, an attempt by local businesses to pan for gold from the few passing tourists who have wandered outside Richmond. By the end of the 1990s, Goldvein held only five hundred inhabitants, just enough to support two Baptist churches, a post office, and a general store. In short, this was not a promising place to launch a new business.

Kovach lived in Goldvein in a single-story house with dark-toned, tongue-and-groove wood siding and an attached carport, all at the end of a gravel drive. He had a magnificent view and a wife who loved him, which for some people would be enough. His wife, Barbara Ellison, made a good living as a photographer for a big camera manufacturer, Canon. Her job was teaching Canon customers all over the country how to take artsy pictures. She'd show them the right aperture settings and shutter speeds, which lenses to use, that kind of thing. They had no children.

The couple had come to Goldvein via a roundabout path. Kovach was born in Alaska, where his father was stationed in the army. Like a lot of military families, his moved around a lot until finally his father got a job at the Pentagon. That's when they settled on the Virginia side of Washington. His mother, whom Kovach referred to as "a West Virginia debutante," had been a stewardess who met his father on a flight to Alaska. Family lore said she was descended from the Clark half of Lewis and Clark. Kovach contended the explorer gene manifested itself in him from an early age.

"As soon as I could walk and talk I wanted to be outdoors," he said. He wanted to know about plants and bugs and rocks. He learned about camping and canoeing and backpacking in the Boy Scouts, earning the rank of Eagle, he said. In school, his best subjects were in science—particularly biology and geology.

As a teenager, he tried the vagabond life, bumming around Europe. The onetime Eagle Scout became a hippie, a laid-back, long-haired wanderer. Yet he also regarded himself as a man of God, an unordained itinerant street minister.

His calling, he said, was to help anyone in trouble, even if all he did was listen to their litany of woes. But he was no amen-shouting deacon. He felt that many of his fellow Christians were hypocrites who didn't understand the true purpose of the gospel. Unlike them, he said, he wasn't "going to church for the fashion show or the guilt dump or to buy insurance."

Unlike some of his fellow believers, Kovach could not point to a single conversion experience, a moment on the road to Damascus where God knocked him flat with a blinding light. Instead, he said, his attitude toward God was something he had always felt in his heart.

"I've just got my own thing going on," he explained. "When I wake up in the morning, I say: 'Hello, God, I'm going to be the best Mike Kovach I can be today.' That's my prayer."

Jesus was a carpenter. Kovach found work as a carpenter, too, doing trim and finish work wherever he could find someone who needed his services. In the late 1980s, though, the construction industry hit a slump and money got tight. He and some friends from his hippie days organized a round-robin Wednesday barbecue. Each week one of them would throw a feast for the others, so at least once a week they would all eat well. Soon other people were joining in. At one barbecue, he met Ellison, already working for Canon. The carpenter and the photographer hit it off, but he says they left the feast thinking their tastes were so different that "this is never going to work." Eventually, to the surprise of their friends, they wound up getting married.

"My buddies were all taking bets on whether the marriage would last six days or six months," Kovach said, laughing. "They're all on their third wives by now, and I'm still with my first wife."

Ellison particularly liked shooting pictures of flowers. When she was growing up in Illinois, she wrote in a memoir: "My mother had a series of fantastic gardens where she spent many hours a day tending her flowers. The way of spending time with her was to get my hands in the dirt and learn all I could about the flowers."

One day in 1991 Ellison brought home a moth orchid, one of the easiest orchids to care for. She had seen it at a plant fair and bought it on impulse. She put it in a sunny spot in the living room, where it thrived despite being neglected.

At that point, Kovach had been praying for God to point him toward a new career. A few weeks after his wife brought home the moth orchid, Kovach began thinking about that plant, and about orchids in general. Then he got the sign he had been waiting for, albeit from an unlikely source.

"Something inside said, 'Get up off the couch and look out the window,'" Kovach told a reporter in 1996. "So I did. In front of my house about five cars had just pulled up. It was the neighbor's high school kids. It was June. They all got out in their tuxes and evening gowns for the prom. They all had corsages and boutonnieres."

He looked at the high school kids and their flowers, then looked back at his wife's orchid. With minimal care, the moth orchid had sprouted fourteen big flowers. An idea dawned.

"Light bulbs kind of went off," Kovach said. "I know what a corsage cost. I kind of went, 'Aha!'"

Goldvein's miners would have recognized the sensation.

Kovach built a greenhouse behind his house—not a big, fancy one, as the more serious orchid growers have, but something modest, befitting a beginner. Meanwhile he started reading everything he could find on orchids.

He found in their intricacy signs of the deity he worshiped, a creator whose blueprint for the universe encompassed even the smallest details.

"I see these flowers, and I cannot deny the existence of God," he explained once.

However, he soon learned that selling corsages and boutonnieres in a small Virginia town would not bring him the financial success he sought. Instead, like Lee Moore, he launched a mail-order nursery business. He started traveling to orchid shows in other states to show off his flowers and attract customers. His wife got her chance to shoot a lot of her favorite subject, documenting his 8,000-plant inventory with photos he could then display for potential buyers. They called the business Southwind Orchids.

Kovach began pestering orchid experts for answers to his many, many questions, not just about flowers but also about the nursery business.

He struck up an acquaintance with a bombastic Texan named George Norris who, like Kovach, ran an orchid business out of his home. Norris called his business Spring Orchid Specialties, "Importers of Rare and Unusual Orchids." Norris, who started his business in the mid-1980s, was prone to sending out e-mails IN ALL CAPITAL LETTERS. In every newsletter and price list he sent out, he SOUNDED LIKE HE WAS YELLING. By the late 1990s, Norris was raking in thousands of dollars a year in profit, and had begun using his newsletters as a platform for his views on more than just botany. Fellow orchid enthusiasts knew Norris to be a staunch Republican who was, as one put it, "patriotic to the point of arrogance, quick to take offense at any seeming slight of his beloved country and government."

Following Norris's lead, Kovach began importing orchids from overseas, bringing them in from South America and Asia at wholesale rates and then selling them at retail prices. In 1996, upon Norris's advice, Kovach flew to Peru for the first time to buy orchids. He stayed there from September 25 to October 16, nearly a month, and according to the permits he carried, he brought back more than 1,100 orchids.

For this trip, Norris helped set Kovach up with a supplier in Peru that Norris used frequently, Manuel Arias Silva. Arias was an unfailingly polite man sometimes called "El Professore" because he had once been a teacher. The bombastic Norris and the obsequious Arias had been friends for more than a decade at that point. In 1988, Norris had spent two weeks staying with Arias and his family, collecting plants from Peru and checking out Arias's budding nursery operation.

By the time Kovach met him, Arias was a courtly gentleman in his early sixties, with heavy jowls and eyebrows so thick they looked like rabid caterpillars. He had been married for more than thirty years to the same woman, and the couple had raised two sons. The boys were burned in a fire in the late 1980s. George and Kathy Norris helped arrange for Arias's sons to get plastic surgery in Texas, and let the boys stay at the Norris home for six months while recovering—a sign of how close the two orchid growers were, despite hailing from different countries and cultures.

Arias's nursery, in the capital city of Lima, bore the simple yet elegant name "Orquidaria," although it also went by the name "Peruflora." He ran it with his father and one of his sons. With Norris's help, Orquidaria soon became one of the best-known orchid exporters in Peru, and thus Arias was one of the best people in Peru for a novice like Kovach to get to know during his first trip to the country. A few years after Kovach's visit, though, El Professore would become a fugitive from justice, sought for his role in a long-term scheme to smuggle orchids into the United States.

Despite Arias's polite façade, "you had to be on your toes to negotiate with him," Kovach said years later. Kovach particularly liked Arias's father, who "only wanted to sip cognac, smoke cigars, and dance the tango," he said. All in all, he judged the proprietor of Orquidaria and his family to be "good people."

Of course, he added, "old man Arias stiffed me for $900." Kovach said George Norris's most trusted Peruvian partner had charged him that much for obtaining shipping permits that, he later learned, cost only seventy-five dollars. The overcharge helped pay for a new pump for the Orquidaria greenhouse. Kovach shrugged off the con.

"I still got what I wanted for the price I wanted to pay," he said. "Besides, these people, they're living in a poor country."

Through experience, Kovach had learned that every orchid transaction in a foreign country involved a little corruption—finessing a permit with a judicious bribe, paying someone to look the other way or to leave your shipment alone.

"Everywhere I went, you've got to have the envelope and the hand shake," he said.

At first he phoned the U.S. Fish and Wildlife Service to try to report wrongdoing. Because he had no proof, his calls were to no avail. Eventually, though, he came to view the pay-to-play world of orchid collecting as being little different from what happens in Washington, D.C., where big companies donate to campaign funds so they can get favorable treatment from Congress. He didn't begrudge a few lowly customs officials asking for a taste of the action.

"I got to where I looked at it as their retirement fund," he explained.

Finding a way of sliding around the rules was just the price of succeeding in the orchid business, it seemed. Kovach explained his views in a 1998 letter to Vietnamese orchid suppliers: "In our business, the largest margin of profit is being able to be consistent in providing species that are endangered, and in constantly being the first to provide new and/or rare plants."

Over time, he became adept at sliding things past the inspectors. On Valentine's Day 2000, Kovach sent a letter to a Panamanian orchid collector giving him a list of orchids he wanted to gather prior to making a tour of Midwest orchid shows in March and April. He asked to sleep in the collector's chicken-house hammock for two nights during his visit. Kovach told his Panamanian friend he would need some pre-approved export permits for the orchids so he would not have to wait around while the paperwork was being processed. Kovach wrote that he might wind up with some orchids not already on his list that needed special export permits, but "I can fudge similar-looking species into listed batches—since no taxonomist will be reviewing the order."

Kovach is the pivotal figure in this drama. Without him, none of what followed would have occurred. His account of what he did and saw and said is crucial.

He has told his story repeatedly—talking to reporters, giving handwritten accounts of his actions to federal investigators, even penning a first-person piece for an orchid-collectors' newsletter. The problem is, none of his stories completely jibes with the others. Sometimes he portrays himself as a noble savior of rare plants, a servant of science. Sometimes he comes across more as a bold entrepreneur, seizing his chance at a big payday—his gold vein, if you will.

Even Kovach calls himself a walking contradiction. In one breath, he says he was "a big sap" who naively let others exploit his gullibility. In the next, he portrays himself as a savvy businessman who knew what the law required and followed it to the letter—but then ran afoul of overzealous law enforcement agencies looking to score publicity points.

To Lee Moore, who is something of an expert on the subject, Kovach came across as "a bullshitter."

According to Moore, Kovach claimed to be a former U.S. Army Green Beret, skilled in all the ways to kill an enemy. He said he had seen action in Vietnam—a story Moore found downright implausible, given Kovach's comparative youth. (Kovach says it was his father who was the Green Beret, not him.)

Yet despite that, they regarded one another with some affection. Kovach explained: "I could generally trust Lee. He knew I would hold him to whatever he promised to do. But I could never trust Chady. She was too greedy."

Nevertheless, Kovach's various accounts of what happened don't agree with what Moore and his wife say occurred, either.

For instance, Kovach says he made his second trip to Peru on May 11, 2001. This is the trip on which both he and Lee Moore say they met by accident on the flight back to Miami. However, according to a written account that Kovach gave to the U.S. Department of Agriculture a year later, "this trip was specifically to begin a contract orchid farm/lab on a friend's farm. . . . I spent most of this trip supervising the erection of a shade house and installation of a water cistern and pump house."

Kovach did not name his friend, but he was talking about Moore. In another version of his story, Kovach says he had "needed someone to share land and local labor to really efficiently mass-produce species orchids for some time." In that account, he names Moore, and says The Adventurer was "receptive to the deal"—but puts the date of their discussion in 2002. No matter what the date, Moore adamantly denies they discussed going into business together prior to Kovach's 2002 trip.

During his two-week visit to Peru in May 2001, Kovach did some exploring around Moyobamba, looking for plants that would be "starter or brood stock" for this orchid farm/lab, he wrote.

In one account of his travels, Kovach said he hired a driver to take him miles beyond Moyobamba, finding that the local orchid collectors had stripped the roadsides of the most interesting native species. While driving around, he had the driver pull over at a rustic truck stop with the overly optimistic name of El Progresso. At the truck stop stood a crude wooden building, the South American counterpart to the classic American roadside diner. In the El Progresso diner, the food items on the menu were *sopa de caldo* (old hen soup) and *cuy* (guinea pig).

"You actually go into the kitchen to choose the *cuy* you want for lunch," Kovach wrote.

At El Progresso, Kovach met Faustino Medina Bautista, a copper-skinned farmer with thick black eyebrows, a bulbous nose, a beer-belly paunch, and ten children. He and his family ran a small, wood-framed stand full of plants for sale to the passing tourists. The family told him they had something special for the discerning collector. They took him to see it growing in a field, Kovach told federal investigators a year later. But Kovach wrote that he was not sold on the mystery plant, not just yet.

"I was unsure what it was (out of bloom) and knowing I was coming again next year, waited," he wrote in 2002.

When he saw it again the following spring, though, he knew what it was. He had struck the mother lode, the gold vein of all gold veins for an orchid collector. He could at last point to an accomplishment to rival, if not exceed, anything The Adventurer had ever done.

What he didn't know at the time was that others were on the hunt for his prize as well.

5

The Holy Grail

On the whole, the flower looks like some alien, anomalous
creature, seeming to transcend the vegetable world and at
times emanating an indefinably sinister air. It looks for all
the world like a visitor from an unknown planet.

Luigi Berliocchi, *The Orchid in Lore and Legend*

The biggest orchid show in the United States takes place every spring in one
of the unlikeliest spots imaginable—not in a convention center or a hotel,
but in an open field in a rural area about thirty minutes south of glittering
Miami. Yet it attracts attendees from Australia, Taiwan, the Philippines, Bra-
zil, Thailand, and, of course, Peru. Between eight thousand and ten thousand
orchid fanciers flock to the show.

They all converge on the Redland Fruit & Spice Park just outside the small
town of Homestead. According to one of the organizers, Martin Motes of
Motes Orchids, holding the annual Redland International Orchid Festival
in this open-air park turned out to be the key to its enormous popularity.

"There's no other event that I know of where there will be so many [or-
chids] and people can see them in the clear light of day," Motes said. "Fluo-
rescent lights tend to skew some color ranges, so that reds and blues tend to
shift. Under some other types of lights, yellows to orange shift, so you're not
seeing true colors."

The Redland show started as a way to cope with a disaster. Homestead
had been Ground Zero for the damage caused by Hurricane Andrew in 1992.
While the disaster drove away some growers, such as Bob Scully, others
chose to rebuild. The ones who rebuilt their operations decided to put on a
show to let everyone know the Redland growers were back in business.

They designed the Redland show to appeal to every level of expertise. The festival offered classes on plant care for casual orchid fanciers, while for the more serious hobbyists there were lecturers from around the world discussing the species grown in their countries. There was a competition, of course, to attract the orchid fanciers eager for the adulation and envy that a blue ribbon can bestow. Of the fifty vendors who were approved for participation, many sold orchid-related gardening supplies along with a rainbow of orchids at varying prices.

The most expensive orchids were not on display for the general public. Their vendors knew to keep those special flowers out of sight, and offer them only to the right buyers—the ones who knew how to keep a secret, the ones they were sure weren't government snoops out to bust a careless smuggler.

Ted Green flew in from his home in Hawaii for the sixth annual Redland show, which ran from May 16 to May 18, 2002. Green was in his seventies and had been raising orchids for decades. He had long been a vocal critic of the laws governing the trade in orchids, complaining that they were not only unfair but counterproductive. Everyone in the orchid community knew him, both for his orchids and his opinions. As Green strolled around the Redland show, one of the vendors beckoned him to come closer.

"Want to see something really special?" the man asked, reaching beneath the drape covering the display table. From under the cloth he pulled a spectacular orchid, one that Green had never seen before.

But this was a slipper orchid, and Green had no interest in those. He said no thanks and walked on.

Other people at the Redland show saw or at least heard about this amazing new slipper orchid. Word was, it came from Peru. The rumored price: $10,000 per plant.

One of the judges picking the winners at the 2002 Redland show was a member of Selby's OIC staff. John Beckner, a balding, heavyset man, had once been a teacher. Although he had worked for Selby for years, he still had a teacher's didactic manner. This was far from his first Redland show. Beckner hailed from Miami originally, so he was accustomed to making the long drive across the state.

On the last day of the Redland show, Beckner said later, he was chatting with a couple of orchid growers he knew when they mentioned about the rumors they had heard about someone selling a $10,000 orchid from Peru.

Beckner's first reaction was to blurt out: "Don't tell me that! I've got a credit card in my pocket with that exact credit limit. Don't put temptation in front of me like that!"

His second, more serious, reaction was to wonder if Lee Moore might be the one hawking this plant.

"I've known Lee since the '50s, and I figured if something new had been found in Peru, I figured he'd be involved somehow," Beckner explained. He did not know that Moore wasn't an approved vendor at the 2002 show.

Beckner's friends gave him directions to the table where they had heard the Peruvian plant might be for sale. He set off walking. The show was huge and sprawling. The temperature was above 90 degrees. The steamy South Florida heat made sweat roll down his sides and back.

After walking for a while, Beckner decided he'd gotten turned around somehow and missed his target. He spotted a booth selling soft drinks and stopped to buy a two-dollar Pepsi.

While he was paying, a couple more friends hailed him, and he wandered over to sit with them. He asked if they had any idea where this mystery flower might be. They said they hadn't seen it, either. Finally he gave up, tracking back to the parking lot. He drove home with the air-conditioner turned up full-blast.

Later, much later, he wondered if the story had gotten tangled somehow. It could have been that someone was just showing pictures of this flower and taking orders for it.

"There would be nothing wrong in itself with that," he said.

Beckner wasn't the only Selby orchid expert who had been at the Redland show. Bob Scully, the new chairman, was there as well, judging the show at his old Redland stomping grounds. But Scully said later he didn't see any undiscovered Peruvian plants. He didn't even hear the same rumors Beckner had heard. But soon he'd hear plenty.

Beckner loved to be the first one in the OIC to report the latest stories going around the orchid world. His coworkers knew he collected gossip the way kids used to collect baseball cards. On his first day back at work after the Redland show, Beckner immediately told all of his OIC colleagues about what he'd heard, about how someone was showing off this new orchid and charging thousands of dollars for it. He told them that this mysterious Peruvian flower might turn out to be the next big thing to sweep the orchid world, the next *Phragmipedium besseae*. If only he'd actually seen it!

Beckner's tales from the Redland show only served to whet the orchid boys' appetites.

Then, on Monday, June 3, a Texas orchid grower named Dave Hunt e-mailed Wesley Higgins some photos of a big, flashy purple orchid.

"Wes, do you recognize this species?" Hunt asked in his terse e-mail.

Higgins thought the pictures were stunning. He asked Hunt where he'd gotten this new slipper species.

"I don't have it," Hunt replied via e-mail. "The pictures were sent to me from Peru. I hope to have more info later. The flower is supposedly 15 cm [centimeters] across!"

The orchid boys all studied the photos sent in by Hunt. Taking an especially close look was Scully's old friend John Atwood. The New Englander specialized in slipper orchids, and this clearly was one he had never seen before.

It wasn't easy to give a definitive answer based solely on pictures, but the OIC's experts decided this was the real deal.

"We were glad to see the pictures but couldn't do anything more" about the new species, Dalström said. Not without actually seeing the orchid in question, that is.

The Selby experts feared they might be too late, though. The photos Hunt sent them came from a Peruvian nursery called Vivero Agro-Oriente, run by Renato Villena and his daughter Karol.

Vivero Agro-Oriente had been one of just two Peruvian vendors among the sixty at the Redland Show. Vivero Agro-Oriente's Karol Villena was the orchid vendor that Beckner had heard might be selling the new orchid for $10,000 at the Redland show. (The other Peruvian booth at the show had been run by a grower named Alfredo Manrique, who had not figured in any rumors—yet.)

Agro-Oriente sent its photos to other orchid growers besides Hunt. George Norris, the bombastic Texas orchid grower who had counseled Kovach years before—and was himself a vendor at the 2002 Redland show—later reported getting the same pictures from Karol Villena.

"IT IS A GREAT PLANT, AND OBVIOUSLY SOME PEOPLE ARE GONNA MAKE SOME MONEY WITH IT," Norris wrote in one of his typical all-caps e-mails.

With all the photos floating around on the Internet, Higgins said later, the Selby experts figured some rival taxonomist must have already seen the plant and set to work giving it a name and a formal scientific description. They all agreed that the most likely one to beat them to it would be a California botany professor named Harold Koopowitz. Like Atwood, he was an expert on slipper orchids, and he might already be writing up a description for *Orchid Digest* magazine, where he was editor. There was little they could do about that without having their hands on the real flower.

Very soon, though, the orchid boys would get a chance to see this new flower in person, courtesy of the president of Southwind Orchids and his friend Lee Moore.

⚬ఞ

Lee Moore's wife, Chady, heard about the mysterious Peruvian flower before her husband did. She said she first heard about it from a rival orchid grower. He told her that a competitor, Renato Villena, was selling an amazing new slipper orchid.

The rival said he knew about this orchid because he had helped Villena's daughter Karol "pack them to take to the orchid sales show in the Redland," Chady Moore said.

The Adventurer's wife said later she dismissed the story because the man had described an orchid too fabulous to be true: "If you're in the orchid-hunting trade, you always hear tall tales about the Next Big Thing out there." This was, she said, "like too many other stories I have heard over the years."

Still, she knew Renato Villena had the ability to pull off a coup like this. After all, his Vivero Agro-Oriente was the same Moyobamba nursery that had helped her husband get that *Cattleya mooreana* with a seedpod into the United States in 1991.

Villena, a slender, hawk-faced man, had deep-set eyes and a mass of dark hair so wavy it would make a surfer swoon. He harbored political ambitions, and had launched a campaign for vice president of his region. There was a time when Moore and Villena had been good friends and even discussed going into business together, but it didn't work out, according to Moore. Moore no longer considered Villena an ally—quite the opposite, in fact. He described the proprietor of Vivero Agro-Oriente this way: "He's a short, gnome-like creature with a very nice smile on his face. When you meet him, you'd say, 'What a nice guy.' But he's a God-damned thief, a liar, a heinous S.O.B., in a word."

When Renato Villena wanted to attract some American buyers, he would dispatch his daughter Karol to the United States to make the rounds. She was more fluent in English than he was. She would set up booths at various orchid shows around the country—including the Redland show. But she said she did not take illegal orchids to the 2002 Redland show, despite the rumors John Beckner heard.

According to Karol Villena, on May 4, 2002, as she prepared to leave Lima for the Redland show, her father sent her photos of a spectacular new slipper orchid, the same photos Dave Hunt later sent Higgins. She said he told her that he had found someone selling them at a roadside stand two days before, so he bought two of them—one in flower, one not.

She intended to take the photos with her to the Redland show—not the actual flowers—but in her rush to make the plane she forgot them, she said. She left the envelope of photos in her apartment in Lima. So she called her brother and asked him to scan the photos into his computer and e-mail them to her. That way she could take her laptop to the Redland show and let certain customers view the pictures. She said she was able to show them to a few people who visited her booth, folks who would be interested in and knowledgeable about slipper orchids. She said her only interest was in identifying the orchid, not selling it.

However, she said, "it was difficult to have a computer during the exposition. I was very busy with my booth so I just asked people around if it was a new species. . . . But people that had other booths said that they thought it was *Phragmipedium schlimii* from Colombia, and someone else said from Ecuador. I was very disappointed to hear this and I just concentrated to my stuff."

She figured once she got back to Peru, she could e-mail the photos to some experts for their opinion—Dave Hunt, George Norris, and others—and that's what she did. Meanwhile, though, other collectors would soon be chasing the same flower.

On May 2, 2002—two weeks before the Redland show, and the very day that, according to his daughter, Renato Villena bought that new orchid—Lee Moore sent Kovach a fax suggesting dates for them to travel through Peru together. They had talked of taking a trip together, and now the time had come to plan it.

"I am looking at a ballpark date of the 23rd for us to go down," Moore scrawled in longhand on his stationery, which bore the letterhead "Lee Moore The Adventurer."

Moore told Kovach they should spend four or five days in Moyobamba, and "after that we plan to go to the new area I spoke of." They would return to the United States around June 6, he said.

On May 21, 2002, Kovach and his wife caught an evening flight to Miami on U.S. Air out of National Airport in Washington, D.C. They boarded a flight to Lima the next day. They spent their first night in Peru with the Moores, then flew with them to the town of Tarapota. That was as far as commercial airlines could take them. The only way to get to Moyobamba was by car.

The drive from Tarapota to Moyobamba took four hours because the road through the mountains was unpaved, Moore recalled later. There were plenty of huge potholes requiring drivers to slow down to a crawl.

"We drove across at night," Moore said. "That's the time when bandits wait at these potholes for cars to slow down or stop. So we got to one pothole and our driver stopped, and two bandits in ski masks jumped out and yelled, 'Hands up!'"

According to Moore, his wife, Chady, leaned forward to hiss at the driver, "If you don't put your foot on that gas pedal *I'll* kill you." The driver floored it, and the car roared past the bandits.

"And where was Michael, the Green Beret guy, who said he was a commando?" Moore said, cackling. "He hid under the seat!" (Kovach does not mention this incident in any of his accounts.)

Kovach later told federal investigators that he and his wife spent the next day touring several nurseries around Moyobamba, buying plants. Among the ones he visited: Vivero Agro-Oriente, owned by Renato Villena.

In an affidavit to investigators, Kovach wrote that he bought some orchids there, and that Renato Villena agreed to take care of preparing all his export paperwork for all the orchids he had bought and all the ones he was going to collect. In none of his accounts does Kovach mention seeing the new orchid at Vivero Agro-Oriente that Chady Moore had heard about and that Karol Villena says was already there. Nor does he mention hearing about it from either Renato Villena or Mrs. Moore. He did, however, complain that in their dealings, Renato Villena conned him out of some money with a scam involving a fake tax—just as Manuel Arias Silva had done six years before.

Early on the morning of May 26, 2002, Kovach and his wife drove up into the mountains looking for orchids. Moore says he had told Kovach that was the right place to go looking. He didn't go with them, he says, because he was supervising some construction at his Nuevo Destino nursery.

There were four people in the hunting party that day. The Kovachs sat in the back. They had hired the Moores' driver, Jose Mendoza Gomez— the one who had driven past the bandits—to take them where they wanted to go. Gomez brought along his toddler, explaining it was his turn to watch the boy.

Kovach told Gomez to head north to a village called Chachapoya. By the time they arrived at 9:30 a.m., Gomez's son had become carsick, so they stopped in the village to buy something to settle the boy's stomach. Then they began to backtrack back toward Moyobamba, "in particular looking for slash, roadwork, treefalls etc.," Kovach wrote.

The Peruvian authorities had been busy building new roads through the jungle to connect the more remote villages, making it easier for farmers to carry their produce to other towns for sale. Kovach explained that orchids found along the side of such new roads "usually will die, so we rescue them; better in cultivation than dead."

However, as they drove south, opportunities both for photographing flowers and harvesting them from the wild seemed sparse close to the road, Kovach wrote. The Moyobamba orchid collectors had stripped the landscape of everything they could carry.

Meanwhile the sun dipped lower on the horizon. "I became concerned about being on the road after dark," Kovach wrote. "The threat of armed robbery and/or terrorist assault increases exponentially after dark."

So instead of trolling slowly for plants by the roadside, they decided to head straight for El Progresso "as I knew of a roadside plant vendor there," he wrote.

"As we approached the place, we saw several tables to one side of the lot with shade covers and potted orchid species," Kovach wrote in a newsletter for orchid collectors. "Even from thirty to forty yards away, it was obvious that many beautiful, unusual things abounded here."

They pulled in and bought some bottles of a yellow soft drink called Inca Kola—more popular in Peru than either Coca-Cola or Pepsi—to quench their thirst. They skipped ordering any guinea pig for a late lunch and instead strolled around looking at the plants for sale at Faustino Medina Bautista's stand, the one Kovach said he had visited the previous year.

Medina and a young woman he identified as his sister approached the couple to negotiate on the prices. Ultimately they agreed on fifty cents to $1.50 each for the *maxillarias* and other species Kovach wanted.

Kovach wrote that he was just reaching for his wallet "when the young woman told me that she had some plants in the back of the building. I asked if she wanted me to pass through with her. She told me that there were only a few and that she would fetch them."

When she returned, Kovach couldn't stop gawking at this vision before him.

"I was struggling not to let my jaw scrape the ground," he told a reporter six months later.

He recognized the thing she carried as resembling a slipper orchid, but it was bigger than any slippers he'd ever seen. Its stalk rose a full foot. And the flower! The petals seemed as broad as a boulevard, their color a shade of pinkish-purple so rich and deep that it could have been cut from one of Gorgeous George's wrestling costumes. It looked like a frozen explosion, a freeze-framed blast of raspberry fireworks painted on the richest velvet. Truly this was a find to eclipse Libby Besse's long-ago discovery, and maybe every other astounding orchid discovery since William Cattley first coaxed a flower out of some packing material.

"I guessed that it was a new species, maybe even a new genus," Kovach wrote later.

When Kovach asked the price, Medina told him, "Venta soles." That was the equivalent of $3.60.

"Now, you must consider a cultural note here," Kovach wrote. "If I don't try to negotiate a lower price, I have committed two social faux pas. First I have insulted a hard-working man by showing contempt for the value of money. Second, I am a person who is a fool and deserves no respect as a result."

So he tried to haggle. To his dismay, Medina stuck to his guns, even when the Moores' driver stepped in and asked why he was being rude. Kovach, realizing the farmer knew this flower was something special, agreed at last to pay the asking price.

"We then loaded our neatly boxed plants into the car and proceeded down the road to Moyobamba," he wrote.

Kovach couldn't wait to brag about his find to Moore. Although it was late when Kovach and his wife returned to their hotel, he called Moore.

"You ought to see this plant I found," he told The Adventurer. "It's got to be something new."

In one account he gave investigators, Kovach said that the next morning he mailed all the plants he had collected "to a friend's farm" and then he and his wife set off to tour Peru since his wife had never seen the countryside.

In the version he wrote for the orchid-collectors' newsletter, however, Kovach says that the next morning he and his wife had breakfast with the Moores, and then he showed the flower to them.

They were duly impressed at finally seeing this vision they had heard about. Moore, remembering Kovach's wish to someday have a flower named after him, says he told Kovach: "This is your chance. You've got the Holy Grail of orchids."

They snapped a few photos of Kovach's find. One shot showed a potted plant sitting on the hood of the white car that had taken Kovach to El

Progresso. It looked like a freakishly large and poorly placed radio antenna with the most garish antenna-topper ever manufactured. Another showed a close-up of a somewhat wilted bloom, which was still big enough to cover the palm of Chady Moore's hand. A third one showed Kovach himself, smiling at the camera and holding the flower in front of his chest.

They were excited about the commercial possibilities, Moore said later. They discussed a partnership where Moore would grow the orchids in Peru and ship them to Kovach to sell to collectors in the United States. They could foresee making a fortune.

Right about then, according to Kovach's account for the orchid-collectors' newsletter, Renato Villena showed up on a motorbike.

Even though Moore and Villena regarded each other as competitors and enemies, according to Kovach the proprietor of Agro-Oriente "joined us for coffee while Lee and I began to talk to him about my desire to buy plants and to accommodate my collected plants in the order."

Although all of a vendor's plants might be collected from the wild, Kovach wrote, government officials in Peru's version of the U.S. Fish and Wildlife Service, the Instituto Nacional de Recursos Naturales, or INRENA for short, treat them as if they are greenhouse-grown. More importantly, from his point of view, they treated smaller shipments as noncommercial, he wrote.

If a shipment were small enough, then it didn't matter whether the shipper's intention was to sell the plants. They would still be classified as noncommercial, and thus would not need certain commercial permits, he wrote.

"At any rate, Senor Villena assured me that there would be no problems," Kovach wrote. "He would take care of interfacing with officials from INRENA. . . . Renato said that for a small fee he would handle the cleaning of the collected plants and arrange for and complete the inspections. He would walk my paper through the agencies and meet with the local head of INRENA."

Kovach did not define what he meant by "interfacing" with INRENA, although it suggests the greasing of skids through personal charm, long friendship, or something sleazier. INRENA inspectors were not regarded as paragons of rectitude. A year later, the *New York Times* reported that an investigation of INRENA found that fourteen of the agency's twenty administrators had probably been involved in corruption.

However Villena achieved the feat of sliding the orchids through the bureaucracy, he promised he would then send all of Kovach's plants—including Kovach's dramatic El Progresso purchase—along to Lima by bus, Kovach wrote.

Michael Kovach knew he had found the Holy Grail of orchid hunters, but Lee Moore says he told Kovach he would never get a permit to get it out of Peru. Photo courtesy of Lee Moore.

Kovach and Moore then spent the rest of the day in a taxi, running around Moyobamba procuring steel cable for a new greenhouse at the Moores' farm. The next morning, Kovach, Ellison, and Lee Moore boarded a plane for Lima. Chady Moore stayed behind to take care of farm business.

Her farm business included making a trip over to Vivero Agro-Oriente. When she walked into Renato Villena's greenhouse, she said, she saw the flowers that had been in the photos that had been e-mailed to Dave Hunt and forwarded to Selby—lots of them.

"I couldn't believe the magnificent sight," she wrote. "He had more than two hundred of them in flower."

She says Renato Villena told her, "Chady, Chady, we're millionaires!"

As she gazed around at all the blooms in the Vivero Agro-Oriente greenhouse, Chady Moore said later, a single thought leaped into her mind: "If they have it, why not *me*?"

Instead of rushing back to the United States with his find, Kovach spent the next few days showing his wife the beauty of Peru's countryside.

"We drove through the market towns ablaze with the colors of fresh produce and native costumes," he wrote later. As they drove through the mountains, "llamas and alpacas munched around the rocks, while their progeny mugged for my wife's camera. . . . As soon as we hit 12,500 feet, orchids of all varieties were everywhere. We slowed down and began orchid spotting."

After all, Kovach had orders to fill back home—and anyway, his Moyobamba order hadn't reached Lima yet.

Meanwhile Chady Moore told Gomez to drive her to El Progresso. When she visited the roadside stand, though, she learned the price had doubled for the spectacular slipper orchids. They were now six soles, not three. She bought seventy-four of them, even though they weren't in flower, and took them back to the Nuevo Destino greenhouse to start growing them.

Finally, on June 2, the Kovachs arrived at the Moores' home in Lima. According to Kovach, the flowers shipped by Vivero Agro-Oriente arrived on a bus an hour later. Shortly after that, Chady Moore arrived, carrying the permits for INRENA that Renato Villena had prepared for Kovach.

The paperwork, Kovach wrote, consisted of three items: "a receipt for our purchased and collected plants from Senor Villena's nursery," a tax receipt from Peru's Department of Agriculture, and a permit from INRENA called a "phytosanitary certificate" verifying that the plants were clean of any disease. He had a total of 364 plants, he wrote. Two hundred of them were *Psygmorchis pusillas*, prolific little devils he gave away for free at workshops designed to hook the average person on orchids. To more serious growers, they are regarded as little more than weeds.

Moore says Kovach knew the El Progresso orchid needed a special permit to be taken out of the country. He also knew that Peru would be unlikely to give him such a permit because he was a foreigner and the orchid appeared to be a rare species, perhaps even an endangered one.

Yet it was Kovach's shot at the kind of glory that Moore had long enjoyed. And Moore, who had made plenty of trips to Sarasota, knew just where he should take it.

Moore says he told Kovach: "Take the God-damned fucking thing up there to Selby. If you try for a permit, you'll never get a permit."

Chady Moore, too, urged him to hurry up, before the pictures and plants already sent out into the world by Vivero Agro-Oriente beat him to the punch. She says she told her husband, "Tell Michael if he wants that plant named for him, he should run right to Selby Gardens."

Yet Kovach and his wife lingered in Lima one more day.

"We bought gifts at the Indian Market, then headed toward the main plaza in Lima," he wrote later. "Upon arrival we found that it was a holiday. . . . The air was filled with choral music as church choirs competed for honors. This was the feast day for the Blood of Christ Festival of the Catholic Church. We toured the cathedral, where I had a significant faith experience."

The "experience," Kovach said years later, consisted of a tingling along his spine and a wave of emotion that reduced him to tears. When that happens, he said, "you know you're in the presence of something unusual."

He knew he was about to embark on an adventure that was likely to change his life, but he also felt a sense of being on the verge of some great trial, something that would test his resolve and his faith. The message he received that day, he said, was: "No matter how this goes down, Michael, it's going to be all right. Hang on."

Yet still they did not leave Lima. Instead, from the church, the Goldvein residents then walked down to tour the Museum of Gold, which displays the pre-Columbian artifacts that Lee Moore and other adventurers hadn't smuggled out of the country. Kovach judged its treasures to be "truly remarkable." Then they went back to the Moores' house and, as Kovach put it, "packed our treasures," ready to catch their flight out in the morning.

Kovach packaged his divinely beautiful find in the most mundane of containers. He wrapped it in a swatch of newspaper, slid it into a cardboard tube, and stuffed it and the other plants into a suitcase with his dirty laundry.

At the Lima airport, their paperwork from Renato Villena sped them through inspection and they stepped aboard a plane home. The flight, he wrote later, seemed pleasant.

Their destination: Miami, then Selby Gardens and, soon thereafter, Kovach hoped, the realms of immortal botanical glory. He didn't know someone was already aiming at that same destination—but in a way that honored Peru, not an American tourist.

6

The Rival

The majority of these botanists fully believe they
are above the law. . . . They are an arrogant and
remarkably self-righteous lot.

Eric Christenson, orchid taxonomist

Marni Turkel didn't really like slipper orchids. She understood why some people swooned over them, though. The flowers could be big and showy, and they couldn't be easily cloned like other types of orchids. Since no one could create millions of identical blossoms, that left the ones that grew wild or in greenhouses. But slippers grew and matured slowly. As a result, newly discovered slippers tended to remain valuable rarities a lot longer than other orchids.

Still, she regarded slipper orchid fans as being "kind of crazy." When word first got around about Libby Besse's discovery of *Phragmipedium besseae*, she said once: "They went nuts. They were willing to pay any amount for it." Even though all slipper orchids were on an international list of endangered species, it hardly discouraged people from buying them. In fact, the difficulty of obtaining them made them even more desirable.

"Because you're not supposed to have them, people want them," she explained. "It's like an illicit drug."

Turkel preferred miniature tropical orchids, known as "botanicals," that are almost the opposite of slippers. Because botanicals are not flashy, they have little commercial value, but they suited her tastes better. She had been growing them since 1980 in her San Francisco greenhouses. She had traveled far and wide to seek them out, even venturing down to Peru with her friend and sometime collaborator Eric Christenson.

They made an odd pair. Turkel, a gentle Californian with glasses and graying hair, ran a pottery and ceramic design company and grew orchids only as a hobby. Then there was Christenson, a pugnacious, heavyset Florida resident whose thick beard and bushy eyebrows gave him a passing resemblance to Bluto from the Popeye cartoons. But his voice was no growling bluster. He generally spoke in a light, confiding tone, except for when his words carried a load of heavy sarcasm. He lived for orchids.

Turkel, who first met Christenson when he spoke at a meeting she attended in 1986, regarded him as a brilliant if eccentric scientist and writer. Although they lived on opposite ends of the country, they worked together on a number of magazine articles, and he sometimes used her photos to illustrate the pieces he wrote solo.

He really needed her help on their trip to Peru in February 2002. Despite his vast knowledge of the country's plants, Christenson had not learned Peru's national language. But Turkel spoke and read Spanish fluently, so she could interpret for him.

One of the stops on their tour was the Vivero Agro-Oriente. Turkel had met the owner's dark-haired, broad-faced daughter, Karol Villena, a few times at orchid shows in America. On this trip to Peru, Turkel finally met Karol's father, Renato Villena. She liked him, and she regarded Karol Villena as a friend.

So Turkel wasn't too surprised when, on May 22, 2002, Karol Villena e-mailed her some photos of a big purple slipper orchid her father had come across. The Villenas didn't want to sell it to her, she explained, just wanted her to tell them whether it was a new species of orchid, or one that—like the *Cattleya mooreana*—had been discovered years before but not seen since.

"It was big and flashy and new," Turkel said years later. "She just wanted an identification."

Turkel translated the e-mail and sent it along to Christenson, the expert. Clearly excited, Christenson rifled back a request for the plant's dimension, a request she quickly translated into Spanish and sent back to Peru. Soon Renato Villena e-mailed back a drawing he had made of the plant that included exact measurements. She translated it into English and forwarded it to Christenson.

Christenson alerted the editor of the American Orchid Society's magazine, *Orchids*, to get ready for something big. He would be offering a scientific description of a new orchid that was sure to cause a stir.

He hadn't actually seen the plant himself, just the photos. But he wasn't going to let that stop him.

⟶✢

In the Garden of Eden, Adam named everything. These days it's more complicated. There are strict rules on publishing new scientific names, rules laid down by the International Code of Botanical Nomenclature. Scientists called taxonomists specialize in making sure that the naming of new species is carried out properly.

The science of taxonomy owes its existence to a Swedish pastor who was once mocked as a provincial boor. In 1732, the pastor, Carl Linnaeus, invented the method still used today for labeling and classifying different types of plants. His was one of about fifty classification systems in use in the late 1700s, but his system was so easy to grasp that it is the one that eventually triumphed. You could say it was based on sex: it required comparing how the plants reproduced.

Taxonomists hold an obscure yet powerful place in the field of biology—the power to give new discoveries a name. When they name a new species, the name must clearly describe some aspect of its character or appearance. That way other scientists can easily see how this new discovery fits in with other organisms in the same group.

The American Orchid Society's (AOS) list of approved taxonomists in 2002 consisted of just twenty-three experts, none in Peru. Seven of the taxonomists on the list were affiliated with Selby Gardens, more than any other botanical garden. They included Selby founder Carl Luer; its first director, Cal Dodson; artist Stig Dalström; the gossipy John Beckner, systematics director Wesley Higgins; and his mild-mannered predecessor, John Atwood of Vermont.

There was an eighth AOS-approved taxonomist in Sarasota: Christenson. But he wanted nothing to do with the orchid boys at Selby Gardens. Over at Selby the feeling was mutual. Christenson regarded Selby's scientists as a pack of lying, hypocritical scoundrels. They reviled him as a hateful, and possibly violent, ex-employee.

Yet Christenson's initial interest in plants took root in a peaceful place, the placid suburbs of Connecticut. His father would come home from a corporate job, mix up a martini, then take an old hunting knife and set to work slicing the dandelions out of their otherwise perfect lawn.

"It was his way of relaxing," Christenson explained. "I accompanied him, but concentrated on the flower borders and other ornamental plants. The natural progression during my teen years was simply from flowers to wildflowers, to wild orchids, to tropical orchids."

He bought his first orchid when he was fourteen. In college, Christenson earned a bachelor's degree in horticulture, then a master's in genetics, and a Ph.D. in orchid taxonomy from the University of Connecticut. He gravitated to taxonomy because, he said, "I always scored through the roof on math, and working with orchids is all about pattern recognition. If you have to stop to think about why a *Dendrobium* is a *Dendrobium*, you'll never do well with identifying a family like orchids."

He was no shrinking violet when it came to fieldwork, either. Once, in India, as he strolled through a cardamom plantation, he discovered leeches had attached themselves to his ankles. He calmly picked them off and kept going.

Like Lee Moore, he had species named after him. In fact, a whole genus from Asia bore the name *Christensonia*.

Christenson took a job at Selby Gardens before completing his doctorate, and soon became director of its micropropagation laboratory. The lab was trying to clone orchids, particularly a species called *Phalaenopsis*, so that was his primary project. He also wrote a three-part history of Selby for the American Orchid Society.

In five years there, Christenson developed a distinct distaste for many of his coworkers. Christenson concluded that Beckner was a "blowhard botanist," acting as if he knew everything although he had published very little in the way of discoveries. He found Atwood to be painfully naïve. He particularly disliked Dalström, whom he accused of smuggling orchids into the United States from Peru.

He contended for years afterward that he saw Dalström unpacking an illegal shipment of *Phragmipedium besseae*, dirt still clinging to their roots. Christenson said he complained about Dalström, but no one at Selby would do anything about it. Instead, he said, his boss ordered him to write up a grant proposal to help pay for propagating the smuggled flowers. (Dalström contends Christenson was mistaken, that he had the proper permits for the plants, and that even after he proved to everyone at Selby he was innocent, Christenson continued spreading the smuggling story anyway. In turn, Dalström began referring to the portly Christenson as "the Blob.")

Christenson regarded the gardens' top management as the chief reason for the staff being so dysfunctional. One executive, he became convinced, was a serial sexual harasser. He believed another was a bigot and a Holocaust-denier.

Eventually, he said, he recognized the pattern that made Selby so dysfunctional. Too many of its scientists had gone through the same graduate degree programs. The place had become too insular, so the scientists and leaders had no appreciation for what might be going on elsewhere in the world, he contended. They especially cared nothing for the exotic lands where most orchids grow, taking a jingoistic, me-first approach to their work. Thus, he said, their attitude became, "We're white, and we're going to do whatever we want, and fuck the Third World."

Christenson made no secret of how he felt about everyone, either. When he quit, nobody asked him to reconsider or missed him when he was gone.

After leaving Selby, Christenson stuck around Sarasota, making a living as a freelancer. He wrote hundreds of articles and provided taxonomy for pay. He joined forces with a former airline pilot named David Bennett who had moved to Peru. Together they published an ever-evolving inventory of the orchids of Peru, an inventory that Christenson's former coworkers often contended was full of errors.

Christenson's big ambition was to write an encyclopedia of every orchid species in the world, but a simmering conflict with officials from the American Orchid Society, which was supposed to publish the book, scuttled that project. It would not be his last conflict, either, as he burned bridges with many of the orchid world's biggest names.

"He's brilliant. He's the closest thing to a real genius I've ever run across," said Harold Koopowitz, editor of *Orchid Digest*. "But he can be very difficult. He eventually antagonizes everybody he works with."

In between his scientific studies and his writing, Christenson engaged in a long-running feud with his former employer and everyone who worked there. Christenson contended that Selby's smuggling dated back to its founding. He once wrote that Carl Luer and Luer's wife "have probably illegally smuggled the largest number of orchids out of Latin America and into the United States than any other individual[s]."

When he alerted other organizations about what he saw going on at Selby—the American Orchid Society, for instance—he said his complaints met with indifference. In some cases, he faced defiance from orchid fanciers who contended smuggling was the only rational response to the rampant habitat destruction occurring throughout South America. The argument was a horticultural variation on Lee Moore's contention that smuggling antiquities out of Latin America was the only way they could be studied and preserved in the United States by institutions that were better equipped than the ones in their countries of origin.

He grew to scorn all botanical gardens, not just Selby. He believed they were all guilty of preaching conservation while swiping rare plants from distant lands, just because they could.

"Everyone treats it with a kind of nudge-nudge, wink-wink," he complained. "This is what all botanical gardens are doing. . . . The problem is the hypocrisy."

—⚶—

Much as Selby's staff might scorn him, Christenson had a point. U.S. officials acknowledge that a lot of orchids that are supposed to be protected by law wind up being smuggled into the country to satisfy the desires of collectors—some of whom clearly know better.

When a new species is discovered, some collectors and growers are particularly eager to get their hands on it before anyone else—and before anyone gets legal permission to possess and sell it. It's not just out of pride, either. There's an economic motive.

"They want to be the first ones to have it and the first ones to hybridize it, because then when it becomes legal, they have a jump on everybody," explained Robert "Roddy" Gabel, the U.S. Fish and Wildlife Service's resident orchid expert.

The people caught smuggling aren't on the fringes of the orchid world either. They have included orchid show judges, major nursery owners, even the president of an orchid society. Sometimes the smuggling involves just a handful of flowers. On the other hand, in 1997, officials at Mexico City International Airport seized a shipment of 843 plants being sent to Australia by Mexico's biggest orchid exporter.

Even though post-9/11 America boasts of its tighter borders and tougher security measures, the smuggling of flora and fauna such as orchids remains a pursuit that's both popular and lucrative. If anything, it's become more diverse than it used to be.

"Almost anything in nature can become contraband," journalist Craig Welch wrote in 2010. "Fish eggs. Baboon noses. . . . Crooks ship stolen monkey blood through Memphis and banned seal oil through Louisville." Smuggling is nearly recession-proof, Welch noted, because "in good times, the wealthy demand new delights; when economies tank, enforcement gets curtailed."

Some of the orchid smuggling is fairly blatant. Some Asian companies advertising their orchids on eBay offer to ship their orders in boxes labeled "children's clothes" or "toys," Gabel said.

Some smugglers follow a subtler method, mislabeling the rare orchids in a shipment as more common species that they resemble. If the orchids aren't in flower, picking out what's what can be nearly impossible, even for an expert, Gabel said.

The mislabeling can be as simple as pulling flowers out of the ground and labeling them as greenhouse-grown species, something Arias had a reputation for. In one e-mail Marni Turkel sent to Karol Villena, she wrote that Christenson's description of the new orchid would not give any specifics that might help smugglers: "He is not going to put the location of the collection, only that it is Peru. He doesn't want Arias coming to rip out every *phrag* in the north."

Still, getting such rare gems out of their native country can require the judicious application of cash, which helps drive up the price. Marni Turkel contended that the main thing limiting Karol Villena's ability to sell Peruvian orchids was her inability to figure out which officials most needed bribing.

Botanical garden employees have not been immune to the temptation to smuggle orchids, Gabel said. Gardens such as Selby have special permits allowing them to ship endangered orchids under certain circumstances, say from one scientific institution to another. That allows staff members of those institutions to carry orchids back and forth, even between countries, without needing individual permits. But that special permit does not allow them to pluck orchids from the wild and bring them into the country. For that, they would need to get a permit just like anyone else, Gabel said.

Gabel said that from time to time federal investigators have run across a scientific institution that, as he put it "has not used their permit appropriately." When that happens, he said, federal officials take the view that the employee involved has made a mistake. Instead of prosecuting anyone, "generally we counsel them on what is and isn't allowable. . . . They get fairly wide latitude."

To Christenson, letting a botanical garden and its staffers off with a warning seemed ludicrous. To him, the botanists on a garden staff should be above reproach, and they should know the consequences are dire for abusing their employers' special permit.

Without facing the prospect of any punishment, some botanical garden scientists have come to regard themselves as somehow beyond the law, said Koopowitz. They believe that their devotion to science allows them to disregard the rules by which commercial traders must abide.

Christenson's frustration about these issues mounted, and his feud with Selby took on a darker tone. In 2001, he accused Meg Lowman of trying to get around a different law. He accused her of engineering a Selby scheme to swipe copyrighted orchid descriptions that he had published.

Eric Christenson wanted to name the new orchid species after Peru, instead of a person. He didn't know Selby Gardens would beat him to the punch. Photo courtesy of Eric Christenson.

He sent a particularly fiery letter about it to Luer's wife. Christenson wrote that he had heard that Selby employees were saying they could no longer attend orchid conferences for fear they might run into him "because I am 'insane' and will try and 'murder them' at the conferences. Such fucking bullshit."

Christenson went on to describe Luer himself as "a slime of major proportions—a perfect match for the illegal and criminal activity that is the Marie Selby Botanical Gardens." When he referred to Lowman, he used a four-letter word many women find particularly offensive. He warned that she and Luer would soon learn "there are repercussions to their attacks."

Selby officials circulated the letter far and wide as proof that their chief critic had come completely unglued.

Now Christenson studied the photos and drawings that Marni Turkel had forwarded to him from Agro-Oriente. He thought of Renato Villena as little more than a peasant dirt-farmer. But he knew these pictures Villena had sent were his connection to something amazing—the most stunning new *Phragmipedium* species in at least the past twenty years, maybe even the past century.

He also knew he could not ask Villena to ship him one of the slipper orchids so he could examine it personally. He knew what the consequences would be for anyone caught with a slipper orchid.

"Anyone with half a brain cell doesn't go near them," Christenson explained later. "They're the pandas of the orchid world. . . . When somebody shows up with an orchid like that, you either quietly tell them to go away or you call the cops."

Instead, Christenson e-mailed Marni Turkel a set of detailed instructions on how Karol Villena should prepare what taxonomists call a "type specimen" to take to Lima. In Lima it could be put into the collection of the Museo de Historia Natural, run by a scientist named Ricardo Fernandez, known as Peru's preeminent orchid expert.

Then Christenson set to work writing up a description of this new plant. He had written so many that he didn't need very long to get it right—less than an hour, in fact.

He started off by noting that the discovery of the *Phragmipedium besseae* "forever changed the way we look at South American slipper orchids." This new species, he wrote, had "flowers that rival those of the famed *Phrag. besseae.*"

But what to call it? That was the thorniest question of all.

Turkel, in forwarding Christenson's instructions, wrote to Karol Villena that he said she had found something no one had seen before—and therefore naming it was tricky. She warned the Villenas "not to sell or give a plant to other people until it is described" or it could wind up bearing "the name of the wife of some rich German."

The Villenas had inquired about the possibility of naming the flower after their family: *Phragmipedium villenorum.* Turkel warned them that could lead to "the name of your family" being "in close association with a lot of problems . . . when plants leave Peru. The police of various countries are waiting for people who sell plants such as this. I am sure that you understand that you should be very discreet in this. The plant is worth thousands," she wrote.

Instead, because this was going to be such a big discovery, she told Karol Villena, Christenson thought it would be more appropriate to name the plant for where it had been found: *Phragmipedium peruvianum.*

Such a showy flower should bear a name honoring its country, not a mere person, Christenson reasoned. He finished up the description using that name and sent it off to the AOS.

In early June, Christenson got an e-mail from Harold Koopowitz. The *Orchid Digest* editor said a grower had just sent him pictures of an amazing new

Phragmipedium from Peru—the same photos that had been shot at Agro-Oriente and circulated via e-mail to Christenson, Dave Hunt, George Norris, and others.

Koopowitz, who in a few years would write the definitive book on tropical slipper orchids, wanted to be the first to describe this new species. He was already thinking about flying down to Peru so he could see it in person. But he wanted Christenson's help with the part of the description that had to be in Latin.

Christenson's reply: "Sorry, Harold, you're too late. I've already described it."

Christenson's description would be published in the July 2002 issue of the American Orchid Society's *Orchids* magazine, under a headline calling it "the most glorious new *Phragmipedium* in two decades." The magazine would be mailed to subscribers on June 17, 2002.

Under the rules of taxonomy, as of that mailing date, Christenson's description would be the officially accepted one . . . unless, of course, someone beat him to it.

7

The Race

Only for some of us does collecting become an
obsession. All obsessions are dangerous, and their intensity
can create astonishing human stories.

David Stuart, *The Plants That Shaped Our Gardens*

The Kovachs landed at Miami International Airport a little after 11:30 p.m. on
June 4, 2002. The flight had been "pleasant and uneventful," Kovach wrote
later. "Barbara and I wheeled our luggage up to customs just shy of midnight."

What they did next became the subject of a great deal of dispute.

Miami's airport is the busiest in Florida, primarily because of its proximity
to Central and South America. More than 16 million international passengers passed through its gates each year in the first decade of the twenty-first
century, so many that it ranked third in the country for the number of international passengers. It handles more international freight than any other
airport in the country.

For that reason, Miami International has a long history of being the con-
duit for smuggled contraband. In 1986, a federal grand jury indicted twenty-
three Miami baggage handlers on charges of smuggling up to $1 billion
in cocaine into the country through the airport. Two years later, customs
inspectors seized an entire L-1011 jetliner owned by Eastern Airlines. They
had found 56 pounds of cocaine hidden in a mailbag, encased in plaster and
wrapped in rugs to throw off drug-sniffing dogs.

Miami is also considered to be the third-most popular entry point in the
United States for smuggled wildlife. Federal inspectors working the Miami
beat have run across every creature imaginable, from monkey skulls used
in Santeria rituals to boa constrictors stuffed with cocaine. Lots of wildlife

smugglers are amateurs, like the one who tried sneaking more than forty Cuban finches into Miami by hiding them inside hair rollers taped to his legs. An inspector noticed his pants didn't hang quite right, which led to a search.

But there are plenty of professionals, too—often people in the legitimate wildlife trade who have slipped across the line. One notorious smuggler indicted in Florida boasted to an undercover federal agent that he could acquire any kind of wildlife, depending on "how much certain people get paid."

Why Miami? It's not just the geography. A 1994 report by the U.S. General Accounting Office found Miami's airport had the lowest rate of inspections in the country. On their best days, inspectors peek into only three out of every ten legal shipments. They don't have sufficient staff to stand watch at the baggage carousel all day and night.

The airport's loose security has attracted more than just animal smugglers. Plant smugglers have exploited Miami's weaknesses as well.

On July 22, 1998, George Norris, the Texas orchid dealer who had counseled Kovach before his first trip to Peru, sent a letter to Manuel Arias Silva, "El Professore," whose Orquidaria had supplied Kovach with plants and permits on that trip two years before. In his letter, Norris—for once not using ALL CAPS—complimented Arias for smuggling some illegal orchids to him in a shipment of legal orchids sent through Miami. Arias was slipping the shipments past the Miami inspectors by labeling the plants as if they were fairly common orchids, *maxillaria*, when in fact he was shipping Norris the more valuable slipper orchids that *maxillaria* resemble when not in flower.

"This shipment was great. It went through inspection in one and a half hours," Norris wrote. "They did not open very many bags. They know that you have really clean plants and just do not look. But this is only Miami.... Houston would be much tougher. Please make a note to not ship except to Miami.... They do not want to take time to unwrap and then have to re-pack."

Kovach, however, carried no big boxes or bags for inspectors to pull apart. All of his orchids were tucked into his luggage, and perhaps that's why he was treated the way he was.

He says that upon arrival at U.S. Customs, he told inspectors that he had live plants that required inspection by the U.S. Department of Agriculture. Normally live plants would be taken to a USDA building called "the smokehouse," where they could be inspected by plant experts and fumigated to eliminate pests.

But that's not what happened to Kovach.

"The customs officer marked my declaration accordingly and pointed me to the inspection area," he wrote later. "My bags were placed onto the image scanner." When he again mentioned needing a USDA inspection, he wrote:

"I was ignored. . . . I was waved on with almost no verbal reply. . . . One inspector, as an afterthought, finally turned and said, 'Oh, I'll need that,' referring to my customs declaration form."

With that, Kovach and his wife walked out of the airport without ever opening their bags.

Kovach and Ellison went to a hotel for the night, determined to get up early the next morning, rent a car, and make the four-hour drive to Selby Gardens.

They would have just forty-five minutes to spend in Sarasota before they had to race back to Miami—otherwise they would miss their flight back home.

⁓ঙ

The morning of Wednesday, June 5, 2002, started out as a typical workday at Selby's 7-11 building. In the herbarium, elderly volunteers toiled away pressing plant specimens and filing them away in the proper drawers.

Stig Dalström was busy sketching at his drawing table. He worked in the room that was supposed to be for visiting scientists. It had become his de facto office, decorated floor to ceiling with his drawings and paintings. John Atwood, the part-time orchid expert from Vermont, was at work in that room, too.

In the next office, Wesley Higgins sat at his computer, tapping on the keyboard. Higgins shared the office with the OIC's orchid-collection curator, John Beckner. But Beckner was out that day—in preparation for an overseas trip, he had scheduled a visit to his doctor for vaccinations.

Their two-man office didn't offer a lot of room, and despite Beckner's absence that day, it was more cramped than usual. Cal Dodson, the gardens' first director, had dropped by. Dodson owned a well-appointed home in Sarasota, and when in town he stopped in frequently to see how everyone was doing.

Two more visitors were in Higgins's office, too—a pair of American Orchid Society judges named Jim Clarkson and Mark Jones. The two men were friends of Higgins, visiting from the north side of Tampa Bay. They had shown up to chat with him a bit. They wanted to take him to lunch.

When the Kovachs drove into Sarasota, they followed Lee Moore's directions along U.S. 301 and made a beeline for the 7-11 building rather than wasting time over at the tourist-friendly part of the garden. But when Kovach stepped through the front door with his plant, he discovered, to his disappointment, that nobody was there to greet him.

He heard voices and followed the sound back to the herbarium. The volunteers at work proudly showed him what they were doing. But they told Kovach all the scientists were busy. Whatever he had to show them, it would just have to wait.

Kovach, afraid of missing his flight, played his trump card. He showed the women his flower and told them he had just arrived with it from Peru. At that point, Kovach wrote, one elderly volunteer grabbed her walker and told him: "Your God is good to you. Follow me."

Accounts vary as to who in the OIC saw it first, but Wesley Higgins and Stig Dalström both say it was Dalström. The artist says he stepped away from his drawing board and into the hallway and saw Kovach walking up with a wilting flower in hand. Though it clearly had seen better days, the blossom's size and color caught Dalström's attention immediately.

Dalström viewed Kovach's orchid not only as a great scientific discovery, but also as a harbinger of a far brighter future for the poor, neglected OIC.

"I immediately realized that what he held in his hand could mean great publicity if handled correctly, which would stir the sleeping board members and demonstrate that we actually existed," Dalström said later.

The artist escorted Kovach back to Higgins's office. As the door swung open, Dalström said, "Hey, look at what this guy's got."

As Kovach walked in, holding the plant ahead of him, he wrote later, the Virginia nurseryman was greeted by "a simultaneous wave of eye-widening and mouth opening."

"To say that it created quite a stir is to put it mildly," Dalström wrote a few months later.

This was just the reception Kovach had hoped for. Higgins, glancing at the man carrying the magnificent new flower, could see that Kovach "had the look of a proud new father on him."

Someone asked Kovach what he thought he had there. He said that while it might look like a slipper orchid, "I'm not sure. It's just different, and big. It could be a whole new genus."

Someone expressed doubt about that analysis. Someone, Kovach doesn't mention who, insisted it had to be a *Phragmipedium*—a slipper orchid from South America.

Higgins then tapped a few keys on his computer keyboard, called up the e-mailed photos Dave Hunt had just that week sent the OIC, and informed him that the Agro-Oriente photos showed the same flower now before him.

"Someone is advertising them on the web with this photo," he told Kovach, according to Kovach's account.

"You're joking," Kovach replied, not mentioning Chady Moore's warning

Wesley Higgins tapped a few keys on his computer keyboard to show Michael Kovach that Selby scientists had just seen photos of the orchid he now held in his hand. Photo courtesy of Wesley Higgins.

about the Villena family—or that his own sales receipt came from the Villenas' nursery. "I mean, I just found this a week [to] ten days ago."

According to Dodson, Higgins had those photos close at hand because he had just shown them to Dodson when Kovach walked in with the exact same flower.

"I knew as soon as I saw it that it was an undiscovered species," Dodson said. "Then in walks this guy holding a plant of this thing in bloom."

In Dodson's version of Kovach's visit, Dodson immediately asked him what would turn out to be a crucial question: "Do you have a legal permit for that plant?"

Dodson says Kovach "acted shocked" when Dodson told him: "That plant is illegal in this country. It's an undescribed *Phragmipedium*."

According to Dodson, Kovach recovered his sangfroid and replied, "Oh no, I've got permits to cover everything."

Kovach "assured us that he had all the necessary papers and that he would fax copies promptly upon his return to Virginia," Dalström wrote later.

Atwood, the slipper orchid expert, figured they were too late to be the first to describe this new orchid. If there were pictures flying around on the Internet, then surely someone had already beaten them to naming it. The rules of taxonomy said that the first one to get the description published and into the mail would be the winner. Still, he wrote later, "I got a pad of paper, anyway, on which to make a description at least for the files, if not for publication."

The orchid boys began questioning Kovach about where the plant grew, and he answered as best he could. According to Kovach, Dodson asked him what he would like to call his discovery. (Dodson says he does not recall this.)

"I thought, 'Well, why not? I've worked long and hard; it can't hurt,'" Kovach wrote.

According to his own account, Kovach replied: "Well, if it is not dependant on plant structure, or any violation of protocol or taxonomy regulation, I'd kind of like to have it named after me, if that's okay."

They assured him it was fine. According to Kovach, Dodson then asked him to spell his name and inquired, "What Latin end do you want on it?" They sounded out the possibilities and finally "I picked 'ii' because it was the easiest to pronounce," Kovach wrote.

Thus the scientists set to work preparing a description of what would become known as *Phragmipedium kovachii* (pronounced Frag-mih-PEE-dee-um ko-VOCK-ee-eye). Everyone began "passing it around and working on it," Higgins recalled.

According to Kovach, Higgins then pulled him aside and "informed me there had been a buzz about this plant, and bragging by Dr. Eric Christenson of his describing a super *phrag* from northern Peru. He informed me that this had been going on since the Redland show . . . and that a race for access to the plant had developed. He said it looked like I had won that race. I informed him, somewhat taken aback, that it is interesting to win a race one had not entered. I told him my main concern was to get it to science, and get it protected status."

Higgins recalls a different discussion. He says he never mentioned Christenson's name, and in fact did not know Christenson was involved at that point. Instead, he said, Kovach "asked me if Selby wanted a plant to grow, and I declined the offer."

Higgins didn't turn down the offer of a new orchid because he was squeamish about its legality. Instead, he explained later, he was just concerned that the plant would die because "a high-elevation plant would not survive in the Florida heat."

Kovach said no more about the offer, Higgins said later, but the scientist got the impression that there were more *Phragmipedium kovachii* stashed in his car.

Kovach also had a brief discussion with the two American Orchid Society judges visiting the OIC, Jim Clarkson and Mark Jones. According to Kovach, Clarkson and Jones wanted to buy whatever extra new orchids he had with him. In Kovach's version of events, he said he explained to them he didn't have any more for sale.

Kovach says that answer didn't sit well with them, and later would cause him trouble.

Now he was ready to go, but there was one last bit of business to deal with: the fee. Normally, Selby's OIC charged twelve dollars per plant for an official identification. Under the circumstances, Higgins and his colleagues waived the charge.

Then Kovach ran for the car and, "blazed, flush with excitement, back across Alligator Alley," he wrote. The couple made their plane in Miami and flew north, giddy at having accomplished everything they had set out to do.

Meanwhile the OIC, which had been so quiet, now had turned into a buzzing beehive.

While Higgins says that "winning the race" discussion with Kovach never happened, Selby's orchid boys did see ahead of them a race of some kind, one that they now had a shot at winning.

According to Higgins, they initially assumed that Harold Koopowitz, the California-based editor of *Orchid Digest* and a widely known expert on tropical slipper orchids, was the man to beat. There had long been an East Coast–West Coast rivalry among orchid experts. The Selby scientists were part of the East Coast contingent that included the American Orchid Society organization based in Delray Beach, a three-hour drive across the state. They figured Koopowitz and the West Coast gang had probably gotten a jump on this find.

But then Cal Dodson called up a former grad student of his who happened to be the editor of *Orchids* magazine and learned the truth. They weren't racing Koopowitz. They were racing their most hated critic, Christenson. Now they had an even bigger reason to want to be the first.

According to Dalström, though, it was more than just a race for glory and the sweet taste of revenge. He contended that getting that orchid named first was a matter of life and death for the OIC:

"We're an organization, we depend on reputation. We depend on publicity . . . to get funds and sources and support, and we wanted to describe this thing." Selby's OIC had to be the first to do it, he explained, because "nobody wants to fund researchers that are lagging behind."

Stig Dalström, who knew from his fieldwork that Peru is a place where everything is difficult but anything is possible, worked all night on the illustration for the new orchid find. Photo courtesy of Stig Dalström.

Atwood and Dalström worked through the night of June 5 and into the early morning of June 6 on the scientific description of Kovach's plant. For Dalström, this meant trying to revive the wilted thing that Kovach had handed over by floating it in a bowl of water. He needed to pump up the lip of the flower, which now resembled a deflated balloon. He also used the photos e-mailed by Dave Hunt, as well as the pictures that Kovach had brought back with him, to flesh out his drawing.

Dalström did a black-and-white sketch and later a color version showing the flower growing in its natural habitat. He finished the black-and-white drawing about 3:00 a.m., so weary from such intense concentration that he felt cross-eyed.

The ever-methodical Atwood, meanwhile, checked Selby's voluminous reference files. He had to be sure nothing like the *Phragmipedium kovachii* had been found in the long-forgotten past. Then he took the plant to the mounting room to press and dry it, preserving it as the type specimen—proof that the orchid really existed and had not been conjured out of thin air. He took an extra step, too, one that later led to tremendous controversy—but at the time, no one objected.

Meanwhile Higgins took a 1-inch slice off a leaf and preserved it in gel as a DNA voucher, another piece of proof that it existed. The flower, once Dalström was done with it, was put into a bottle of alcohol as another voucher specimen. They left the bottle on Beckner's desk, a surprise for the man who always liked to be first with the latest news.

Atwood's written description began by alerting readers that this was something special: "While biologists marvel at the biodiversity of the ocean's depths, etc., striking novelties within relatively accessible lands continue to appear, surprisingly even among the most cherished plants."

Just like Christenson, Atwood mentioned the sensation caused by Libby Besse's flower and other surprises over the years. The haste of writing so quickly led to a typo in a discussion of possible pollination methods, where he mentioned "a humming bird" instead of a hummingbird—a minor misstep that Christenson later carped about.

After that prelude, Atwood got down to brass tacks: "Recently, Michael Kovach discovered a new *Phragmipedium* with large purple flowers in northeastern Peru." He pointed out that Kovach's orchid "differs from all other species in the genus by the huge flowers that range in color from pinkish to dark purple."

Somehow the name of Faustino Medina Bautista never came up.

On the afternoon of June 6, 2002, Higgins e-mailed Meg Lowman and Bob Scully to tell them about what had happened. Neither had been around Selby the day before. Lowman was on vacation, and Scully was visiting a client in South Florida.

"A new purple species of *Phrag* came into the OIC yesterday," Higgins wrote them. He said it could be a more momentous find than any previous Selby discovery: "This could be bigger than *P. besseae.*"

Higgins did not attach any photos of the new orchid to his e-mail, even though he had pictures from both Dave Hunt and Kovach that he could have used. Higgins says now that he just didn't think about it. Instead he focused on which of Selby's publications they should print as a special issue—its scientific journal, *Selbyana*, or its quarterly newsletter, *Tropical Dispatch*.

In the e-mail, Higgins didn't mention Christenson's name but told his bosses that time was of the essence: "We need to publish next week to be first."

Scully, who had just returned from his trip to South Florida, shot back a response to Higgins in a half hour. The veteran orchid grower called the discovery "a fabulous opportunity" and added, "Hope there is a way to get this in print . . . soonest."

Scully mentioned a concern about "logistic and then economic questions" over publishing a special issue of *Tropical Dispatch*, then asked who was "doing the Latin" for the description. The Latin section of the description must conform to very specific rules, which is what had led Harold Koopowitz to call Christenson.

"John Atwood has written the article (with Latin), and Stig has finished the drawing," Higgins replied. "We are ready to go to press!"

But there was a problem, a big one. Dalström was working at his desk when Higgins waved Kovach's paperwork in his face.

As Dodson had feared, it wasn't as kosher as Kovach had said it was.

Lowman, as usual, was not in town.

But for once she wasn't out giving a speech or serving on a panel. She had taken the week off from Selby out of maternal guilt. She felt guilty about missing her sons' special moments. Now one son's rowing crew would be competing for the national championship. She had missed all his previous races and she had vowed not to miss this final race. She did do some work from home early in the week, spent Wednesday packing suitcases, and then on Thursday she accompanied her sons to the race in Cincinnati

When they reached Cincinnati, they ate at a chain steakhouse. She went back to their hotel room and threw up. The woman who ate crickets for hors d'ouevres got food poisoning off a Midwest T-bone and spent the night hugging a toilet.

By the next morning, Friday, she had recovered enough to check her e-mail. That's when she saw for the first time the e-mail exchange between Higgins and Scully about the new orchid. Although she wasn't an orchid expert, she knew this was an important discovery—one that could yield a bonanza of favorable press.

"It is great news! Congratulations," she told Higgins in an e-mail. "Please figure out what is best for the orchid world."

She told him she had alerted the gardens' publicity and marketing experts about what was happening so they could help get the new flower's description published as soon as possible.

She asked if the gardens could publish a special edition of *Selbyana* or *Tropical Dispatch*. And she asked if the word could be passed along to the

Sarasota Herald-Tribune, too, getting this news out to the wider world beyond orchid fanciers.

Higgins's reply laid bare the real issue:

"The only way we can get this into print before two others that are intending to publish is to issue a supplement to *Selbyana*. We are holding a department meeting this morning to discuss the matter."

Although he did not name the "two others," it was a reference to Christenson and to Koopowitz, whom the orchid boys still figured might have a shot.

The news left Lowman elated. She called Higgins for details "and was told that the orchid was spectacular," she wrote later. "He also said the collector's permits were in order. The only hiccup mentioned was a potential threat from a rival orchid taxonomist"—namely Christenson. "The research staff seemed concerned he might exhibit violent behavior if Selby Gardens identified and published a description of this fabulous new plant before he did."

Actually, Higgins explained years afterward, Lowman had misinterpreted what he said about the permits. He did not mean that they were in order. All he said was that the customs inspectors in Miami had not seized Kovach's shipment so apparently the government had no objections to what Kovach had done.

Still, Higgins called Kovach in Virginia to ask him to send to the OIC copies of all his permits. When Kovach faxed the papers to him, Higgins could see he was missing something crucial, a particular permit required for transporting endangered slipper orchids from one country to another, but he didn't ask why.

The special Friday staff meeting involved figuring out, as Dalström put it later, "what we should do, because this was sort of a hot potato, a screwball that someone threw at us."

Higgins outlined the issue in an e-mail Friday morning to Scully and Lowman: "Cal reports that the new species will be published in AOS *Orchids* with a publication date of 25 June by Christenson. . . . We have the ability to beat the AOS to press. However, Cal recommends that we drop it since it will cause many hard feelings and may have institutional repercussions. What do you think?"

The group gathered in their usual place for staff meetings, in what used to be the 7-11 house's garage. Now it was known as the "mounting room," the place with the plant dryers used to create type specimens. The men pulled out the chairs set up around the big wooden table and sat down to wrestle with the problem.

Higgins's meeting of the 7-11 brain trust included Dalström, Atwood, Beckner, and three scientists from outside the OIC: the thick-bearded bromeliad expert Harry Luther; research director Bruce Rinker; and plant-collections director Bruce Holst, who was also in charge of *Selbyana*. Also sitting in, albeit not as an employee, was Cal Dodson. He was the only one who had been through something like this before, thanks to the *Phragmipedium besseae* furor.

They reviewed their options. On the one hand, they had the plant in hand, and a chance to beat everyone to what they all agreed would be the biggest orchid discovery in a century. On the other hand, they risked running afoul of the law, both in the United States and Peru.

Dodson and Holst didn't like the situation. Although Kovach's flower had no fragrance, they thought it reeked of unnecessary risk. They both voiced strong objections to doing anything with Kovach's orchid other than shipping it straight back to him.

"It's a grim mistake, and Fish and Wildlife will be all over you," Dodson told the group. The plant was clearly illegal, he said, and he had "seen how bad things can get if you push official people."

But the rest of the orchid boys did not want to let it go. Some privately regarded Dodson as a loose cannon. What was he even doing at the meeting?

In their view, by publishing this identification, Selby's OIC would get all the recognition and face no actual risk. Kovach was the one who brought it into the country. He was the one who said his permits were in order. Who were they to question his presumed innocence?

"If there's a problem, it's down on Kovach," Atwood said.

According to Dodson, though, the clincher came when Higgins told the rest of them, "I already have orders from above."

When Dodson asked who the orders came from, Higgins named Meg Lowman. She had called that morning and told him to publish the piece, he said.

"I don't believe Meg knows what she's getting into," Dodson replied. "I think you're going to be in a world of hurt."

No one, not even Dodson, suggested calling the authorities, Higgins said later.

At last the scientists who wanted so badly to win the race against Christenson figured out how to satisfy everyone. They would publish the description as planned, but with an additional author listed, one from Peru: Ricardo Fernandez, a boyishly handsome orchid expert who oversaw the herbarium at the University of San Marco in Lima. He and Dalström were friends, so he would be amenable to helping Selby out.

In addition, instead of keeping the type specimen that Atwood had prepared at Selby the way they normally would, the orchid boys would ship their dried plant to Fernandez. That way it would be housed at a scientific institution in its native country. (They did not know Christenson had told the Villenas to take his type specimen to Fernandez, too, so Fernandez would wind up with both of them.)

Including a Peruvian author would mean no one could complain about gringo scientists grabbing the glory from the Third World. Returning the plant to Peru would blunt any criticism of Selby for keeping something that was legally questionable.

With no further objections, the publication of a special issue of *Selbyana* got a green light. Problem solved. Meeting adjourned.

The publication was credited to Atwood, Dalström, and Fernandez, but Fernandez did no writing. He just reviewed what Atwood had written and gave it his approval.

Only later did Dalström realize that Higgins and the other Selby employees at the OIC had allowed the announcement of this earthshaking discovery to be handled by three people who were not full-time Selby employees. Atwood was a contractor, Dalström a freelancer, Fernandez an employee of a different institution. Dalström wondered if that was done by design, to make it even less of a risk for Selby and its science staff. But by the time he figured it out, the deed was done and no one could turn back the clock.

Higgins and Cal Dodson served as peer-reviewers on the piece, despite Dodson's open misgivings. It was a shortcut, a way to speed up the normal process of sending the piece to scientific reviewers outside the authors' institution. Higgins and Dodson made sure the science—if not Atwood's spelling—was sound and the proper format followed. Once they were done, the piece could proceed to publication.

Lowman got one more e-mail, this one from Bruce Rinker, the director of research. He "confirmed that the orchid boys had all the proper permits," she wrote later, "but repeated their fear of repercussions from the antagonist down the street."

He also reported the plan to return the orchid to a Peruvian institution, "as a gesture of good will to the orchid's country of origin," Lowman wrote. "Thus I would never see this orchid, but since I was not an aficionado, I never gave it a second thought."

Scully stopped by Selby on Friday to chat with the one of the institution's administrative staff members. While he was there, he recalled later, Rinker walked in grinning and told them both that they were now sure Kovach's papers were in order and they were ready to publish.

But Scully got a different opinion from Dodson, who tracked him down to warn him about the danger involved. Dodson told Scully that publishing the orchid's identification would be "a terrible mistake."

Scully's reply, he said, was dismissive: "We're going to do it anyway."

The following Monday, June 10, Lowman—back in Sarasota after watching her son's crew place ninth in the nation—sent an e-mail to Scully, all of Selby's scientists, and several other Selby employees.

As of 11:00 a.m., she wrote, *Selbyana* was "printing a supplemental issue that describes an exciting new orchid species. This orchid comes from Peru and with it probably come the passionate and emotional repercussions that often accompany orchid activities."

Without mentioning Kovach by name, she wrote that "a bonafide collector of orchids brought this specimen to the OIC for the purposes of describing and publishing it," and that's just what the OIC was prepared to do.

"I recognize that there has been a lot of discussion of the pros and cons of publishing this new orchid species," Lowman wrote, "but it all boils down to the fact that the function of our OIC is to do just this—identify orchids and publish new orchid species."

She acknowledged that "there may be jealousy and controversy arising as to who should be publishing this species description, but Wes and John wrote a very good and accurate description which is exactly what Selby Gardens' OIC needs to do in cases of new specimens." (Why she thought Higgins had cowritten the description with Atwood is a mystery.)

A half hour later, Scully sent an "amen"—showing that, at least this once, he and Lowman agreed on something: "Congratulations to all involved in this one. . . . It has been said that those on top typically attract the greatest amount of comment from detractors. Move on stalwarts. Let us hope there will be other similar opportunities not too far ahead in our future. Well done!"

Selby's press slowly began cranking out the special *Selbyana* supplement. It ran for three days straight. Meanwhile the staff began mailing out copies to subscribers in thirty-eight countries. Officially the mailing date, the one that counted for taxonomic purposes, was June 12—beating *Orchids* magazine, and Christenson's description, by five days.

On Friday, June 14, *Selbyana's* most important subscriber, Bob Scully, e-mailed Lowman and Luer that his copy had just arrived: "Great job getting that piece produced so quickly and so well. This should really open some eyes."

Meanwhile Beckner went to a meeting of the Florida West Coast Orchid Society, where he announced the big discovery, and "everyone was excited."

Christenson was supposed to speak at that meeting, too, Lowman noted in an e-mail to Scully, "but he never showed up."

"The orchid world seemed thrilled" by what Selby's OIC had pulled off, Lowman wrote later. She noted, too, that the "apparent dedication of the research staff was timely, since salary reviews were only a month away." One of the scientists, she wrote, "reminded me at our brief Monday meeting that in his opinion the processing of this major new orchid warranted a big raise (for him)."

Lowman wrote later that she expected some very different rewards for the description of *Phragmipedium kovachii*. She hoped the acclaim for this discovery would "provide a long-sought spotlight for orchids at Selby. I was relieved, hoping it would ease a sense of growing jealousy and tension directed toward the successes of canopy ecology. . . . I hoped this discovery would prompt new initiatives by the orchid staff for increased funding, productive science, and public support."

On June 18, Selby's marketing director put out a press release touting the new orchid's discovery and Selby's role in it. Like the official description in *Selbyana*, it included the photos of the flower in Chady Moore's hand and the potted plant sitting on the hood of the car Kovach had used.

"This has got to be one of the most important plant discoveries for Selby Gardens and for the entire orchid world in the past 100 years," Beckner said in the release.

The *Sarasota Herald-Tribune* ran a story on the discovery. It quoted Beckner as saying that the commercial possibilities for this new flower were equally exciting: "It is going to open up a whole new line of orchid hybridizing."

Christenson called up his friend Marni Turkel and told her what had happened. Contrary to the expectations at Selby, she said, he was neither violent nor even angry. Instead, all he said was, "Well, that's taxonomy."

Kovach, back in Virginia, phoned Lee Moore down in Miami to crow about his triumph.

"He called me and said, 'Well, it's officially named for me now,' and I said, 'Congratulations,'" Moore recalled. "Then the shit hit the fan."

8

The Investigation

With most species of orchids, it is often not the fittest
but the most deceptive that survive.

James J. Angleton, CIA counterintelligence chief
and orchid grower

The letter from Lima arrived via fax in Arlington, Virginia, at 3:32 p.m. on
June 26, 2002. Before anyone could pass it along, the bureaucrats had to find
an employee who could translate it from Spanish.

The subject line said, "*Phragmipedium kovachii*, colectado y exportado
ilicitamente"—in English, "illegally collected and imported."

The letter came from a top official at Peru's INRENA, writing to the U.S.
Fish and Wildlife Service to complain about what Kovach and Selby Gardens had done. Although Carlos Salinas Montes said he was "pleased to address the matter," he was just being polite. INRENA was not pleased, that
much was clear.

"In reference to this, we inform you that a specimen or specimens were
collected and exported without authorization. . . . We ask that you please
seize these precious Peruvian specimens and that we coordinate our action
for their return to Peru," the letter said.

Then came the kicker, aimed directly at Selby: "We also ask your country's scientific institutions to please establish arrangements with the respective . . . authorities, regarding the origin of the plant material they will be
researching."

Along with the letter came a copy of Dalström's drawing of the *Phragmipedium kovachii* as reproduced in the special *Selbyana*; a copy of Kovach's

INRENA permit for his shipment that made no mention of any slipper orchids; and an enlarged version of the picture of Kovach's wilting bloom in Chady Moore's hand, one of the photos that had appeared in *Selbyana*.

INRENA officials clearly were embarrassed by what Kovach had done. When the news about *Phragmipedium kovachii* first broke, INRENA officials already had their hands full with a more violent emergency in their own backyard. A mob of loggers protesting a new law cracking down on illegal mahogany harvesting had burned down INRENA's headquarters in Puerto Maldonado, then set fire to the impound lot, which held about 10,000 feet of illegally cut lumber. The ringleader of the fiery insurrection, despite facing criminal charges, was subsequently elected governor of the state.

Now, in the middle of all this uproar over mahogany, some gringo snatches the world's biggest orchid discovery in a century out of Peru's hands and smuggles it to the United States? And he's going to grab all the glory for himself with not a word for Peru? No, this simply would not do. INRENA demanded action, pronto.

Kovach didn't know about the INRENA complaint just yet, or that the weight of the federal government was about to fall on him. But based on what he was hearing from other orchid collectors, he had started getting worried—worried enough to do something unusual.

He phoned a U.S. Department of Agriculture agent named Marty Feinstein to talk about how his orchid had come into the country.

After listening to Kovach's story about being waved through customs in Miami, Feinstein told him he had handled the situation poorly. Should that ever happen again, Feinstein told Kovach, he should "take personal responsibility" for making sure the plants were properly inspected by a USDA official.

The next day Kovach sat down and penned a lengthy, handwritten letter to the USDA agent, saying he wanted to "clarify my right and proper legal standing as a properly permitted live plant importer." He said he also wanted to alert the USDA and other federal agencies "to persons involved in attempts to smuggle these . . . plants into the U.S. from Peru."

Kovach wrote that these crafty smugglers—and he named several names, including Renato Villena—had been spreading rumors casting suspicion on him so federal officials would be less likely to pay attention to the real culprits.

Although a mere twenty-two days had elapsed since Kovach first walked through Selby's doors, a lot had already happened. Kovach, who had once craved fame like Lee Moore's, had discovered that this kind of notoriety wasn't all it was cracked up to be.

"The plant has great commercial value, and many normally rational vendors and collectors seem to have succumbed to greed-motivated forms of insanity," he wrote to Feinstein, sounding exasperated.

Ever since word got out about the new orchid, Kovach wrote, "I have been bombarded with calls" from people wanting to buy one. Most callers said they were willing to wait for nursery-raised plants, he wrote, not mentioning where those might come from. However, he continued, "many vendors and especially breeders want them now, but are too cagey to allude to an alternative source, other than to state, 'I can get them elsewhere.'"

Some vendors had even "urged me to sell them my plants (at fire sale prices) to avoid confiscation and prosecution!" he complained. "So I'm being threatened by American vendors . . . if I don't sell them the plants I don't have, and sell them quick and cheap." In fact, he wrote, "three such individuals have stated that my price is too high, and they can get the plants in July for $500 U.S. per plant."

He blamed "political and ego issues" for stirring up such a ruckus. Specifically, he blamed Eric Christenson for the failed attempt to name the plant after Peru, and he blamed the American Orchid Society for publishing Christenson's description in its magazine even after the Selby description hit the mail. Because Christenson and the AOS were beaten by Selby, "they got mutually embarrassed and discredited and will have to print an apology," Kovach wrote to the USDA.

But the origin of his biggest trouble, he wrote, lay with the two orchid judges who had been visiting Selby's OIC when he walked in with his new flower. He didn't recall their names, he wrote to the USDA agent, but they were "unhappy, because of jealousy and greed" when he refused to sell them the plant "on the spot." As a result, they "began a rumor that I had smuggled a number of plants into the U.S. and had them for sale. Then the rumor took on a life of its own."

Kovach insisted he brought in just one plant, which he gave to Selby, and "my only intent was scientific description." He did not intend making a mint off the discovery, he wrote—although he contradicted himself in another paragraph.

Back in Peru, he wrote, Renato Villena had sent workers out to strip the mountainside of this valuable orchid. As a result, he wrote, "it has taken most of my time and no insubstantial amount of out-of-pocket investment to protect the plant colony from him and his ilk." Kovach wrote that, rather than let Agro-Oriente pull all the plants out, he had sent someone to pull them out of the wild first—not exactly an environmentally friendly move, but logical for a cut-throat businessman. Then, he wrote, he had them moved "to a friend's farm in northern Peru, put under armed guard, and initial steps taken to artificially propagate them en masse. I will sell *none* until the survival of the species is assured." He did not name the friend—not then, at least.

Kovach's letter produced a split among USDA officials, according to an e-mail that Feinstein sent to several colleagues. Some wanted to yank Kovach's federal import-export permit, shutting him down. They also wanted to slap him with a civil court fine for breaking the law. That would send a strong message to smugglers, they contended.

Others, including Feinstein, thought that approach would be counter-productive. Feinstein contended that they should cut Kovach some slack since he had "come forward voluntarily. . . . If we are to encourage others to emulate his example, we would be well advised to tread lightly because a heavy-handed approach would be the sort of misstep that would spread like wildfire throughout the industry. I would not expect too many others to be so openly cooperative." However, Feinstein conceded, "I'm not certain as to how much of his motives are altruistic as a steward of the environment."

Meanwhile, though, another federal agency was swinging into action. Responding to the complaint from Peru, U.S. Fish and Wildlife Service assigned one of its Virginia-based investigators, Mary Holt, to find out what had happened with Kovach. She was perfectly suited for the job.

Special Agent Holt worked for the wildlife service's law enforcement branch in Richmond. At that point Holt—a tall, athletic woman with blond hair and an engaging smile—had been a wildlife officer for eight years. She had spent four years as a military policewoman for the U.S. Air Force, working as a dog handler, among other duties. She had earned a bachelor's degree in wildlife biology from the University of Massachusetts. That led to a three-year stint as a wildlife inspector for the Fish and Wildlife Service—in other words, she knew what it meant to check shipments of flora and fauna as they go through airports, to make sure nothing is being smuggled. Holt was no slouch as an investigator. She had just finished up a successful case in which she and her colleagues nailed two people and a Virginia corporation for smuggling Native American remains as well as wildlife. The case resulted in prison time and a big fine for the principals and the forfeiture of the vehicles involved—a feat that led to her getting her picture published in the agency's national newsletter, posed next to one of the confiscated vehicles.

Agent Holt called up Kovach to tell him she wanted to talk to him about orchid smuggling. She didn't mention that he was the one suspected of smuggling. She did tell him that she would be asking him for a sworn affidavit, though.

On July 16, 2002, Agent Holt drove to Goldvein and questioned Kovach at length. In Holt's report, Kovach doesn't look quite so noble as he portrayed himself in his own writings. He comes across as more concerned about fame, expense, and convenience than with helping the causes of science and plant conservation.

Holt began their conversation with a time-tested investigative technique: She played dumb.

She told Kovach that she had never investigated a case involving orchids before. She wanted his help figuring out who was smuggling orchids into the country. Kovach, flattered, couldn't resist giving her a tutorial on his favorite plants. He showed off all of his hard-won knowledge, making it clear he was an expert on the subject and not some amateur who had stumbled on the discovery of the century by accident.

According to Holt's report, Kovach knew he had found the type of orchid that requires a special export permit from Peru "and that he should've had a permit to bring the species into the United States."

But Kovach contended that doing it the right way would have taken way too long, Holt wrote. "Kovach wanted to get back to the United States and get the *Phragmipedium* . . . published and have it named after him so it appeared he discovered the plant first," she wrote. "Since he was only over there a total of two weeks, it would have taken too long to wait for a . . . permit to be issued."

How long? Kovach told Holt he figured it would take two to three weeks to get the special permit because he would have to go through a broker from Peru—say, Renato Villena. The broker would have to travel to Lima to obtain the proper paperwork from government officials there.

Then there was the added cost. "Kovach said he would have to pay all travel expenses of the broker ($60) and pay for the permit ($35)," Holt wrote. "So it would have been an additional $100 just to get the permit."

Even before Holt arrived at his house, Kovach had begun scratching out a six-page timeline of his trip to Peru, Miami, and Sarasota, scrawling it onto a legal pad just like his letter to the USDA. When he was done, he signed it for her as his sworn affidavit, and she attached it to her report.

As with his letter to the USDA, the timeline makes no mention of Lee or Chady Moore, only referring to "friends" in Peru. But as he wrote, Kovach went beyond a mere recounting of his travels. He turned it into a narrative, telling in some detail what happened that afternoon in El Progresso when the woman went behind the shack:

"She reappeared with a plant in flower, and then apologized that it was the only plant out back. The plant was a large, single flower slipper, dark pink. At first I thought it was an escaped or traded-for hybrid. Suspect it was a new species. I negotiated a price and purchased it."

Kovach's affidavit was all that Agent Holt carried away from the interview. Although INRENA had asked for the return of Kovach's Peruvian prize, Holt did not at that point search or seize anything from his greenhouse—not yet. She needed to build the case against him and establish a probable cause for a crime. Until then, she wrote, "Evidence is being retained and cared for by the subject."

About a week later, though, she drove back by his house, making sure she had the details right for the next step in the Virginia end of the investigation.

After Agent Holt left with his affidavit, Kovach called up Lee Moore to tell him about her visit.

"He told me on the phone, 'I told 'em I went down there for humanitarian reasons to help the peasants,'" Moore said years later. "It was so much bullshit, I didn't even listen."

When Agent Holt checked with the USDA, she learned that Kovach had previously gone through the proper steps to import rare orchids from overseas. He had done all the right things to import orchids during his first trip to Peru in 1996, when he dealt with Manuel Arias Silva, and then again on a trip to Vietnam in 1997.

Therefore he knew how the system was supposed to work. Therefore, she figured, he knew that he had broken the law by smuggling the Peruvian slipper orchid past customs in Miami.

She asked agents in Miami to pull Kovach's customs paperwork, because, she wrote, "he may not have declared the plants he brought with him."

When Agent Holt got a copy of the form from Miami, she found that it said only that he carried "plants." Not "slipper orchids." Not even "orchids." Just "plants."

Holt still had questions about Selby's role, too. She wrote in her report that she needed to "find out their relationship with Kovach. . . . Was there any type of commercial transaction between Kovach and [Selby] when he gave them the *Phragmipedium* specimen? Did Kovach give them any other orchids that he brought back from his recent trip to Peru? (If he did, they need to be seized.) What has Kovach given them from his previous trips to Peru?"

Before Holt could dispatch an agent to question Selby's staff, though, rumors about the investigation began spreading throughout the orchid community. It was like someone in a small town spotting the state police pulling up at the mayor's house with lights flashing. Soon everyone would know it happened and there would be a dozen interpretations of what it meant.

A Canadian orchid grower named Peter Croezen did the most to get the word out. Croezen, a retired high school teacher, had made numerous trips to Peru and took a strong interest in what happened there. He had spent years working with Peruvian orchid growers, teaching them how to propagate their orchids via mass in-vitro propagation in a lab so they wouldn't have to strip the jungles bare.

Croezen had already talked to Eric Christenson about the new slipper orchid that Karol Villena and her father had found, and that Christenson had written up for publication in *Orchids*. He fully approved of how Christenson had handled the situation—leaving the plant in Peru—and of the name he'd chosen for it.

But then Croezen saw the Selby Gardens' press release about the special *Selbyana* publication. He could foresee Selby's actions undoing all of his hard work in Peru as collectors plundered the jungle searching for more of Kovach's flower. Worse, in his view, was the fact that the new name honored an American exploiter instead of the country where the flower grew.

"I was asked, by my angry Peruvian friends in orchids, to help them find justice in the USA," he said. "Peruvians are a very proud people. They do not like to be ripped off by foreign visitors."

To make things more personal, Croezen said, he knew exactly where Kovach had stumbled across the most amazing orchid discovery in a century. He knew because Croezen had been there himself six months before. He'd been riding past El Progresso with some Peruvian friends when they stopped at Medina's roadside stand.

"Faustino came up and offered us an 'orchid with a big red flower,'" Croezen wrote later on an orchid-collectors' web forum. "If we could wait 15 minutes, he would get one for us. It was late in the afternoon, our drivers said that we did not have 15 minutes to spare, for we needed to get to our hotel in Chachapoya before darkness set in." So Croezen said no thanks and they drove off—thus missing out on the glory of discovery and leaving it for Kovach to claim.

Now Croezen was determined to challenge what Selby had done with this orchid. On July 18, 2002, Croezen booted up his computer and clicked around on the Selby website until he found a place for comments. He filled out a form that allowed users to send a message to the gardens' staff. In it, he blasted them for accepting Kovach's orchid.

"From information I received the flower you identified was brought into the USA illegally," he wrote on the form. Not only that, he added, but it appeared the reason they broke the law was "that there was a concerted effort to beat Dr. Eric Christenson to the publishing of this new species."

There was only one solution, Croezen warned Selby: "The proper thing to do is to admit to the truth and withdraw the name *Phragmipedium kovachii*."

Croezen's message ultimately went to Wesley Higgins, who wrote a rebuttal e-mail that mostly dismissed Croezen's complaints as illegitimate rather than offering a defense.

Higgins wrote that the laws that were supposed to protect rare species "cannot protect a spectacular species such as *Phragmipedium kovachii*." Taxonomy is a highly competitive field, he wrote, so of course Selby moved quickly—and anyway, Christenson's name for the plant would have been "inappropriate" because people had once referred to another plant by that same "peruvianum" name.

As for withdrawing the name Selby used? "The code does not allow an author to withdraw a validly published name," he wrote.

Croezen read this and concluded it was "cover-up B.S." He fired back an e-mail to Higgins saying so and again urging Higgins to withdraw the name.

"We exchanged a few e-mails in which I was calling a spade a spade," Croezen said later. Then Croezen posted on his orchid business's website a few quotes from what Higgins had said regarding Selby's policies on dealing with orchids such as Kovach's.

Higgins, believing his comments had been taken out of context, then posted their entire exchange—including the contents of what he called Croezen's "emotionally charged e-mails"—on an orchid growers' LISTSERV called the *Orchid Guide Digest*, where it fueled more widespread debate.

Meanwhile Eric Christenson sent Croezen a four-page letter dated July 23, 2002, giving his detailed analysis of the situation, including his assertion that Selby was "a rogue institution that is deeply involved in illegal and criminal activity." The calm demeanor that had so impressed Marni Turkel was gone. He went on to slam Higgins, Atwood, Carl Luer, Cal Dodson, and a number of other targets. He wasn't shy about it either, sending copies of the scathing letter to some forty recipients other than Croezen.

Croezen, of course, posted this missive from Christenson on his website as well, giving it even wider circulation.

"I right away received all kinds of angry e-mails from people Eric had accused of one thing or another," Croezen said. "They told me Eric was a liar and called me some names as well. My standard response was, 'Sue Eric Christenson!' No one ever did."

In his letter, Christenson reported—without naming his sources— that Kovach's orchid-collecting expedition was "led by the infamous Lee Moore. . . . The only real danger to the plants in the wild is Lee Moore, who has purportedly made an exclusive deal with the actual plant collector for all future plants of the species."

As far as Christenson was concerned, the "only bright light in this quagmire" was the U.S. Fish and Wildlife Service. "They are the only government agency that seems to give a damn" about orchid smuggling, he wrote.

When Croezen posted Christenson's response on his website, he replaced Moore's name with a series of Xs, making it say, "the infamous XXXX." Moore knew who they were talking about, though, and leaped into the fray, incensed at being labeled "infamous" and yet not given full credit for his swashbuckling past.

"I enjoy a good reputation and I am well respected in INRENA and by the world over for my work done in Peru," Moore wrote in an August 7, 2002, e-mail that Croezen dutifully posted on his website. "Now I strongly suggest that you and Mr. Christenson consider a retraction of the defamatory remarks . . . and that any further reference to me in this matter may result in serious legal consequences."

Moore also faxed a scrawled letter to Kovach to alert him to what was being said on Croezen's website:

"Check it out now! . . . Guess who the infamous XXXX is and you supposedly went on a collecting expedition with XXXX which is illegal in Peru." Moore then asked Kovach, somewhat plaintively, "Why did he not write my name?"

Moore wasn't the only one incensed by the material on Croezen's website. Wesley Higgins filed a complaint with Croezen's Internet service provider that the Canadian grower was posting libelous material. Croezen refused to take it down, and the service provider refused to take action unless someone filed a lawsuit. No one did.

So the flame war continued playing out in the public arena, much to the delight of other orchidophiles, who found the whole spectacle quite entertaining.

"It was great theater," Christenson said afterward.

⁓੪

Inevitably, word of the raging orchid controversy reached the ears of someone in the press. On August 10, 2002, the *Miami Herald*'s veteran gardening writer Georgia Tasker broke the story on the paper's front page.

"A new 'slipper orchid' found in Peru could be the most important orchid discovery of the past 100 years, and it's turning the highly competitive industry into even more of a hothouse," Tasker wrote. "Some say the orchid is being smuggled into South Florida. . . . And the U.S. government is investigating the man whose name the orchid bears."

Years later, Tasker said she couldn't remember exactly who in the South Florida orchid community had tipped her off.

"*Everybody* was talking about it," she said.

She called up Kovach in Virginia and interviewed him about how he'd found the orchid being sold from a roadside stand after seeing it there the year before. He sounded excited, she recalled later, and very sure he had done the right thing. He also told her about seeing the orchids in 2001, on his earlier trip.

"I got to this place on the side of the road in northern Peru where a guy had a little stall," Kovach told her. "We stopped, and they said they'd take me to their property. That's when I first saw the plant."

Tasker wrote that Kovach saw "a small colony of the rare orchid" growing on a cliff some 500 yards from the road.

"Obsessed, Kovach returned to the area this spring," Tasker wrote. "He found the orchid but noticed many had been stripped from the cliff. He learned word had been spreading among the Peruvians and had made its way onto the Internet."

"People began to move very fast," Kovach told her. "So I packed one up and headed home."

The rest of her story covered all the bases with admirable thoroughness. She quoted Kovach on how he brought the orchid to Selby. She reported about how Peru had complained and thus spurred the ongoing Fish and Wildlife Service investigation. Tasker quoted sources from the American Orchid Society in Delray Beach about how the new orchid was producing a buzz of excitement worldwide. And she reported how Christenson had been beaten by Selby, and now called Selby "a rogue institution involved in an illegal act."

The Fish and Wildlife Service, Tasker said later, had been very open and cooperative with her. "They wanted to get the word out" that they were digging into who had this illegal orchid, she recalled.

In fact, she said, the one person who wouldn't say much at all was someone she regarded as a longtime friend: Bob Scully. Tasker had known Scully for years. She had even—at his and his wife's insistence—stayed at the Scully home in Sarasota once. But when she called up her old friend to ask him about the new orchid and the investigation, "he wouldn't say a word. I think he wanted to deflect everything off him. . . . He just got weird." (Scully says he does not recall this.)

So it was up to John Beckner to defend Selby's actions in Tasker's story, as he explained that they had shipped their only specimen to a scientist in Peru. However, Beckner's defense sounded like a debate among football fans about a disputed call: "If we looked at a plant, held it in our hands and sent it back, is that possession?"

She also quoted Meg Lowman attacking the antismuggling law that had apparently been broken, noting that "what we're seeing here is that it's just blocking the progress of science. The bigger issue is how come the hillside was denuded."

The *Miami Herald* reporter told her readers that other *Phragmipedium kovachii* plants been smuggled into the United States to be sold on the black market. It would provide a rich payday for someone, she predicted.

"The commercial potential of the plant could be the stuff of dreams," she wrote.

One South Florida orchid grower quoted in Tasker's story said his customers were approached about buying the illicit orchids "with an asking price of a whopping $10,000 for two."

Years later, Tasker explained that, like Beckner, she had heard about the under-the-table sales at the Redland show, but "I never could find out exactly who had it. It was just too hot for anybody to talk about it."

In her story, though, she did name one person who was peddling the new *Phragmipedium* to South Florida buyers. It was none other than Lee Moore.

Tasker reported that Moore had phoned one of Florida's best-known orchid growers, Martin Motes, to ask "where he could best market the orchid."

So Tasker, well aware of Moore's past, called up The Adventurer. But Moore told the reporter that he wasn't smuggling Kovach's namesake plants into the United States. He was just looking ahead. Moore said he had phoned Motes because he was growing some of the new orchids at his Peruvian nursery "and was seeking advice on potential buyers and the right price," Tasker wrote.

Tasker noted that Kovach and Moore were working hand-in-hand, writing that they "recently reached a business agreement. Kovach . . . said he has hired Moore to be his Peruvian contract grower."

Martin Motes wasn't the only person Moore phoned about buying the orchid. He also called up Harold Koopowitz in California. In addition to teaching and writing about orchids, Koopowitz co-owned a nursery that specialized in slipper orchids. Koopowitz said Moore offered to sell him the new orchid for "several thousand dollars." But as soon as Moore mentioned that it was a slipper orchid just found in Peru, Koopowitz cut him off. He knew what that meant.

"I wouldn't touch it with a ten-foot pole," Koopowitz said.

Even Bob Scully got a call from Lee Moore, about a month after the special *Selbyana* publication came out.

"He said he was seeking information on people who might be interested in buying his collection of *Phragmipedium kovachii*," Scully said. "I told him that I certainly wasn't interested. I'm not one who would want to exploit nature for money."

Years later, Moore said that while he had *Phragmipedium kovachii*—or "Pk" as he sometimes called it—growing in his nursery in Peru, he had also handed off a piece of one to a friend near Miami who was an expert on growing orchids from seeds in flasks.

"I can tell you truthfully that I brought a seedpod of the Pk to him to put into a flask when it was first discovered and not named yet but it did not germinate," Moore said. "The flask failed." He did that "before all of this bullshit started and no one was concerned about it at that time."

Three days after Tasker's bombshell in the *Herald*, the *New York Times* followed up with its own story, headlined "New Orchid Species Leaves Admirers Amazed." This piece was far more sympathetic to both Kovach and Selby. It barely alluded to the investigation and Peru's complaint, and there was no mention of smuggled orchids selling for $10,000, perhaps because the *Times* reporter lacked Tasker's Florida sources.

Instead, the *Times* piece quoted Wesley Higgins boasting about how quickly Selby's OIC had produced its description of the plant: "We went from totally unidentified species to being published in eight days, validly, in the scientific literature." (Christenson, who wrote his in less than an hour, later scoffed that the worked-all-night story just showed how inept Selby's OIC staff was.)

Despite its shortcomings, the *New York Times* story did offer a detail about

Kovach's trip to Moyobamba that contradicted both his USDA letter and the affidavit he wrote for Agent Holt.

In this version, Kovach told the paper that after buying his first slipper orchids in El Progresso, he returned to the truck stop "three days later to buy additional plants."

But on his return, the paper wrote, "he found that what had been a mossy slope of 500 of the new orchids had been stripped clean, even of inch-tall seedlings."

"They were gone," Kovach told the paper. "There had been armies of people plucking the plants up."

After that story ran, Moore faxed Kovach a note coaching his protégé on how to make his story sound less incriminating.

"There are a couple of points that you should try to clean up which look bad for you," Moore warned Kovach. "This thing is getting blown way out of proportion."

Moore told Kovach to stop telling anyone he returned to El Progresso three days after his initial plant purchase because "it indicates that you were set on depredation by getting more. This looks bad. It looks better that you left the very next day after 'purchasing' that one plant than to go up looking for more."

He advised Kovach to "tell that they misunderstood what you said and that it was Chady that went there and found that Renato had wiped them out which is the fact. Stick with the facts and we can't go wrong or contradict each other."

However, the relationship between Kovach and Moore was becoming somewhat strained. The pair had talked about pooling their money to buy some of the land where the new orchid grew, Kovach said later. But when Kovach called Moore to set up the transfer of funds, Moore told him not to worry. He said Chady had gone out and bought the land herself. No need for Kovach to invest anything—although that meant the Moores, and not Kovach, owned the land.

"I liked Lee. I trusted Lee," Kovach said. "But Chady was greedy."

Agent Holt read the newspaper coverage with interest and attached it to her next report. Beckner's argument that Selby Gardens had sent the plant back to Peru raised a new question. If that was true, she noted, then Selby should have paperwork proving it.

Lowman was in her office, penning thank-you notes to donors, when a pair of Holt's colleagues showed up unannounced to inquire about Kovach's orchid.

"It was presented to me as something routine," Lowman recalled later. "They showed up to say hey, we're looking for this orchid."

Lowman told the agents they didn't have any illegal orchids because the staff had immediately returned the orchid in question to Peru. The officers said thanks, then headed over to "the Far Side" to question Higgins and the other OIC scientists who had met Kovach and seen the plant.

Based on what they heard from Beckner, Higgins, and others, Fish and Wildlife Service agents in Texas then paid a visit to Dave Hunt to ask him about the pictures he had e-mailed to Selby Gardens.

Under questioning, Hunt yielded a detail that he hadn't mentioned to Higgins: He had had a chance to buy the new orchid shown in the e-mails before Kovach got there.

After he got the photos from Agro-Oriente, Hunt told the investigators, Karol Villena had called him to offer to sell him the new orchid. A phone call, of course, leaves no written record. Karol Villena told him that Agro-Oriente had had the orchids in their greenhouse for some time, but no one realized what they had until one plant finally produced one of those spectacular flowers, Hunt told the investigators.

Villena's asking price, Hunt said, was $5,000 per plant. However, she made it clear that that price didn't include shipping or handling. Instead, it would require him to make a trip to Peru—although how he would get his purchase home, she couldn't say.

"She told me, 'You could come get it, and what you do with it after that is up to you,'" Hunt said years later. He said he declined her offer.

In the meantime, a University of Florida orchid scientist friendly to Selby contacted Dodson and Dalström with more disturbing news. She had just returned from Peru, she said in an e-mail. While there, she had talked to officials from INRENA, and they were seeing red over what had happened with Kovach's orchid.

She warned her Selby friends that INRENA had demanded a Fish and Wildlife Service investigation "and they want these specimens and/or live plants to go back to Peru." In addition, she wrote, "they asked us if there was any possibility to change the kovachii name because he is an illegal plant collector."

She asked Dodson and Dalström to send her copies of any permits Kovach had been carrying so she could try to straighten things out for Selby, explaining, "This thing is getting a bit international."

Dodson forwarded the e-mail to Higgins, who sent her a reply pointing out that the only orchid Selby had had was now back in Peru. As far as Selby Gardens was concerned, that was that.

She wrote back to tell him that INRENA did not see it that way.

"From my friend I heard this morning that INRENA is putting a lot of pressure and I think they want to make a scandal out of this," she warned Higgins. "I hope everything will calm down soon."

Just to be on the safe side, *Selbyana* editor Bruce Holst e-mailed Ricardo Fernandez in Lima to ask if he'd received the orchid they mailed back.

Yes, Fernandez replied in broken English, eventually he had gotten it, although someone else at the museum had opened it before him. Fernandez implied he had had a run-in with the INRENA authorities over the orchid, but offered no details about what a lot of hot water he was in.

What he didn't say was that INRENA had sent a letter to the director of the museum where Fernandez worked. INRENA demanded an explanation for why Fernandez was working with American smugglers.

Fernandez had to explain to his boss that he was innocent. He really didn't do anything to enable smuggling. All he did was read over some of the language in the description. He had been so excited about the discovery of such a spectacular new orchid species, and about getting a little bit of the glory from helping Selby with it, he just didn't consider that there might be criminal implications.

In his e-mail to Holst, Fernandez noted that "I have no read anything about the comments on *Phrag. kovachii/peruvianum*, but I suppose this is very controversial."

The controversy was about to get a lot wilder.

The knock on Kovach's door came about 8:30 a.m. on August 22, 2002. The people on the porch called out, "Federal agents!"

Kovach and his wife, Barbara, opened the door, looking dazed. Then they swung it wide to let in a team of four armed Fish and Wildlife Service officers accompanied by two state game officers.

The team's leader, Agent Holt, carried a search warrant, signed by a judge, allowing her to seize any of Kovach's business or personal records, including photos, invoices, telephone bills, bank records, price lists, receipts or anything else relating to the shipment of orchids "from 1997 to the present." She was also allowed to confiscate "all orchids that were brought in from Peru and/or foreign countries on or about June 4, 2002." To be sure the team grabbed the right plants, Holt had brought along someone who seldom got a chance to go on a raid: the agency's top expert on orchids, Roddy Gabel.

Gabel already knew Kovach's name. A few years before, Kovach had called Gabel's office to report orchid smuggling he said he had witnessed in Vietnam. But he had no proof, Gabel recalled, so the Fish and Wildlife Service could do nothing about his allegations.

Now, facing a raid team looking for evidence of orchid smuggling in their own home, Kovach and his wife "were obviously taken completely unawares," Gabel said years later. "I think they were still asleep."

They were—until they saw all the armed officers waiting outside the door. The sight of all those guns woke them faster than a blaring alarm clock.

"They came in like a fricking SWAT team," Kovach recalled years later.

The officers told the couple they weren't allowed to touch any of their belongings during the search because it was potential evidence. Then the agents set to work rooting through the house, examining every scrap of paper they could find.

"They also videotaped the whole inside of the house, in case they had to come back, so they'd know where everything was," Kovach said. "It's total fascist, Gestapo nonsense."

Gabel, meanwhile, headed for the greenhouse to look for illegal plants.

Roddy Gabel, the Fish and Wildlife Service's top orchid expert, helped search Michael Kovach's greenhouse for contraband plants. Photo courtesy of Roddy Gabel.

He wasn't impressed by what he saw there. Despite his big-time discovery, Kovach struck Gabel as strictly a small-timer, with a greenhouse to match.

"It was really a backyard hobby greenhouse, not like you see with some people who have acres and acres of glass walls," he said.

As Gabel examined Kovach's plant collection, nothing struck him as out of the ordinary. All the labels appeared to match what was growing in the pots—the *maxillarias*, the *psymorchis*, the *odontoglossums*, the *epidendrums* and so forth. He saw no sign of *Phragmipedium kovachii*.

Nevertheless, Gabel and his colleagues seized 385 orchids, which according to Kovach were the ones he'd toted in two suitcases through the Miami airport. The Peruvian plants—even the plain ones—all went into a truck headed for the U.S. Botanical Garden in Washington, D.C., to be held as evidence.

During the two-hour search, Holt also seized a laptop computer, lots of business receipts and records, and one item that Kovach said later made him particularly angry: his draft proposal for a reality television show called "The Orchid Hunter," which was to star one Michael Kovach.

"You know that show *The Crocodile Hunter*? I was experimenting with a show that could be like that," he told a reporter several months later. "This week *maxillaria*, and next week *kovachii*."

On the same day Holt and her colleagues were searching Kovach's house, agents from the St. Petersburg office of the Fish and Wildlife Service served similar papers on Selby Gardens, giving the recipients a similar shock.

The document they delivered was addressed to the gardens' comptroller, as custodian of records, but the intended recipient balked, Lowman said. So the executive director went to see what the agents wanted.

What Lowman found awaiting her brought her up short. It was a subpoena from a federal grand jury seeking any and all documents regarding the *Phragmipedium kovachii*.

Until that point, Lowman said, "I knew of no reason to be concerned" about the federal investigation. But when she saw agents seizing records and documents—and doing so on behalf of a grand jury—"obviously my hairs were up and I was thinking something was up."

She called her husband, the lawyer, and in talking it over with him she decided that perhaps she didn't know the whole story of *Phragmipedium kovachii*. Although the orchid boys assured her they had the situation under control, she wasn't so sure.

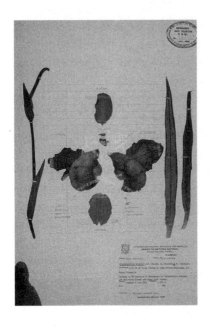

By sending the type specimen back to Peru, Selby's orchid experts thought they would satisfy any objections. But Bob Scully could tell something was missing. Photo courtesy of Stig Dalström.

She had already gotten an intimation of this, courtesy of her board chairman. Scully had asked to see a Xerox copy of the herbarium specimen they mailed back to Peru. He took one look at it and pointed out to Lowman that something seemed a little off. There appeared to be a part of the plant missing. Now what could that mean?

After talking to her husband, Lowman decided what she needed to do was compile a detailed chronology of what happened that day in June while she was traveling to Cincinnati. She sent an e-mail to every staff member she knew to be involved in the *Phragmipedium kovachii* discovery, asking each to write her a memo about what they had seen and done. She sent the request to Higgins, Beckner, Dalström, Harry Luther, and several others she thought had been present.

The next morning, she woke up and in a flash realized she had left someone off her list: Atwood.

He was only a part-timer, as far as Selby's management was concerned, since his salary was paid partly by the Missouri Botanical Garden. But his was one of the three names listed in the *Selbyana* description as author, so he needed to be queried as well.

Bleary-eyed, she climbed out of bed and sent him an e-mail up in Woodstock, Vermont, asking Atwood what he remembered of the events from two months before.

"The Fish and Wildlife visited Selby with a subpoena yesterday, because for some reason, the Peruvian government thinks we still have one of the *Phrag*. plants," she wrote to the scientists. "This is pretty standard procedure on there [*sic*] part, but it really means we have to get our facts and data organized. Can you please write to me, by Monday, a full account in your words of the entire episode—how many plants, the timetable of how things happened, your take on Michael's paperwork, and any other steps and facts that will be useful for me to put together all the correct information as we move forward."

In response to her request, Lowman wrote later, she got back seven versions of Kovach's visit to Selby, and "not one of them [was] altogether consistent with the others. . . . The only issue that the staff seemed to agree on was that they considered this to be the most exciting orchid discovery in over a century. Some claimed this large, showy flower could be worth millions of dollars in the world of horticulture."

The most alarming response came from the mild-mannered Atwood. Instead of e-mailing her back, he called her long-distance, sounding "anxious and upset and distraught," she said.

Despite the assurances everyone at Selby had given the Fish and Wildlife Service and the *Miami Herald*, the OIC staff had not, in fact, sent every bit of its *Phragmipedium kovachii* to Ricardo Fernandez in Peru. As Scully had suspected, a piece of Kovach's plant wasn't saved as part of the herbarium specimen.

Instead, like Lowman's last e-mail, it had gone to Vermont.

9

The Last Condor

Part of the allure of these plants has to do with the forbidden
nature and illegal status of some of the wild slipper orchid
species. . . . All of this has engendered a certain mysticism
and mythology about the slipper orchids.

Harold Koopowitz, *Tropical Slipper Orchids*

Back on June 5, 2002, when Atwood took Kovach's plant to Selby's herbarium to prepare the dried specimen, he didn't use all of it.

Scully was right when he told Lowman something was missing. Not all of the plant had been mounted on paper as the type specimen. Instead, Atwood had removed part of the stalk for the type specimen, added the dried flower that Kovach had brought in, but held back a clump of old growth.

Thus, when the herbarium specimen was packaged up to ship to Lima, "there remained a piece of the living plant for Selby to grow, but it lacked living roots," Atwood wrote in the letter he finally e-mailed Lowman on August 23. "Although no formal arrangements were made, the first priority was to assure the health of the plant."

Telling the story years later, Atwood explained that he did not do this on his own. He was doing something he and his colleagues agreed was the right thing to do. He said the thinking of the orchid boys went this way: Selby's primary goal was conservation. Here was a plant that no one had identified before, a rare tropical slipper orchid at that. No one knew how many others there might be. There might be only a handful of them. This might even be the only one left. But pressing the plant would kill it.

Would you kill the last California condor? The last manatee? The last Florida panther?

"Shouldn't we save a little piece of it?" Atwood asked.

Besides, wouldn't it be a nice coup for Selby's OIC if they had one to display? To study? To make their own, a signature species of Selby, the way they did *Phragmipedium besseae*? Imagine how people would flock from around the world to see it! Imagine how other orchid scientists would envy them! Think of what it would mean!

Everything hinged on whether Kovach's permits were in order, Atwood explained in his letter to Lowman. If the permits were legal, then they could legally keep a piece. A live *Phragmipedium kovachii* "would be a valuable asset for our institution," he told Lowman.

Or, as he put it more bluntly years later, "We did want to keep the plant alive if possible . . . since it was such a botanical sensation."

Even if Kovach's permits weren't legal, they thought Selby Gardens might find a way to hang onto it anyway, an angle that they could exploit. Thus, Dalström wrote in his own letter to Lowman, a group of the OIC scientists agreed someone should "cultivate it for the time being, until a definite decision could be made about the fate of the plant."

Who made this fateful decision? "All of us who were present," Atwood said years later.

He identified the colleagues who made the call to keep the piece of a plant as Wesley Higgins, Harry Luther, John Beckner, Cal Dodson, and Bruce Holst. Although Atwood did not name him, Dalström himself says he was part of the group, too. However, Higgins has repeatedly insisted he wasn't present for this discussion and didn't know what Atwood had done until later.

When the orchid boys were discussing it, they thought the bigger question was not so much whether to do it, but how. Because the orchid came from a high altitude in Peru, they knew it would not survive Sarasota's summer in one of Selby's greenhouses. Selby simply wasn't equipped to keep it cool.

The Atlanta Botanical Garden had just opened a new cooling facility for plants that came from places like the Andes. But they feared that Atlanta's scientists would not give Kovach's orchid the kind of daily attention it would require.

There was another way. Atwood, the resident expert on slipper orchids, was just about to leave for his childhood home in Vermont, where he took care of his ailing mother. The summer there would more closely match the

John Atwood kept mum about the slipper orchid he was growing on his Vermont farm because he feared unscrupulous collectors would come after it. Photo courtesy of John Atwood.

Andean climate than Sarasota would. Night-time temperatures would be no higher than 60 degrees.

Thus Atwood's colleagues agreed that he should take it home with him. Atwood, however, wasn't so sure.

When he was younger, doing field research in Borneo, traipsing through rough mountain terrain, Atwood had lost count of how many leeches he had picked off his body. He dismissed the multitude of bites as "a little bit icky, but they don't hurt." Leeches didn't bother him a bit. But this! This made him squeamish. Taking this rare slipper orchid with the iffy provenance back to his cherished family home and trying to keep it alive—this, at last, was something that gave the man pause.

"It was quite a responsibility," Atwood explained. "There were rumors that people had paid $10,000 for one of these. It felt funny taking something back to Vermont with that kind of value on it. I really didn't want that."

But he knew that if he refused, the plant would die. He did not want that on his conscience. So he swallowed his objections, packed this sliver of a slipper in his luggage, and headed for home.

When he got to the Vermont farm, he gathered up some sphagnum moss, which he knew would make an ideal growing medium, and used that in potting his *Phragmipedium* piece. He set the plastic pot outdoors, on a picnic table, and tended it carefully for the next two months.

Later, after the lawyers got involved, and he was testifying under oath, someone asked him whether anyone had ordered him to keep his *kovachii* a secret.

"Was I ever told to keep confidential?" he replied. "I think it was kind of implicit in the fact that here we had a plant that by some accounts somebody had paid $10,000 for one of these things. . . . You might attract some very interesting people to a remote hillside up in Vermont, so I wasn't used to going around and telling people."

Nevertheless, he couldn't keep it to himself. Not entirely.

"What I did do is I went to a Unitarian church service in which we have a session of sharing of joys and concern," Atwood said. "And I reported this wonderful lady slipper orchid that I had a hand in describing at a church service, not having any idea of what this was going to turn into."

Atwood knew his slippers. By mid-August, he had managed to coax Kovach's plant into producing five new roots and a single new shoot.

Encouraged by this success, Atwood had begun plotting his triumphant return to Selby. Perhaps he could design a new cool-storage facility like Atlanta's as a place for Selby to grow this orchid and others like it. He was sure this would earn the OIC the respect it deserved—and not just the OIC.

"I was going to become a big hero," Atwood said, then sighed heavily.

Although Atwood had been distraught on the phone with Lowman, in his e-mail to her he took a bolder tack. He argued that neither he nor anyone else on Selby's staff had done anything wrong.

Their loyalty was to science alone, he argued. The job of enforcing the law should be left to the police.

"Do we at Selby Gardens have any responsibility to prove that any plant submitted is legal?" he asked. "We believe we had no basis on which to reject it on the mere possibility that the plant might be illegal. We leave that to the border authorities."

Atwood's argument, which would be repeated in various iterations by other Selby defenders, would be sure to draw a frown from any veteran lawman. To them, it would be like an auto dealer accepting a trade-in Ferrari from someone with no title papers and claiming it was up to the police to catch car thieves. Anyone who made such an argument would likely wind up charged with dealing in stolen property.

Lowman, reading through Atwood's account and that of his colleagues, realized she had stepped into a valley of venomous snakes like the ones she had seen around the gympie-gympie trees in Australia. This time there was little chance of tiptoeing away.

The OIC's defense of "we sent it back to Peru" would clearly not hold up now, since they had not sent it *all* back. Atwood's piece of the plant ruined that argument. The Peruvian authorities could not be persuaded that Selby had only good intentions.

Realizing what was at stake, Lowman decided that she needed someone to pull her—and Selby Gardens, of course—out of danger. Someone who had a special knowledge of how to deal with this kind of complicated mess.

She called her husband again, and at his suggestion she started looking for a law firm that could provide the kind of help she needed. She finally settled on Holland & Knight's Washington, D.C., office, signing a contract with them on August 28, 2002, just five days after getting Atwood's e-mail.

"The gardens has hired some very capable legal counsel in Washington, D.C., that I found," she wrote in an e-mail to Atwood. "I am very optimistic that we will have a successful outcome. Just grow that plant and keep it safe."

Lowman picked the firm because, although the lawyers charged $400 an hour, they had experts on staff skilled in dealing with complex endangered-species cases.

And this one looked like a doozy. It involved not just federal wildlife law but also an international treaty, one that everyone in the orchid world regarded as an abomination: the Convention on International Trade in Endangered Species.

10

The Law and the Loophole

*Instead of protecting the wild orchids, they have fostered
an illegal black market and made the gentle art of flower
breeding into a criminal activity.*

Harold Koopowitz, *Tropical Slipper Orchids*

Guido Braem speaks four languages and travels the globe lecturing about
orchids. He has a Ph.D. in taxonomy. He edits a scientific journal and has
written hundreds of scholarly articles.

But he may be best known in the orchid world for punching out a cop.

To understand why someone like Braem would do something so violent
requires rewinding the clock to 1973, the same year Carl Luer twisted a bank
president's arm to launch Marie Selby Botanical Gardens.

On February 12, 1973, delegates from eighty nations converged on Washington, D.C., to discuss a thorny issue: the international trade in wildlife.
They knew they could not control poaching as long as there was an unregu-
lated international market where anyone willing to pay the price could acquire any species, no matter how rare. What they needed was a treaty among
all the nations that spelled out the rules for legal trade, one that gave them
power to combat poaching and smuggling.

Previous treaties, some with quaint, Monty Pythonesque names, had attempted to deal with the same problem: the London Convention Designed
to Ensure the Conservation of Various Species of Wild Animals in Africa
Which Are Useful to Man or Inoffensive (1900), the London Convention
Relative to the Preservation of Fauna and Flora in Their Natural State (1933),

the Washington Convention on Nature Protection and Wild Life Preservation in the Western Hemisphere (1940), and the Algiers African Convention on the Conservation of Nature and Natural Resources (1968).

But all of those treaties suffered from limitations that eventually made them unworkable, tied as they were to colonial rule or to protecting only a region and not the entire globe. Poachers and smugglers could be clever and determined, and so the law had to be made tighter. Now the time seemed to be right to take that step.

The late 1960s had brought a fresh wave of attention to the problems of pollution and environmental exploitation. In 1970, 20 million Americans—10 percent of the country's population—took to the streets for the first Earth Day protests. A number that big made Congress sit up and take notice. Soon it began passing new legislation, such as the Clean Air Act and the Clean Water Act. Similar pro-environment activism occurred on the global level, pushed along by an organization called the International Union for the Conservation of Nature, or IUCN for short.

The IUCN had been the first organization to prepare a list of endangered species, a project spearheaded by a scientist named Lee Talbot. The IUCN had also been pushing hard for a treaty to combat poaching. By 1973 Talbot, an ex-Marine who enjoyed driving race cars and climbing mountains, had landed a job working for President Richard Nixon's White House Council on Environmental Quality, and he was determined to see the IUCN's goals carried out.

"I made it clear that I came in with an agenda," said Talbot, who played a crucial role in writing such legislation as the Endangered Species Act and the Marine Mammal Protection Act.

In 1972, the United Nations Conference on the Human Environment, held in Stockholm, adopted what it called its "Action Plan for the Human Environment." Recommendation 99.3, pushed by Talbot's friends at the IUCN, called for a new treaty "on export, import and transit of certain species of wild animals and plants."

Talbot convinced his White House bosses that the United States should be the host for a discussion of this proposed treaty, and he served as the American delegation's chief scientist. At the 1973 convention, the delegates spent three weeks debating what such an agreement should say. One of the big arguments: whether this treaty should cover not just animals but also plants.

The original negotiations leading up to the conference had originally covered only animal species. But two weeks before they convened, the IUCN urged that the convention follow the Stockholm recommendation, adding plants, too.

"Various kinds of trees, orchids, and cacti are a big part of the international trade," Talbot explained.

Most of the objections to including plants such as orchids came from the British, he said. "They argued, 'Our customs people wouldn't have a hope of identifying different kinds of wood or orchids.' So there was some kind of a dust-up over that. They wanted to limit it to just animals."

In the end, however, the IUCN proposal carried the day with the delegates, most of them from Third World countries weary of their natural bounty being pillaged by their colonizers. On a Saturday morning, March 3, 1973, twenty-one delegates signed the document that they had drawn up. Over the next two years, ten countries, including the United States, officially ratified it. When the tenth country stamped its approval, the treaty took on the force of law. That happened in 1975, the same year Selby Gardens and its OIC officially opened for business.

The treaty said the delegates recognized that "wild fauna and flora in their many beautiful and varied forms are an irreplaceable part of the natural systems of the earth which must be protected for this and the generations to come." Trade would be allowed, but only if it did not doom the species to extinction.

The public heard little about this treaty, officially called the Convention on International Trade in Endangered Species of Wild Flora and Fauna, or CITES—pronounced "SIGH-tees"—for short. Yet it proved so popular among the government agencies in charge of wildlife protection that by the time the treaty's thirtieth anniversary rolled around in 2003, more than 160 nations had signed up to enforce its rules, which by then covered thirty thousand species.

The CITES treaty that won approval in 1973 built on the earlier treaties' approach to ensuring commerce did not trample on conservation. But it also included a provision that set up a decision-making body to periodically adjust the treaty's language and its species lists—an innovation credited with keeping the treaty functional for thirty years, although it also has generated controversy over such issues as adding polar bears, bluefin tuna, and all kinds of sharks to the list.

What marked CITES' biggest departure from its predecessors, though, was the recognition that some species may be more endangered than others. As a result, different species needed greater protection than others.

The lists of species covered by CITES were included in the treaty as a series of three appendixes. The most critically endangered wildlife, the ones that needed the tightest control on trade, were listed as Appendix I. They were the ones "threatened with extinction which are or may be affected by trade," yet could still be traded under limited circumstances with special CITES permits.

Anyone who wants to ship something listed in Appendix I to someone in another country must get an export permit from the country where the shipment originates and an import permit from the country where the shipment is headed. The government agencies in charge of issuing the export permits must determine that "such export will not be detrimental to the survival of that species," while the agencies in charge of importation permits must decide that "the specimen is not to be used for primarily commercial purposes"—but scientific purposes were supposed to be all right.

The Appendix II list covers species that face extinction only if there were no regulation of trade, or are so similar to species on Appendix I "as to be indistinguishable." They, too, may be traded with special CITES permits, but unlike Appendix I species, they can be shipped for commercial purposes as well as for science.

The species listed in Appendix III are the ones not covered by the first two lists that are still under regulation by a member country. The other countries must help prevent any cross-border trade in those.

The rules about the species listed in those appendixes cover not just live wildlife but also their parts—crocodile purses, rhino horns, and tortoise-shell combs, for instance. The parts business can be a lucrative one. One smuggler offered to sell an undercover officer a carving made from a narwhal tusk for $10,000 and bragged that he had access to $250,000 worth of similar stock. Since the animals listed in the appendixes were usually killed by poachers to obtain those coveted parts, it made sense to include the parts under the law, too.

Except that's how Guido Braem got in trouble.

The largest single group covered by CITES, representing about 75 percent of species on all three appendixes: orchids.

Initially, all orchid species were put on the Appendix II list, meaning trade is allowed with a CITES permit. Getting such permits can be difficult, involving bureaucratic delays and, from time to time, the need to bribe some foreign official, but it's not impossible.

The attitude that most orchid collectors have toward CITES and its

Although he speaks four languages and has a Ph.D. in taxonomy, Guido Braem is better known for punching out a customs official over an orchid collected in 1905. Photo courtesy of Guido Braem.

permitting system is best summed up in Florida orchid grower Mary Motes's comic novel *Orchid Territory*.

In Motes's book, one of the main characters, a veteran South Florida orchid grower, tells a group of people at a Christmas party, "In the old days . . . any hobbyist who spoke a little bad Spanish could go down to Guatemala, Peru, wherever, and round up a cab driver, show the village kids a plant, offer two cents each, and come back the next day to mounds of orchids by the road."

When one of the partygoers says something complimentary about CITES, the elderly orchid grower gives the man a sharp look.

"Orchids, the largest family of flowering plants on earth and the whole damn *family* is on the list!" she barks. "It's as daft as putting a hold on all *Compositae*"—the common dandelion.

What happened to Braem is, to many orchidophiles, the perfect illustration of just how daft the rules are.

In 1986, Braem was writing a book about Asian slipper orchids, the *Paphiopedilums*. He wanted to take a look at the original type specimen of one particular flower. It had been collected in 1905 from an island off the coast of Thailand, and since then had been kept in a jar of alcohol at a museum in Copenhagen. Braem called a Danish colleague and asked that he ship the specimen to him in Germany for inspection.

But the jar was held up at customs. When Braem drove over to see what was wrong, the customs officer told him he was being charged with smuggling a protected species. Braem had not obtained a CITES permit for the transfer of this orchid specimen from Copenhagen, and there was no bill or invoice as required either, the officer said.

Braem objected, strenuously. Surely CITES covered only live plants, not pickled ones that had been sitting in a jar for more than eight decades, he contended. And the flower was a loan, not a sale, so of course there could be no invoice.

Braem argued for an hour and got nowhere. Then he noticed the officer smirking at him.

"He knew he had me by the balls," Braem later told Eric Hansen in *Orchid Fever*. "I didn't like his attitude, so I just leaned over the counter and punched him in the face. He hit the floor like a sack of potatoes."

Braem wound up charged with assaulting a civil servant, orchid smuggling, and tax evasion. He paid a fine that went to charity, and all charges were dropped. As for the pickled specimen, it went back to Copenhagen without Braem ever seeing it.

Months later, after disposing of his criminal charge, Braem climbed in his car and drove to Denmark just to gaze upon it—hardly a triumph for the cause of conservation, and certainly not what the delegates in 1973 had in mind. But his was far from the only troubling case.

In the 1980s, an adventurer named Henry Azadehdel became one of the most prominent and prolific orchid hunters in the world.

He regularly brought back rare orchids to be studied by scientific institutions in Russia, Germany, and England. Scientists at the Royal Botanical Gardens, Kew, sent him written requests for particular orchid species they wanted for their research, and Azadehdel filled the orders. He even had a slipper orchid named for him: *Paphiopedilum henryanum*.

Then, in 1987—a year after Braem punched out the smirking customs man—British police arrested Azadehdel, snapping on the handcuffs at Heathrow Airport. In his luggage they had found thirteen *Phragmipedium besseae* seedlings. He had neither the required CITES permit for trade in Appendix II plants nor the phytosanitary certificate attesting that the orchids had no diseases or parasites. A search of his home turned up three hundred more orchids that the authorities deemed suspect in origin.

The newspapers ate it up, dubbing him an "orchid pirate." The tabloid

Weekly World News ran the story under the breathless headline, "Raider of the Lost Orchids!" and depicted him as an evil Indiana Jones. Prosecutors contended that his correspondence with the botanical institutions had been a ruse designed to tease out information from the scientists about where he should hunt for rare orchids to plunder. They wanted to make an example out of him, to scare other plant smugglers.

Eighteen months later, in 1989, Azadehdel pleaded guilty to smuggling the original thirteen *Phragmipedium besseaes*. The plants seized from his house turned out to have the proper documentation—but they were not returned.

As Azadehdel stood before a judge at the Old Bailey to be sentenced, the judge said: "The destruction of rare species is not caused by overenthusiastic collectors but by cynical and ruthless commercial exploitation and trafficking for profit. If ever a trade wants discouraging, it's this."

He then sentenced Azadehdel to a year behind bars, making him the first person in Britain ever imprisoned for orchid smuggling. He was also fined 10,000 pounds—about $16,000—and ordered to pay the same amount in court costs.

Eventually, though, an appeals court reduced it to the five weeks he had spent in jail after his initial arrest. The higher court dropped the order to pay court costs and reduced his fine to a mere 2,500 pounds (about $4,000). The appellate judges pointed out that if the courts imposed such a stiff sentence for mere flowers, how could they punish ivory poachers, who by comparison made really big profits?

"Dealers in rare orchids must be laughing all the way back to the jungle to carry on their iniquitous trade," fumed an editorial in *New Scientist*.

However, Eric Hansen's book *Orchid Fever* contended that most of Azadehdel's collecting work wound up benefiting the botanical gardens' scientists, not putting money in Azadehdel's pockets. Hansen reported finding documents that showed that one of Azadehdel's own customers, Dr. Philip Cribb of the Royal Botanic Garden, Kew, had denounced him to the CITES authorities—even as Cribb continued accepting wild-collected orchids from him.

After he walked out of jail, Azadehdel was discovered to have had a number of aliases that included "Henry X," a sign that there may have been more to his shadowy activities than anyone suspected. Today he is better known in England for his claims about UFOs and alien abductions than for the controversy over his orchid-smuggling case. But his crime left its mark on those who followed.

The same year Azadehdel stood in the dock, the CITES committee in charge of reviewing plant species decided to move most of the tropical slipper orchids up to Appendix I, thus stopping all legitimate international trade in wild *Paphiopedilums* and *Phragmipediums*.

Their concerns were fueled not only by Azadehdel's case but also by the rediscovery of an orchid that had been considered lost, the *Paphiopedilum sanderianum*. Soon after it was rediscovered in the wild, ads popped up offering the plant for high prices—a clear sign that someone was stripping it from the jungles of Borneo to make a tidy profit.

Although no studies had been done of how abundant these and all the other slippers might actually be in the wild, the committee decided they all needed the toughest protection available under CITES. They made that decision based on records showing how many slipper orchids were being traded legitimately under Appendix II rules. Some of the trade levels seemed to the committee to be extraordinarily high.

However, according to Harold Koopowitz, those trade numbers were misleading. The numbers appeared to show how many plants were being sold. Actually, he explained, orchid traders were selling them by the growth—the fan of leaves produced during a single season—and not by the plant.

"What this meant for the trade numbers was simply that they were inflated," Koopowitz explained. "A thousand plants recorded in the trade may have represented only a hundred plants taken from the wild. Efforts to point this out were ignored."

Nobody at the CITES plant committee had any hard numbers on how many slipper orchids might still be in the wild, or what the real trade numbers might be, Koopowitz said. Worse, the committee never bothered to consult with the group of orchid experts who are supposed to advise them. Had they done so, he said, they would have learned that the experts believed that putting all tropical slipper orchids on the Appendix I list was "neither desirable nor recommended."

Before the new rule took effect, collectors rushed to grab as many of them as they could, anticipating that closing off legitimate trade would drive up both demand and the black-market price. It was like a return to Victorian days, when orchid hunters like Benedict Roezl would strip a jungle bare.

"I walked into the nursery of a renowned importer," Koopowitz wrote afterward, "and the entire floor was set up with piles of bare rooted *Paphiopedilums*. Each pile contained hundreds and hundreds of plants. . . . The plants were only collected in those quantities because it was the last time that they could be collected legally."

As he walked past the heaps of flowers, Koopowitz wrote, he couldn't help wondering if the change to Appendix I "had forced a frenzy of overcollecting" which would end up causing them to be endangered rather than protecting them.

"Any remaining respect that I had for CITES and its professed goals evaporated at that point," he wrote.

How effective was this new rule in stopping orchid smugglers? Four years later, in 1993, a postal inspector in California discovered that a box marked "sample material" actually contained sixty slipper orchids. They had come from a nursery in Java run by Iwan Kolopaking, who had long done a steady business in tropical orchids. As with Azadehdel, there was a slipper orchid that bore his name: *Paphiopedilum kolopakingii.*

In September 1994, Iwan Kolopaking's twenty-eight-year-old son, Harto, flew into Los Angeles International Airport carrying 216 jungle-grown slipper orchids in his large suitcases and no CITES permits. He checked in at the airport hotel, and not long afterward he was showing some collectors what he'd smuggled in.

When one of the customers asked Kolopaking how much he wanted for the lot, the answer was $13,000. At that point, another customer identified himself as an undercover officer with the U.S. Fish and Wildlife Service and arrested him.

Three months later Kolopaking pleaded guilty, not just to the sale of those 216 orchids but to smuggling more than a thousand slipper orchids worth an estimated $150,000 into the United States in 1992 and 1993. A judge sentenced him to five months in jail, making him the Henry Azadehdel of the United States, the first person ever imprisoned in America for orchid smuggling.

The prosecutor said such a stiff sentence should serve as a warning to other smugglers. But even Kolopaking's own father didn't get the message, apparently. In 2001, a federal grand jury indicted Iwan Kolopaking on charges he was still smuggling orchids into the United States. The only change: this time they were in boxes labeled "toys."

This, then, is the law that Kovach had apparently violated, and that now had Meg Lowman very worried.

As Dodson pointed out in the staff meeting that Wes Higgins had called, Kovach needed a CITES permit to take the plants out of Peru and a CITES permit to bring them into the United States, and he had provided Selby with copies of neither.

In Agent Holt's affidavit applying for a search warrant for Kovach's house, she wrote that he did not commit this crime by accident.

"Kovach admitted that he knew he was importing CITES Appendix I and Appendix II orchids," she wrote. "Kovach also had knowledge of the CITES Convention and the provisions for exporting CITES Appendix II orchids. Kovach told your affiant that he didn't have time to obtain the necessary CITES permit."

However, Agent Holt noted, Kovach had hit upon what would prove to be a possible loophole in the law.

"If Kovach had applied for a U.S. permit it would have been denied because he would have to state the species to be imported into the U.S. and he would need to have written permission from Peru that [the plant] would be legally acquired," the investigator wrote.

But how could he state the species name for the permit if the orchid didn't have a name yet?

Selby's orchid boys were also familiar with CITES and its quirks. One orchid expert quoted repeatedly by reporters writing about all the previous orchid-smuggling cases was none other than John Atwood, then heading up Selby's OIC.

A story by *New Scientist* on the Azadehdel case included a warning by Atwood that targeting the people who collect rare orchids from the wild would never stop the illegal trade. Instead, he said, the authorities should target the dealers and buyers.

"Until you eliminate the greedy 'I want,' you'll never get anywhere," he said. "The whole system is a villain. Consumers are villains, the vendors are villains. There is a lot of ignorance along the way."

Then, in 1995, Atwood told a reporter covering the Iwan Kolopaking case that slipper orchids were now the most commonly smuggled type of orchid in the world, explaining, "They're so valuable, so desired, and so slow to grow."

Yet, like all orchid fanciers, Atwood's Selby colleagues had nothing good to say about CITES protection for orchids. In the August 1991 newsletter published by the Orchid Conservation Committee, John Beckner blasted the treaty.

"Whether CITES and the Endangered Species Act, after nearly two decades, have saved a single orchid species, is not known to us," Beckner wrote.

"We do know they have resulted in the destruction of plants, the obstruction and discouragement of private efforts and the tying up of much precious time and energy in paperwork and rituals demanded of growers."

The main flaw in CITES could be found in the T in its name: It focused solely on "trade." It did not say one word about the destruction of habitat, which is a larger threat. Farmers and road builders could cut or burn thousands of acres of jungle and kill untold numbers of rare orchids, and CITES could not touch them, orchid experts pointed out. But let some botanical Samaritan try to save a few plants by uprooting them and taking them to another country to grow, and the CITES authorities would scream bloody murder, the orchidophiles complained.

The rules made no sense in other ways as well. Why require onerous rules for species of orchids for which there was little commercial demand, such as the little botanicals that Marni Turkel favored? Clearly those weren't being threatened with extinction by trade since there was hardly any trade to speak of, yet they were listed in Appendix I just like the slipper orchids.

And what about loosening the CITES rules for shipments of hybrids that were so clean they were clearly grown in a greenhouse and not in the wild?

Roddy Gabel, the Fish and Wildlife Service's resident orchid expert, had tried his best to get the CITES authorities to fix what was wrong. He kept running into the same problem that the British had identified back in 1973.

"There's been a fairly substantial effort over the years to look at whether we could identify the heavily traded genera and de-list others that weren't threatened by trade," Gabel said. "The problem was, when orchids are out of flower, they're hard to distinguish from one another, and it wasn't possible to exempt some but not others."

When the CITES plant group convened in Chile in 2002, he said, "we wrote a proposal to exempt large commercial shipments of more than a hundred plants that were clean and uniform in appearance, so they would likely be artificially propagated."

But the delegates from the Latin American countries objected, he said. They did not want the rules to be loosened in any way. They "felt the need to control everything in order to make it all work," Gabel said. "The Colombians in particular were wary. They rotate their [CITES] personnel every six months so they don't get too cozy with the exporters."

Working with the American Orchid Society's Ned Nash, Gabel said, he managed to get the support of the Asian CITES delegates to loosen the rules for some Asian hybrids. The Asians, unlike the Latin Americans, wanted as little regulation of the orchid trade as possible.

So the CITES rules on orchids were looser in Asia, and tighter in South and Central America—the place where Kovach had found his Holy Grail.

Ironically, despite all of the orchid boys' criticism of the treaty, Selby had benefited from the enforcement of CITES.

In 1989, Fish and Wildlife officers seized a shipment of Chinese slipper orchids from a Florida nursery called Limerick Inc., even though the owner contended he had all the proper CITES permits. They then delivered the seized orchids to Selby Gardens.

Selby's executive director at the time told the *Sarasota Herald-Tribune* that the Chinese orchids were being held there under increased security "because it is not uncommon for people to try to recover their property through moonlight raids."

Soon, however, Selby Gardens was itself busy getting rid of the Chinese orchids—sending them to other botanical gardens, distributing them to dues-paying members, or selling them to collectors. As Eric Hansen pointed out in *Orchid Fever*, the owner of Limerick Inc. "could have legally repurchased some of the orchids that had been confiscated from him."

Selby's own rules required the submission of proper CITES permits for plants shipped to the OIC for identification. But so many orchids were sent to Selby each year for identification that "the Gardens does not require the submitters to provide documentation as to the sources of the plants," Wesley Higgins wrote in an e-mail in 2003.

"We follow the standard practice of all botanical gardens," Meg Lowman would later explain to the *Herald-Tribune*, "which is essentially to take people at their word."

Lee Moore said in all his years of shipping orchids to Selby, "nobody ever said boo about permits."

That was never considered to be part of Selby's job, Carl Luer insisted. It's up to the customs inspectors to check permits, not the scientists.

The pugnacious Guido Braem agreed. "Is a scientist responsible for checking the provenance of plants presented to him for a description? Hell no!" he said. "Will I continue to describe plants? Hell yes! Will I ask where they come from? Hell no! Do I care how they get to me? Hell no!"

In short, orchid fanciers, orchid collectors, orchid growers, and even orchid scientists feel about as warmly toward CITES as orchid hunter Joseph Hooker felt toward that "loathsome tick" he encountered in the Himalayas.

So when word of the Fish and Wildlife Service investigation hit the press in August 2002, it spurred a particularly animated debate on the various Internet forums for orchid collectors. Plenty of the participants griped about CITES' flaws, but they had questions, too, the same one Holt had asked: If a slipper orchid wasn't identified, did it automatically get classified as Appendix I? Could Kovach have avoided CITES problems if he'd found someone in Peru to describe the plant? Did Kovach leave some plants behind with a buddy who would now make millions?

And could Selby get off the hook by simply sending the plant back to Lima?

The answer to that one was: Maybe—at least until the Atwood piece turned up.

Under CITES, botanical gardens and other scientific institutions get a break. They can get a special permit under CITES to exchange plants with other institutions that are listed on the CITES registry.

That was Selby's defense, at least until the Atwood piece turned up: The OIC had promptly sent the *Phragmipedium kovachii*–type specimen to another scientific institution, one that was in the flower's country of origin, and therefore Selby had complied with CITES.

According to Braem, the exemption for botanical institutions constitutes a huge loophole. Every institution hides behind that special permit to trade plants that would normally not be permitted out of their home country, he said.

"All botanists who work at a botanical garden know that and take advantage of it," Braem said. "If they would not, they would be stupid. And you show me a botanist who denies that, and I will show you a liar."

However, the CITES rules are still sufficiently cumbersome that, according to a 2007 study, they have made collecting orchids for scientific study far more difficult than collecting bromeliads, which are not subject to similar rules.

According to Braem, the CITES rules are particularly maddening for scientists when the orchid is a newly discovered one such as the *Phragmipedium* that Kovach brought to Selby. As Holt's search warrant affidavit made clear, getting a permit to export it for study requires listing a name, but at that point there is no name. So botanical garden biologists around the world have become accustomed to skirting the CITES rules in the name of science.

"You smuggle or you cheat," Braem explained. "Legally you can't win."

Because botanical gardens such as Selby continue to describe new species that clearly were imported from other countries, Braem said, that suggests they were all "based on illegal plants."

"Everyone treats it with a kind of a nudge-nudge, wink-wink," Eric Christenson said. "This is what all botanical gardens are doing."

⁓❦

As it turned out, though, by sending the type specimen to Ricardo Fernandez, Selby's OIC had blundered across yet another violation of the CITES rules.

The staff had mailed off the *Phragmipedium kovachii*—now a named specimen—without a CITES export permit. That would not be a problem if they had sent it to another institution approved by the CITES authorities since they had a CITES permit for making such institutional exchanges.

But Stig Dalström's assumption that the University of San Marcos had a similar permit turned out to be wrong. In fact, there were no CITES-approved scientific institutions anywhere in Peru. Thus, no matter which Peruvian university Selby's orchid boys had picked as the recipient for the type specimen, the OIC would have broken the law.

Lee Moore couldn't believe it. He fired off a typically blunt e-mail to Wesley Higgins: "What is this shit about Selby being in violation of CITES for repatriating the type specimen to Peru without a CITES [permit]. What bullshit. Did they not ask for it back? . . . CITES regs, as written, now guarantee the extinction of any new species found in the future. No plant can legally be collected in the wild but they say also that no species can receive certification without being legally collected. . . . This is an impossible paradox and becomes the catch-22."

Still, some of Selby's orchid boys refused to take the situation seriously. To Meg Lowman's dismay, where she saw a tightening noose, the orchid boys saw a rope swing.

One scientist—Lowman didn't name him—joked that he would bed the female prosecutor who, their attorneys said, was now running the federal investigation. Surely that's all it would take to satisfy her and save Selby, right?

Another, Lowman said, bragged that he would write the whole thing up as a book, to make big money off the tale. To them what was happening was "merely another chapter in the world of orchid passion and lust," she wrote. "The idea that their institution and perhaps several individuals might be indicted by a federal grand jury on felony smuggling charges did not seem threatening."

Instead of hiding behind the wall of lawyers that Lowman had hired, several Selby scientists appeared on a national television show to boast about what they had done.

Higgins, Beckner, and Dalström all gave interviews to a crew from the Public Broadcasting Service program *NOVA*. They told how Kovach had brought them the plant, and how they then rushed the description into print to earn glory and honor.

"This is the most spectacular, the most sensational, the most incredible-looking orchid in a hundred years or more," Beckner gushed for the TV audience.

Higgins explained to the TV crew that Kovach "requested that it be named after him, so it was given the name *Phragmipedium kovachii*."

That just proved how stupid everyone involved with the flower was, Christenson said later. Bringing that orchid to Selby was "like showing up at a museum with an elephant tusk with fresh blood dripping off the end."

And naming the orchid after the man who walked in with it, he said, was tantamount to telling the people who enforced the CITES rules, "Hey, come arrest me!"

II

~~~

The Circular Firing Squad

I don't want to give the impression that perfectly normal, healthy,
thoughtful, and balanced people are not drawn to orchids. I am
told they exist. I just didn't have much luck finding them.

Eric Hansen, *Orchid Fever*

Agent Holt knocked on the door of John Atwood's Vermont farmhouse on
September 18, 2002. She had brought along a male agent for backup, and was
armed with a load of questions.

When Lowman had informed Selby's new attorneys about what Atwood
had done, they quickly realized how bad it looked. They notified the prosecutor, who notified the U.S. Fish and Wildlife Service, which in turn dispatched Holt to confiscate what Atwood had taken.

The mild-mannered Atwood said later he didn't understand why Holt
had brought along a second officer for backup. Although it's standard law
enforcement procedure, he joked that it was "just in case I might be a dangerous person to deal with."

He lived on a plot of land next to a dairy farm, on a dirt road about 2½
miles off the main highway. This was the same house where he'd grown up,
one that his grandfather had acquired in 1926. Now Atwood and his wife
and daughter had settled there, happy to be away from the rush-hour hell of
Florida.

"I'm pretty strongly rooted here," he explained. "In Sarasota, everybody
seemed to be on their way somewhere else, and they were from somewhere
else."

Even though he had spent nearly twenty years working at Selby, Atwood had never quite learned his route home. All the houses and buildings looked like they came out of a cookie-cutter, he said: "I had to look at the street names to make sure I wouldn't pass my own street."

Yet now that he was back home in rural New England, back to a quiet life of reading and tending to his vegetables, here came an unwelcome reminder of that stressful place: two federal agents to question him about his actions at Selby on the day he had held the most glorious orchid find in a century in his hands.

They grilled him for three hours. The questioning might have gone more quickly if not for Atwood's social awkwardness.

At one point Holt asked him, "Are you holding anything back?"

"Probably," replied the man Eric Christenson found so painfully naïve. "But I don't know what it would be. You have to ask the right questions."

When the agents were satisfied that they had wrung him dry, "they took the plant," Atwood said. "And I got some more sphagnum for them." The agents seemed grateful for that, he said. It's also possible they were just happy to be done with him.

Given his qualms about taking the piece of orchid home, Atwood should have felt a surge of relief to be freed of the responsibility. Instead, he said, "I just felt awful that we had accepted a plant that would create such a conflict with the goals of conservation."

Atwood sent Lowman, Higgins, and two other Selby leaders an e-mail to report that the agents had visited and taken the orchid. He added some peevish comments about Christenson, whom he and everyone else at Selby blamed for stirring up this hornet's nest with the feds and the Peruvians. Atwood contended that Christenson, whom he referred to in the e-mail as EAC, was the one who should be in trouble, not Selby.

"I don't know what to make of EAC's aggravating U.S. Fish and Wildlife Service and possibly INRENA to further his own agendas," Atwood wrote to Lowman. "Aren't there laws against that? What about working for foreign agents?"

Although Peru's INRENA was demanding that any plants or plant material brought in by Kovach be returned, that's not where Atwood's piece of his orchid went. Instead, the agents took it back to Washington, to the U.S. Botanical Garden, where it would be cultivated by the botanists looking after Kovach's other orchids.

They needed to keep this one because it had become evidence in a criminal case—not the case against Kovach, but the case against Selby Gardens itself.

On September 1, 2002, the *Sarasota Herald-Tribune* ran its first story on the investigation into what happened with the *Phragmipedium kovachii*. The story hit all the same points as Tasker's *Miami Herald* piece, but added one intriguing twist: the financial ramifications.

Selby drew its revenue from more than just admissions, plant sales, and big donations. It also depended on grants, many of them from the federal government. In fact, during the 2001–2 fiscal year, Selby received more than $900,000 in government grants. They accounted for a quarter of Selby's $3.6 million budget.

The *Herald-Tribune* story pointed out that every government grant included a condition stating that Selby had to obey all the applicable laws on the books to keep receiving the money. If Selby became a lawbreaker in the eyes of the government, then it could lose all of its federal grants. It was an unnerving prospect for Selby's always precarious financial prospects.

That same day, Lowman called up Scully and invited him to stop by her office. There he found not just the executive director but also the board's treasurer, Joel Fedder. Like Scully, Fedder was an orchid fancier, with his collection on display at his $1 million home on Longboat Key that also featured sweeping views of Sarasota Bay and the city skyline. Unlike Scully, though, Fedder's world extended beyond orchids. He held degrees in both law and accounting, and had carved out a third career as a developer. He collected art as well as orchids, and had recently become an avid kayaker. He counted himself as a fan of Lowman. He had chaired the committee that recommended promoting her to executive director in 1999, and as time went on, she had come to rely more and more on his support in the face of Scully's criticism.

Fedder and Lowman explained to Scully that the federal investigation appeared to be aimed not only at Kovach but also at Selby Gardens. They told him about Atwood keeping a piece of the plant, and how that must look to the Fish and Wildlife Service.

When Scully heard about his friend Atwood keeping part of the orchid, he said, "Oh my God!"

But he didn't blame Atwood. To him, this was further proof of Lowman's shortcomings as executive director, proof that her absences left the staff with no guidance. She was always gadding about giving speeches and not minding the store the way she should.

Then Lowman and Fedder showed him the contract with Holland & Knight, the one Lowman had already signed. Scully's mood turned even darker. To him, Lowman was making up for the consequences of her own errors by blowing large sums of money on Washington lawyers when he knew some perfectly good ones worked in Florida.

Even worse, in his view, was the fact that she had not bothered to get the board's approval before signing a contract with the law firm. She hadn't even given him, the board chairman, a heads-up about it, much less sought his advice. Now it was too late.

Scully had to break the news to the rest of the board. He waited until they were all together at a board retreat in the dark-paneled comfort of the St. Petersburg Yacht Club, then dropped the bombshell. They didn't like it any more than he did, and they took it out on their chairman.

"I was crucified by the other board members because I had not told them before," he said.

Some of them also blamed Lowman, just as Scully did. Although Lowman enjoyed tremendous popularity among the donors, some of the board members agreed with Scully that their director seemed irresponsible and flighty.

They were already annoyed about how she had handled another project. A donor had given the gardens a big contribution in exchange for an agreement to spend some of it on building a new wedding pavilion that would bear his name. But the cost of the pavilion kept rising, eating up the contribution to the point that none of the gift was left to spend anywhere else in the gardens. The board members held Lowman responsible for what they regarded as a waste of money. Scully wasn't the only one who had started thinking that Lowman should be fired.

Many of the board members feared the expense of the investigation more than the investigation itself. They worried that fighting the federal government would bankrupt Selby, which despite its recent prosperity still had not entirely recovered from the drop in donations after 9/11. They also wondered about Lowman's insistence on sticking up for her staff and fighting any charges. Did she defend them because to do otherwise would be admitting her own errors?

One board member, a vivacious middle-aged brunette named Caren Lobo, owned a popular store in downtown Sarasota called Sarasota News & Books. Her husband, a former member of the Clinton administration, now ran the Tampa public television station. Because of her husband's government experience, Caren Lobo knew full well how a lengthy investigation—such as the ones involving the various Clinton-era scandals—could bog down an institution, blocking it from getting any work completed.

Lobo urged the board to quickly cut a deal with federal investigators and end the case. She suggested they just tell Agent Holt, "We were excited and we made a mistake, a horrible mistake and we'd like to apologize."

But Lowman, when she met with the board members, persuaded them to hang tough. She argued that the OIC staff was innocent. To cut a deal would be to admit guilt.

Privately, Lowman wanted to fire Atwood, as well as some other members of the OIC, for causing this foul-up. Holland & Knight's attorneys had talked her out of it. Hold off until the investigation is over, they counseled, because firing anyone now would make Selby Gardens look guilty. Because that's what the attorneys told her, that's what she told the board to do, too: Keep fighting. Don't yield an inch.

One board member who strongly agreed with Lowman's hang-tough strategy: Carl Luer, the gardens' founder.

"The gardens committed no crime anywhere along the line," he insisted years later. The OIC staff wasn't responsible, he said, because "they didn't collect the species."

Their only blunder, he believed, was Atwood keeping that one piece. "He should not have done that," Luer conceded. "He knew better than that."

Yet even Luer, who owed his seat on the board to Lowman, felt no love for the embattled executive director—although not for the same reasons as Scully. He disliked her efforts to broaden Selby's focus beyond just plants to look at tropical ecology as a whole.

"She was great at fund-raising and everything around that," he said. "The problem with her was that she was not a botanist . . . and she hired people who were not botanists."

In the end, the board reluctantly approved Lowman's hiring of the attorneys. Each time the attorneys' bills came due, they paid them. But silently they blamed Lowman for this drain on their precarious finances.

"We were always hopeful this thing was going to blow away," said one board member, avuncular, gray-haired Bob Richardson, a past president of the Greater Sarasota Chamber of Commerce. Instead, he said, "it just kept escalating as time went on."

One reason people in trouble hire Washington attorneys is because they enjoy greater access to Washington decision makers, people who can wave a hand and dismiss a case before it gets started.

Thus Selby's newly hired attorneys set up a meeting with Agent Holt's superiors at the U.S. Fish and Wildlife Service in Washington. But someone at the Department of Justice got wind of the meeting, Scully said, and as a result "the prospect of getting the case scuttled just evaporated."

Instead of wiping the slate clean, he said, "the effort may have steeled the prosecutor in her determined effort to make an example out of Marie Selby Botanical Gardens."

With Scully's approval, Lowman quietly contacted the head of the Missouri Botanical Gardens to ask him to get in touch with other botanical gardens asking them to send Selby some money to help deal with the government's investigation. After all, what was happening to Selby could have happened to any of them. Perhaps they could even band together to fight this intrusion into their scientific mission.

The answer to this quiet initiative was a deafening silence, Scully said later. Nobody felt the slightest twinge of empathy for Selby Gardens, at least not enough of a twinge to offer any help.

"Other gardens may have been interested enough to follow the case from afar as it developed," he said. "But amazingly almost no institution understood . . . the case's implications for all botanical gardens."

The growing controversy over the *Phragmipedium kovachii* fascinated everyone in the orchid world. It was, Harold Koopowitz joked, like watching a wrestling match on cable TV, with bellowing combatants and soap-opera story lines.

Selby and its adherents were in one corner, and Christenson and his adherents in the other. Rumors swirled about who was doing what, their spread fueled by gossip, snarky comments, and half-baked theories spread among users of the various orchid-grower web forums.

On September 2, 2002, the Texas grower George Norris sent one of his all-capitals e-mails to Wesley Higgins to ask him to sort out what was really happening.

"I KNEW THERE WAS A LOT OF FLACK ABOUT THIS PLANT," he wrote to Higgins. "IT WAS OFFERED TO ME BACK IN MAY BY KAROL VILLENA IN MOYOBAMBA BUT I KNEW IT WAS TOO HOT AND PASSED. KINDA GLAD I DID."

Then he got down to brass tacks: "WHAT IS YOUR TAKE ON ALL THIS. IS EVERYONE LYING OR IS THE TRUTH BURIED IN THERE SOMEWHERE. MIKE KOVACH WON'T RETURN MY EMAILS AND LEE MOORE IS CALLING EVERY WEEK OR SO WANTING TO SELL SOME HE HAS JUST BROUGHT BACK. SO WHAT'S THE DEAL."

"All the stories keep changing," Higgins replied, "but obviously the truth is out there somewhere."

Maybe, Norris wrote, but it seemed like there were too many versions of what happened floating around: "TOO MANY DIFFERENT STORIES, NOBODY WILL RECOGNIZE THE TRUTH IF IT DOES SURFACE."

Then Norris contributed some stories of his own.

"I KNOW THAT LEE MOORE HAS BROUGHT IN ABOUT 20 AND A BUNCH OF SEED PODS," he wrote to Higgins. "HE SOLD THEM ALL FOR $2000 EACH AND DOWN. HE WAS WANTING $500 FOR THE SEED PODS. HE SAYS HE HAS 250 PLANTS IN A SECRET LOCATION NEAR MOYOBAMBA AND WILL BE GETTING THEM IN. I THINK HE IS GONNA TRY TO GET A CITES [permit] FOR THEM AS A HYBRID PHRAG. HE HAD BETTER BE CAREFUL AS THERE ARE A LOT OF RED FLAGS UP ON THIS ONE."

Norris told Higgins he had heard through the grapevine that Peru's INRENA might soon grant permits to certain growers to legally collect some of the new orchids from the wild. However, he said, INRENA would not allow them to be exported. But then he pointed out a way a smuggler might get around that.

"HOW WILL ANYONE KNOW THE DIFFERENCE WHEN IT IS OUT OF FLOWER," he wrote.

However, Norris backed away from the implication of that sentence, instead predicting that in short order the *Phragmipedium kovachii* would show up for sale all over the United States: "THEY WILL BE COMING BUT I WILL BE WELL CLEAR OF THEM."

In the end, Norris wrote, "I DON'T KNOW HOW MUCH IS B/S AND WHERE THE TRUTH IS. IT IS FUN TO WATCH FROM A DISTANCE BUT ONLY FROM WAAAAAAAY-BACK."

Soon, though, Norris would put himself front and center.

The uproar over Kovach's orchid wasn't confined to the United States. It had created quite a stir in Peru as well.

In a classic case of shutting the barn door after the horse has run off, IN-RENA swooped in on Faustino Medina's roadside plant stand and ordered it closed. That didn't stop him from selling plants, though. He just went mobile. Lee Moore still saw him wandering around the town square in Moyobamba, carrying a tray of orchids for sale—including more *Phragmipedium kovachii* that his family had dug up and brought in from the countryside. To

Moore's amusement, Medina sometimes sold his plants to passing tourists right in front of the local INRENA office.

Chady Moore focused on a bigger business rival, the Villenas. She had found out that she could buy thirty minutes of airtime on Peruvian television for just $200, so she did. She used her time to broadcast a blast against the Villenas and Agro-Oriente for exploiting one of Peru's natural resources.

The Spanish-language broadcast included footage of Faustino Medina at his roadside stand, a ball cap pulled low over his forehead. He talked about how he had sold his special orchid to Kovach, to the Moores, but especially to the Villenas. He said they bought between 150 and 200.

In the show, an interviewer named Lino Gordillo showed the mountainous roadside terrain where Medina's family had first found the flower, and asked about what happened after he made his sale to Kovach.

"Many people are looking for this plant from top to bottom and can't find it," Faustino said. "I'm very grateful to God to give me the opportunity to find this plant."

The interviewer asked Faustino if it seemed fair that the orchids he had sold for a pittance now sold for a small fortune. No, he replied: "I should earn at least half that."

The rest of the show portrayed the Villenas—to their dismay—as greedy scoundrels out to rape the Peruvian environment.

"From this day the media in the city attacked us saying bunch of lies and many ugly things about our family and professional life," Karol Villena wrote later. "This affected us very much [so] that we decided to defend ourselves and said what happened in order to clarify things."

However, the family couldn't counteract how the unfavorable publicity had hurt Renato Villena's budding political career. He was forced to drop out of the campaign for the regional vice presidency.

Then Lee Moore tried cutting off their American customers. He e-mailed Marni Turkel to warn her against any further association with Karol Villena.

"Your name came up several times last week during our press conference and TV interviews in Peru concerning e-mails you had sent to Karol Villena in the month of June which she presented in support of Agro-Oriente's part in the depredation of *Phragmipedium kovachii*," Moore wrote her, copying the e-mail to a raft of other Americans. "However, your letters to her raised questions about the legality of plants that you had obtained from her. The director of INRENA was present and questions were raised about certain species you had mentioned in these letters."

Since Turkel had previously ordered orchids from Agro-Oriente—although not Kovach's orchid—Moore wrote: "Don't you realize that you are in possession of illegal plants and are ordering more? . . . Can you tell me why you should not be prosecuted for the same crime that Kovach is being accused. What is the difference?"

Moore's accusations were one more salvo in what was becoming a war of words over the *Phragmipedium kovachii* case. But as each claim and counterclaim shot through the orchid world, it soon turned into a circular firing squad, with every crack of the rifle bringing down not only the target but also the shooter.

And so, as Moore was loudly denouncing the Villenas and everyone connected to them, someone he had regarded as a friend was about to denounce him.

~⚹~

Just as the United States has the American Orchid Society, so Peru has the Club Peruano de Orquideas, or the Peruvian Orchid Club. Like its American counterpart, the Peruvian Orchid Club, since its founding in 1985, has gone through its share of political infighting and cliquish sniping.

But the club members were united in their dislike for what Kovach had done. They believed the orchid he found should have been named *Phragmipedium peruvianum* to salute their country's natural assets, not named for some American tourist who had done nothing for their country beyond spend a few dollars at a roadside stand. They sent INRENA a statement from the club supporting its enforcement efforts and lamenting that the discovery of this flower, "instead of bringing unity to the scientific community and the orchidologists, had produced confrontations and some greedy human beings."

They didn't buy Kovach's claim that he didn't realize he had a slipper orchid until Selby's OIC told him. One Peruvian Orchid Club member told the *Sarasota Herald-Tribune* that would be "like if a gynecologist would say he did not know the difference between men and women."

The members of the Peruvian Orchid Club tended to be either commercial nurserymen or wealthy hobbyists who had the time and money to devote to their favorite pursuit. One of the latter group happened to be a short, dark-haired eye surgeon named Dr. Isaias M. Rolando Castaneda. Dr. Rolando began growing orchids when he was fifteen. In 1985, right after he completed his bachelor's degree in medicine, he became one of the club's founders.

Three years later, during his term as president of the club, Rolando got involved in a project that would become his proudest achievement, as well

Dr. Isaias Rolando Castaneda flew to Washington to tell investigators they should check on Kovach's connection to Lee Moore. Photo courtesy of Tatiana Fasenando.

as one of his biggest headaches. The owner of a hotel being built near the ruins of Machu Picchu asked him to help rescue orchids from the grounds that would otherwise be wiped out during construction. Rather than merely moving the plants, Rolando oversaw the design of a garden walk that would showcase those orchids and others collected from throughout Peru. The garden would both attract tourists visiting the Incan ruins and serve as a rescue center for orchids from around the country that were threatened by new roads, power plants, and other changes occurring as the ancient country entered the modern age.

In designing what became the Orchid Trails at the Inkaterra Machu Picchu Pueblo Hotel, Rolando consulted with the experts at Selby Gardens. He even spent twelve weeks in Sarasota doing an internship with the OIC.

Not everyone at Selby took a shine to the bubbly surgeon. Stig Dalström, for instance, later joked that if he was going to shake hands with Rolando, he'd first coat his palm with sand to counteract the doctor's natural slipperiness.

Dalström was not alone in that assessment. George Norris, the Texas orchid dealer who had helped arrange Kovach's first trip to Peru, contended Rolando was in fact "one of the big-time orchid smugglers. I never particularly liked him. He's a shady figure."

When the Machu Picchu hotel was first opened, Rolando basked in the praise for his Orchid Trails project. But then it became the target of critics who complained about the removal of orchids from the wild to decorate the grounds of a hotel for foreign tourists. In response, Rolando painstakingly removed all the orchids that did not belong in that region of the country, said his longtime friend Alfredo Manrique. But that didn't silence the complaints, Manrique said.

Over the years, Rolando had documented with photos nearly every species of Peruvian orchid. He had a reputation for being able to tell at a glance any Peruvian orchid species. When he decided to do something, he let nothing get in his way.

In early October 2002, the doctor flew up to Washington determined to do something about the *Phragmipedium kovachii*.

He met with Agent Holt and a Spanish-speaking colleague of hers as well as a federal prosecutor. By way of introduction, so they would know he was a serious man, Dr. Rolando mentioned that he was not just an orchid club member and a surgeon. He also "claimed to be a close friend of the prime minister of Peru," the Spanish-speaking agent wrote in his report.

The doctor had an intriguing piece of information to deliver to the U.S. authorities. He also had two requests.

Dr. Rolando said he had heard from fellow orchid collectors in Peru that the roadside vendor who had dealt with Kovach that fateful day in May 2002, Faustino Medina Bautista, had sold the gringo tourist a total of three plants, not the single plant that Kovach had claimed in his affidavit.

However, no matter how many he bought, they were all illegal because "Peruvian law does not allow the collection of these specimens without a permit." In other words, Faustino Medina wasn't supposed to have plucked them from the wild, much less sold them to Kovach.

But that wasn't his main point. No, the doctor wanted to put the investigators on the trail of what appeared to be a conspiracy.

"Dr. Rolando mentioned that Kovach has a partner named Lee Moore," the Spanish-speaking agent wrote. "He said that Moore is not allowed entry in several countries because of Moore's smuggling activities with plants, archaeological artifacts, etc. Rolando claimed that Moore had obtained hundreds of these plants from the same collector in Peru and that the plants were imported into the U.S. He stated that plants were being identified as something else in order to export them. He suspects that the plants are being kept somewhere in Miami, Florida."

The doctor urged Holt and her colleagues to fly down to Peru and interview Faustino Medina to get the real scoop on the connection between Moore and Kovach.

The doctor had something other than smuggling he wanted to discuss, though. It was a matter of national pride.

"Dr. Rolando stated that Peru is concerned about damages to habitat due to illegal collection of orchids," the agent wrote. "Rolando's main interest was to seek assistance in dismissing . . . the scientific name given to the Peruvian orchid published by Selby Garden since the study of this plant was based on illegally obtained material by Kovach."

However, Holt told him that botanical nomenclature wasn't really something the Fish and Wildlife Service dealt with much.

After Dr. Rolando left, Holt wrote some notes of her own: "There is speculation that Kovach ultimately brought this plant in for his 'business partner,' Leeman Moore, who lives in Miami, Florida, and is married to a Peruvian national," she wrote. "It is further speculated that Moore told Kovach to smuggle the plant in and then (for his trouble) have it named after him to allow Moore to maintain a low profile. . . . In the meantime, while the new orchid hits publication, Moore has stockpiled approximately seven hundred of the orchids in Florida. He has more at his nursery in Peru. The ultimate goal is to sell the plants for $10,000 apiece while they are still hard to find."

This was not the first time Moore's name had come up in the investigation. He had been quoted in the *Miami Herald* as looking for buyers for the orchid. More importantly, he had sent several faxes to Kovach that Holt had found while serving the search warrant on Southwind Orchids. The fax Holt found particularly intriguing was a brief note that Moore had scrawled in the margin of a fax dated August 7, 2002. It was the fax that he'd sent to Kovach urging him to look at the awful things Eric Christenson had said about Moore on Peter Croezen's website.

Moore's note in the margin said: "Priority mail today $1,260.—You will need this—Anyway I have enough small ones for us when the [*sic*] get bigger—"

Although Moore didn't say what "the" meant or what was going to "get bigger," it seemed a safe assumption that Moore was sending Kovach money, perhaps as part of a business transaction. Could it be Kovach's split from the sale of some of the new orchids from Peru, perhaps to some unscrupulous collector in the United States?

Now here was a Peruvian doctor, an influential orchid collector, claiming that Moore, a veteran smuggler, had smuggled hundreds of *Phragmipedium kovachii* plants into the United States to sell.

Holt had to go talk to The Adventurer.

The trip was delayed by other events, but a few months later Holt and a prosecutor flew down to Miami to see Moore. They were now keenly interested in talking to him. In an e-mail to Stig Dalström that became evidence in the case, Moore had boasted: "You know that I am directly responsible for the discovery. I took Kovach to Peru and sent him to the man that found it originally. I told him if he wanted his name on it that he would have to cut his trip short and go straight to Selby. I would have liked to have my name on it, but I foresaw what would happen, which did."

Moore alone greeted the investigators at the door. His wife was down in Peru. He invited the two women into his first-floor apartment in suburban Kendall. The place was decorated with artifacts he'd hung onto over the years and photos of himself and his wife from back in their glory days when they looked lean and cool and a little dangerous.

The investigators noticed that amid all the artifacts, they were surrounded by plants. While they talked, the feds couldn't help glancing around from time to time, plainly wondering if Moore could be so brazen as to leave smuggled plants out in plain view. Neither of them was an orchid expert, though, and so they couldn't tell whether he had anything illegal sitting out.

Moore told the pair he had had nothing to hide. He boasted that he alone knew the whole history of the *Phragmipedium kovachii*. He had plenty to tell them.

However, Holt observed in her report, he "talked primarily about all the slanderous remarks" that had been made about him by Christenson and other critics, and not about how he had pointed Kovach toward the discovery of a lifetime.

They asked him if it was true he'd told Kovach to take his orchid to Selby Gardens. Sure, he said, "I told him to take it straight to John Atwood."

This seemed like a big break, a clue to what really happened. Moore tells Kovach to take the orchid to Atwood. Atwood winds up running off to Vermont with a piece of the plant. Atwood starts growing the plant, producing shoots, maybe even blooms. Could this be the unraveling of the Selby conspiracy?

Moore had a lot more to tell his visitors. In anticipation of the investigators' questions, Moore had stacked up a pile of files on Peruvian orchids on his coffee table. But whenever he picked up a document off the pile, Holt noticed, he tried to scan the paper before handing it over. She wondered if he was making a last check to ensure there was nothing there he didn't want them to see.

Finally the investigators told him they didn't have time to sit around and watch him read. So Moore agreed to hand over all his documents in return for a promise that they would make copies of everything and return the originals.

Faustino Medina Bautista told the TV interviewer that he'd sold three orchids to "the foreigner"—but he couldn't remember the man's name. Photo courtesy of Lee Moore.

Before they left, though, Moore—noticing how they had been glancing at his plants—took the pair around to his side porch. Holt wrote that he said he wanted them to see "the orchids he had retrieved out of the dumpster that florists throw out." He also showed them seedlings planted in a bottle. Holt thought the seedlings looked like *Phragmipediums* of some kind, so she asked what they were.

"*Maxillaria*," Moore said innocently.

The most important thing Moore handed to the investigators was the videotape from Chady Moore's Peruvian TV broadcast. On the tape, there was Faustino Medina Bautista, the El Progresso flower vendor, talking to interviewer Lino Gordillo about when "the foreigner"—Kovach—visited his thatch-roofed stand.

"I don't remember the foreigner's name," Medina told the TV reporter.

"You sold three plants to a foreigner?" the interviewer asked.

"Exactly," Medina said.

During their visit to Miami, Holt thought she had established a good rapport with Moore. He seemed surprisingly cooperative, albeit a bit shifty. So at her request, a few weeks later more Fish and Wildlife service investigators braved the South Florida heat to visit Moore a second time. This time they brought along an orchid expert from the Florida Department of Agriculture to check the seedlings in the bottles.

But there were no bottles. Moore said he'd already taken them back to Peru.

Following up on Holt's report, they asked him how he knew Atwood would be at Selby when Kovach arrived.

"He's always there!" Moore replied.

Apparently Moore was unaware that Atwood was no longer in charge of the OIC. He didn't realize Atwood only worked in Sarasota part-time now. The feds' hopes of building a conspiracy involving both Moore and Atwood crumbled.

The investigators tried the same tack with Moore that Agent Holt had used so successfully in questioning Kovach. They asked for his help in nailing the big orchid smugglers. But Moore, thanks to his long experience with government officials, was far cagier than Kovach.

When the investigators asked if he knew of anyone in Peru who would be willing to help track down the smugglers at work in their country, Moore gave them a flat no. They asked him to call a few of his contacts in the country anyway, so he picked up the phone and dialed. No one he called even answered. He left messages but no would-be snitches called back, not then and not afterward, either.

Then the investigators asked Moore if he would go to Moyobamba and take a leaf off one of his own *Phragmipedium kovachii* and bring it back to them. That way they could get a DNA sample to be used in identifying any contraband orchids they might find. Oh sure, he said. The agents judged him "more than happy to oblige."

Since he would be helping their investigation, they told him they would arrange to get him the proper CITES permit to carry the leaf out of Peru and into the United States.

Oh no, he said, don't bother with that. A single leaf was so small he could just stick it in his pocket "and no one would ever see it."

The agents didn't appreciate Moore's smuggling joke. They warned him not to try pulling anything like that.

Moore wasn't done teasing them. When they asked him how he knew where to send his own workers to gather the new orchid along the roadside, he laughed at their ignorance of Peruvian geography.

"There's only one road," he explained.

By the time the agents left, they had drawn certain unsurprising conclusions about Moore's character and honesty. They did not go through with the plan to have him bring them a leaf for DNA testing.

However, Moore said later, "I gave them the whole story."

Well, *almost* the whole story.

There was one thing, Moore said, one crucial little detail that he fudged. "But that," he said, "was my one lie."

12

The Stories They Told

*Without a good memory it is of no use trying to be a
botanist; one had better give it up and be a merchant.*

Orchidologist Rudolf Schlechter, quoted in
A History of the Orchid

The *Washington Post* finally caught onto the big story going on in its backyard
around Christmas 2002. A *Post* reporter tracked down Kovach in Virginia for
an interview. He didn't sound like he was having a holly jolly holiday.

"Kovach feels shunned by the 200,000 growers and hobbyists in the United
States," the *Post* reported. "Invitations to speak at orchid society annual
meetings have dried up. Almost nobody buys any of the 8,000 orchids from
Vietnam, Laos and Borneo in his backyard greenhouse. . . . The career Kovach sought to cap with his find is a shambles, he said, all because he dared
to 'exploit an opportunity.'"

Kovach recounted for the reporter once more the tale of his fateful trip to
El Progresso. But this time he added a wrinkle not in his official handwritten
accounts.

Just as Dr. Isaias Rolando had warned federal investigators, just as depicted in the video that Moore had handed over, Kovach said he had bought
three of the orchids. He told the *Post* he "gave two to an American friend in
Peru . . . and saved the third to bring to a U.S. botanical institution for identification, because he said he knew of no Peruvian institution that was up to
the task—and none that would name it for him."

In telling his tale, the *Post* noted, Kovach spoke of his namesake orchid
"with the swagger of a heavyweight boxer on fight night."

Gone was any pretense to being on a humanitarian or conservation mission. Kovach came across as an unapologetic carpe diem capitalist.

"Why is it not okay for me to seek recognition for my work?" he asked the *Post* reporter. "It's okay for the U.S. attorney to try and throw me in jail to enhance his career, but it's not okay for me to exploit an opportunity? Every success story is about someone exploiting an opportunity to enhance their career."

By now Selby's board members were starting to realize that their staff's effort to exploit an opportunity had left Selby mired in what would at best be a lengthy criminal investigation, and at worst an economic and public relations disaster. Attorneys' fees were eating away at the gardens' already tight budget.

To make matters worse, because the OIC had shipped the *Phragmipedium kovachii* to an unregistered institution in Peru, Selby's institutional CITES permit had been suspended until further notice. This crippled the OIC's ability to exchange plant material across international borders.

Now if the scientists wanted to send plants—even pickled or dried specimens, as Guido Braem had discovered, or even seeds—to a colleague, they would have to go through all the red tape of applying for an individual permit. They would have to do the same thing if they needed plants or specimens sent to them from overseas.

The investigation had also turned up some sloppy record-keeping in the OIC, or worse. The permit file containing Kovach's paperwork had disappeared. The pickled specimen of *Phragmipedium kovachii* that Higgins had left on Beckner's desk had disappeared, too. When no one could find it, some speculated that it had somehow been tossed out with the trash. There were other, less savory possibilities. Someone may have stolen it, although to what purpose no one could say. Dalström suspected someone on the staff simply panicked and hid the thing, perhaps even by misfiling it among the fifteen thousand other spirit specimens, making it a botanical version of Poe's purloined letter.

The OIC staff had at last begun to realize the terrible spot they were in. They started to turn on each other—not just with suspicious looks but something worse.

Atwood complained to colleagues at the Missouri Botanical Gardens that he had been informed via e-mail that the locks on Selby's research building had been changed, but he didn't get a key. Then he found out his Selby e-mail address had been deleted, which he feared meant "that the administration is creating a culture of suspicion about me," Atwood wrote to his Missouri colleagues. He fretted that federal agents might "lug me off to prison," and added, "I have never been involved with such intrigue, and if I could have foreseen the ugliness of the situation probably would not have had the courage to accept the plant."

Before long, John Beckner and Bruce Holst both cut a deal with the prosecutor to testify in exchange for immunity from any charges. Their change in status from suspect to informers was not a well-kept secret. Scully and the other board members found out about it because the board had to pay for Beckner and Holst to have their own attorneys advising them. Holland & Knight represented Selby so it would be a conflict of interest to represent the two witnesses against Selby, too. The new arrangement increased the legal bills for the board, as well as the sense of paranoia around the OIC.

Under the pressure of the investigation, "the staff at the research department went totally bananas," Dalström said later. "Instead of staying together and following the procedure we had all agreed upon, there was a lot of finger pointing and forgetting about what had been said, and by whom. Then everybody tried to cover their own backs. . . . It made us all look like idiots."

The investigation into what some were calling "that *phrag*" had also cast a pall over what was supposed to be a prestigious Selby event. Higgins and the OIC were supposed to be pulling together an International Orchid Conservation meeting. The meeting was slated to take place at Selby the following year. But now some participants wondered if Selby was really the right place to hold such an event.

"Their description of a clearly illegal plant promotes and rewards the action of a commercial grower who smuggled the plant," one potential sponsor complained.

Lowman, in an e-mail to Higgins, told the OIC chief to reassure anyone with questions that Selby was cooperating in the investigation and had nothing to hide. She said Higgins should remind everyone that "Selby Gardens operates in the same fashion as Missouri, Harvard and NY [New York Botanical Garden] with regard to the exchange of plant material to and from international herbaria. Nothing different in this case."

Of course, that was Christenson's criticism in a nutshell: The problem was bigger than just Selby. No one at any botanical garden took the law as seriously as the Fish and Wildlife Service did.

Beckner did not relish being a prosecution witness. The man who loved to be the first with the news did not like talking to investigators. He was summoned to Tampa to meet with Agent Holt and the prosecutor. They warned him that if he told them anything that turned out to be false, he could be prosecuted for lying.

As much as he sweated walking around the Redland festival, Beckner sweated even more now. He spent an entire afternoon trying to convince law enforcement that neither he nor his colleagues had done anything wrong.

Because of Atwood, though, they didn't buy it. In fact, they suspected Beckner himself might have an illegal orchid or two hidden away somewhere as well, Beckner said later. He was the one who had reported rumors about the *Phragmipedium kovachii* being sold at the Redland show. He admitted he had thought of using his credit card to buy one. Perhaps he'd gone through with the purchase and hidden it somewhere—maybe with Atwood's help?

"They were clearly convinced we were a gang of conspirators intent on violating the endangered species laws," Beckner said afterward. "I argued with them. It was one of the worst afternoons of my life."

At one point, the prosecutor told him that Selby would have to do something about taking Kovach's name off the plant. That's what Peru wanted, the attorney told him.

"I don't give a damn what Peru wants," Beckner shot back. Under the rules governing botanical nomenclature, the name Selby had used was valid and could not be changed, he said.

But Selby's involvement in the naming had tarred its own name. The Selby staff organized a field trip for some of its dues-paying members to the American Orchid Society headquarters in Delray Beach. Scully tagged along. To his dismay, the tour guide made several snarky comments about Selby and smuggling, prompting Scully to complain to AOS officials about it.

Then, on Valentine's Day, Eric Christenson sent a friend an e-mail with copies cc'd far and wide.

"This is just a quick note with breaking news," he wrote. "Earlier this week a Federal Agent arrived at my front door and handed me a (friendly) subpoena. A Federal Grand Jury has been convened next month (March) at the Federal Court Building in Tampa to hear testimony concerning the smuggling of *Phragmipedium kovachii* by the Marie Selby Botanical Gardens. This is not a rumor—I've got the subpoena to prove it! So the question 'When are the feds going to do something?' has now been answered. This is a VERY BIG DEAL—U.S. Fish and Wildlife does not engage the Justice Department for minor problems."

Then he added, "Please spread the word in Europe . . . that the U.S. Government is going after orchid smuggling at botanical gardens."

And with that, subpoenas began to rain down on everyone.

Throughout the rest of 2003, witnesses were summoned to testify to a grand jury that met in Tampa at the thrusting marble pylon known as the Sam M. Gibbons U.S. Courthouse. The building had been named for a jowly congressman repeatedly reelected because of his skill at funneling millions of taxpayer dollars to his home district.

Grand juries, as the name implies, are larger than the twelve-person jury familiar to anyone who has ever seen a murder trial on TV's *Law & Order*. Federal grand juries meet in secret, sometimes for up to three years, although usually they convene no more than a day or two a week during that time. Their job is not to decide who's guilty, but to question witnesses, review evidence, and decide who should be indicted.

The grand jury investigating the orchid case met in Tampa in an austere and dimly lit room that sometimes made witnesses feel as if they'd been dragged into a star chamber. The jurors sat in chairs arranged in descending rows like movie theater seats. Down at the bottom, in a sort of pit, was where the witness sat, alone. No defense attorneys were allowed inside to speak for the people testifying. Meanwhile the prosecutor not only was allowed in but actually led the questioning of witnesses.

Kovach, as one of the targets of the investigation, was not subpoenaed. But he was still talking to reporters. On March 9, 2003, the *Palm Beach Post* published a story about the investigation in which Kovach named someone new as the reason why he found his flower.

"I still feel really blessed to have been the person to whom God revealed it," he told the *Post*. Despite all his legal woes, he was happy the plant was named for him. If the paper reported his quote accurately, he gave the reporter one of the great malapropisms of all time: "It's like a little piece of immorality."

The first witness stood before the grand jury on March 26, 2003, and swore to tell the truth.

"Thank you," the jury foreperson said. "If you would, please, be seated. Please speak into the microphone and state your name. For the record, please spell it."

"My name is Mary Holt," the investigator told the rows of people facing her. "H-O-L-T. I'm a special agent with the U.S. Fish and Wildlife Service."

Then a prosecutor named Elinor Colbourn took over the questioning,

Elinor Colbourn prosecuted violations of the endangered species laws but often found judges and other attorneys did not take the crimes as seriously as she believed the law required. Photo courtesy of the Colbourn family.

knowing already what Holt's answers would be and what evidence she wanted the jurors to hear.

Colbourn stood five foot two, with long brown hair and hazel eyes that could snap with anger. A 1988 graduate of Yale Law, Colbourn was a senior trial attorney for the U.S. Department of Justice and nobody's fool. Her specialty: prosecuting violations of the laws that protect the environment.

For her it was more than just a paycheck.

"What a pleasure to tell people honestly that you love what you do," she wrote in a Yale alumni publication. "That's one of the great perks of my job."

Colbourn relished being one of the eight trial attorneys in the department's wildlife section, going after bad guys who were beating up Mother Nature. The crimes and criminals could get pretty wild themselves.

"The cases frequently take on a soap opera quality: people who smuggled snakes in their pants, or birds in special vests under their shirts, or whole families who for generations have poached bears on public lands," she wrote.

Some prosecutors are pragmatists who see cases as problems to be solved. They are good at spotting the vulnerability of their own arguments, but sometimes poor at putting across to a jury the importance of right over wrong. Some prosecutors are just the opposite. They come across as true believers, passionate about the virtue of the government's position on a case but sometimes blind to its weak spots. Defense attorneys regarded Colbourn as being an example of the latter category.

She lacked the vanity that drives many lawyers. For instance, she rarely allowed her name to appear in Justice Department press releases about her cases, instead letting someone else take the credit. And she avoided ever letting anyone snap her photo in connection with a case, even when she won an award for her work.

Although she was a mother of three, her work frequently took her to courtrooms around the country. She prosecuted fishing-boat captains in Alabama for smuggling lobsters in from Honduras. She went after a reptile dealer in Orlando for smuggling turtles and snakes from Asia. Sometimes her quarry was someone who believed the laws on endangered species didn't apply to him. In 1999, for instance, she led the prosecution of the curator of reptiles at the San Diego Zoo on felony fraud and theft charges.

What Colbourn found more difficult than getting a conviction was getting everyone else in the justice system to take these cases as something other than a waste of the court's time.

"The greatest challenge . . . is getting judges and other prosecutors to take you seriously," she wrote. "When they are dealing with overwhelming caseloads of murders and big money drug cases, we frequently hear things like, 'But it's just fish.'"

Now, in the grand jury room in Tampa, with twenty jurors looking on, Colbourn took Agent Holt through the basics of the case against Kovach and Selby Gardens. She asked Holt to recount how the case began, how she focused on Kovach, even asked her to spell the name of the flower so the court reporter could get it right. Then she asked where Kovach took the plant when he got to the United States.

"It came in through—it came in through Miami, the Port of Miami," Holt told the grand jury. "And Mr. Kovach transported it from Miami up to Sarasota where Marie Selby Botanical Gardens is located. Marie Selby Botanical Gardens took possession of the plant. There was at least two plants that we know of at this point and one was dried and used as a holotype, which is like a control so that they have a description of the plant. And the other plant they kept. The other live plant they kept. They took the dried plant and sent that one back to Peru."

Colbourn asked Holt if her account about there being two plants might change as she continued her investigation.

"It's possible," Holt said.

Then Colbourn asked the jurors if they had any questions. The foreperson wanted to know how Kovach got his plants through customs in Miami.

"We're looking into that right now," Holt said without elaborating.

There were more questions about Kovach. Was he employed by Selby?

No, Holt said, "he has his own private nursery. It's very small. It's smaller than this room."

"Have you spoken with Mr. Kovach?" Colbourn asked.

"Yes."

"That was not under oath, correct? He was just being interviewed by you?"

"That's correct. However, he did write an affidavit."

"At that time," the prosecutor asked, "did he acknowledge that he had, in fact, brought at least one Appendix I *Phragmipedium* into the country?"

"Yes," Holt said.

One of the jurors chimed in. "What is the value of this plant?"

"We're getting ranges from $2,000 to $20,000 a plant," Holt said.

"One plant?" the juror asked, clearly stunned. "Per plant?"

"One flowering plant," Holt said.

"Ohhh-kay," the juror said.

"I don't have one of those," another juror quipped.

As Colbourn and Holt probed more deeply into what had happened the day Kovach walked into Selby Gardens, they were under serious political pressure.

The Peruvian embassy had demanded to be kept abreast of the progress of the investigation. That put the wildlife agency in a quandary: How could federal officials reassure the Peruvians that the investigation was making progress without disclosing what the grand jury was doing? Grand jury proceedings were supposed to be secret.

When the Fish and Wildlife Service didn't respond at first, the Peruvian ambassador asked again, adding that the nation was still seeking the return of any plants illegally taken from Peru.

The response from the Fish and Wildlife Service basically said: Trust us, we're on the case.

However, the investigators were often distracted by having to sort out truth from rumor and fact from speculation—a common occurrence in the gossipy orchid world.

At one point, Colbourn received a tip that someone had decided to shut up Faustino Medina Bautista permanently. Their tipster said the El Progresso orchid peddler had been poisoned.

Alarmed, she sent a request via Interpol to the Peruvian authorities. Six months passed, and finally word came back that the petal peddler was fine, and their tipster—Eric Christenson—was wrong.

Christenson's own trip to the grand jury went smoothly. His main purpose, he said later, was to "to tell what is normal for botany and how Selby's actions were way outside the norm."

He spent two hours answering Colbourn's questions, testifying not only about what happened with the new Peruvian slipper orchid but also telling his stories about Selby's many other misdeeds.

The grand jury had subpoenaed a dozen Selby employees and board members to get their side of the story. Meanwhile Selby's attorneys negotiated with Colbourn, trying to work out whether there would be criminal charges against the garden or its staff, and if so how bad they might be.

The board's anxiety over the grand jury investigation had exacerbated the long-running feud between Scully and Lowman. Now the board members invited a third party in to act as a referee: David Benzing, a biology professor at Oberlin College in Ohio. He rounded up a group of horticultural experts and scholars to run an audit of Selby's organizational structure and figure out how to fix it.

The Benzing committee found "a deficit in leadership" with Lowman at the helm—but also that she was "a first-rate front person" as the face of Selby. She had "some very substantial strengths that were clearly good for the institution," Benzing told the *Herald-Tribune*. The Benzing report also found that Scully had repeatedly intervened in staff affairs in ways that weren't appropriate for a board member.

The solution: Hire a chief operating officer—something the board had promised to do three years before—and make Lowman turn over day-to-day operations to him or her. That way she could continue representing Selby while someone other than Scully took care of the gardens' daily oversight. The board picked a former COO of the Annenberg Foundation, Shawn Farr, and he came on board in May 2003. His salary: $100,000.

Dalström warned several board members that this move wouldn't work. He figured Lowman didn't want to be Selby's public face, its mascot, with no actual power. She wanted to keep running Selby, even if—in his view—she was running it into a ditch.

By now the uproar over the Peruvian orchid had reached the ears of some editors at *People* magazine, a publication normally focused more on sexy Hollywood stars, not screwy botanical scandals.

Kovach, who had refused to speak with the *Sarasota Herald-Tribune*, gladly opened up for America's premier entertainment publication for a story headlined, "Blooming Mad."

"He's been called thief, smuggler, evil, pariah," the magazine announced. "Armed federal agents stormed his home. He could wind up spending a year in jail. And all because some people believe James Kovach stole a flower."

The magazine briefly recounted Kovach's trip to Moyobamba and his stop at El Progresso.

"At a roadside stand he bought a foot-tall magenta flower for about $3," the magazine told its 3.7 million readers. "'We didn't quite know what it was,' he says, 'but we were pretty-sure we found something special.'"

Kovach told the magazine he had no idea the orchid could be endangered. For a response, the *People* reporter contacted the president of the Peru Orchid Club—which, as it turned out, was none other than Alfredo Manrique, the nursery owner who was one of two Peruvian vendors at the Redland show in May 2002.

Manrique scoffed at Kovach's claim of innocence, insisting Kovach "can't say he didn't know this was illegal. Now, in the orchid world, he is a leper."

While the investigation of Kovach continued, *People* reported, "his income from breeding and lecturing has dried up like a wilted you-know-what. 'My life is ruined,' says Kovach. 'The bottom line is, it's just a flower. Everybody's lost their mind.'"

Except it wasn't just a flower—not a single flower, that is.

Because now Kovach's story changed again.

In June 2003, two months after the *People* story appeared, a newsletter for slipper orchid enthusiasts belonging to the Global Paphiopedilum Alliance published Kovach's first-person account of his trip to Peru and subsequent triumph and travail.

He wrote it, he said in the piece, because all the other stories written about the discovery of his namesake orchid "ha[ve] been at best innocently misinformed and at worst the most heinous lies and perjured slander to protect their own greedy interests."

The story, headlined, "The True Story of the *Phragmipedium kovachii*," is notable as the only account in which Kovach mentions Moore by name. And it's notable, too, for offering a new version of his story about the woman at the El Progresso truck stop.

She walked around back and "then quickly reappeared cradling three pots containing plants with large dark rose flowers," Kovach wrote. "They appeared to be slipper orchids of some kind, but I'd never seen anything like this."

According to this new account, Kovach bought all three orchids—not just one. And what became of them?

"Two plants were placed in the Moores' farm with the intent to use as brood stock," he wrote. Of those two, "one slightly wilted flower was harvested and brought to me. I pressed and dissected it crudely. The third plant came to Lima with my order."

He ended his account by warning his readers against doing what he did.

"In the year that has passed, the forces of greed and envy have stolen my joy of discovery," Kovach wrote. "I have been ridiculed, misquoted, slandered, libeled and had political and economic interests manipulate the U.S. government into an unconstitutional persecution to try to force me out of business."

He urged his readers to "agitate, agitate, agitate" to get CITES changed. In the meantime, he wrote, "pray that if you ever get a new orchid species named after yourself, that it is some ratty little weed, with insignificant green flowers and absolutely no commercial potential."

This was the story Lee Moore had told Holt and Colbourn as well: Kovach had bought three orchids, but left two at his farm in Moyobamba.

That story was a lie, Moore said years later.

He was just trying to help Kovach by backing up his friend's account of what happened, he said. That's why he told Holt and Colbourn that Kovach brought back just one orchid. The truth, Moore said, was that Kovach took all three of those orchids home to the United States. What happened to them after that, Moore said, he did not know.

But since Moore had no great love for the U.S. government, given what it had done to him over the years, he had seen no need to tell Agent Holt all that.

What Moore didn't realize is that Holt and Colbourn didn't believe his story anyway. After all, they had witnesses who'd been at Selby Gardens who said Kovach had had more than one plant that day.

The blond-haired man settled himself in the witness chair and spelled his name, "S-T-I-G, D-A-L-S-T-R-O, with an umlaut, M." He exuded confidence, even with twenty strangers staring at him.

Colbourn asked the standard opening questions, including one about if there was any reason why his memory might be impaired, such as medications or "any head trauma lately?"

"Not really," Dalström said, then grinned. "I met a beautiful girl in Costa Rica but that's—no, I'm fine."

Although he didn't show it, Dalström was annoyed at having to testify. He had expected to be on his way out to South America for a long-planned trip, but then the subpoena landed in his mailbox commanding his appearance in Tampa federal court.

Despite his annoyance, he answered Colbourn's questions with ease—although his fractured sense of the English idiom produced some curious verbiage. When Colbourn asked him about how many plants were named after him, he told the grand jury, "Finding new orchids is very simple if you know what to do, but most of the orchids that are described every year are very insignificant and nobody raises an eyeball."

He went on to tell them about John Beckner going to the Redland show and returning with stories of a thrilling new slipper orchid, and then about the e-mail that Wesley Higgins received from Dave Hunt in Texas with pictures from the Villenas.

Then he got to the part about Kovach's arrival with the plant itself, and the staff's decision to publish the description and beat Christenson to the punch.

"The description of these species was a little bit controversial, for political reasons, in Peru," he testified. "There are people down there with their—with their agendas. And for some reason they wanted to have—they preferred the name *Phragmipedium peruvianum* rather than *Phragmipedium kovachii*, and I can't blame them."

After all, he said, over the years thousands of orchids from South American countries had been named by foreign taxonomists who had little concern about the feelings of the people who lived where the plants grew. It was understandable the Peruvians would want this new one named for their own country.

But Dalström scoffed at suggestions that Selby could now withdraw the *kovachii* name for the orchid and substitute Christenson's proposed name: "My answer to that was you can call it whatever you want, but scientifically it's a done deal, so you might as well get over it. Forget it."

He insisted to the grand jury that Selby had done nothing wrong, legally as well as ethically—in part because of paranoia.

"It was discussed whether we should proceed and describe this species, and in case we did, so how would we do that," he explained. "We wanted to do it—we wanted to do a good case. We wanted to do the right thing. We wanted to send the specimen back to Peru, because we had doubts about Kovach's papers. . . . So we had to discuss well, what if, what if. You know, is someone trying to set us up, because we've heard really strange rumors about people being set up to do illegal things and so on. So we want to be very cautious."

Ultimately, he testified, the scientists decided "that the only way we want to deal with this issue at all would be to invite the Peruvian co-author and send the specimen back to the country of origin immediately, and no matter what, otherwise we—we couldn't touch it."

"So," Colbourn asked, "did all of it go back to Peru, to the best of your knowledge?"

"Yeah, to the best of my knowledge," Dalström replied. But then, as Colbourn began a new question, he backpedaled: "Wait. Wait. Let me rephrase that."

Then he started talking about the piece that Atwood kept, but without mentioning anyone's name: "So we pressed—or somebody pressed some leaves of that, and they were trying to keep the plant alive, because if it turned out that the papers were legal, a living specimen of this species would be a lot more valuable than a dead one."

"Valuable in what sense?" Colbourn asked.

"You know, for—if it's a rare and endangered thing it's better to have it alive so you can propagate it rather than just press the whole thing," Dalström said.

Instead of hammering Dalström for contradicting his own testimony, Colbourn zeroed in on a question about Kovach: How many plants did he bring to Selby?

"He had a plant, but I don't recall how many leaves or parts of the division," Dalström said. "It looked like a single plant with a flower."

"Okay," Colbourn said—but what did he present that was used for pressing?

"He presented a division for pressing, where he got that, I don't know," Dalström said.

He explained to the jurors that orchids produce new growths called "divisions" that can be ripped apart from the plant and grown separately. He said he did not know where Kovach had obtained that particular growth that Selby used for the type specimen later shipped to Peru.

"So the rest of the plant that had the faded flower on it, what happened to that?" Colbourn asked.

"That, Mr. Kovach kept that," Dalström said.

At one point, Dalström confessed that the investigation had made the orchid boys question their own motives and actions.

"We ask ourselves from time to time . . . whether we did the right thing," he testified. "And there's no doubt in my mind whatsoever that we did the right thing."

Harry Luther, who had ridden to Tampa in the same car with Dalström, was next. He stepped into the grand jury room just before lunchtime. He didn't have as much of a story to tell, so he finished more quickly.

When he was done, he said later, "one of the jurors leaving for noontime vittles said 'Can you believe all of this is about a flower?'"

As the investigation continued, Bob Scully repeatedly called Selby's attorneys for updates and even flew to Washington to meet with them.

One day he got a call from Selby's attorney informing him that some of the most damaging evidence in the case had come from none other than Cal Dodson.

When Agent Holt showed up at Dodson's door in Sarasota with a colleague, Selby's first executive director said he'd be happy to talk to the investigators. They sat on his patio for three hours, and he hung his former institution out to dry.

Dodson told them he'd known that Kovach's orchid was illegal the minute he'd seen it. He told them he had said so, both to Kovach and to the OIC staff, even to the chairman of the board.

"I told them nothing but the absolute truth," Dodson said later.

When the gardens' attorney heard about it, "he was beside himself," Scully said. The investigation had taken a dire turn, and now there seemed no way to avoid criminal charges.

To help deal with the continuing bad publicity about Selby's role in the orchid case, the board made another big hire, bringing on board a professional crisis manager. But the next crisis requiring management proved to be internal, not external.

For board member Bob Richardson, a staunch ally of Lowman's, the last straw came in May 2003: "We were sitting in a meeting with the board and Scully was saying he thought Meg hadn't told the truth about what happened."

Richardson, disgusted, stormed out and quit the board on the spot.

Scully says he did not mean that Lowman intentionally lied to the board or the investigators. He just meant that she may have given them inaccurate information she had received from someone on the staff. But that's not how Richardson or some other board members took it.

Richardson had once pledged to donate $100,000 to Selby—enough to cover Shawn Farr's salary as COO. But now the elderly real estate mogul was so furious at what he saw as an attempt to make Lowman a scapegoat that he vowed to withhold the donation. He promised to donate the money to Lowman instead, in case she needed it for her own legal expenses.

Lowman had begun considering that possibility herself. As the gardens' director, she might be held legally responsible for what the OIC had done, even though she had never even touched the orchid.

In the negotiations with Selby's attorneys, prosecutor Colbourn kept bringing up the idea of Lowman pleading guilty to a charge. Some of the board members thought she should go along with the prosecutor's wishes, just to end their agony. She refused.

"I didn't want to be part of the guilty party because I was innocent," she explained later.

So on a trip to Tallahassee, Lowman stopped by to see her old friend Robert Rivas, the ACLU board member she had bonded with during their Leadership Florida sessions. She took the jolly Rivas out to a pizzeria for a reunion dinner. As they ate, she slowly eased the conversation into the story of what was going on with Selby. She explained CITES, the orchid world, and then her own increasingly precarious position.

"I didn't know she had an agenda" when he accepted the dinner invitation, Rivas said later. "I had only the dimmest idea what CITES was, but I pretended I knew what she was talking about. Then the tone began to shift, and all the festiveness of the evening evaporated. I became transfixed. Meg was telling me she was in really big trouble and needed some help."

Rivas instantly agreed. That evening he started boning up on orchids and CITES. Lowman, meanwhile, continued to stand her ground—even as it crumbled beneath her.

The man who showed up to speak to the grand jury in July was looking for work.

John Atwood's Selby employment contract had run out at the end of June. He had been right about losing the key to the research building and his Selby e-mail address: They were signals. Because he had taken a piece of an il-legal orchid to Vermont, the board was not inclined to renew his contract. Besides, with what they were spending on attorneys, the board had to start cutting back on nonessential personnel.

When the Selby job evaporated, Atwood also lost his part-time position with the Missouri Botanical Gardens. But he didn't want to leave Vermont, so he was applying for jobs around the state as a church organist.

As the prosecutor ran through what was supposed to be a routine line of questions to establish his bona fides as a witness, the clearly nervous Atwood went overboard with his honesty, just as he had during his interrogation by Holt.

When Colbourn asked if there was any reason why his memory might be impaired or inaccurate, Atwood startled everyone by saying yes.

"I can relate to you a story of how my memory has worked because I was mentioning to Mary Holt earlier because I'm also a musician," he explained. "I used to play a piece of music in high school and I didn't have the music to it and I thought I could play it by memory. Twelve years after the fact, I played it to a group, having played it a bit beforehand. They played me the actual piece on a recording because I didn't even know who the composer was, and it turned out, in my version, I had fabricated about a quarter of that piece thinking I was playing something that I thought I once knew very well. That was the way my memory worked, so I know one's memory can do things, particularly with lapse of time and particularly with understanding the order of events."

Fine, Colbourn said, trying to get the witness back on track. With the understanding that over time one's memory tends to fade a bit, she said, "have you, for example, taken any medication that would impair your memory?"

"None whatsoever," he replied.

With that out of the way, Colbourn turned to the subject of Selby. Why was he no longer employed there? It was, he said, a financial decision, based in part on how much Selby's board was spending on attorneys.

"My understanding is that it's been several hundreds of thousands of dollars," he testified.

She took him through a description of what happened the day Kovach walked in with the orchid. But when she tried to press him about how many orchids Kovach had, he hesitated to give her an answer.

"This is part of the problem with memory because we are concentrating on the live plant that came in," Atwood explained. "It was a live plant that we were all looking at."

Did he know what he was looking at? "Well," he said, "it was clearly a new species."

And his reaction? "I guess the first question I had was did he have paperwork on these, and I remember him balking just a little bit and then he nodded yes, I do have papers." Because Selby had never set up any protocol for handling a CITES Appendix I plant like that, though "we took him at his word."

What about that piece he took back to Vermont? "The plant was sitting there, maybe on the kitchen table, maybe on the windowsill, and it was agreed upon by all of us that I should take it to Vermont to grow to stabilize,' Atwood said.

Colbourn zeroed in on the paperwork question regarding Kovach walking in with the plant: "So nobody ever expressed any concern to you that the documentation had been incomplete or inadequate?"

"No."

"At any time, including when Ms. Lowman sent e-mails to you?"

"That the documentation was inadequate, to my knowledge, no."

She asked if a CITES permit wasn't absolutely required for importing an Appendix I orchid. Yes, he said, "but there are other ways of getting plants into the United States that I don't know about. We're not law enforcement people."

By the end of July, Atwood wasn't the only Selby employee out of work.

Shawn Farr, frustrated at Lowman's resistance to turning over day-to-day operations, handed in his resignation.

"The working relationship Meg and I had was fine, but she had to go through some transition here of letting some things go," Farr told the *Herald-Tribune*. "The transition wasn't going as quickly as I expected."

Farr's resignation proved to be the last straw for Lowman's critics on the board. She had hired expensive attorneys without asking permission. She wouldn't go along with a plea deal. She continued tussling with Scully, whose term as chairman had ended but who remained on the board and remained popular with a majority of the members. Now the man the board had hired to help her had quit over how she treated him. That was it for her.

Normally the Selby trustees did not meet in the summer so Lowman had planned a rare family vacation, taking her kids camping. Then she was told the board was convening a special meeting to "discuss your job and possible termination." She was not invited to attend. She realized the skids were greased.

The July 26, 2003, special meeting to discuss Lowman dragged on for more than two hours. The board members debated Lowman's job performance as if they were a jury debating her guilt. Some cried bitter tears, wrung out by the emotional strain. Even some people who professed to like what Lowman had done for Selby, people like Carl Luer, couldn't agree to keep her on any longer.

The final decision, by majority vote: Oust Lowman and ask Farr to come back in the hope he could save Selby Gardens from financial ruin.

Scully's replacement as chairman, Barbara Hansen, was a steely grande dame who had served as mayor of the Village of Barrington Hills, Illinois, for twelve years. She had survived four surgeries to deal with pancreatic cancer as well as a near-fatal bout with a staph infection. Now in her seventies, she did not shy away from even the hardest tasks.

Hansen tracked Lowman down and informed her that she had lost the board's confidence. Hansen urged her to spare Selby further bad publicity and resign instead of forcing them to fire her. Stunned at her swift downfall, Lowman agreed.

But word soon spread around Sarasota how Lowman had been shown the door, and the *Herald-Tribune* picked up on it.

"It's a tragedy what happened to her," board treasurer Joel Fedder told the paper. "It's a tragedy for her, for Sarasota, and for the state of Florida."

Farr agreed to return to Selby as COO, thanks to the promise of a 10 percent raise on his $100,000 salary. But in the meantime, Lowman's allies—board members and donors—began bailing out, and taking their money with them. Their vows to withhold promised donations cut the gardens' expected income by hundreds of thousands of dollars, forcing the gardens to borrow money for some scheduled renovations to the mansion. By October, eight trustees had quit. The eighth to go was Fedder, the treasurer.

The turmoil soon claimed another victim. In November, a frustrated Farr quit again, this time for good.

"The end of this story hasn't been written yet," a still angry Bob Richardson told the *Herald-Tribune*.

In October 2003, Bob Scully put on a suit and tie to testify to the grand jury. He figured that, because of his position as a member of Selby's board of trustees, he should appear as businesslike as possible.

Then he walked into the grand jury room and discovered, as he put it, "I'm dressed better than anybody else in the room." The jurors, who had spent months together, wore the kind of casual clothes you might see on shoppers at the mall. Scully was unimpressed.

Scully spent about forty-five minutes answering questions. Right from the start, he believed the prosecutor had ambushed him as hostile.

"She started to threaten me the minute I sat down," Scully said afterward. "She said, 'If you do anything to protect Lowman, I'll send you to jail.'"

Scully would be the last person to try to protect Lowman, but apparently Colbourn didn't know that. However Scully didn't correct the impression.

"I think all I said was, 'Okay,'" Scully said.

He said Colbourn focused a lot of her questions on the e-mail that he'd sent to Higgins the day after Kovach presented his orchid to the OIC. She seemed particularly interested in the sentence where he had described this as "a fabulous opportunity." After all, Scully had been a commercial grower and all of his Tiger Orchid clients were commercial growers.

"She went after me on that," Scully said. "She said, 'You had a commercial intent here.'"

Not true, Scully insisted. "I meant it was a chance for them to be recognized for the work that they do," he explained. "Why shouldn't Selby Gardens tell the world that they gave it a new name?"

By the end of his session, he said, the prosecutor "seemed to get frustrated with me."

Finally, Colbourn asked if Lowman had ever lied to him. Yes, Scully said. But instead of talking about *Phragmipedium kovachii* or CITES permits, Scully launched into a long story about how he believed Lowman had fabricated figures for how much money she had raised for Selby Gardens, as a way to pad her own pay.

That wasn't what Colbourn was looking for, Scully said, "so she dismissed me."

Stalking out, he decided that all the questions he'd heard were "preposterous," a big waste of time.

He had no idea what the final witness would reveal.

13

———

The Judges

The overall desire to possess this plant and be the first
has brought on the overabundance of scandal,
rumors, lies, and more.

Glen Decker, *Orchids* magazine

The last witness turned out to be the first witness: Agent Holt. She made a
return trip to the Tampa grand jury on November 19, 2003, so the prosecutor
could go over the case with her one more time, and raise a new question.

"Agent Holt," Colbourn asked, "in the course of this investigation, have
you had the opportunity to interview a gentleman named Lee Moore?"

Yes, she said.

"Who is Lee Moore?"

"Lee Moore is a friend of Michael Kovach," Holt said. "He has a nursery
in Peru and a nursery in Miami." She didn't mention anything about Moore
and Kovach being business partners, or about Moore's past run-ins with the
law, and Colbourn didn't ask.

Instead, the prosecutor asked, "Did Mr. Moore provide you any documents and/or videotapes during his interview?"

"Yes, he did," Holt said, and told the grand jury about the videotape of
Faustino Medina Bautista giving his version of what happened at the El Progresso roadside stand.

"What does the person on the videotape say about what he sold, how
many plants he sold to Mr. Kovach?"

"In the videotape," Holt said, "he stated three."

Moving on, Colbourn asked what Kovach's paperwork showed when he
went through customs. Just plants, she said, valued at less than $500. Col-

bourn asked what Kovach told her he had left at Selby. The answer: one dried flower and one live plant in flower.

Then she asked about Atwood's piece of the plant, and reviewed what became of it. Next Colbourn asked about the other plant pieces Selby saved.

"Have you ever recovered a pickled specimen of this plant?" she asked.

No, Holt replied.

"Have you ever recovered a DNA sample of this *Phragmipedium*?" Colbourn asked.

Yes, Holt said. That snippet of the plant—the only part of it that Wesley Higgins handled personally—had remained in Selby's possession all these many months. Finally, Selby's attorney had turned it over to Holt just a week before her return trip to the grand jury. It was another black eye for Selby's scientists, another sign that they were either unable to keep track of their own inventory or unwilling to cooperate with the authorities.

Then Colbourn asked about two witnesses who weren't employed by Selby, the pair that Kovach had once told the USDA were to blame for all his troubles. She asked about the two orchid judges who had been visiting Higgins's office that morning.

"What did they tell you about Kovach's departure from Selby Botanical Gardens on June 5th, 2002?" Colbourn asked.

What those two had to say provided the most tantalizing clue of all.

Jim Clarkson and Mark Jones were best friends. Both had served in the military—Clarkson in the army, Jones in the navy—but what brought them together was their love for orchids.

They had gone on collecting trips together overseas. They had really bonded when they went through the lengthy and difficult training to become American Orchid Society judges, a process similar to earning a master's degree in botany. Over and over, when controversies had arisen during orchid shows, the two judges had worked together to deal with the situation.

Holt had phoned both men to schedule separate meetings with them for January 2003. She visited Clarkson first, and to his surprise she brought Colbourn as well.

Then Clarkson surprised the two women by pulling out a tape recorder. He wanted a record of what they all said, he explained. Holt said that would be fine, so long as she got a copy of the tape, too. Sure, Clarkson said.

At the end of their interview, the investigator asked Clarkson not to tell anyone what they had discussed. But as soon as the two women were out the door, Clarkson called his friend to tip him off that Holt was not alone.

When Holt and Colbourn showed up at Jones's telemarketing office to question him, he was prepared. Like many orchid hobbyists, Jones despised CITES and disliked what he regarded as a fumble-fingered attempt to enforce its misguided rules.

"As far as I'm concerned, what they were doing was totally illegal under the Constitution," Jones said later.

First he asked for their names. When Colbourn identified herself as a Justice Department attorney, Jones asked if he needed an attorney, too. No, they said.

Fine, he said, and then just like Clarkson he put a tape recorder on the table and informed them that he would be recording their conversation. He also laid a booklet on the table.

"Here's a copy of the U.S. Constitution," he told them. "If you say there was a crime committed, I want you to show me the section of the Constitution that covers it."

Finally, Jones pulled out a printed copy of the Miranda rights that police officers routinely read to suspects. He read them aloud to Holt and Colbourn: "You have the right to remain silent . . ."

The next forty-five minutes did not go easily. Jones accused Holt and Colbourn of selective prosecution, contending that Eric Christenson deserved to be investigated as much as anyone at Selby. It didn't help matters when Holt asked Jones if he had held the plant Kovach had shown to the scientists to Selby.

"If I held it, would I have been guilty of a crime?" he asked. The answer from Holt and Colbourn: We don't know.

Nevertheless, Jones told them his version of what happened:

On the morning of June 5, 2002, Jones and Clarkson drove down to Sarasota to buy some special orchid fertilizer from a company called Florikan. When they finished that errand, they figured they would drive over to Selby Gardens and treat their friends and fellow orchid show judges, Wesley Higgins and John Beckner, to lunch.

Jones, in particular, loved going to Selby. He had done a lot of research in its library for the scholarly papers he had to submit to become an orchid judge. Higgins and Beckner were not just fellow orchid judges, though. They were people he enjoyed chatting with—and not just about orchids, either, but about broader subjects, such as how civilizations rise and fall. To him that was one of the great pleasures of orchid collecting: that it brought together such articulate, sophisticated people who could talk intelligently on virtually any topic.

Selby had other positive associations for him as well. Once, on a first date, he took a woman to stroll around Selby Gardens. She later agreed to marry him.

That morning, when Clarkson and Jones walked into Selby's 7-11 building, they found Beckner was off for the day, gone to get his vaccinations, but Higgins was in. Instead of discussing the rise and fall of civilization, though, the three men sat around gossiping about "some juicy nonsense that was going on" in the orchid world at the moment, Jones recalled later.

Soon, though, they were interrupted. Someone notified Higgins that a visitor was waiting up front, a man who said he had an orchid to be identified. Higgins was enjoying the conversation too much, though, Jones recalled.

"Ahhh, screw it," Higgins said. "Whoever it is can wait."

Finally, though, the visitor—Kovach—got tired of waiting and walked back to Higgins's office on his own. He was alone, Jones said, no sign of a wife (and no escort from Dalström or any volunteers, either). The man was carrying something.

"He had a box," Jones said. "Inside the box he had plants. They were wrapped up in newspaper. He says, 'I have this plant I want you to identify.' He says, 'I think it's a *Phrag*, but I'm not sure.'"

"Where did you get it from?" Higgins asked, although most collectors are like most fishermen: loath to identify the place where they got their best catch.

"If you're going to identify it," the visitor replied, "I'll tell you where I got it from."

So then, Jones said, "he unwrapped it. Jim sat there and helped him. We pulled it out and went, 'What the hell is this?' And Jim said, 'It looks like a *Phrag*, but that ain't a *Phrag* flower!'"

Two of the plants in the box were in flower, Jones said. One of the flowers seemed a bit wilted, Jones recalled, but the other was so huge and colorful "it blew everything else away." All thoughts of their lunch date went out the window.

At that point, Jones said, Kovach "starts telling us stories about where he's seen it." Kovach talked about finding the flower in the Peruvian Andes. He didn't mention buying it at a roadside stand. "All he said was, 'I collected it up there.'"

Higgins asked about documents, Jones said, and Kovach said he had declared everything when he went through customs and had no problems—

not exactly what Higgins had asked, but good enough to deflect further questions for the moment.

"And about this time is when John Atwood and Cal Dodson walked in," Jones said. "Stig came in with them."

They all began examining the plant, trying to figure out what it could be, Jones said, "and Kovach's comment was, 'If it turns out to be a different genus, I'd like it named after me, and if it's a new species I'd like it named after me.'"

Then someone—Jones couldn't remember who—made the comment, "Wouldn't it be nice to have one?" But Clarkson, who had done his judge's thesis on *Phragmipediums*, said, "These ain't growing here."

The reason: They came from high in the Andes, where the temperatures were far cooler than in Sarasota.

"Then John [Atwood] said, 'About the only place they'd grow would be in Vermont,'" Jones said. "At the time I thought he was just kidding."

What of Kovach's later complaint that Clarkson and Jones had tried to buy some of the new slipper orchids from him? "That's absolute hogwash," Jones said. "I was born, but I wasn't born yesterday."

After all, he pointed out, what would be the point of buying one of Kovach's orchids if it wouldn't grow in Florida's climate?

On the contrary, Jones said, Kovach himself hung onto some of the plants. He wasn't sure how many were in the box Kovach brought into Selby, or how many left with him, but it wasn't a lot. "Fewer than ten," Jones said.

There was one plant in particular that Kovach kept his hands on, Jones said. Although he left the flower itself behind at Selby, Jones said, Kovach walked off with the one plant that had had the most spectacular flower on it.

Clarkson had told Holt and Colbourn a similar story. He said that he was sure Kovach had been carrying not one but three *Phragmipedium kovachii* that day. Kovach had one flowering plant, one nonflowering plant, and one dried specimen, Clarkson said.

How did he know? Because he helped Kovach unwrap the live plants from a newspaper, he explained.

Then, when Kovach left Selby, he left behind a live plant and the dried specimen, Clarkson told Holt and Colbourn. That left the third orchid still in Kovach's possession.

"He said he helped wrap one plant up that Kovach took with him," Holt wrote in her report on the interview.

So Holt, in testifying to the grand jury, said that according to the two orchid judges, "he left with at least one live plant."

Of course, that raised an obvious question—one that Colbourn did not dare ask Agent Holt in front of the grand jury because she didn't have an answer. The question was: If Kovach had more than one orchid that day, what happened to it? Why didn't any other *Phragmipedium kovachii* turn up during her search of Kovach's home? Where did it go?

A week later, on November 26, 2003, the grand jury officially indicted James Michael Kovach on charges of "Smuggling Goods Into the U.S. (Except Narcotics and Liquor)" and "Prohibited Acts—Endangered Species," both of them felonies.

Kovach, outraged, vowed to fight the charges.

"The whole thing was a totally fascist proceeding," he said later. He saw it as part of a continuing campaign to smear his good name, or, as he put it sarcastically, "I'm the guy who slaughtered the last woolly mammoth!"

The grand jury did nothing about Selby Gardens. There was no need. Selby's board and its attorneys had been negotiating the terms of surrender for several months.

"The Justice Department was coming up with as many ridiculous charges as they could," said Higgins, whose position of responsibility made him a target for the prosecution along with Lowman. "They were just beating us to death with it, so the lawyers started negotiating a plea deal."

If Selby balked, Colbourn could simply mention the grand jury. An indictment for a felony would create far more damaging publicity than being charged with a misdemeanor, not to mention ending Selby's access to federal grant money. A felony would carry a greater stigma for any gardens employees or board members who were charged, too. Someone convicted of a felony would lose the right to vote and to own firearms.

"At a certain point, the gardens knew that we had to get past this issue and go forward," Caren Lobo, the bookstore owner, said. "We realized we were facing the power of the federal government, which has all the money and time in the world to do anything they want, and we're just a small garden in a small market." Agreeing to a plea deal "was the best solution to a difficult situation that we could come up with."

The growing stack of legal bills and the loss of major donors after Lowman's ouster put the board under a severe strain that it could no longer bear. It made more sense to cut their losses and move on, Scully explained.

"We were bleeding attorney's fees," he said.

Not everyone wanted to give up, though.

"I voted to fight it and not accept any guilt whatsoever," Carl Luer said. But the elderly ex-surgeon was on the losing end of the vote. Selby would cut a deal and plead guilty to breaking the law.

Less than a month after Kovach's indictment, on December 17, 2003, Colbourn filed a misdemeanor charge against Selby Gardens for "trade contrary to CITES and prohibited acts with endangered species." This was the deal Selby had agreed to with the prosecutor.

She also filed the identical charge against Higgins. The mustachioed scientist had reluctantly gone along with it, because that was what his bosses wanted.

Selby's attorney had discussed with Higgins the possibility of battling on alone, trying to prove he had committed no crime. But the attorney pointed out that he would have to do so at his own expense. The cost, Higgins was told, would be $30,000—minimum.

So Higgins swallowed his pride and his belief in his own innocence and agreed to plead guilty to a misdemeanor. Sure, it would be a blemish on an otherwise spotless life, but as he pointed out later, "I never planned to work anywhere else but Selby Gardens, and as long as I wasn't seeking employment anywhere else it should be okay."

Still, he said, after spending twenty-six years serving his country in the Coast Guard, pleading guilty to a federal charge like this seemed "like a bit of an insult."

The plea agreement for both Selby and Higgins spelled out exactly what they were acknowledging they had done wrong:

"The elements of Count One are:

"First: knowingly possessed;

"Second: a specimen;

"Third: that had been traded contrary to CITES;

"Fourth: knowing that the specimen had been traded, i.e., imported, in some way illegally; and/or

"First: knowingly exported;

"Second: a specimen;

"Third: contrary to the provisions of the Convention on International Trade in Endangered Species of Wild Flora and Fauna (CITES)."

In other words, they were wrong to accept the plant from Kovach, wrong to possess it (even a piece of it, as Atwood had), and wrong to export any part of it back to Peru because they knew that it had been illegally imported by Kovach. Thus the step the orchid boys had taken to protect Selby—returning the specimen to Peru—had shot their employer in the foot.

As part of his plea deal, Higgins also agreed to sit down with Colbourn to discuss turning state's evidence. The evidence she wanted concerned Lowman. The prosecutor clearly did not believe a woman as smart as Lowman could have been so far out of the loop when it came to the science staff's work, not to mention so naïve about the law's requirements.

"What she really wanted me to do is throw Lowman under the bus," Higgins said years later. Although he had no love for Lowman, Higgins just couldn't deliver what Colbourn sought: evidence of something other than neglect.

"She kept trying to put words in my mouth," Higgins said. "She kept fishing for something that would show Lowman knew what we did was illegal, or that she thought the gardens could make money on it."

To Higgins, the prosecutor was the naïve one.

"In a botanical garden," he said, "you don't get rich off discovering new species." Still, he conceded, "Kovach thought *he* would."

After nearly an hour of questioning, Higgins said, "finally they gave up. They weren't getting exactly what they wanted."

Later, when she wrote a report about Higgins's testimony, Agent Holt recounted what he said about Kovach's visit to the OIC and what his colleagues did and said. She did not include one word about Colbourn's questions concerning Meg Lowman.

On January 6, 2004, Selby Gardens, through its attorneys from Holland & Knight, officially pleaded guilty, thus becoming the first botanical gardens in U.S. history to be found guilty of breaking the law. The only board member present was Barbara Hansen, her silver hair gleaming under the courtroom's indirect lighting.

When it came Higgins's turn, though, there was a glitch. The magistrate accepting Higgins's change of plea to guilty balked. The magistrate said he wasn't sure a crime had been committed. But a deal was a deal, and the attorneys persuaded him to proceed, despite his clear misgivings.

Four months later, on April 9, 2004, U.S. District Judge Susan Bucklew officially sentenced Selby Gardens to the penalty that its board had agreed to accept. Selby would serve three years of probation and pay a $5,000 fine, which was of course a far more lenient penalty than the potential maximum fine of $100,000.

"I suppose you'd say it was a slap on the wrist," Barbara Hansen told a reporter for the *St. Petersburg Times*. "We didn't think we were doing anything wrong, but it turned out we did, and we're sorry we did."

At Colbourn's insistence, Selby's trustees had agreed to some special conditions on the institution's sentence—conditions that orchid fans viewed as evidence that the Justice Department didn't know anything about how either the orchid world or the science of taxonomy works.

Selby had to agree to write a letter to all the other botanical gardens, explaining what the OIC staff had done wrong and warning the others not to make the same mistake. Selby had to take out a full-page ad in *Orchids* magazine—headlined "Please Learn from Our Experience"—detailing its criminal acts and apologizing for them. Finally came the condition that had orchidophiles around the country rolling their eyes: Selby agreed to petition the international scientific body in charge of naming species to withdraw the name *Phragmipedium kovachii* and substitute the name Christenson used, *Phragmipedium peruvianum*.

"It's not a good idea to name an orchid after anybody who brought it into the country illegally," Hansen explained to the *Times* reporter. But orchid experts knew that such a petition would likely be doomed to failure.

After dealing with Selby's penalty, Judge Bucklew sentenced Higgins to two years of probation with six months of house arrest. He also was hit with a $2,000 fine.

On his way out of the courthouse, Higgins stopped off at the probation office and wrote a check for the full amount of his fine. Later, Atwood and other friends and colleagues made some phone calls on his behalf, and sympathizers in the orchid community reimbursed him for some of it—but ultimately they would be unable to make up for everything he was going to lose.

Even after nailing Selby and Higgins, Colbourn continued pursuing Lowman, determined to get her convicted of something as well.

"There were facts in the mix that they really stretched to be incriminating in some way," said Lowman's Tallahassee attorney, Robert Rivas. "They kept offering more and more favorable plea bargains, and she kept rejecting them. They just wanted somebody who was at the top."

Rivas, spoiling for a fight, wanted to push the government into officially charging her and then taking the case to trial. He was sure he could not only get her acquitted but also embarrass the prosecution. He said his attitude toward the Justice Department could be summed up in four words: "You ain't got shit."

But Lowman's husband urged caution, Rivas said. He pointed out that no one could predict how a trial might turn out. Better to keep an open mind, and an open ear, to any offers. So the negotiations continued.

Even as Lowman and Kovach continued struggling against the government, though, there was another struggle under way—one that would determine the fate of not just the *Phragmipedium kovachii,* but of all future orchid discoveries.

14

The Hike from Hell

We are abysmally ignorant of the ecology of tropical
orchids. Nearly all the attention has been focused on their
taxonomy, the distribution of orchid plants or how they are
pollinated. We know very little about how they "fit" into
their environment.

Harold Koopowitz, *Orchids and Their Conservation*

The first picture Glen Decker saw of a *Phragmipedium kovachii* was the one
that showed a slightly wilted bloom stretched across Chady Moore's hand.

Decker's first impression: Had to be fake. *Had* to be. Somebody must be
playing around with Adobe Photoshop. No way a slipper orchid blossom
could be bigger than someone's hand. Just not possible.

When he found out it was real, Decker knew he had to have one. No matter what it took, no matter how he did it.

Decker, a brash and bearded New Yorker, had been growing orchids since
he was fifteen. He now ran a business called Piping Rock Orchids. He was
a good businessman. He didn't mind if he sometimes had to cut a few ethical or legal corners in his pursuit of profit. When it came to his favorite
flowers, he was willing to admit he had an addiction. He called himself an
"orchid-holic."

So when he got wind of an upcoming expedition to Peru to see this amazing orchid in its native habitat, he didn't let anything stop him from signing
up.

"I invited myself along," he said.

The expedition had been cooked up by none other than Dr. Rolando, the eye surgeon who had taken a strong personal interest in the fate of the famous flower.

As usual, his critics figured this for some slick maneuver. Rolando had recently paid for Ricardo Fernandez, the Peruvian expert who had coauthored the special *Selbyana* publication, to travel to Selby for further research. In an e-mail to Stig Dalström about how he would come up with the money for Fernandez, Rolando wrote, "The Peruvian jungle will provide Ricardo's ticket."

Dalström took that as a hint that Rolando might be involved in some orchid harvesting that INRENA would frown on.

Others viewed Rolando as a man who was fiercely proud of his country and its natural bounty, and who wanted to show it off to foreigners. That's why he wanted to organize this trip.

"He wanted to promote all things Peruvian," *Orchid Digest* editor Harold Koopowitz said. "He saw this as an opportunity for Peru."

At a London orchid show in early 2003, Rolando tracked down Koopowitz and proposed the trip to see *Phragmipedium kovachii* growing in the wild. He wanted Koopowitz to write a big feature on the orchid for his magazine and publish some artistic photos of it, too.

"He kept bugging me," Koopowitz said. "He said, 'Why don't we go down there and look at it?' So we ended up with an expedition."

As the trip took shape, Koopowitz and Decker made for an odd pair. They even sounded like opposites. Decker, the aggressive businessman, spoke with something of a Noo Yawk accent. The more reticent and bookish Koopowitz had a silky British voice that made him sound like the villainous James Mason in *North by Northwest*.

They rounded out their group with a botanical artist from Brooklyn named Angela Mirro; a professional photographer salivating at shooting pictures of the notorious orchid; and several others interested in being among the first U.S. citizens to see this plant in its native habitat. They departed for Lima in May 2003, while Elinor Colbourn and the grand jury in Tampa continued digging into what happened with that first *Phragmipedium kovachii*.

Once the group landed in Peru, they were joined by the nursery owner Alfredo Manrique, who like Karol Villena had been showing orchids at the Redland show in May 2002. Manrique stood six foot two with pepper-and-salt hair and glasses. Everyone, even Lee Moore, praised him as a nice guy. Decker saw in him a fatal flaw when it came to business.

"He wouldn't do anything remotely illegal," Decker said. "He's a Boy Scout."

Alfredo Manrique worked for months to get government permission to gather just five *Phragmipedium kovachii* from the wild. Photo courtesy of Alfredo Manrique.

Thus, while other Peruvian orchid collectors had been stripping the countryside of wild *kovachii*, Manrique had spent three months patiently negotiating with INRENA officials to get a permit to legally collect them. He was the first one to ask, and eventually the first one to have his request granted.

Manrique wanted to cultivate the new orchid through a process called micropropagation, a process for asexual reproduction of plants that he had learned from the Canadian expert Peter Croezen. It was a way to flood the market and wipe out the incentive to smuggle the wild orchids out of the country.

If Manrique's plan worked, Koopowitz was convinced it could show the way to deal with all future orchid discoveries, still comply with CITES, and also protect orchids growing in the wild. But a lot could go wrong, too. Manrique risked wasting a lot of his time and money on it, and losing out to less scrupulous orchid collectors.

The tour group took a side trip to view the ancient ruins of Machu Picchu, where Rolando's orchid walk entertained tourists. Then they flew to Tarapota. In the airport there, the same one Kovach had passed through just a year before, Koopowitz noticed a poster that he found striking. The poster, he wrote later, featured "a poor photograph of *Phragmipedium kovachii*, proclaiming it a protected plant."

Koopowitz did not know it, but the photos on the INRENA warning poster were the same ones published in *Selbyana*: the potted flower sitting on the hood of the car, and the wilted bloom in Chady Moore's hand—the photo that had gotten Decker so excited. It was like a wanted poster that accidentally showed the suspect as he was escaping from jail.

Outside the airport sat a van with three men inside: a hired driver; Chady Moore's friend Manuel Camacho Vela; and Camacho's seventeen-year-old son, Juan. Camacho, whom Lee Moore considered the sharpest wild orchid hunter in Peru, told them he knew a farmer who had recently found two thousand of the newly discovered orchids on a piece of remote land. He had arranged permission for them to photograph the plants.

The next day Rolando's tour group slung their gear into the van and drove up into the mountains to see the plants. As they drove, a tropical shower began pouring down. It was still pouring when they reached the small farm where they would have to begin hiking into the jungle.

As a result, most of the slipper safari crew—including the professional photographer—decided to leave their gear behind rather than risk getting it soaked. It wouldn't be that far anyway. Rolando had said the site was fairly close to the road, maybe just a ninety-minute hike along gentle slopes. They could return the next day, when the weather might be better, to take photos.

Decker and Koopowitz opted to bring their cameras anyway, just in case the next day's weather turned out to be even worse. While the others were wearing sneakers or hiking boots, Koopowitz and a few others slipped on gumboots that they believed would work better under such adverse conditions. Koopowitz's knee-high boots were brand-new, and he was glad they weren't too tight on his toes.

They all shook hands with the farmer and set out to see the orchids he had found. The group climbed a ridge above the farm, then clambered along a slippery path down the other side.

"The footpath seemed muddy and I was pleased with how well the traction on the new gumboots worked, congratulating myself on my sensible choice of footwear," Koopowitz wrote afterward. "I was to regret this later on."

The path began climbing upward again, a steeper climb now. Thanks to the rain, the route had turned into a thick quagmire.

They came to a stream and realized they would have to ford it by jumping from rock to rock. That's the point where Angela Mirro and the other women in the group decided to turn back. Rolando and Camacho's son volunteered to show them the way back. The rest of the men pressed on.

Soon the rain let up and the skies cleared. The mud-spattered travelers dawdled a bit, pausing to enjoy the wide variety of flowering orchids they spotted along the way—*Maxillaria, Masdevallia, Epidendrum,* and what Koopowitz called "a stunning *Stenorrhynchos* with an inflorescence of brilliant scarlet bracts and flowers. The heads were bent like a shepherd's crook."

As they struggled upward, Koopowitz became the first to slip and fall into the mud. His colleagues laughed. He had lost a bet. He would have to buy everyone drinks at the end of the day. Soon, though, the others flailed their arms and fell as well. Slipping and sliding, the muddy crew pressed on.

By then Koopowitz had noticed something was wrong with his boots. Finally he figured it out: they were a half size too big. Whenever a step went wrong and he sank ankle deep into the mud, his struggles to get free would accidentally pull the boot off his foot. Then he would have to perch one-legged until he could work the boot free and put it back on.

"The others, of course, thought this was a great joke," Koopowitz wrote later.

Soon they ran across an old homestead, apparently uninhabited but for a pair of dogs, some ducks, a cow, and a mule. The livestock had deposited their own smelly contributions amid the mud, making the terrain even worse than before.

Yet the group kept going, crossing more rivers. Feeling exhaustion creeping up on him, Koopowitz pointed to his watch and, using sign language, asked the farmer and Camacho how much longer until they reached their destination.

"*Viente minutos,*" they said. Twenty minutes.

Thirty minutes later, the sun had come out and heated up the air so everyone was sweating. Koopowitz asked his question again, and got the same answer.

By now the hikers were hungry and thirsty, and thinking with regret about all the backpacks they had left sitting in the van. In addition to the camera equipment, the backpacks had contained their food and, more importantly, their water.

Koopowitz asked a third time how much further, and a third time was told, "*Viente minutos.*" He checked his watch. Four hours had passed since they had set out on what Koopowitz now regarded as "the hike from hell."

If they turned around and headed back, they still might not reach the farm by sunset.

"There was no way we could negotiate the path in the dark," Koopowitz said. "In that case we might as well lie down and die. This was almost an attractive alternative."

At last, four and a half hours after they started, they rounded a bend in a river and saw ahead of them a steep cliff.

"There, perched on the cliff, were hundreds of *Phragmipedium kovachii*," Koopowitz wrote. "Somehow we had made it."

The orchids grew in enormous clumps on the steep and unshaded incline, amid hummocks of brown moss that apparently served the same purpose as the sphagnum moss that Atwood had used in Vermont.

Exhausted and filthy, the group spent an hour at the site, taking photos, checking the soil acidity, measuring the leaves. They were determined to make the most of their visit since none of them ever wanted to return.

At one point, they spotted some other travelers—a trio of young men, coming up the path after them. Camacho signaled for Koopowitz and the others to pretend they were watching birds in the trees across the river, not the flowers. If the locals knew what was here, and what it was worth, they would strip the place bare. Once the intruders had gone past, Decker and his fellow orchid-holics could go back to drinking in the amazing sight they had struggled so hard to reach.

Now Decker and Koopowitz learned the real reason they had been invited on the hike. The farmer who owned the site viewed them as potential buyers.

"He offered us all the plants for $10,000," Decker said.

Decker found the offer tempting.

"This was the most magnificent orchid found in a hundred years or more," he said. "Everyone was licking their chops to make money off of it."

But first they had to get back to civilization, back to their gear—and their water.

On the return trip, they no longer dawdled to look at the wild orchids along the path. And nobody was joking about slipping down or buying drinks. The travelers just wanted to make it back alive.

This time the hike took them three long, miserable hours. Koopowitz tore the nails on several toes. The lack of water took its toll on them all.

"Coming back, my legs were cramping because I was dehydrated," Decker said. "I could only walk fifty or sixty feet and then I'd have to stop."

He would stride ahead of the group, "and then I'd wait for them to catch up with me. But at one point it was just sit on a rock and say, 'Come back and get me tomorrow.'"

To lighten his load, Decker finally paid one of their guides to carry his gear for him. The price turned out to be a high one.

"I learned a lesson there," he said. "Bribe the guides before you start. It's cheaper."

Somehow they made it back to the van, piled aboard, and headed for their hotel. Koopowitz checked his watch. Their hike, start to finish, had taken nine hours.

On the drive back, they stopped at a small roadside restaurant for dinner. To get into the café required climbing four small steps to the door.

"Each step was only about four inches high," Koopowitz wrote later. "They might as well have been four foot tall. My body had had enough."

The next day, Camacho guided Alfredo Manrique back up the path to collect his five legally sanctioned orchids. He offered to take the others, but according to Koopowitz they "blanched at the idea" of making that trip again.

Instead, Decker said, he and Koopowitz discussed the farmer's offer, the pros and the cons.

"Harold and I sat there all day trying to figure out how to do it," Decker said. They knew if they bought the plants, they would have to move them to someplace secure, where no one could steal them.

"But they were illegal to collect as well as illegal to export," he said. That meant no digging them up and moving them unless they wanted to risk getting in trouble with the Peruvian authorities.

Ultimately they had to say no thanks. The only orchids collected on their trip were the five that Manrique had permission to pluck. Fortunately for Angela Mirro, one of them then bloomed in his greenhouse so she was able to produce a painting for Koopowitz to publish in his magazine.

"It was incredible," Mirro said later. "Nobody had ever seen anything like it. The petals were very velvety. It was just—" she paused, searching for the right word "—*luscious.*"

Later, Mirro returned to Peru to paint an even better *kovachii* bloom in Manrique's greenhouse. That *kovachii* painting wound up being displayed in the Smithsonian Institution in 2010 as part of a special exhibit about endangered plants called "Losing Paradise?"

Although he had to pass up buying the field full of orchids, Koopowitz didn't leave completely empty-handed. He brought back his photos and an exclusive cover story for *Orchid Digest.*

He also brought back something he didn't want.

Glen Decker's obsession with the *Phragmipedium kovachii* survived "the hike from hell," but he reluctantly passed up the offer to buy an entire field full of them. Photo courtesy of Glen Decker.

"I picked up a dreadful disease while I was there, Oroya fever," he said. The disease can be fatal if left untreated.

Fortunately for Koopowitz, after he landed in an emergency room with what everyone figured must be a heart attack, a doctor who learned he had visited Peru looked up the symptoms and made the correct diagnosis.

"It's spread by microbacteria," Koopowitz said. "It has a long incubation period so it developed six or seven months after the trip. It came from a sand fly bite."

Decker came home from Peru with his own disease—orchid addiction—showing no sign of abating despite his horrible experience. He was even more determined to get into the *Phragmipedium kovachii* business. He cut a deal with Manrique to distribute whatever he could grow from micropropagation, assuming INRENA would give its blessing. Peter Croezen cut a similar deal for the right to sell Manrique's *kovachii* in Canada.

Six weeks after their trip, Decker said, he got word that someone else had gone to the site they had visited and stripped it of every single orchid. It was as if hook-handed Benedict Roezl had risen from the dead to begin wreaking havoc on the jungle once more.

Clearly, there was still a thriving black-market demand for the infamous flower.

Not long after the group left Peru, rumors began to spread about the Koopowitz hike.

One version said that the *Orchid Digest* editor and his friends were the ones actually responsible for stripping the site. Another said that his group had taken so many rare orchids out that they needed a helicopter to carry all the bags. Decker laughed about that one. If only there *had* been a helicopter!

One of the people spreading the rumors was Manuel Arias Silva. "El Professore" had gotten the second license from INRENA to collect five and only five *Phragmipedium kovachii* for micropropagation, just like Manrique.

In July 2003, Arias sent an e-mail about that to his Texas customer George Norris, the grower who wrote everything in all capitals. Norris then forwarded Arias's message to dozens of people, including Wesley Higgins, Bob Scully, Dr. Rolando, Karol Villena, Lee Moore, and even Kovach himself.

Norris explained he was doing this because Moore was spreading lies about who was yanking all the *Phragmipedium kovachii* plants out of the jungle to sell to collectors: "LEE IS ALSO MY FRIEND BUT I DON'T AGREE WITH HIM SHIFTING ALL THE FAULT TO OTHERS."

In the letter that Norris forwarded, Arias dropped his usual polite façade. He first blasted his Peruvian competitors: "Lee Moore and Karol Villena never received permission to collect any plants of *kovachii* and [it] is not possible they will receive Peruvian CITES in the future."

Anyone buying plants from them or any of several people he named as their friends—including Dr. Rolando—"can never legally sell this plant or any hybrids made from it," he wrote.

Then Arias attacked the Koopowitz expedition.

"Manrique, Rolando, and some Americans collected many plants in May of this year," Arias wrote. "This was three weeks before I collected my five plants. I have seen many collected plants of *kovachii* with other people and I know some have already been shipped out of Peru. One of the Americans here was the editor of the *Orchid Digest* magazine. It is probable he will publish an article about the habitat for the *kovachii*. This will further damage the dwindling stock of plants still remaining in the wild. This should not be allowed to happen but it is beyond my control."

Arias boasted that he had "collected in this area, just myself and my worker, and took the allowable five plants. . . . My plants are all legal."

Not so The Adventurer, he contended. Arias wrote that Moore "is still taking small quantities of these plants and green seed pods illegally to the U.S. to another secret greenhouse in the Miami area where they are being quietly sold."

Moore, he wrote, used to work closely with the Villena family, but not any more: "At this time, he and the Villenas are at war in competition over illegally collected *Phrag. kovachii*."

A week after passing along Arias's complaints, Norris sent out a second e-mail to scores of people. This one advertised his upcoming sales, including one very special item: "IT IS ALSO POSSIBLE THAT WE MAY HAVE SOME VERY LEGAL *PHRAG. KOVACHII* (COMPLETE WITH GOOD CITES DOCUMENTS) AFTER THE FIRST OF THE YEAR . . . AND THEY WILL NOT REQUIRE BANK LOANS AND CO-SIGNERS TO BUY THEM. THERE WILL NOT BE MANY, MAYBE ONLY 10 BUT . . . THEY WILL BE LEGAL TO OWN."

He ended it with, "GOOD GROWIN' Y'ALL, THE OLD ORCHID WRANGLER."

Among the people who received Norris's prospectus was Eric Christenson. The freelance taxonomist found the claims of legality more than a little dubious.

Christenson immediately forwarded Norris's e-mail to Agent Holt.

"It is truly inconceivable that INRENA would give permission to anyone to export *Phragmipedium kovachii*," he wrote. "I just thought that you should know that the rumors are starting that legal plants of this species are a possibility."

What Christenson didn't know was that the Fish and Wildlife Service was already investigating the Norris-Arias orchid-smuggling connection.

The tip came in April 2002, two months before Kovach's visit to Selby Gardens upset the Peruvian government.

An American orchid grower was showing off his collection to a Fish and Wildlife Service agent and mentioned, in passing, that a lot of orchid fanciers suspected Norris of dealing in contraband plants.

When investigators checked with USDA offices around the country, they learned that several of Norris's orchid shipments had been regarded as highly suspect.

So the feds set up a sting. They arranged to have someone buy some Peruvian slipper orchids from Norris, then ask for the CITES documents that showed they were legal plants.

At first Norris put the buyer off. Eventually, though, he sent the buyer a document that looked legitimate. When Fish and Wildlife Service experts studied it closely, though, they could tell it was fake.

In October 2003, three months after Christenson sent Agent Holt his note about Norris, Fish and Wildlife Service agents got a judge to sign a warrant and raided George Norris's home.

They spent more than three hours searching his office and greenhouse. They found no illegal orchids, but they hauled off twenty boxes of files as well as his computer.

They also had him write a short affidavit, just like the one Kovach wrote for Agent Holt. In it, Norris contended that the only plants he imported from Peru were "artificially propagated." However, he added, his definition of "artificial" meant any plant that had ever been touched by human hands, specifically including "potting, planting, mounting, watering, trimming, fertilizing, or anything else done by someone to the plant."

Still, the raiders told him he wasn't being charged with anything—not yet. When they left, Norris regained some of his normal bravado.

"Let me assure y'all that they are just fishing . . . and they won't find nuttin," Norris boasted in a posting on the *Orchid Guide Digest*'s Internet forum (where his penchant for capitals was for once toned down).

He mocked the raiding party as "the Plant Gestapo" and insisted, "I have always obeyed the laws, my plants are all legal and they won't find anything except some really terrible jokes on my computer."

Not one of those three statements turned out to be true.

A sympathetic Arias sent Norris some money for a lawyer, and a letter saying in somewhat fractured English that he was "surprised by the incursion . . . to your domicile."

But in a way, Arias wrote, it was understandable because everyone was on edge at that moment, and all for one reason: "The authorities of my country are very worried by the illegal exit of *Phragmipedium kovachii* plants."

15

The Courtroom Drama

We have strict statutes and most biting laws, the needful bits
and curbs to headstrong weeds.

William Shakespeare, *Measure for Measure*

Facing the power of the federal government, Kovach felt more alone than
he'd ever felt in his life.

He knew the charges against him could send him to prison for years. He
knew he also risked a fine of up to $100,000. He knew, too, that any allies he
might have once had in the orchid world had melted away.

He had once believed the entire membership of the American Orchid Society would rise up and rush to his defense. When they did not, Kovach drew
his own conclusions about why.

"Half of them are smugglers themselves," he said later. "The other half are
liars and hypocrites."

He couldn't look to the experts at Selby Gardens for help, either. The prosecutor had listed two of them, Stig Dalström and John Atwood, as potential
expert witnesses. They would testify that any orchid grower would know a
Phragmipedium when he saw it.

When Kovach talked about the case, he sometimes cast himself as a lonely
patriot whose dissent regarding the current regime had put him in the government's crosshairs.

"There was a political aspect to this," he said years later. "I was very anti-
war and anti–George Bush, and I made that clear to people in my lectures."

He said that his actions at the Miami airport had exposed a weak link in the nation's security. "Remember, eight months after 9/11, we embarrassed the hell out of" the Transportation Security Agency, he said. As a result, "they were out to get me."

Initially Kovach had relied on the advice of a Virginia lawyer. But once he was indicted in Tampa, he hired two Tampa attorneys more familiar with federal court there.

Jack Fernandez and Robert Hearn made a perfect legal team. Hearn, slender and bald before age forty, excelled at digging into legal minutiae and producing air-tight motions. Hearn could see a case not only as a legal problem but also as a philosophical and moral one. He wished Kovach had come to them while the grand jury was working on the case, not after.

"We wouldn't have let him be indicted," he said.

Fernandez, a Tampa native, was the son of a chemistry professor. He was more than a decade older than Hearn, with a thick head of brown hair and a mustache flecked with gray. A back-slapping extrovert, Fernandez had served in the navy as a fighter pilot before attending law school. He relished the combat of court, the need to think on your feet and respond in a split second. He had been a federal prosecutor prior to going into private practice, so he knew how to see a case from the other side.

Fernandez flew to Virginia to visit the new client and his wife. The three of them sat on Kovach's front porch, sipping iced tea and watching the sun set over the mountains. Their conversation ranged far beyond the case itself.

"He is an absolutely lovely guy," Fernandez said. "He's a Renaissance man. If you want to talk about Shakespeare, he can talk about Shakespeare."

When the attorney wandered through Kovach's house, he noticed that "every wall was absolutely covered with photos of orchids." But when he looked in Kovach's postraid greenhouse, he recalled years later, "it was absolutely devastated. They took everything except some crappy-looking weeds."

As Hearn and Fernandez pored over the case files, they were struck by how much effort the government had put into prosecuting their client over a flower. Hearn joked more than once that "whatever part of my taxes went to fund this prosecution, I want my ten cents back. That's not what I'm paying the government guys to do."

The attorneys decided that the best evidence for the defense was Kovach himself. They liked the story he told, the one about how he'd tried to do the right thing in Miami. They liked that he said his only intention was to protect his namesake orchid. They liked that he had contacted the USDA before anyone ever told him about the investigation.

Before the pair could file their first motion, though, their case got a big assist from one of the prosecution's key witnesses.

Stig Dalström had been in Sweden all summer. As a freelance artist, he could take his vacation whenever he wanted. He usually spent it fishing in his native country.

But instead of enjoying his angling, he said, he kept thinking about his grand jury testimony, the testimony that said Kovach had kept an orchid. He spent so much time distracted by it that it had ruined his trip.

Now, with Kovach already indicted, Dalström wanted to change his story.

"During the summer in Sweden I spent a lot of time trying to remember what exactly had happened and I realized to my great surprise . . . that I wasn't sure anymore," he explained years later. "The more I thought about it, and talked to the others involved, the less certain I became. I therefore had to revise my statement."

So he went back to the grand jury to rewrite his story.

The prosecutor wasn't happy about it, he noticed. Colbourn, he said, "was quite pissed with me at that time. I think she gave me the Evil Eye more than once in that courtroom."

She asked him again about the events of June 5, 2002, and what Kovach did: "Did he bring a plant into Marie Selby Botanical Gardens?"

"Yes he did," Dalström said.

"Or more than one plant?"

"No," Dalström said. "I only saw one plant. I may have said in the past that it was my understanding that he gave me—he gave a division of that plant to make the herbarium specimen, but since you asked about that specifically last time, I've been thinking a lot about that. As far as I remember, there was only one plant. I never saw more than one plant."

Dalström said seeing Kovach's big flower had confused him.

"Well, when I took off the flower and the spike, the beauty—what I saw, what I was in awe at was the beautiful flower," he said, stammering. "When you take off the flower and the spike, all of a sudden you see ratty-looking leaves and it's not as impressive anymore. I think that's what fooled me. I just didn't, you know, combine the beautiful flower that he had with that little ratty-looking thing he gave for processing because the flower and the spike had been taken off."

When he left the witness stand, Agent Holt gave him a warning: If the case ever went to trial, the prosecutor "didn't want me anywhere near a courtroom," Dalström said later. It was easy to understand why. At best, he muddied the waters. At worst, he could give a jury grounds for reasonable doubt.

Still, Colbourn had two other witnesses who had sworn that Kovach had kept at least one of these valuable plants—the two American Orchid Society judges who were friends with Wesley Higgins. She had Higgins's version, in which Kovach offered to give Selby a second plant, implying he had more illegal orchids with him. She had the video from Lee Moore in which Faustino Medina said he'd sold Kovach more than one flower. And she could use Kovach's own shifting stories, which contained enough potentially damning lines to cause his attorneys headaches.

Smart lawyers know that when you are unlikely to win on the facts, you attack the law. So that's what Kovach's attorneys tried next.

The motion Kovach's attorneys filed sought to dismiss the indictment against him. A motion to dismiss an indictment is an uncommon strategy in federal court, one that usually fails. But Hearn and Fernandez decided they had a pretty good argument, so why not give it a shot?

Their argument had been anticipated by some of the impassioned debate on the orchid growers' Internet forums. It went like this: CITES Appendix I forbids all trade in tropical slipper orchids such as *Phragmipedium kovachii*. But the new orchid that Kovach had found was not officially classified as a new slipper orchid species until the special issue of *Selbyana* went out in the mail. Until the orchid was officially named, therefore, Kovach could not have broken the law.

Even then it wasn't officially included on the Appendix I list, the attorneys contended, and could not be until the officials in charge of CITES put it on there.

In federal court, a motion such as this goes first to a magistrate, not the judge. The magistrate hears the oral arguments for and against it, then makes a recommendation to the judge overseeing the case. By making the magistrates deal with the preliminary skirmishes, the judges are free to concentrate on their trials.

The magistrate overseeing Kovach's case, Thomas Wilson, had worked for the Justice Department for nine years before he was appointed to the bench. He had been a magistrate for more than thirty years. With his long experience, he was not an easy man to impress or confuse.

At the hearing, Hearn and Fernandez spent nearly an hour pitching their argument to him. Colbourn used just thirty minutes rebutting it. Then Kovach's attorneys were allowed ten minutes to reply. Two weeks went by, and then the magistrate announced his recommendation.

"The defendant . . . concedes that he cannot identify any language in

CITES that restricts its scope to species that have been formally identified taxonomically," he wrote. "To the contrary, CITES, on its face, applies to all species of *Phragmipedium*, whether formally identified or not."

In the end, the decision hinged on three letters. Wilson pointed out that Appendix I of CITES protects the genus "*Phragmipedium* spp." but does not specify which species that means.

"The abbreviation 'spp.' means that *all species* of the genus *Phragmipedium* are protected," he wrote, underlining "all species" to emphasize his point. "Furthermore, it has been recognized that the use of 'spp.' is not merely a shorthand way of including all previously identified species of a genus, but rather a method of insuring that newly discovered species are protected as well."

Whether Kovach knew what he was carrying was contraband was a question that the prosecution would have to deal with in a trial, he wrote. But that was not enough to toss out the indictment. He recommended the charges stand. Despite strenuous objections from Kovach's attorneys, the federal judge overseeing his case agreed.

In the meantime, though, another smuggling case hit the headlines.

On March 3, 2004, Manuel Arias Silva landed at the Miami airport on his way to the Miami International Orchid Show. When he got to U.S. Customs, he handed over a declaration form that said he didn't have any plants with him.

Immigration officials, acting on a request from the Fish and Wildlife Service, detained him. In his luggage, Fish and Wildlife Service agents found thirteen orchids.

After letting him sweat for an hour, they took the sixty-nine-year-old "El Professore" to an interrogation room. They read him his rights, then said they wanted to ask him about slipper orchids—illegal slipper orchids.

Through an interpreter, Arias denied doing anything wrong. He said he had permits for everything, and "the only species of orchid he knows is illegal is *Phragmipedium kovachii*." He told the agents he had "never exported this species of orchid." In all his years in the business, he said, he "has never violated the law."

After an hour of hearing his repeated denials, the agents told Arias they didn't think he was being honest. They put him in a car to drive him to a federal detention center, where he would be held until he could see a judge to set a bond.

Riding in the car was the interpreter, a wily old federal investigator named Jorge Picon. A balding man with a gray mustache and calculating eyes, Picon was not only the special agent in charge of the Miami law enforcement office of the Fish and Wildlife Service. He was also the only agent in the Miami office who spoke Spanish—a situation he had repeatedly urged his bosses to rectify, a suggestion they had repeatedly ignored. Because he spoke Spanish, Picon often worked cases undercover, adopting the guise of "Senor Blanco," a shady Colombian in cowboy boots who dabbled in smuggled wildlife. Picon could be creative on these undercover cases, showing a flair for drama. Once he dressed another agent in a gorilla suit and sold the "ape" to a Mexican zoo official shopping on the black market.

Picon, only months from retirement after thirty years with the agency, knew all the tricks for how to draw out a suspect's secrets. During the ride to jail, he and Arias began chatting in Spanish, and at one point Picon stopped the car to buy Arias some fruit to eat.

Arias still did not confess to any crimes. But during his car-ride chat with Picon, he tried to save his skin by naming several other people involved in smuggling. These people, he said, were the ones smuggling the notorious *Phragmipedium kovachii*—not him.

Arias explained to Picon how they did it. Most of the time the contraband orchids were not shipped straight to the buyers, Arias said. Instead, they went by a more circuitous route, "exported to Ecuador and then shipped to Poland," Picon wrote in his report on their chat.

One collector in New York, Arias said, "has received up to twenty-five *P. kovachii* that had been shipped from Peru to the United States through Ecuador. He advised that these shipments were disguised as hybrid plants."

However, nothing Arias said was big news. Picon and his agents had heard all the same rumors before, and Arias offered them no corroboration that could lead to an arrest. So off to jail he went for two days, until a judge set a bond for his release until trial.

As soon as George and Kathy Norris heard what had happened to Arias, they scrambled to sell their Peruvian friend's flowers for him at the show. The Norrises guaranteed his $25,000 bail and $175,000 surety bond. They did it "because he was a close friend and there was no one else in the country to do it," Mrs. Norris later testified.

Arias had to give up his passport and agree to stay in the United States until his trial, so he moved in with the Norrises in Texas. However, Arias and Norris soon learned they were not just in the same house. They were in the same boat.

A federal grand jury meeting in Miami had indicted not only Arias but also George Norris. The indictment said Norris had been buying illegal orchids from Arias from 1998 until October 2003, when the feds searched his home.

Investigators said Arias would get INRENA permits authorizing the export to Norris of certain numbers of artificially propagated specimens of orchids. But then his packages would also include species not covered by the permit, plants he had paid people to pluck from the jungle. Arias would disguise them with fake labels and pack Styrofoam around the roots to make them look like they were produced in a greenhouse. Sometimes he would stack the legitimate plants on top and hide the smuggled ones underneath, counting on the inspectors to check only the top layer of flowers. Later, he would send Norris a key to identify the mislabeled plants. That way the Texan would know which ones were the ringers, the ones his customers would pay top price to obtain because they were forbidden fruit.

Much of the evidence cited in the indictment came from a series of e-mails and faxes between the two men that Fish and Wildlife Service agents had found when they raided Norris's house. For instance, in one all-caps message, Norris wrote to Arias: "AS ALWAYS, YOU CAN ADD ANY INTERESTING PLANTS THAT YOU GET BEFORE SHIPPING. MIAMI DOES NOT MATCH PLANTS TO THE CITES OR COUNT THE NUMBER OF PLANTS." And Arias, in a reply to one of Norris's requests for slipper orchids, told him, "Is possible to send *Ph.* Species only with other name (*Maxillaria*)."

Most of the messages between the two men about their illicit activities concluded with expressions of deep affection, such as "With much love and hugs to you all."

The indictment of superpatriot Norris undercut Kovach's argument that left-wing politics had put him in the Bush administration's crosshairs. If that were the case, Norris would have been immune from prosecution. Unlike Kovach, though, Norris appeared not to take the charges seriously.

In an interview with the *Houston Chronicle*, Norris pooh-poohed both the feds and the law they had charged him with breaking: "Selling these flowers doesn't diminish their number in the wild at all. It's not like we are constructing pipe bombs or selling pedophile material. We're talking flowers."

The indictment listed all the types of flowers that Arias had shipped to Norris under false labels. There were more than two thousand orchids covered by the charges, worth an estimated $45,000. Not one was a *Phragmipedium kovachii.*

Norris flew to Miami and voluntarily surrendered. He, too, was thrown in a holding cell pending a bond hearing. The other inmates—drug dealers and men prone to violent crimes—wondered why this gray-haired Texan had joined them. When he explained he had been busted over illegal orchids, one asked, "What do you do with these things, smoke 'em?"

Looking for a break, like Arias, Norris sat down with Colbourn and other prosecutors and investigators to blow the whistle on his fellow smugglers. Like Arias, he talked about people he'd heard had bought fake CITES certificates to hide their crimes. He named people he believed had a thousand or more smuggled *Phragmipedium kovachii* that had been routed through Ecuador. Some of the *kovachii* were shipped from Ecuador to Germany, to Austria, to Poland, he said. One Peruvian, he said, "brings in illegal orchids in his carry-on luggage into the U.S."

The hot spot for finding illegal *kovachii* and other smuggled orchids, he told the investigators, was the Redland show. He repeated the story that Chady and Lee Moore had circulated about Karol Villena hawking *kovachii* under the table at the 2002 show. He said that despite the furor over Kovach, a major Ecuadorean importer had smuggled in *kovachii* to sell at the 2003 show, too.

So in the days preceding the 2004 Redland show, agents swooped down on some of the people and businesses that Norris had identified. They intercepted a shipment from the Ecuadorean orchid nursery that Norris had named. It contained nearly fifty orchids that weren't included on its CITES permit, so they confiscated them all. None were *Phragmipedium kovachii*, though. The seizure led to no charges.

At the show, agents casually walked around Karol Villena's booth. They brought along an orchid expert who charged the government $100 an hour to serve as an inspector. Their expert reported seeing strong indications that "many of the orchids on display were wild-collected."

But without a warrant allowing them to confiscate Villena's inventory, the expert couldn't risk spending much time examining the plants. Norris told the agents they were missing out, because he was sure she "had brought the *Ph. kovachii* from Peru into the United States smuggled in her purse," they wrote in their report. They did not, however, arrest her, either.

But there was one man Norris named that they thought was worth interrogating.

At 9:30 a.m. on May 14, 2004, the springtime temperature in Miami was already above 80 degrees and climbing. Alfredo Manrique stepped off a plane from Peru and, for the first time in his life, a customs official did not

immediately stamp his passport and allow him to proceed to the luggage carousel.

Instead, he was pulled aside to a glassed-in immigration office that foreign passengers had nicknamed "the fish tank." After cooling his heels there for a bit, he was allowed to retrieve his luggage—which immigration officials then searched. When they found no contraband plants, they stamped his passport at last.

But he wasn't free yet. Manrique had shipped orchids to Miami ahead of his flight, expecting to display and sell them at the Redland show. He learned that the plants he had shipped ahead of him had been seized. They were being held at the USDA's plant inspection and fumigation building, known colloquially as "the smokehouse"—the building Kovach had skipped visiting when he landed in Miami two years before. Manrique was told he'd have to go retrieve the orchids in person.

At the smokehouse, when he peeked through the windows, he saw five Fish and Wildlife Service employees in full uniforms, wearing pistols on their hips and latex gloves on their hands. The uniformed officers were digging through boxes of orchids and snapping photos of the plants.

They called Manrique inside. There he met two men, one in uniform, one in more casual clothing. They showed him their credentials. One was an agent of the U.S. Fish and Wildlife Service. The other worked for the USDA.

They said he wasn't under arrest. They just had some questions. He said he'd to try to answer them.

They quizzed him about his facilities in Peru, what he was doing in Miami, how he got permits for export. They asked him if Peruvian inspectors took bribes. Manrique said he never paid any bribes. They asked if INRENA was corrupt. He said he didn't know about that.

Then the agents got to the point.

"They told me that someone tipped them against me and Karol," Manrique recalled later. "Then they said if I had any clue about who was their informer. I said that the only name that come to my mind was Manuel Arias Silva."

Manrique told the investigators that he had probably been accused only because Arias wanted to get rid of a competitor in the *kovachii* business.

"I am the only one allowed to have the plants legally," Manrique told them. "If they destroy my reputation, then they could get someone else to do it. We are talking of millions of dollars."

They told him it wasn't Arias that fingered him, but they didn't say who had.

About 4:00 p.m. they told him he could go to his hotel, but without his orchids. He would have to come back to the smokehouse the next day at 9:00 a.m. They asked his permission to search his orchid shipment. Sure, he said, no problem.

When he came back the next morning, they made him wait outside for more than an hour. Finally, the two investigators who had questioned him came out pushing a cart. On it were his plants.

They said they had found nothing amiss. They gave him their business cards, thanked him for his time, and told him he was free to go.

Manrique frowned at being targeted by some unknown enemy. Despite the agents' denials, he was sure Arias was behind it somehow.

Manrique and his orchids arrived at the Redland show about 2:00 p.m. on its second day. Everyone seemed surprised to see him. They had heard he was in jail.

Manrique got another surprise a little later. He spotted Arias himself, out on bond and recently relocated to a friend's house in Miami, walking around the show with his held high as if nothing was wrong.

George Norris was there, too. When he saw Arias, his old friend told him, "Good-bye, George." Norris says he had no idea what was about to happen.

~ 🙰

Unlike Kovach, Arias did not put up much of a fight against his charges. On May 13, 2004, just two months after his arrest, El Professore stood up in a Miami courtroom and pleaded guilty to smuggling orchids.

The judge set a sentencing date for several months later, giving the probation office time to write a report recommending whether to send him to prison. Meanwhile Arias obtained a new passport and, shortly after his surprise appearance at the Redland show, hopped a plane for Lima, never to return.

"He up and scooted," Norris said later. "I can well understand why he did it. I would've gotten the hell out of Dodge too if I could have."

Arias sent the judge a letter from Lima to apologize, sort of.

In it, Arias said he had fled because his wife was sick and needed him. He said he wanted "to express my true feelings of sorry for the offenses committed and to assure sincerely, from the very deep of my heart, that I will never, for what the rest of my life, intend any action that incur in any other offence like those I pleaded guilty to before your court."

He closed by saying he "would only like to implore for your mercy and pray God for a day in which this nightmare my family and I are living be over some day. You have my word that these mistakes will never happen.

Manuel Arias Silva (*left*) enjoyed a close relationship with officials such as Betty Millian (*right*), the top CITES expert in Peru. When the U.S. Justice Department tried to extradite him, he hired a former prime minister to argue his case. Photo courtesy of Stig Dalström.

May God compensate your mercy and compassion. I beg your pardon and implore your mercy. God bless you."

The plea for mercy would have carried more weight had the author shown up in person. Since he did not, the judge sentenced him in absentia to twenty-one months behind bars, three years of probation, and a $5,000 fine.

In an odd bit of boasting, the Justice Department sent out a press release trumpeting the sentence, yet failing to mention that the guest of honor had skipped the party.

Reporters in Peru tracked down the gentlemanly "El Professore" at his home. They confronted the fugitive in his driveway. They asked him about fleeing from American justice and leaving his partner holding the bag. The ever-polite Arias surprised them.

"Far from offering a response," they wrote, "Arias decided to throw insults."

Colbourn tried to extradite Arias from Peru. He hired an influential former prime minister as his attorney in Lima. The case went all the way to the top of the Peruvian government. Ultimately, the president and cabinet rejected the extradition demand. Peru refused to return Arias to the Americans. He would remain a free man—as long as he never again set foot in the United States.

Because Arias had fled the country, the Norrises lost the $200,000 they had put up to help their longtime friend get out of jail, putting the elderly couple even deeper in a financial hole. Abandoned by the man he had regarded as his friend, Norris now had to battle on alone, just like his old protégé Kovach.

The last defendant in the Selby case finally cut a deal, too. But it was such a comedown from what the government had been seeking that the Justice Department didn't bother with a press release.

Meg Lowman had avoided being indicted by a grand jury or charged by prosecutors. She repeatedly refused a deal. She said she had "steadfastly refused to admit to any wrongdoing, because I had done nothing wrong."

After her ouster from Selby Gardens, Lowman had landed a new job with another of Marie Selby's causes, teaching at New College in Sarasota. Even with the new job, though, she found herself in the same situation as Selby Gardens' trustees, fretting about the mounting legal cost of fighting the government.

Given the acrimony over her departure, Selby's trustees weren't inclined to help. However, her contract gave her an added incentive to fight on. It said that as long as she was not found guilty, Selby would have to pay her legal bills.

"If she took a guilty plea," explained her attorney, Robert Rivas, "then she had no right to get reimbursed for her attorney's fees."

Ultimately, though, Lowman hit a limit. She agreed to an extremely favorable deal "in order to stop the financial bleeding," she said. But she did so in a way that she believed would still require Selby Gardens to pay Rivas for his work.

She agreed to accept the equivalent of a speeding ticket. It even looked like one.

The Fish and Wildlife Service issued Lowman a "notice of violation" that said she had "aided and abetted the possession . . . of at least one specimen of a species of tropical lady slipper orchid, namely *Phragmipedium kovachii*, that had been traded contrary to the provisions of the Convention on International Trade in Endangered Species" and that she had "concurred in and allowed the re-export to Peru" of the specimen.

The penalty: a $450 fine.

The beauty of it was that when she paid the ticket in February 2004, it erased the crime from her record. It was as if she'd never been charged—unlike her former employer.

"It was considered a civil infraction," Rivas said. "It was impossible to say no to that." The fact that the Justice Department issued no press release "tells me they considered it more of an embarrassment than a victory."

However, because she was not completely absolved, Selby's board took that as justification to refuse to pay her expenses.

Lowman turned to her many supporters in the Sarasota community for help. Friends of hers began publicly prodding the board members to come up with the cash. They wrote a piece for a local magazine about it. One even tracked down a Selby board member on the golf course to twist his arm. Scully said it felt like a shakedown.

It didn't work. They wouldn't pay. Lowman won her battle with the government, but lost her war with Selby.

Kovach's attorneys tried negotiating a plea deal, too, but Colbourn wouldn't offer anything less than a trip to prison.

"All the government wanted him to do was plead to a five-year felony," Fernandez later complained in court.

It didn't help that Kovach's record wasn't as spotless as, say, Wesley Higgins's. Kovach had racked up a charge of driving under the influence some years before. Worse, when he initially turned himself in after his indictment, he flunked his first drug test. The ex-hippie tested positive for marijuana.

His attorneys tried the same tactic Selby had attempted, going over Colbourn's head to try to persuade higher-ups at the Justice Department to give Kovach a break. They also tried appealing to the local U.S. attorney to pull the rug out from under the Washington prosecutor. They got the same result as Selby. Nothing would stop Colbourn's relentless pursuit of their client.

Meanwhile, Colbourn signaled that she was going to bring in Lee Moore to testify against his onetime partner. She filed a notice that an "unindicted co-conspirator" would be offering evidence in the case. She didn't specify what his contribution would be.

Kovach's attorneys flew The Adventurer to Tampa to take his statement. This was an unusual event in Moore's history, being on the same side as the federal government for a change. He says he really wanted to help his friend from Virginia. But even as he answered their questions, Moore could tell his version didn't fit what the attorneys wanted to hear.

"Kovach had twisted everything," Moore said. "If he'd just told the truth. But he said he went down there on a humanitarian mission to help people."

Moore's version portrayed Kovach as a sharp businessman out to make a buck, just like Moore, and "that's why they didn't use me for a witness."

The defense next tried attacking Agent Holt. They asked for her personnel records and any notes she took while interviewing Kovach. Their argument: She had it in for him and had skewed her reports to make him look bad. Colbourn objected, and the magistrate sided with her. Those matters were immaterial to the case at hand, he said.

With a trial date looming, Colbourn began sending subpoenas to Peru. She even made arrangements for bringing in the still-alive Faustino, sending him bus fare out of Moyobamba to catch a plane to Lima so he could then fly to Florida. After all, he could testify about how many orchids he sold Kovach.

Kovach's attorneys decided they were out of options. They might have rolled the dice, relentlessly mocked Colbourn for focusing so many resources on what they regarded as a minor infraction, and hoped for a jury to laugh the prosecutor out of court. But even if they had won at trial, Fernandez said, "I was personally afraid even if we got an acquittal the government would have continued trying to destroy this man."

So with Kovach's reluctant blessing, they finally agreed to a deal.

On June 11, 2004, two years and six days after he walked into Selby's OIC, and about a month before trial was set to start, Kovach stood at the lectern in a nearly empty courtroom in Tampa and pleaded guilty to one count of illegal possession of an endangered species and one count of illegal trade in an endangered species. In exchange for his plea, which avoided the expense of a trial, Colbourn dropped the felony charge.

The sentence would be up to the court. Kovach's attorneys hoped they could persuade the judge to give their client probation, not prison time. Colbourn, of course, hoped for the opposite.

Kovach, in entering his guilty plea, made it clear he wasn't happy with the outcome.

"There's a lot of questions about this case in my mind," Kovach told the magistrate who accepted his plea. "But it's resolution time."

As part of the plea, Kovach had to recount his crime all over again—and told a slightly different story from the versions that came before.

He told about stopping at El Progresso, and how the vendor "said they had something in the back, and brought this out. I wasn't sure at first what it was. It was too big, too colorful. It didn't fit the description of other orchids in that family."

Kovach told the magistrate that he was "under a mistaken impression" that he did not need a permit for an orchid that had not yet been officially named. He also blamed his lack of fluency in Spanish for misunderstanding Peruvian rules on exporting plants.

Sentencing was set for November 1. The Department of Justice put out a press release announcing Kovach's guilty plea that made no mention of either of the two women who had handled the case, Holt and Colbourn. Instead it quoted a man—an assistant attorney general who had had nothing to do with the prosecution of Kovach, Selby, or Higgins.

Seven days after Kovach pleaded guilty in Tampa, George Norris followed suit in Miami.

"He said it was the hardest thing he's ever done in his life, because he didn't believe that he had done anything wrong," his wife, Kathy, said later.

Norris's attorney tried to convince the judge to give him a break because the Texas orchid dealer was sixty-seven. The attorney questioned whether the Bureau of Prisons would be able to keep up with Norris's required regimen of two insulin shots a day. She suggested he might need a heart bypass. And she pointed out Norris's many good works, including letting Manuel Arias Silva's two sons stay at his house when they needed plastic surgery for their burns. She also reminded the judge that a lot of people had written to the court urging leniency (although one letter from a slightly confused orchid grower urged the judge to give the confessed smuggler "impunity" not immunity).

The prosecutors—one of them Colbourn—scoffed at those pleas for mercy. Despite his age and condition, he managed to run his orchid business just fine, they pointed out. While Norris took in Arias's sons, he didn't pay for the boys' care but just gave them a place to stay, they noted. Since Arias was his business associate, providing temporary housing for the sons was just smart business practice, they contended.

As for all those letters begging for leniency? Most of them were from people "who have never met Norris or do not know him well," the prosecutors wrote.

The prosecutors' arguments carried the day. The judge rejected any leniency for the Texan.

George Norris, Kovach's original mentor on collecting Peruvian orchids, was sentenced to seventeen months in a federal prison. Now only Kovach was left.

But before Kovach got his turn in front of a judge, Selby Gardens' leaders got a taste of how the case would forever haunt their institution.

16

The Scarlet Letter

There is that in the glance of a flower which may at times
control the greatest of creation's braggart lords.

John Muir, *A Thousand-Mile Walk to the Gulf*

Even though Selby Gardens' trustees had pleaded guilty in January 2004 to
breaking a law designed to conserve orchids, Selby was still scheduled to
be the site of the second International Orchid Conservation Congress that
spring.

The congress had been planned for two years, every event meticulously
choreographed in advance. Selby's remaining leaders were determined to
see it through. So despite the fact that a judge had put the gardens on probation in April 2004, the congress proceeded a month later, just as it was supposed to.

And even though Wesley Higgins had just been sentenced to house arrest and probation for his role in that crime, he was still scheduled to be the
chairman of the May 2004 event. Fortunately the judge had said he could
delay serving his sentence until after the conference was over.

Selby's leaders hoped the orchid congress would help restore their reputation and funnel some additional funds into the coffers. In the months leading up the conference, one of the administrators asked several OIC regulars
to suggest ways Selby might make some money from the event. Did Dalström have any ideas?

"Sure!" said Dalström. "Sell T-shirts with pictures of the *Phragmipedium
kovachii* on it."

After all, he pointed out, Selby already possessed his full-color painting of
the orchid. Why not make use of it?

The administrator blanched and said no way. "He was scared," Dalström said.

Actually, according to Higgins, Selby's leaders felt they had no choice but to turn down that moneymaking opportunity, given the prosecutor's search for some sign that Selby was going to profit from the illegal orchid. With Selby still on probation, they feared that being caught selling *Phragmipedium kovachii* souvenirs could be just the thing to bring the wrath of the federal government back down on their heads all over again.

Dalström, unfazed by the reaction, asked if it would be all right for him to print up a bunch of T-shirts on his own and sell them—not to help Selby, but to boost his own bank account. He was told he could do it so long as he didn't sell any of them on Selby's grounds.

"I sold them out of the trunk of my car in the parking lot," Dalström said, chuckling.

At eighteen dollars apiece, he made a bundle. It seemed as if every conference attendee wanted one of the shirts as a souvenir. Many of them wore Dalström's artwork as they walked around the conference, so that the flower showed up everywhere like hundreds of scarlet letters—a repeated reminder to Higgins and the rest of the Selby orchid boys about what they had just gone through.

The pressure proved to be too much for one of the invited speakers. Ricardo Fernandez, the Peruvian orchid expert who had coauthored the *Selbyana* piece, was supposed to fly in to attend the conference, but he had gotten cold feet. Manuel Arias Silva's arrest at the Miami airport in March had spooked him. Then he got e-mails from Peter Croezen warning him that associating with Selby Gardens would likely result in him being handcuffed as well.

A nervous Fernandez passed the e-mails along to Higgins and Dalström, seeking their advice.

"Well," he asked, "shall I travel to Sarasota via Fort Myers on April 9 or not??????? I would like to have guarantee I will not have any problem with the USA Justice Dpt., please advise me about this matter. Please make sure that I will not be arrested in airport if not I will not be able to travel."

The baby-faced Fernandez expressed regret for ever getting involved with the *Phragmipedium kovachii* in the first place. Instead of bringing him glory and renown, it had caused him all sorts of headaches.

"I must tell you that when Stig invited me to be the third botanical author of *P. kovachii* I did not know that it was a smuggling," he wrote. "It would be very disappointing to me and very sad that I would be involved in a judicial scandal because I agree to be the Peruvian botanist to help for describing

P. kovachii. I did not realize that this would be very risky to my career and profession."

Although Fernandez skipped the congress, which ran from May 15 to May 22, 2004, plenty of other players in Selby's drama showed up. It almost seemed like the climax of a mystery, when all the suspects gather in the dining room and the detective exposes the culprit over the veal cutlet.

This climactic gathering would have required an extremely spacious dining room, though: about 130 people attended. Still, that was fewer than the 200 that Selby had hoped to see.

Some of the people involved in the case were not invited, of course—Eric Christenson, Lee Moore, and Michael Kovach, for instance.

The attendees included Phillip Cribb of Kew Gardens, the former associate of Henry Azadehdel who had helped lead the push for putting all tropical slipper orchids on the Appendix I list under CITES. A year later Cribb would write a piece on *Phragmipedium kovachii* in which he rated it "critically endangered." Also there was Ted Green, the Hawaiian orchid grower who had walked away from an offer to buy the new *Phragmipedium* when it was being sold on the down low at the 2002 Redland show. Green, a staunch opponent of Cribb's work on moving all slipper orchids to Appendix I, was there to blast CITES as a failure that hadn't saved any species but had led to the spread of graft and red tape. That message was one with which the congress's recently convicted chairman wholeheartedly agreed.

Harold Koopowitz, who had seen the new orchids in the wild during his "hike from hell" and had passed up a chance to buy one from Lee Moore, flew in from California. Koopowitz's "hike from hell" tour guide, Dr. Isaias Rolando, soon arrived from Peru, even though Croezen had also urged him to stay home, in his case as a protest against Selby's crime. Rolando had been invited to talk about his pet project at the Machu Picchu hotel, though, so nothing would keep him away. It was probably good that Fernandez would not be there, too, because the two had quarreled a few months before at a Peruvian Orchid Club show. Fernandez complained in a letter to Dalström that during their fight, "Rolando attacked to me he tore/broke my Paphiopedilum flowers I presented." The pair had been friends since they were seventeen, but their relationship would never be quite the same after the fight.

Roddy Gabel, the Fish and Wildlife Service orchid expert who had helped with the search of Kovach's greenhouse, flew down to serve on a panel with Ted Green on, of course, the treaty that had tripped up Selby. In fact, Gabel was there to talk about a subject near to the orchid boys' hearts: The requirements that CITES imposed for scientific institutions such as Selby to move CITES-listed species internationally. Of course, while Selby remained on probation, Selby's special CITES permit remained suspended, so the OIC still had to apply for its CITES permits on a case-by-case basis.

Even though they were guests of Selby, both Gabel and Rolando were confronted by an angry Scully.

With Gabel on the dais, the ex-Selby chairman stood up in the back of the room and challenged him "in front of a lot of people about how CITES impacts commercial trade in orchids," Scully said. "But I couldn't pin this guy down. I tried to get him to admit they did a poor job of training their inspectors." After all, he pointed out, when Kovach walked into the Miami airport, "they let this guy through."

Afterward, Gabel said he wasn't sure what Scully's point about the inspectors was supposed to be.

"I don't know how inspectors are supposed to find smuggled goods," he said. "That's the point of smuggling. Kovach should have declared the plants and shown them to an inspector, and I believe he knew that was what he was supposed to do."

Rolando got another blast from Scully over Peru's role in instigating the *Phragmipedium kovachii* scandal.

"I did call out Isaias," Scully said. "I said I thought the Peruvian people had been a little disingenuous. After all, they did issue a permit to him that was enough to make him think it was okay to go forward. It looks ridiculous for them after the fact to start screaming."

Despite his past complaints about Selby, despite Scully's outrage, Rolando had arrived at Selby Gardens determined to put the acrimony behind him, Higgins said.

"Isaias had recanted some of the things he'd said previously," Higgins said. "He even presented me with a pin from the Orchid Club of Peru."

A month later, the diminutive doctor sent Higgins an e-mail that said: "Congratulations once more for a very good IOCC at Selby. Against many bad people trying to destroy Selby's reputation. You now know I am in your side. And we know who is in 'the other side.'"

The doctor had a reason for shining up the Selby scientists, though. The Peruvian Orchid Club still wanted everyone to stop using Kovach's name for the new slipper orchid. They wanted it officially renamed "*peruvianum.*" It was a matter of national pride, he said, and he hoped Selby—as the source of the offending name—would go along with the Peruvians' wishes.

"Many people here still believe the name *Phragmipedium peruvianum* should be reconsidered," he wrote to Higgins. "I know this is very difficult to happen, but please let me know the status of this particular situation."

That was, of course, part of Selby's sentence—although that fact meant primarily that Colbourn and her colleagues "had no clue" about how taxonomy works, Higgins said.

Selby "is not an institutional member of the International Association of Plant Taxonomists," he pointed out. That meant Selby really had no standing to make such a request.

The association meets every five years, and by the time Selby had been sentenced, the deadline for submitting a change for the upcoming meeting had already passed, Higgins pointed out. That meant the name-change request, even if it came from some other qualified source, would arrive too late.

He probably could have steered the Department of Justice straight on those matters, Higgins said, except that after being badgered by all the lawyers over his guilty plea, "I was not in the mood to help."

So Selby submitted a letter to the association that had been approved by the Justice Department, but Selby's leaders had no real expectation that anything would come of the request. Sure enough, the submission was ignored and Kovach's flower name remained unchanged.

Meanwhile, though, Selby itself was undergoing some changes now that Lowman and her supporters on the board were gone.

The change in the gardens seemed clear to those who attended the next Orchid Ball. Lowman's absence took all the fun out of the fund-raising. The event was now all about business, as Selby's leaders tried desperately to make up for all the money her departure had cost them.

With Lowman out of the picture, no one was left to advocate for her pet projects, either. The board members who had sided with Scully shut them all down. They ditched everything, from her proconservation mission statement to her Center for Canopy Ecology. Selby would go back to basics, back to the study of epiphytes, primarily orchids. After all, that's what it was set up to do in the first place.

But the trustees struggled to find a replacement for Lowman. No one seemed interested in leading a scientific institution that had broken the law and, under the pressure of a grand jury investigation, jettisoned its executive director.

Selby's guilty plea had been designed to put the case behind them. But the continuing headlines about Kovach's court battle kept reminding the public about Selby's role in what had happened.

Fortunately for Selby, the fall of 2004 would bring the final showdown over Kovach's case, a chance for Colbourn to lay out her case and explain, at last, what she believed had really happened.

17

The Final Showdown

When it's all over, this will make the best book you've ever seen.

Michael Kovach to the *Miami Herald*, 2002

The big windows that line the main hall of the fifteenth floor of the Sam Gibbons U.S. Courthouse offer a sweeping panorama of smoggy downtown Tampa. The view stretches from the kitschy pink awning of the wig emporium in the next block to the graceful minarets of the University of Tampa, perched on the curving banks of the distant Hillsborough River.

Step inside Courtroom 15-A, though, and once the doors close there's a feeling of being cut off from the world. All sounds are muffled. Thickly varnished wood and rigid marble define the parameters, with nary a curve or bend, nothing but corners. The room has more angles than a law library.

This would be the arena for Kovach's last stand, as his attorneys tried to keep him from going to prison the way George Norris did.

The bench sits beneath what looks like a gigantic slab of wood that makes it appear the judge and court clerk are housed in a shoebox diorama. About ten minutes before 9:00 a.m. on November 1, 2004, a white-haired man in a black robe stepped through the door at the back of the diorama and settled himself into a high-backed chair.

This was U.S. District Judge Steven Merryday, who had been on the bench for nearly thirteen years. He grew up in rural Palatka and his aw-shucks manner still reflected his upbringing, despite the fact that he had graduated with honors from the University of Florida and served as student body president in his first year at law school.

As a judge, he specialized in complex and controversial cases, such as the one that ended forced busing for one of the local school systems. In his time on the bench he had made one major slip: a drunk-driving arrest in 1994. But he didn't try to pull rank on the arresting officer and afterward issued a public apology.

Around the courthouse, Merryday was also known (and sometimes mocked) for taking his time with cases, asking lots of questions, joshing around with potential jurors. Jury selection in his courtroom was known as a "Merryday marathon." But it was because of Merryday's inquisitive nature, his knowledge of the law, and his reputation for fairness that Kovach's attorneys had advised their client to plead guilty, hoping the judge would agree to a sentence of probation instead of prison.

Now Merryday peered through his glasses at the attorneys arrayed before him and said, "Well, good morning."

At one table sat Elinor Colbourn and Agent Holt. At the other were Hearn, Fernandez, and their client, Michael Kovach. Kovach was dressed just like an attorney in a blue suit, a blue Oxford button-down and a paisley tie, but his long ponytail gave him away as a defendant hoping to make a good impression.

The attorneys all introduced themselves to the judge, and Fernandez pointed out that Kovach's wife, Barbara Ellison, sat in the gallery. She wore a black dress with what appeared to be silver vines climbing from hem to collar. Around her neck hung a small gold crucifix. A couple of newspaper reporters sat near her, but she ignored them as best she could.

At that point, the judge asked the attorneys to step up to the clerk's table "so that we might see and hear each other more clearly."

Then the judge looked at the defendant. "And you are James Michael Kovach?"

"That's correct, sir."

"Do I pronounce that correctly?"

"Yes, you did, sir."

Satisfied, the judge shuffled his papers and recited for Kovach what crimes he'd pleaded guilty to committing, then explained that "it is my responsibility to determine a lawful sentence in light of matters brought to my attention by a pre-sentence report by the United States Probation Office, by the United States this morning through Ms. Colbourn, by the defense this morning through Mr. Fernandez and Mr. Hearn, as well as by yourself. You have an opportunity to speak to the court with reference to your sentence and I'll recognize you in a few minutes for that purpose."

Actually it would be nearly three hours before Kovach could speak again.

First came Colbourn's turn to talk. What she was about to do was rare in federal court practice.

Normally, when probation officers prepare a presentencing report for a judge, they consult with the lead investigator about what it should say. The report usually echoes the views of the prosecution, and so prosecutors rarely object to the contents.

But Colbourn objected—and objected strongly—to several points in Kovach's presentence report, points that might lead the judge to give the defendant something less than a prison sentence. Her first objection brought in new evidence about what Kovach had done while he was in Peru.

Colbourn said the judge's calculations about what sentence to give Kovach should take into account that the offense "creates a significant risk of infestation or disease transmission potentially harmful to, in this case, plants."

Why? Because, she said, Kovach's phytosanitary permit, the one he said he got from Renato Villena at Agro-Oriente, didn't cover what he said it did.

To begin with, she said, bear in mind that Kovach had plenty of experience with importing orchids. He'd done so, and done it properly, several times over the years. So when he got to the Miami airport, he knew the right way to bring in plants. He knew that once he'd cleared Customs, he was supposed to take his plants over to the USDA's smokehouse to be checked to see if they were disease-free. But he didn't.

"So he knew what was required," Colbourn told the judge. "He didn't do it."

Still, he had a permit from Peru that said the plants he brought with him were clean, the so-called phytosanitary certificate. All along, she said, Agent Holt and everyone else had simply taken him at his word that the phytosanitary certificate allowed him to take plants out of Peru—maybe not the new slipper orchid he'd found, but the other, more common orchids he'd acquired.

But then Holt had sent INRENA an inquiry about Kovach's papers. INRENA's response, according to Colbourn, was: "That document you sent us is only for movement inside of Peru. It's not a phytosanitary certificate as defined under the treaties and legal requirements." The certificate clearly said, right on top, that it was for "*mobilization dentro linatia,*" which meant "inside the country"—in other words, not for export.

Fernandez defended his client first by attacking the prosecution.

"I have probably been in front of this court a hundred times and I don't think I have ever had such a profound disagreement with another lawyer who I stood before this court with as to the application of the guidelines and what happened in this case," he said, his baritone voice ringing off the marble walls. "The undercurrent of Ms. Colbourn's discussion here appears to be that Mr. Kovach is just fundamentally a liar."

The person who obtained that phytosanitary certificate for Kovach—Renato Villena—told him it was sufficient, so Kovach believed it to be sufficient, the attorney said. For Colbourn to now claim to have information from Peru saying otherwise ought to be considered hearsay, and thus inadmissible as evidence.

Besides, he said, "there is no evidence here before the court today that there was any infestation problem." After all, Kovach himself had meticulously cleaned off the plants he had bought before he left Peru. If there were some problem with them, he contended, then surely the staff at the U.S. Botanic Garden, which took possession of Kovach's plants after Holt confiscated them, would have mentioned it.

As for what happened at the Miami airport, Fernandez said that both the defense and the prosecution had tried, in vain, to get either a witness or a videotape showing what had happened the night Kovach and his wife passed through Customs. No one could come up with either, to their frustration.

"I have been through that process down at the Miami airport a few times," Judge Merryday said.

"Have you?" Fernandez asked.

"Yes. I have some idea what it looks like down there on the average day."

"Well," Fernandez said, "I have never brought in plants, I don't know, Your Honor . . ."

"Oh, I have never brought in plants," Merryday said.

"It looks like you would be in big trouble if you did," Fernandez joked.

Colbourn was not amused. For one thing, she said, INRENA's responses to Holt's inquiry were not hearsay. The responses were all in writing, and she had copies of the documents available for everyone to read. To claim it would be inadmissible in a sentencing hearing "boggles my mind," she told the judge.

The reason why the U.S. Botanic Garden didn't complain about any infestation, she said, was because the gardens staff also fumigated all of Kovach's seized plants "because these were plants that had been seized that had been imported illegally."

The judge, without ruling immediately, turned back to Colbourn and asked her to explain her other complaints about the presentencing report.

Her next point, she said, concerned Kovach's knowledge of orchids: He used a "special skill" to commit the crime, and that made his crime worse.

Not only did he know he had a tropical slipper orchid, she said. He also knew how difficult it would be to tell a slipper orchid from another orchid species, *maxillaria*, she said. So he bought a lot of *maxillaria* too and hid his special plant among them. Even the way he carried the plants showed his intent, she contended.

"Now, Mr. Kovach historically from the records that we have seen ships product back and forth," she said. "In this case he went over and he hand-carried it back."

Then, she said, when Higgins called him in Virginia to ask for his paperwork, he sent Selby everything but the CITES permit he did not have, explaining that he had to leave that at Customs.

"Well," Colbourn said, "he knows that's not true. He has imported these kinds of plants before."

Fernandez retorted that that was hogwash.

"Your honor, I can go down to Peru and find a plant that is highly beautiful and bring it back," the defense attorney said. "I don't have a special skill."

The ability to identify an orchid that beautiful as something worth buying didn't require any training or education, he said. Then he addressed the prosecutor's larger point about his client's motives.

"Ms. Colbourn is operating under this kind of conspiracy theory where Mr. Kovach is this bad man who tried to set up all these things," Fernandez said. "But the fact is, he brought a plant to a place that could identify it, and ensure that it did end up on CITES Appendix I and be protected."

Colbourn's theory about Kovach was based on a faulty premise, he contended.

"There is a misperception in this case that Mr. Kovach is a high-rolling greenhouse owner," Fernandez told the judge.

Fernandez told the judge about going to visit his client at home: "It is a little clapboard house in Virginia. It's a very beautiful setting. And his greenhouse is a little room not a whole lot bigger than this table here. I mean, it's a little bigger than that, and he never made any money doing this. So if he is such a great orchid enthusiast—I don't mean any offense to you by this—he would have made a lot more money. He didn't make any money doing this."

"I notice the probation officer in Virginia visited the house and gave a similar description," the judge said.

"Well, I wanted to see it for myself, your honor," the defense attorney said. "I mean, because Ms. Colbourn was telling me what a bad person this is. This is a guy who loves orchids and he's probably—probably the damage that has been done to this orchid has been by press release, not by Mr. Kovach. Mr. Kovach got it identified and now it is a protected plant."

For that reason, the judge not only should refuse to send Kovach to prison, Fernandez argued. He ought to give Kovach an even more lenient sentence than the sentencing guidelines called for. He didn't call for giving Kovach a medal, but he came close.

Then Fernandez explained to the judge the real reason his client pleaded guilty. The reason, he said, had nothing to do with the *Phragmipedium kovachii*.

As Colbourn had pointed out, Kovach more than once had bought or collected orchids in other countries and brought them back to the United States. He could do that with Appendix II orchids because he had a permit from the USDA to import those on a regular basis.

The only problem, Fernandez explained, was that Kovach had tripped up. He had let that USDA permit lapse in May 2002, just prior to his trip to Peru.

As a result, *any* orchids he brought to Miami, even the ones he considered roadside weeds, were illegal.

Although Kovach subsequently renewed that permit from the USDA, Fernandez explained, "there was a gap in time when he couldn't bring these plants in. This is what Mr. Kovach pled guilty to. He didn't plead guilty to this overarching conspiracy that Ms. Colbourn is trying to paint."

The slip with his USDA permit proved what an amateur he was, Fernandez told the judge.

"He's a self-trained guy," Fernandez said. "He's got a little greenhouse in the back, that's what he is. It's not a special skill, number one. And number two, he didn't use it to perpetuate this crime. The crime here is not having a permit. I would say that reflects a *lack* of skill, that he was unable or that he neglected to renew his permit. That's all that we have pled guilty to here."

Colbourn couldn't believe what she was hearing.

"I'm sorry, your honor," she said. "A lapse in a permit?"

"A lapse in permit," Fernandez insisted.

"He had a permit, and it lapsed?" the prosecutor said, sarcasm dripping from her voice.

"If the *court* has a question, I'll answer it," snarled Fernandez, no longer willing to play games with Colbourn.

"Let's direct your comments to the court, if you have them," the judge agreed.

"I'm sorry," Colbourn told the judge. "I apologize, your honor."

"That's all right," the judge murmured. Then he asked for her next objection.

And that's when she really blasted Kovach.

Fernandez had boasted to the judge how much his client had cooperated with the authorities. Kovach reported his potential violation to the USDA. He even wrote the agency a letter explaining why he'd done what he'd done, Fernandez pointed out. Kovach freely answered all of Agent Holt's questions on her first visit to his farmhouse, too, the attorney said, and even gave her a written affidavit. It was only when Holt returned with an armed squad of officers and a search warrant that he quit talking to her.

But that's not the way Colbourn saw it, not at all.

Sure, Kovach gave a written statement to the USDA. Sure he wrote an affidavit for Holt. However, she said, "those documents all contain false statements right out of the get-go."

That's why, she said, the judge should give him a stiffer sentence—for obstructing justice.

For one thing, she said, Kovach's Agro-Oriente invoice said he had 566 plants. But then he told Agent Holt the invoice was made up before he'd collected any plants and he'd really only brought back 385. Taking Kovach at his word, that's how many her search team confiscated.

As a result, the prosecutor said, "there are arguably some 140, almost 200 plants out there that were illegally imported as it turns out now without a phytosanitary and we have never been able to find them. . . . Whatever he produced is what they took."

Then there's the matter of how many slipper orchids he bought at El Progresso, she said.

"He made a statement at the time of this initial interview—and has never made a statement to the government, I mean, come back and corrected that statement or done anything otherwise since—'I went down there, I bought one *kovachii*, I bought *one kovachii*.'"

Holt took him at his word, Colbourn said, until Dr. Rolando flew to Washington to tell her different:

"Isaias Rolando came over from Peru and asked to speak with Fish and Wildlife Service authorities about this case and said, 'I know the guy who sold the stuff, he sold him *three*.'"

Initially that didn't seem significant, Colbourn conceded, until Kovach started telling reporters that he did indeed buy three of the plants, not one.

Then the investigators began toting up what the witnesses said about it: Dalström seeing Kovach walk out of Selby's OIC with a plant (at least initially) as well as the taped statements of the two orchid judges, Mark Jones and Jim Clarkson.

Colbourn said the two orchid show judges were "essentially the closest thing we have found anywhere in this case to a disinterested third-party witness." Despite their obvious loathing of the government and CITES, both of them said Kovach left Selby carrying at least one orchid.

Clarkson, she said, "stated quite unequivocally that Mr. Kovach left with one of the plants. In fact, he helped wrap it back up."

Kovach, she pointed out, had more recently told reporters that he had bought three plants but left two of them in Peru with his friend, Lee Moore—although Kovach contended he and Moore didn't really know each other well.

Moore told the same story, but Colbourn didn't buy it.

"All of the papers show that he came back here to get this named after him because that was his spectacular find," the prosecutor said. "To say that he just left two with Mr. Moore, who he describes as a mere acquaintance in his papers—and we'll look at that in a moment, too—just doesn't make sense."

The bottom line, according to Colbourn: "Our belief is certainly, by a preponderance of the evidence, he brought more than one plant in here, and he lied about that."

The judge looked at her. "And how," he asked, "is your investigation materially obstructed by the difference between three plants and one?"

"They are unaccounted for," Colbourn replied. "They weren't looked for. We don't know if he sold them. We don't know if he has tried to propagate them. You know, he says they are in Peru but he's never turned them over to Peruvian authorities or contacted Peruvian authorities about doing so. He has never discussed with us through his counsel or otherwise providing any cooperation in that regard in turning over those plants. They have simply disappeared."

Fernandez, when it was his turn, admitted, "I'm not even really sure where to begin."

The judge, taking a cue from Lewis Carroll, told him, "Begin at the beginning, continue until the end, and then stop."

First of all, Fernandez said, Agent Holt's report about her interview with Mark Jones did not mention multiple plants. It only mentioned one, he said.

The judge turned to Colbourn for an explanation. She put the blame on her investigator.

"The report does say just one," she conceded. "Agent Holt reviewed that tape with me last night and agrees that she actually omitted incriminating information from that tape in her report."

"Incriminating?" Fernandez interjected.

"She omitted incriminating information," Colbourn repeated, "and we have the tape here as well and we are happy to play it."

The judge wondered if that was worth the trouble. The court reporter would have to transcribe the whole thing while it was playing, he explained. Then he asked Fernandez if Clarkson's tape also offered contradictory stories.

"Clarkson does say that—" the attorney began.

"Does say what?"

"That there was three plants, and he took one with him," the defense attorney conceded.

But then he brought up Dalström's conflicting testimony and the letters and e-mails to Lowman from the other Selby scientists "that said there was only one plant and nobody took anything."

He made an argument similar to the one that George Norris had predicted in his e-mail to Wesley Higgins: With so many conflicting stories, nobody knew the truth.

"You know, there is all kinds of speculation here that Mr. Kovach brought in a whole bunch of these *Phragmipedium kovachii,* but that's just speculation," he contended. "There's no proof of that. You know, these plants are such that you can rip them apart. When you clean them, you can take them apart. . . . So Mr. Clarkson could have seen that."

Caught up in his argument, his voice rising, Fernandez insisted that "there is utterly no proof whatsoever—period! none!—that Mr. Kovach brought into this country more than one plant. . . . I think she'll even admit that other than—"

Colbourn cut him off with a firm, "No, your honor."

"Well," Fernandez conceded, "maybe she won't."

He went on to talk again about Atwood and Dalström, saying they only saw the one plant, the one Kovach left at Selby. He scoffed at Colbourn's insistence there must be more than that. He also mocked the government's effort to throw Kovach in prison for one, two, or even three flowers.

"I have got to tell you," he told the judge, "that this case has been investigated more than any case I have ever seen in my life, both as an assistant [U.S. attorney] and a defense attorney."

And yet, he said, no investigator ever went back to *ask* Kovach to clarify what he meant. His affidavit about how many plants he bought at El Progresso "is ambiguous," Fernandez said, and not sufficient to prove he tried to obstruct the investigation.

Fine, the judge said, and are there any further objections?

Yes, Colbourn said, just one more: Acceptance of responsibility.

Sure, Kovach had pleaded guilty, but he had lied all along the line, she said. That should count not only as obstruction of justice but also as a sign that he refused to admit that what he'd done was wrong, she said.

At that point, the judge noted, "you people have been standing for an hour and fifteen minutes." He joked, "It's my way of wearing you down." As soon as Colbourn signaled she was done, the judge called a short recess. Everyone exhaled.

⸺⸱⸻

Ten minutes later they were all back in their places, and it was Fernandez's turn to object to items in the presentencing report. He wanted to knock out the sections recommending stiffer punishment. That meant attacking not just CITES, but also his own client.

The probation officer's report recommended enhancing the sentence because the crime involved an Appendix I plant, and also because Kovach knowingly violated the law.

Fernandez told the judge that Kovach had initially thought he might have a new genus of orchid, and thus one that wasn't covered by Appendix I. Kovach had said so to both Stig Dalström and Mark Jones, he told the judge.

"In fact, the very evidence that Ms. Colbourn cites for the proposition that he brought in more than one plant is the same evidence I would use to say that Mr. Kovach thought it was a new genus," he said. Since he didn't know whether it was a new genus, the defense attorney asked, how could he be accused of knowingly violating CITES?

At that point, Fernandez apologized to the judge for briefly misplacing his copy of the probation officer's presentencing report. The judge joked that there were so few copies "you should retain it, it may sell at a premium on eBay someday."

"Don't say that, your honor," Fernandez replied, "because we are now getting into the pecuniary gain part."

That was Colbourn's cue. The prosecutor began by responding to Fernandez's first two arguments. She reminded the judge that the issue of whether Appendix I covered a newly discovered plant had already been dealt with by the court.

The defense's argument, she said, "is the equivalent of saying that even if it was described, every time you went in the forest and you picked up something, until some scientist positively identifies it for you as being that, it's not that—which isn't true." Even if you don't recognize it, she said, "it is what it is. A violet is a violet."

As for whether Kovach knew what he was doing, Colbourn said, "of course Mr. Kovach knew. He's an orchid hobbyist, enthusiast, a dealer. He runs a nursery."

Then she pulled out some of the evidence Lee Moore had handed over and began to outline the prosecution's theory of what *really* happened.

First the prosecutor told the judge she wanted to bring to his attention Chady Moore's own history of the discovery of *Phragmipedium kovachii*.

Her history took the form of a long e-mail Lee Moore sent to Peter Croezen, written in August 2002, right after the *Miami Herald* story first broke the news of the investigation. In it, Colbourn pointed out, Mrs. Moore talked about how she had heard about the new orchid. She had heard the story from people around Moyobamba who knew that Renato Villena at Agro-Oriente had some of them.

"This is before Kovach ever comes to their place and ever finds the *kovachii*," Colbourn explained.

So as soon as Kovach returned from El Progresso and showed off his new purchases, Chady Moore told him someone else had beaten him to the plant, someone who she heard had taken some of them to the Redland show near Miami.

"Now, these are cohorts in time with Mr. Kovach," Colbourn said, but then Fernandez interrupted.

"Cohorts of what?" he asked. "Cohorts of what? I didn't catch that, your honor."

"Colleagues of his, or the people he is in Peru with, at the time of his collection," Colbourn explained, then returned to outlining the plot.

She next pulled out an e-mail that Lee Moore had sent to Stig Dalström, responding to questions the Swedish artist had sent him. She began reading it out loud in court, but censoring some of the salty language.

"You know that I am directly responsible for the discovery," the prosecutor read. "I took Kovach to Peru and sent him the man that had found it originally. I told him that if he wanted his name on it, he would have to cut his trip short and go straight to Selby. I would have liked to have had my name on it, but I foresaw what would happen, which did. I also advised him Murphy's Law and it did happen. Oh, the cost of fame. I have had my bouts with the USDA and did not need any more. I am too old and too tired of this expletive."

Then she began to explain about Kovach and Moore: "He went down by prearrangement with Mr. Moore. . . . Mr. Moore directed him to this person. His wife had already had discussions that there was this new *Phragmipedium*. They brought it in."

Fernandez jumped in to attack The Adventurer's credibility.

"Mr. Moore is a crank," he said. "I mean that in the old-time sense of the word. Even the government doesn't believe him."

Fernandez insisted his client's actions were never part of a moneymaking scheme involving Lee Moore.

"I submit to the court that if Mr. Kovach had an impulse towards pecuniary gain, he would have been much smarter to keep his mouth shut and keep bringing in these plants and selling them for $10,000," Fernandez said. "Mr. Kovach has made no money from this plant. He never sought any money from the plant."

Fernandez said Colbourn was just grasping at straws. He reminded the judge about how, in a motion regarding sentencing, Colbourn had noted Kovach's comment to the *Miami Herald* about writing a book, and how she contended that was another way he planned to profit from his crime.

"If I had been through what Mr. Kovach went through, I'd write a book too," Fernandez told the judge. "Except it wouldn't be about *Phramipediums*. It would be about what Oscar Wilde talked about, the grinding heel of justice on top of him."

There was also the matter of Kovach's proposed reality show. What about the outline for "The Orchid Hunter" that Agent Holt had seized during the raid on his house?

"Well, whatever," Fernandez said, sounding disgusted, as if reality TV weren't worth his time. "I have got nothing to say about that."

The upshot of it all, Fernandez said, is that "there is no proof that as to this plant . . . that there was any motive to personal gain, to pecuniary gain."

The judge turned to the prosecutor and asked, "What says the United States, Ms. Colbourn?"

Colbourn was ready. She had compiled all the evidence for Kovach's trial, and now it lay stacked at her fingertips. She had gone through it again the night before. This would be a compressed version of her closing argument, stitching the whole story together for what was, in effect, a jury of one.

First she held up the fax that Lee Moore had sent Kovach prior to the May 2002 trip to Peru, setting up the dates for their joint excursion.

"Mr. Kovach's papers describe Mr. Moore as a mere acquaintance," Colbourn said. "It clearly goes a great deal more than that."

Next she pointed out that Kovach's own affidavit to Agent Holt said he had gone to Peru "to collect orchids and to discuss species production facility."

"He goes down there, he pursues that, and describes this person as a partner of his," the prosecutor said.

Then she brought out the fax that Moore sent to Kovach after the *Miami Herald* story appeared, the one coaching him on what to say to the press. This was the fax warning him not to mention going back to El Progresso because it "indicates you were set on depredation by getting more. This looks bad."

"This is a relationship," Colbourn said, her voice firm, her tone one of clear certainty. "I mean, this is sounding an awful lot like a conspiracy at this point with these kinds of statements about, 'This is how you project what happens.'"

Then the prosecutor pointed out to the judge what Moore had scrawled on the side of another fax, the one that he'd sent Kovach to complain about Croezen posting the Eric Christenson letter on his website and deleting his name with a series of *X*s. The note, she said, was "very significant." She read aloud what Moore had written:

"Priority mail today, $1,260. You will need this. Anyway I have enough small ones for us when the get bigger—" Colbourn looked up and said, "It's very difficult to interpret that any way other than Mr. Moore is trying to send Mr. Kovach money—pecuniary gain."

Colbourn next brought up the taped interview with orchid judge Mark Jones: "Mr. Jones says that Mr. Kovach told him when he was at Selby that day that he was going to be producing or trying to produce seedlings. Now this matches with the whole relationship with Mr. Moore. It matches with the $1,260 being sent."

Meanwhile, she pointed out, Chady Moore's own statement talked about going back to El Progresso herself to obtain as many of the plants as she could.

"Now that," Colbourn said, "has got to be for a commercial purpose. I mean, they're saying we're trying to propagate these, we want to sell them. We are a commercial nursery."

Her final piece of the puzzle, she said, came from Kovach's own words, his very first account of what happened. It was contained in the letter he'd written to the USDA on the same day the investigation began.

Colbourn read aloud to the court the part of the letter talking about how Kovach was being threatened by orchid dealers who wanted to buy the new Peruvian orchid. It was the part about how the dealers threatened to report him to the authorities if he didn't "sell them the plants I don't have and sell them quick and cheap."

There Colbourn paused.

"Now all of that sounds like he really doesn't have the plants," she said, "until you get to this next line. And here's the kicker, as he writes, 'Three such individuals have stated that my price is too high and they can get the plants in July for $500 U.S. per plant.'"

Colbourn looked up at the judge.

"How can his price be too high," she asked, "if he didn't have any and didn't have a price?"

Getting the plant named after him, getting Selby Gardens to publicize it—that constituted the marketing for his product, she contended. Thanks to *Selbyana*, people in the orchid world knew who found the plant and who might be able to get more for them: the guy whose name was on the new orchid, Michael Kovach.

The judge was intrigued, but he had a question.

"The issue is not whether this had commercial consequence or might have resulted in a commercial gain, even a sharp commercial gain," he said. "The question is whether the initial offense was committed for that purpose."

"Yes, your honor."

"And how would one in my position glom onto that conclusion, as opposed to that it had that happy consequence?" the judge asked.

Simple, Colbourn replied, then ticked off two points.

"One, of course, we contend that he kept some of the plants so that he could propagate them, so it was an illegal importation of the three plants, not one.

"And secondly, to get a CITES permit, you have to be able to identify what species it is you are exporting. So if you are going to start engaging in serious commercial trade, you have got to have a way to legally transport them. So you bring it in, you get it named, and then you have got something to start putting on CITES—had this, of course, not escalated as it did into the case that it did."

Fernandez, of course, disagreed.

"Mr. Kovach got zero," he contended. He labeled Lee Moore's e-mails and faxes as "self-serving" because "Mr. Moore was a guy who was way more involved than Mr. Kovach." As a result, Fernandez said, "I think the court should reject them out of hand."

He then accused Colbourn of taking Kovach's statements out of context. The single line about prices in the USDA letter, Fernandez said, accompanies statements about how he doesn't have any of the plants to sell.

"There is no evidence of any other plants that Mr. Kovach was going to sell," the defense attorney insisted. "The plants were two left with Moore in Peru and one that he turned over to Selby. If there was a pecuniary—"

Suddenly Fernandez stopped and asked the judge, "Am I making any sense at all?"

"No, I understand you," the judge said. "I think that you both have made yourselves pretty clear."

The prosecutor reminded the judge again about how Kovach's story kept changing. She contended that Kovach had only reported himself to the USDA because he thought other nursery owners might be about to turn him in.

"As far as his actions bringing the species to the attention of the world, it did," she said. "Our argument of that would be, that's the problem."

First there was a race to publish the name, she said, and then "there was this mad race and everything was stripped from the hillsides. So I just don't see that bringing it to the attention of the world is necessarily a good thing here."

Kovach's actions were not those of someone concerned about the good of the plant, she told the judge.

"If he really was concerned with the protection of the plant, he wouldn't have brought in one plant to have it dissected and killed and left the other two and not reported anything," she told the judge. "If he was really that concerned, you go to somebody in Peru to identify it properly. You ask for the right permits, which he knew how to do. He told Agent Holt in this initial interview, 'Yeah, I knew, but it was going to take too long. It was going to cost a hundred bucks. I didn't have time for that. I just brought it home so I could get it named after me.' There was no conservation motive here. He wanted something named after him to become somewhat immortal."

She reminded the judge about how Kovach, in writing to an orchid vendor in Panama two years before his fateful trip to Peru, had talked about how he knew to mix up species to fool inspectors. She also reminded him about the planning that went into coordinating the trip to Peru with Moore, his erstwhile partner. Even taking Kovach at his word, she said, he brought in a single flower that was then killed by dissection and sent back to Peru— hardly a conservation-minded move.

That's when Fernandez jumped in: What about the piece that Atwood saved?

"If we are sitting here arguing whether the plant was murdered by Mr. Kovach so he could have it named after him," he said, "that's just flat not true."

All the witnesses testified that Kovach, when he walked into Selby's OIC, "was like a little kid," the defense attorney said. "He walked in there, he was so happy and so excited and ebullient that he had brought this plant to Selby Gardens. I mean, this picture being painted of Mr. Kovach is this dark, underworld figure who murders plants, and it is just not so. He brought one plant back. There is no proof he brought anything more than that."

The connection with Lee and Chady Moore, the suggestion they were all involved in an orchid-smuggling plot together, "there is no evidence of any of that," Fernandez contended. As for the e-mails that Moore produced, the defense attorney said, "I don't know what kind of threats Ms. Holt went and made to Chady Moore or Lee Moore."

That brought Colbourn charging in. "Your honor, I object to that," she barked.

"Wait just a moment," the judge said in a soothing voice, then let Fernandez continue.

"I don't know what kind of threats were made to induce him to send these things," Fernandez repeated, not mentioning to the court that he and his partner had deposed Moore themselves. "I don't know what was said. I have no idea what happened in that part of the investigation."

As for Kovach, he said, well, his client should have renewed his USDA permit "but everything else he did, he did right, and I'm asking the court to recognize that."

Colbourn fumed at Fernandez for attacking Agent Holt. She told the judge she had accompanied Holt to interview Moore, and no threats had been necessary. She accused Kovach's defense attorney of slandering the investigator because they had nothing to counter Lee Moore's evidence.

When Fernandez offered to substantiate his allegations, Colbourn urged him to try. But the judge interrupted the spat to tell them that wasn't the issue of the day, so he didn't have time for it.

At last, it was time for Fernandez to try out what might have been his closing argument for a jury of one.

"I think the court is getting some flavor—if you don't have it already, I certainly didn't have it—it's almost a religious fervor with these plants, with these orchids. It's the most extraordinary thing I have ever seen." The whole case, he said, had become "wild and woolly, it's a bizarre thing."

He warmed to his subject: "But at the end of the day, what you have here is you have a guy who lives in a clapboard house in Virginia—a very beautiful house, a very beautiful place, with a wife who loves orchids. He went down—he saves his money, what he makes, to make one or two trips a year to places like Vietnam, Jamaica, Peru, and he meets people down there who have a similar love of orchids."

Now the attorney's voice took a rueful tone. "In the past he has always gone and gotten the CITES permits. He didn't do it this time for reasons that, that, you know, we can dispute until the cows come home. He knew to do it. He had done it before. I can only conjecture that the reason he didn't do it here is because he felt it wasn't necessary or maybe he cut a corner, and he's pled guilty to that."

And what did Kovach get for cutting that corner? Federal agents "come in, you know, with their guns on, and they ravage his house. I don't understand why that would be. I suppose that's not a mitigating thing [but] I think it goes to the issue of how much does a man have to be punished for doing what this man did."

The investigation had itself become the punishment, Fernandez told the judge.

"And I'm just asking the court to send him back to Virginia and let him sit on his front porch and try to grow his orchids again. His business is destroyed. He's a good man. I think Barbara, his wife, would like to speak to the court in mitigation as well. She accompanied him on this trip as she does on the other ones. And I want the court to let him go home."

"All right," the judge said, "have her step up to the clerk's table and we will hear what she has to say."

Barbara Ellison rose from the gallery and stepped forward to her husband's side.

"Good morning," the judge told her.

"Good morning," she said. "Well first of all, I just wanted to say—let you know that my husband is a kind and generous man, and in the past he has done a lot for people in different countries. He has donated lab equipment in the name of conservation. So I just wanted you all to know that—that he loves the plants and so I do too. We are both very much in love with orchids and it has been our life for the past several years together. And I am just asking for your leniency, and that's it."

With that, she turned to go sit back down, and it became, at last, Kovach's turn to speak on his own behalf. There was a time when he expected to testify in court, at length, about what he'd done. But now he told the judge, "Thank you, your honor. I'll try to keep it brief."

He had memorized his statement and recited it straight through, but still mangled the second sentence a bit.

"I have been involved in conservation for the twelve years that I have been involved in orchids. In fact, there are places in Jamaica that would not have orchid conservation programs had my participation not been involved. I love these plants, and I did what I did without violating any laws as I understood it. However, I did follow apparently the wrong procedure, and for that I'm very sorry and in the future I would make a much stronger effort to verify the credibility of the people I'm doing business with overseas and their governments. Thank you."

Now it was all up to the judge.

To begin with, Merryday thanked the attorneys for bringing him such an interesting case.

"We don't have a lot of prosecutions under this statute," he said mildly. "This marks one in my soon-to-be-thirteen years, and I appreciate your figuring, representing your respective sides."

Then the judge set to work, going through Colbourn's arguments against following the probation officer's recommendation. He overruled Colbourn's concern regarding the risk of infestation as a reason for giving Kovach a stiffer sentence. Then he overruled her point regarding the use of a special skill, too.

"While I would agree that his knowledge of this matter allowed him to identify the object which became the opportunity for this offense," the judge explained, the prosecutor had not proven that Kovach had used "some highly specialized skill in the facilitation or concealment of his crime, and I distinguish between spotting the opportunity for the offense and facilitating or concealing the offense."

Next the judge tackled the question of whether Kovach obstructed justice. He ruled that Colbourn had not established that it was "a material obstruction of justice." Merryday said he agreed with the probation office report that Kovach had demonstrated an acceptance of responsibility for his crime. The reason: Just twelve days after the judge shot down his motion to dismiss the case, his attorneys filed a notice saying he would change his plea to guilty. The short time period for the turnaround suggested the required acceptance of responsibility.

Now came the crucial question: Did Kovach do what he did for money? Or for the love of orchids?

Merryday said he had struggled with that one "because I can't tell what his motivation was." He then struggled to explain what he meant.

"The question here," he said, "is not whether a gain was possible. The question here is not whether a gain occurred. The question is not whether there is a gain to be had. The question is whether, at the time of this offense, it was committed with the material objective of pecuniary gain, as opposed to any of the other competing possibilities—whether it was to have the thing named after him, or because of a feeling of elation at having identified some heretofore unidentified plant. I'm not sure how one ultimately figures out why Scott Fitzgerald wrote *The Great Gatsby*, or why Stephen Hawking labors against his illness to prove black holes, or why other people do other things. But unless a satisfactory showing can be made that it was for pecuniary gain rather than for some, I suppose, some other purpose, the enhancement is not justified."

Still, he admitted, it was "a close call."

At last it was time to talk about what sentence to give Kovach.

Colbourn noted that the federal sentencing guidelines called for a range of up to six months behind bars. She pointed out to the judge how all of the factors that could have piled more time on top of that had been close calls at best.

"At this time," she said, "we would still be moving for a prison sentence of at least four months for this defendant within that range."

The government would also like to see a fine, she said, but not a high one because "frankly that would probably just penalize his wife more than it would penalize him."

"Anything, Mr. Fernandez?" the judge asked.

"Slightly," Fernandez said, annoyed with what he viewed as an insult aimed at his client's manhood. "I agree that there should be no fine imposed, but Mr. Kovach is a working man, he's not indolent, and I don't know what the intent of that was."

The four months in jail, though, was unacceptable, he said. He contended Kovach should face no jail time at all, given everything else he'd already been through.

"This has been a very punitive thing to have happened to Mr. Kovach," his attorney said. "He is a law-abiding citizen. His past is not checkered. He has a wife who loves him. I can tell you there is no likelihood of—what do you call it when you do it again?"

"Recidivism," the judge prompted.

"Got it, recidivism. And that's punishment enough. I'm asking you, your honor, to send him home."

But Merryday still had a question: What about his marijuana use? Did Kovach need to go to a substance abuse program? Fernandez said he could ask Kovach, but the judge instead addressed the defendant's wife.

"Is your husband needing some assistance with substance abuse?" he asked.

"He does not, sir," she replied.

Fernandez jumped in then to say Kovach was even giving up smoking cigarettes "because she's teaching him to play the mandolin in return."

"Mr. Kovach is not a narcotics or marijuana user?" the judge asked.

"Not at this time, sir," his wife replied.

At last, the judge was ready. He stared down at the defendant standing before him.

"Let me say this, Mr. Kovach," Merryday began. "Some of these things are ambiguous. . . . I guess I am resolving some doubts in your favor, owing to your status as a first offender and the fact that some of the consequences that could have occurred apparently did not."

Any future offenses, though, would undoubtedly lead to a prison sentence, the judge warned him.

"I'll be honest with you, Mr. Kovach," Merryday said. "Some of your explanations here are very nearly, 'The dog ate my homework,' but not qualitatively the same."

Kovach hung his head and shook it slightly.

Despite Kovach's lovely home and loving wife, the judge said, those factors don't matter to the law and the sentencing guidelines. Don't get crosswise of the law again, he warned, "because it comes at you like a freight train."

At last, having lectured the defendant, the judge announced, "James Michael Kovach is placed on probation for two years, that's two years as to each of count one and count two, those terms to run concurrently." That meant they would run at the same time and not be stacked up to make a total of four years.

Kovach could serve his probation in Virginia, the judge said, but he could not travel outside the United States—no more trips to Jamaica or Vietnam or Peru. Merryday also ordered mandatory drug testing and fined him $1,000.

The judge asked if either attorney had any objections to the sentence. Colbourn, reluctantly, spoke up. There was an issue regarding fairness in the punishment the judge had just meted out, compared to what the other defendants received.

"It may be belated," she said, "but since you have decided against the prison term, I would request that you give some consideration to community service time, given that Mr. Higgins was given house arrest for just receiving the plant."

"Is there some particular community service that you had in mind?"

"No, your honor," Colbourn said—then quickly added, "Preferably not something involving orchids."

Fernandez mentioned that Kovach was already helping out at a food bank for the poor in Virginia. The judge said he didn't know anything about the place, which made him cautious. A couple of times in the past, he said, he had seen "some insulting wild cards dealt to defendants" in the name of community service, so he usually avoided including that in any sentence. He would not order community service for Kovach.

Thus, thanks to Merryday's caution, Kovach the smuggler got a lighter sentence than Higgins the scientist, who got house arrest.

Then, in a final, brief discussion about the sentencing guidelines with Colbourn, Merryday revealed the real reason he had not put Kovach behind bars. He didn't know it, but it was similar to the British appellate court's decision on Henry Azadehdel's case.

Just the other day, the judge told the attorneys, he had visited the federal prison in nearby Coleman and had seen how crowded it was with drug traffickers and so forth.

"Prison square footage is a scarce national resource," Merryday said. "While I am certainly not suggesting that violations of this statute are not sufficient to warrant incarceration, because that's flatly not the case, I'm not sure that given the cost and the like . . . that that's what's called for right here under the circumstances of this case."

And that was that. The judge told the attorneys, "Thank you all very much for your spirits, and we are in adjournment." Then he stood up and stepped through the door behind the bench, closing the last chapter on the *Phragmipedium kovachii* case.

The Kovachs declined to speak to reporters as they hurried from the courtroom. So did the attorneys.

Photographers are not allowed to shoot pictures inside a federal courthouse. They have to catch their subjects on the sidewalk outside. Before Kovach's sentencing, a newspaper photographer snapped a picture of Kovach and his wife walking into the courthouse, both looking tense.

A photo snapped moments after they walked out showed Kovach's face wreathed in a big, beatific smile.

"I felt relieved," Kovach explained later. "I also felt like, under the circumstances, we truly had won a victory."

But the story of the *Phragmipedium kovachii*, the one Kovach had thought might someday make a good book, had not reached the end. Not quite.

Epilogue

The Stuff That Dreams Are Made of

The concentrated romance, mystery, and tragedy built into
the story of orchid collecting are rarely considered when we
enter a greenhouse. . . . And yet, there are many species which,
whenever seen, suggest to the student of orchid history events
full of fascinating associations and uncanny experiences.

Oakes Ames, "The Dean of American Orchidology,"
quoted in *A History of the Orchid*

As soon as Chuck Acker saw the story in the Chicago paper about the *Phragmipedium kovachii* case, he knew he had to have one.

He was cuckoo for slipper orchids anyway. Once he'd seen a photo of this big beauty and heard about the controversy, "I went ape about it," he said later.

Acker, who lived in Wisconsin, had never imported any foreign plants. He had to make quite a few calls just to find out who might have a line on these new orchids. Finally someone gave him Lee Moore's number in Miami.

"I called him up and introduced myself and he said, 'WHAT? Who are you?'" Acker said, chuckling.

Moore, suspicious of a call from a complete stranger, took down Acker's name and number and promised to call back. Eventually he did, this time sounding a bit friendlier. Moore said he didn't have any *Phragmipedium kovachii* for sale right then, but he could help Acker in another way.

"One thing led to another, and all of a sudden I'm going to Peru with him," Acker said.

Acker and his fiancée flew down to Miami and met Moore. Then they joined him on a flight to Lima. "Then he hooked us up with his favorite hotel," Acker said, "and then the next day he set us up with his guide."

Acker regarded Moore as an entertaining character, not some legendary icon. The way he acted around his wife, Chady, cracked him up.

"He was smoking, and his wife was always mad at him for it," Acker said.

The guide Moore had recommended took the couple up to Moyobamba. After what Acker's fiancée referred to as "the death march," they got far enough up into the mountains to see a hillside covered in *Phragmipedium kovachii*.

But none of them was in flower.

They toured Moore's nursery and then visited Alfredo Manrique's nursery, too. Moore also took them to see a few private collections. He knew who had what.

"I wouldn't want to mention the names," Acker said. "One gentleman had a lot of these plants. I'm not sure it was legal for him to have them. He had twenty of them."

At last Acker got to see a *kovachii* in bloom—even held a blossom in his hand. But afterward, back home in Wisconsin, he decided that wasn't enough. He talked to his best friend, another slipper orchid fanatic named Jerry Fischer, and told him, "We've *got* to get those plants."

Fischer knew how, Acker said. Unlike Acker, Fischer had connections in Peru. He had been importing orchids for some time from a grower named Manuel Arias Silva, he said. Arias's nursery had a license from INRENA to collect *Phragmipedium kovachii* from the wild, just five, for propagation in vitro. Then they could put the results into flasks—sealed vessels filled with a jelly-like solution of agar. The seedlings grow in the enclosed, sterile environment until they are large enough to be potted. Arias's *kovachii* flasks were now available for sale.

Arias had such good relations with INRENA's top CITES officials that he became the first nursery owner to get permission to ship his flasks of *kovachii* out of Peru. He also enjoyed a distinct lack of competition.

When Manrique sought permission to ship his flasks out of Peru to his partners, Glen Decker in New York and Peter Croezen in Canada, INRENA officials repeatedly turned him down. Not until Manrique finally sought the help of Dr. Isaias Rolando was he able to successfully appeal the decision to the head of the agency.

The Moores had a bigger problem than bureaucratic red tape. Someone broke into Vivero Nuevo Destino and stole the lab equipment that Peter Croezen had given them. They had their legal *kovachii* plants, but they couldn't micropropagate anything. Years later, photos of the *kovachii* still appeared on their website as if it were for sale, but the fine print said it wasn't really available.

So while Manrique appealed his case and the Moores tried to figure out where their equipment had gone, Arias was the only game in town.

Still, Moore warned Acker against getting involved with the Arias family. They were a shady bunch, he said. But Acker had also been told that Peruflora was now being run by Arias's son Manolo, who promised the nursery would be run more professionally.

So in 2005—even as the elder Arias was battling extradition—Acker and Fischer flew to Peru to meet with young Manolo, a slender, serious man with dark hair and glasses. There was no sign of the burns he had once suffered, the ones he recovered from while staying with George Norris in Texas.

The younger Arias showed the two Americans around his lab, and then came the moment Acker had been waiting for.

"The flasks looked beautiful," Acker said. "He told us which crosses were which, and then he left us alone in the lab for an hour to pick which *kovachii* we wanted."

Once they were done, he said, "Manolo packed them up and we flew out the next day."

Back home in Wisconsin, Acker waited impatiently for his new orchids to sprout. He found himself "acting like a mother goose looking after her goslings. I was constantly viewing them and admiring their progress, as well as checking for contamination."

Acker notified his customers that he expected to have the fabled *Phragmipedium kovachii* for sale very soon. When the announcement went out, he was stunned by the response.

"It was like a feeding frenzy," he said. "I was overwhelmed with orders. I sold out in a couple of days."

Soon, though, Acker noticed something odd about his plants. They were all growing—but most of them were growing far more rapidly than he had been led to believe was normal. He clipped off a few pieces and shipped them to experts at the University of Florida to have the DNA checked.

The results floored him.

"Most of the flasks I brought back were mislabeled and they weren't *kovachii*," Acker said. Instead, most of what he'd brought home were hybrids, a cross of *Phragmipedium wallisii* with *kovachii*.

This was, for him, not just a disappointment but a financial calamity. He had collected a deposit from each customer worth half the price of each orchid, for a total of $6,500.

"I obviously had to refund the customers' money," Acker said. "And I told Manolo, 'You need to write a letter of apology.'" Acker says Peruflora refunded his money, which took a bit of the sting out of the debacle.

Eventually, from the one flask that contained what it was supposed to contain, Acker coaxed one single *Phragmipedium kovachii* into flower. He got it to bloom just in time for Wisconsin's 2009 Orchid Quest show. As a result, he became the first U.S. grower to successfully bloom a *Phragmipedium kovachii* plant from a flask, as well as the first to display a blooming specimen at a judged event.

Needless to say, it won Best in Show.

Despite that triumph, the whole experience left Acker feeling like he'd gone over Niagara Falls in a barrel: shaken up and amazed that he'd survived. He and his new bride agreed there was something about that orchid, something a little sinister.

"We called it the *kovachii* curse," he said.

Although Harold Koopowitz had hailed the five-plant permits issued by INRENA to Manrique, Arias, and Moore as the best way to protect new plants like the *kovachii*, in 2006 INRENA threw the Peruvian orchid community a curve.

The bureaucrats in Lima issued Decreto Supremo No. 043-2006-AG. The decree said nurseries could no longer export any orchids that were produced by any method other than in-vitro propagation. No wild-collected plants, and not even any nursery-grown ones, could be shipped overseas. Surely that would put a stop to smuggling those slippers.

The announcement caused an uproar. Manrique called it "an act made by people that say that they protect the natural resources of Peru, but know nothing about how the orchid market works."

"What are the exporters now expected to do with the thousands of orchids that we have been reproducing and propagating over many years?" Chady Moore wrote in a letter to INRENA. "These plants now have no value because they are prohibited for exportation."

Mrs. Moore wrote that she knew just who to blame for this ill-considered decree: Manuel Arias Silva. "El Professore" was claiming to have produced in-vitro orchids in just two years, which she said everyone knew to be impossible. The United States might consider him a fugitive from justice, but in Peru he still wielded plenty of political clout.

"It is obvious that this new decree was designed to benefit only one orchid exporter . . . in order to obtain a monopoly of orchid exportation in Peru with the blessings of INRENA," she wrote.

Her protests were for naught. Four years later, the decree still stands. As does the name of the accursed orchid.

Selby's court-ordered request to rename *Phragmipedium kovachii* failed miserably, just as Higgins and all the other orchid boys expected. But that was not the end of the effort to change it.

In 2006, a Dutch taxonomist named Paul van Rijckevorsel picked up the cause. In the November issue of a publication called *Taxon*, he proposed renaming Kovach's orchid, giving it the identity Christenson had intended, *Phragmipedium peruvianum*.

Sure, he wrote, it would be a bit of a pain to change the name after four years. But it would be worse for the "credibility and good reputation of botanical nomenclature" to let Kovach's name stand unchanged, he argued.

"After all," he wrote, "just about 'every rule in the book' was broken here. . . . Allowing this publication to stand may well send out the message to the world that the botanical community considers violation of CITES, blatant 'name hunting,' and criminal convictions as acceptable parts of the process of describing a taxon."

Higgins—now finished with his probation and able to speak his mind— fired off a rebuttal. He pointed out that the rules did not say it was wrong to name a plant after a convicted criminal. In fact, he contended, changing the name now "would create chaotic consequences for the stability of botanical nomenclature."

Not even Peru's top CITES expert backed the change. One reason: Just as Arias had once pointed out, Christenson's source, Renato Villena, did not have state permission to collect the orchids, either.

"Thus, under Peruvian law both type specimens are associated with illegal actions," Betty Millian, Peru's top CITES expert, wrote in a 2008 response in *Taxon*. Anyway, she wrote, changing the name now "would create a dangerous precedent for the chaotic rejection of any publications that include undesirable names."

Ultimately the committee in charge of naming plants ruled that the name Selby had produced, the one naming the plant after Kovach, would remain in place and that "the committee should confine itself to issues of plant nomenclature rather than indulge in questions of moral judgment or political or legal correctness."

Thus, for good or ill, Kovach's name is likely to remain on his plant forever.

While the debate about the name of the orchid continued, the man who had pushed the hardest for Selby to change it stirred up an even bigger controversy.

In April 2007, Dr. Isaias Rolando complained on the Slipper Talk Internet forum that nobody really cared about all the illegal *Phragmipedium kovachii* flowers being smuggled out of Peru. When people on the forum asked him if he wasn't stepping on toes in Peru by highlighting the smuggling, he replied that he just wanted to protect the remaining wild population in Peru.

"I am only exposing facts," he wrote. "If you feel offended, very sorry and my best apologies. But how can we deal with the fact that there is a business in the market that were CONVICTED by the U.S. Department of Justice?"

He promised to tell, at last, the true history of the notorious orchid. Chapter 1 began a dozen years before Kovach arrived at the El Progresso truck stop, he wrote.

"In 1990 visiting Moyobamba and Vivero Agro-Oriente, Renato Villena told me the story that some locals have mentioned to him about a '*zapatito azul*,'" the doctor wrote. "That time it was difficult to believe the existence of such a 'blue' color in a *Phragmipedium*, but after the appearance of *Phragmipedium besseae* anything could be possible, but certainly not a blue pigment in an orchid."

Then, he wrote, in 1997 a farmer named Juan Perez Rojas discovered the fabled *zapatito azul* on land his family owned near Venceremos, in an area well known to orchid collectors.

"One of these orchid collectors was Renato Villena and knew about this new and incredible orchid from that area," Rolando wrote. "He started to study the new *Phrag* since 1999 and took him and his authorized firm more than two years to obtain enough material to send it to orchid taxonomists and finally Dr Eric Christenson was able to write the original and legal description of the new discovered *Phragmipedium peruvianum*."

But another collector, Lee Moore, got wind of what was going on, Rolando wrote: "Rumors of the blue *zapatito* took him and his friend Kovach to travel to the area. Another local farmer, Faustino M., also collected some plants and with his family he used to sell orchids in his farm aside the highway when Mr. Kovach arrived, bought some specimens, took them out of the country and illegally introduced the plants to the U.S."

Afterward, he wrote, unscrupulous collectors stripped that area, as well as a second one he called "Habitat No. 2."

"Habitat No. 2 was depleted . . . yes sure, after collecting permit No. 2. Who did this? You all know that convicted person," he wrote, in a not-so-subtle dig at Arias.

The people most responsible for stripping the jungle of the orchids "have already been convicted by U.S. Department of Justice but escaped from U.S. and cannot travel anymore because Interpol is after him," Rolando wrote. "That is why the son is doing and perpetuating their illegal commercial activities."

The Peruvian Orchid Club had voted this fugitive smuggler out of its membership, Rolando noted. The vote, he said, was unanimous. Yet the man stayed in business.

"How can he export? With the help of some bad officers at INRENA," Rolando wrote. "I am sure when the new president will know about this illegal activities he will stop that business. All his plants should be confiscated and returned to where they belong: the Peruvian jungle. He always exported but wild collected material, for the last 30 years at least."

Smuggled *Phragmipedium kovachii* were scattered all over the world, he wrote, calling them "pk" for short.

"Do you know that there is a country in Europe having a full greenhouse with hundreds of PK?" he asked. "Do you know that there are thousands of pk in Ecuador? . . . Do you know that pk was in Taiwan even before the description of the new specie?"

The doctor admitted he might be crossing a line by posting the accusations he'd made, even though he hadn't named any names.

"Am I clear enough?" he wrote. "I know that posting this facts I risk my life, because I have some real enemies that act very badly when they are exposed . . . you will see." He concluded with "VERITAS ILLUMINATIO MEA IN GOD I TRUST."

Rolando's posting touched off a flurry of comments among the other Slipper Talk users. Peter Croezen, for instance, pointed out that Manuel Arias Silva and George Norris had not been convicted of smuggling *Phragmipedium kovachii*, but of smuggling other species. Rolando promised to explain the connection in a later posting, but he never did.

Instead, in May 2007, the diminutive eye doctor posted a dramatic update.

"It is happening already," he wrote. "The 'others' are acting against my reputation at my university and threatening members of my family. I have a pregnant wife at this moment and she just mentioned to me that the phone and the e-mail are constantly receiving very dirty messages and warnings. My friends, family and lawyers consulted recommended me to stop all communications. I deeply regret to decide not to continue with this. I will only stay as an observer."

That was his last post. But he was not quite done with the fabulous *kovachii*.

In January 2008, a jubilant Rolando brought *Phragmipedium kovachii* to Miami—legally. The venue: the 19th World Orchid Conference and Show at the Sheraton Miami Mart Hotel and Convention Center.

Rolando, with his government contacts, had gotten permission to take some *kovachii* plants as well as some hybrids to the show and sell them. The prices would be $50 to $100 for seedlings and $120 for a plant that was nearly ready to produce a flower—a far cry from the $10,000 price tag at the 2002 Redland show.

"Finally, after five years of working very hard, now we can say the species is commercially available," Rolando told the *Miami Herald*.

Yet, despite his vow on the Slipper Talk forum to keep mum, Rolando could not resist mentioning smugglers and their well-heeled customers.

"The main profit is already out of the country," he told the *Herald*. "There is a big black market, and it does not belong to any Peruvians. I know who they are but I cannot say."

Before long, Rolando was mired in a different controversy. He was accused of plagiarism by a former employee of Manrique's. His university opened a formal inquiry. Rolando's spirits sank.

On the night of July 15, 2008, Rolando visited one of Lima's most exclusive country clubs. He had hoped his good friend Manrique would accompany him there.

"He tried to contact me that afternoon to join him to take a sauna bath at the Club Regatas," Manrique said, but they missed connections. As a result, Manrique said, "he went alone. He took a sauna bath and then went to have a frugal dinner."

About 8:00 p.m., a body plunged from the building's upper floors to the pavement below.

The headline in the next day's *El Commercio* reported, "Doctor Found Dead at Club Regatas Lima." *La Republica* reported that he'd apparently clambered over a railing and "launched himself into the void."

Was it suicide? Initially the police said that appeared to be the case, and one of the Lima TV stations claimed there was a suicide note. There wasn't. Eventually the authorities decided it was an accident, Manrique said, but he doesn't buy it. He still believes the despondent Rolando jumped. So does Ricardo Fernandez, Rolando's friend since they were teenagers. He's convinced Rolando suffered from a psychiatric disorder that drove him to jump.

Other theories abound, though, most of them based on Rolando's reputation and the circles in which he moved.

"There's been a lot of talk in the orchid world that he might have had help," said Wesley Higgins. "He's made a lot of enemies over the years."

"He was always a wheeler-dealer," said Glen Decker, Manrique's partner in the in-vitro propagation project. "Maybe he wheeled and dealed once too often."

The mystery doesn't surprise George Norris. "That's the way he lived his life," said Norris, who made it clear he didn't mourn Rolando's passing. "He was always undercover."

Lee Moore wondered if Rolando had somehow gotten in over his head with people smuggling things other than orchids. The Adventurer is convinced Rolando did not kill himself. His wife Chady is just as convinced that he did. The couple has argued about it, their voices rising in anger and frustration.

"He was too happy!" Moore insisted. "Give me a reason why he would kill himself!"

Easy, his wife said. Rolando was despondent because he owed too much money and couldn't pay it back.

Chady Moore said she had friends in Peru who told her about the night he died: "He received a phone call, he excused himself, and then walked out and jumped."

Moore shook his head, still unconvinced. Heavy debts didn't seem to him a good reason for anyone to commit suicide. After all, he and his wife had run up some $300,000 in debt and had to file for Chapter 7 bankruptcy protection in 2009, he pointed out. (Of course, their filing made no mention of their Peruvian holdings.)

Could Rolando's mysterious death be another instance of the Curse of the *Kovachii*?

Manrique takes a philosophical view—one that puts Kovach's infamous orchid in the same league as a famous movie icon, the Maltese Falcon. The little statuette was "the stuff that dreams are made of," but pursuing those dreams brought out the worst in everyone who chased it.

Sure, Manrique said, everyone involved with the plant has seemingly become mired in bad luck. But that's not because of the plant itself, he explained. It's because of what they thought it could do for them.

"The *Phrag kovachii* history is made on dreams, tales, and rumors," he said. "People dreamed on being famous or getting rich in no time."

They were so intoxicated by the sweet future that seemed to be offered by this stunning flower, he said, that they forgot one of the maxims of the orchid business:

"If you want to earn a million bucks selling orchids, start investing ten million."

Still, what happened at Selby Gardens after its guilty plea in the *kovachii* case might be further evidence of a curse.

In 2005, Selby sold the old 7-11 building and moved its scientists into some newly refurbished quarters on the main Selby campus. The same year the OIC moved in, John Beckner left—he won't say why. He contemplated writing a book about the *Phragmipedium kovachii* controversy, but after working on it for a while, he gave up. If he wrote down everything he knew and heard, he explained, he feared he would wind up in some sort of legal trouble. Instead, he's writing the story as fiction.

"It's a murder mystery," he explained.

Thanks to Beckner's departure, Stig Dalström finally landed his dream job, a full-time position with Selby Gardens as orchid curator. He didn't hold it long.

The loss of so many donor dollars during the Kovach case hurt Selby, and so did having to borrow money to complete a major renovation of the gardens' mansion. When the real estate meltdown hit Florida, Sarasota's economy suffered badly. By 2008 Selby's tax return showed a deficit of more than $1 million.

In February 2009, Selby's trustees, fearing bankruptcy, hired a new CEO. Thomas Buchter had been director of horticulture at the Holden Arboretum in northeastern Ohio. He was a botanist, but not an orchid boy.

Buchter's mission was to cut expenses wherever possible, just like the general who'd once replaced Cal Dodson. As one of his first cuts, Buchter laid off seven employees, including both Dalström and Higgins.

For Higgins, this was a disaster.

His six months on house arrest hadn't bothered him much. He could still drive back and forth to work, and he and his wife had never gone out on the town much. The one part of his sentence that seemed like a punishment was the requirement that, during his probation, he had to document all his finances for his probation officer twice a year. It was like being required to do your taxes every six months.

Still, Higgins had done so well on probation that, at the suggestion of his probation officer, he applied to end it early. Despite Colbourn's objections,

Judge Merryday agreed, and Higgins was a free man after thirteen months.

But now, thanks to Buchter's budget cutting, Higgins was out of work. The full impact of his reluctant guilty plea hit home. Every place he applied for a job, he had to fill out a form that asked if he had ever been convicted of a crime. Every time, he dutifully checked yes. Every time, that single check mark outweighed his employment at Selby, his doctorate, his Coast Guard service, and his previously clean record. No potential employer ever got past it.

"I can't get to the interview stage," he said with a sigh.

Dalström, on the other hand, was not a bit discouraged by this sudden turn in his fortunes. He had a better, brighter future in mind. Like Kovach, he had already begun working on plans for a reality TV show. He even filmed a pilot episode. He called it *Wild Orchid Man*. The star, of course, would be Stig Dalström.

Until the show caught on, though, Dalström had decided to take a job down in Peru working for one of the most prominent orchid growers there: Manolo Arias Silva.

With both Higgins and Dalström out, that effectively shut down the OIC. The books and computers and specimens were still there, sitting in the brand-new OIC, but as Carl Luer bitterly pointed out, "Nobody's running it."

The shutdown sent a wave of outrage through the local orchid community. When the Sarasota Orchid Society held an advance screening of the *Wild Orchid Man* pilot episode during its regular meeting on Selby's grounds, the star could not attend because he—like Eric Christenson, the ex-colleague he had taunted as "the Blob"—was now forbidden to set foot in the place.

"Stig was not permitted on Selby property. Well, now it seems Selby will not be allowed on our property," the president of another local orchid society wrote in his club's newsletter, banning Selby participation in its events.

Then the unthinkable occurred: Harry Luther quit. The bearded bromeliad expert, once so in love with Selby that he called it home, saw what had happened to his fellow scientists and figured his neck would be the next one on the chopping block. He took a job in Singapore as assistant director of its national parks board.

"I spent thirty-plus years at Selby, but it looks like it's crossed the tipping point, no longer the institution that I joined in 1979," he explained.

Buchter insists Selby is just as committed as ever to plant science, as well as tourism and weddings. Someday, he said, when the finances permit it, he would gladly restore what he'd cut. But by 2011 that day had still not arrived.

Buchter's office features a wide variety of botany-related artwork. One of the most stunning pieces hangs directly across from his desk. It's what the Selby CEO sees whenever he raises his eyes from his paperwork.

"Most people don't have to be told what that is when they walk in," Buchter said, chuckling.

It's a painting of the *Phragmipedium kovachii*, depicted growing on a mountainside in Peru. The artist: Stig Dalström.

⁓⁂

The fact that Dalström and Christenson were both now pariahs at Selby did not make them allies. As the years went by, Christenson picked fights with his few remaining friends. He pushed everyone away. Soon even he and Turkel parted company.

Isolation took its toll. In April 2011, Christenson's letter carrier noticed that mail was piling up at his house and asked a neighbor to check on him. Inside the house, it wasn't pretty. Christenson had been dead for a week and no one had noticed. He was fifty-seven.

His obituary in the *Sarasota Herald-Tribune* glossed over much of his career but highlighted his battle with Selby during the *kovachii* controversy. "He was well known before that time," Turkel told the paper, "but the *kovachii* incident made him famous around the world."

⁓⁂

Another of the *kovachii*'s ill-fated pursuers, George Norris, served his prison time and was released on April 27, 2007. He went home to Texas to rebuild his shattered life.

Two years later, though, his cause was taken up by a conservative think tank, the Heritage Foundation, which had never been much of a fan of endangered species protection anyway. The Heritage Foundation held up Norris's case as an example of bureaucracy run amok and the frivolity of environmental regulations—rather than as an example of an unscrupulous businessman who gained an edge over his competitors by breaking the rules they were all supposed to follow.

A report posted on the foundation's website described Norris's crime as merely "a paperwork violation: He had the wrong documents for some of the plants he imported but almost certainly could have obtained the right ones with a bit more time and effort." Of course, that was an inaccurate statement for the Appendix I orchids, which weren't to be traded at all. The report also made no mention of how, over the years, Norris had told Arias the way to hide the illegal orchids, or how he counseled him to send them through Miami to guarantee the shipment lighter scrutiny.

Although now a free man, "Norris has lost his passion for orchids," the 2009 report said. "The greenhouse is abandoned. Broken pots, bags of dirt, plastic bins, and other clutter spill off its shelves and onto the floor. The roof is sagging. A few potted cacti are the only living things inside it, aside from weeds."

Norris told the foundation's writer that he had trouble sleeping at night because "I still have prison dreams." He paused and looked down at the floor. Then the man who used to write everything in ALL CAPS said, in a quiet voice, "It's utterly wrecked our lives."

That same summer, Norris's wife, Kathy, was called to testify before a congressional subcommittee investigating the consequences of "overcriminalization" in America. She echoed the Heritage Foundation report, insisting the federal government had sent her husband to prison over a minor infraction, making an example out of a sick old man.

"This 'crime' is one committed by everyone who imports orchids because otherwise it would be impossible to do business at all with most foreign sellers," she testified. "Manuel and George probably could have gotten the right paperwork for all of them, but it would have taken months and cost a fair amount—that's how foreign governments work. So this really was a paperwork violation." No one on the congressional subcommittee challenged her assertions.

A year after the Heritage Foundation report painted such a dire picture of his circumstances, Norris seemed more like his bombastic and opinionated self. In an interview, he called Christenson "a ratty little sumbitch," made snide comments about Isaias Rolando, and contended he had been the victim of "a prosecutor on a rampage." He called his conviction for smuggling "this little nitpicking thing."

As for Norris's co-defendant, the one who had skipped the country to avoid prison, he was still a free man. Norris says they're still friends and occasionally still communicate with each other. "He's really in his twilight now," Norris said.

In September 2010, a Peruvian newspaper called *Peru.21* published a story on criminals from Interpol's most-wanted list who were loose in Peru. Among those pictured: Manuel Arias Silva.

A few days after the newspaper published his photo and name, describing him as a fugitive, Arias quietly set up a booth at an orchid show in Lima. The next booth over belonged to none other than Lee Moore. The Adventurer, upon spotting his nemesis so close by, couldn't resist asking how he was doing.

"Everything's fine," Arias replied imperturbably, according to Moore. Then El Professore settled in to sell a few flowers, and so did Moore. The two longtime adversaries sat placidly side by side, hawking their wares to the passersby, just two old men trying to make a buck off of found beauty.

Up in Vermont, John Atwood gave up on botany. Orchids had brought him so much heartache that he went back to his first field of study, music. The man who successfully cultivated a *Phragmipedium kovachii* on a picnic table now spends his days repairing pipe organs.

"I changed directions," he explained. "I don't think about epiphytes and tropical research anymore."

He still grows about a dozen orchids at home, but that's his only connection with the past. Yes, he said, they are slipper orchids. No, none of them is a *Phragmipedium kovachii*.

The one *kovachii* he did successfully cultivate, the one that was confiscated by Agent Holt and sent to the U.S. Botanic Garden, did not do so well south of Vermont. The garden staff reported that it died in custody.

As Higgins likes to point out, that means the only piece of the plant ever sent back to Peru—as INRENA requested in 2002—was the piece that Selby itself sent to Ricardo Fernandez at the University of San Marco.

Ultimately, Higgins contended, what Kovach and Selby did benefited the plant that bears Kovach's name.

Before Kovach showed up in Sarasota with his orchid, the plant was being sold for high prices on the black market. Now, thanks to them, there are plants produced by people like Chuck Acker. The result is that "they've taken it off the black market, and now it's out in the public market," he said.

But that's little comfort to Michael Kovach.

Kovach still lives in Virginia, in the little clapboard house up in the hills where miners once searched for gold, where the feds once searched for smuggled plants.

Agent Holt showed up there in February 2005 to bring him back the boxes of files she had confiscated three years before. She went over the list with him, but when she asked him to sign a receipt, he refused "because no one from the U.S. government had told him the truth since the investigation had begun," Holt wrote in her report.

She eventually cajoled him into signing her receipt, but he added a note that said: "Signed under protest; item-by-item inventory not provided at time of search; must go through all items to insure nothing is missing."

Kovach did not get back his orchids. The eight plants still living of the 385 that Holt had seized from Kovach in 2002 were officially handed over in 2005 to the caretaker that had failed to keep Atwood's sliver alive.

But that was fine with Kovach. He had decided to give up the orchid business. Southwind Orchids is no more.

He's also given up trying to make the big score, the big discovery. He and his wife get by on her salary from Canon, he said. They don't need more than that, he said, although his battle over his namesake orchid cost him $130,000. He and his wife refinanced the house and burned through money he'd inherited from a well-off uncle, too. They spent every penny they had on his defense just to avoid prison.

For the first year he was on probation, Kovach didn't do much beyond taking guitar lessons. He didn't bother looking for work, given his conviction. Then his probation officer told him he had to find a job. He persuaded the music store where he took his lessons to hire him. He sold guitars there for three years.

Like Atwood, Kovach now devotes himself to music. He doesn't tour with any bands, just plays guitar and sings for any group in the region that needs a journeyman to fill in during a performance. He prefers bluegrass, but these days the demand is mostly for old rhythm and blues tunes. He doesn't mind.

"All I have to do is chop chords so I can sing," he said.

He does still tend a crop, but it's vegetables now. He said he grows them for a food bank for the poor, although lately the farm had gone fallow because he was battling pancreatic cancer. As of November 2010, he said, his prognosis was good.

He tries not to think about how his glorious career as an orchid hunter crashed and burned. Nobody but him really cared about the plant, he contended.

"All anybody gave a goddamn about is the money," he said.

When he does ponder what happened to him, he can't help but feel bitter. He's convinced the Moores—and specifically Mrs. Moore—concocted a plan to use him as a stalking horse. They sent him to Selby to get this dramatic new discovery named after him, thus drawing all the attention to the bumbling amateur from Virginia. Meanwhile the Moores quietly pursued control of as many plants as they could get their hands on in Peru, he said.

Moyobomba embraced the orchid's notoriety in the hope of attracting tourists. There is a statute of Kovach's orchid erected downtown, and even a disco opened bearing the flower's name. Photo courtesy of Stig Dalström.

"I'm sure she set me up," he said. "Everybody used me as a scapegoat. I'm just the dumb, happy Christian who goes around trusting everybody. I'm a sap."

Despite Moore's new revelation about the three orchids, despite the stories of the orchid judges, despite Higgins's impression otherwise, Kovach still contends he brought only one *Phragmipedium kovachii* to Selby Gardens. Everything that happened, he said, "was over just one flower—just one."

The whole ordeal, he said, "was a nightmare." He'll never get over it, he said, because "you never get over not getting justice."

Dalström, as he was about to leave for Peru to go work for Manolo Arias Silva, listened with a quizzical expression on his face as a visitor to his small but tidy Sarasota apartment told him about Kovach's bitterness. Dalström was bound for Moyobamba, which has eagerly embraced the notoriety that Kovach's discovery generated. The town square now features a large, purplish-pink statue of the flower Kovach bought at El Progresso. There is even a disco that bears the famous flower's name.

When the visitor finished the story, Dalström chuckled and shook his head.

"I don't know what he's got to be bitter about," said the man who made a tidy profit selling *kovachii* T-shirts. "He got the plant named after him. Isn't that what he wanted?"

Acknowledgments

No author writes alone. My primary thanks go, as always, to my wife, Sherry, who for months on end put up with orchid books and court files scattered from the dining room table to the bedroom floor, and listened without eye-rolling as I prattled on about international endangered species law.

My heartfelt gratitude also goes to Gisella Canepa-Bosco for her crucial work translating documents and even video from Spanish into English. Without her help, this book would lack some of its most important details.

I was greatly aided by a number of my colleagues at the *St. Petersburg Times*. My editor, Roy LeBlanc, graciously read the manuscript and suggested ways to improve its flow—so you, dear reader, should thank him too. Caryn Baird, the Indiana Jones of document research, dug up all sorts of valuable background material for my initial stories, which benefited the book version immensely. Artist Don Morris updated and expanded the map that ran in the newspaper to better suit this book's ambitions. Paul Jerome, whose technical savvy is exceeded only by his patience, provided me with some badly needed help in dealing with the photos and video. As always, I owe a tremendous debt to editor Neil Brown for granting me permission to plumb the resources of Florida's largest newspaper, as well as to my attorney, Alison Steele, whose advice is worth its weight in gold (which, fortunately, is not the way she bills).

My thanks go to orchid experts extraordinaire Paul Martin Brown and Scott Stewart, who vetted this manuscript for accuracy. If I have still blundered into errors, that's my fault, not theirs. Documentary filmmaker Rich Walton helped me in ways too weird to recount. The folks at the University Press of Florida were wonderful, as always, especially Meredith Morris-Babb, Catherine-Nevil Parker, Susan Murray, Dennis Lloyd, and Stephanie Williams.

Finally, I must give a special shout-out to Boy Scout Troop 305 and Scoutmaster Tim Bulu. They tolerated me dragging a laptop along and working on this book during our summer camp in Georgia. Despite the scorpions, skunks, and blistering heat, our campsite proved to be the ideal place to get a lot of writing done. The lack of any Internet access or cell phone service may have had something to do with it.

July 2011

Notes on Sources

Most of the information in this book came from interviews I conducted, documents provided to me by the people I was interviewing, federal court records, and the investigative files of the U.S. Fish and Wildlife Service. In these notes, where it says the information came from an interview, it means an interview with the author. Where it mentions internal e-mails, memos, and other documents, I will, when possible, cite their source. The federal court records come from three cases. The two filed in the U.S. District Court in Tampa are *United States vs. James Michael Kovach*, Case No. 8:03-cr-00457, Middle District of Florida; and *United States vs. Marie Selby Botanical Gardens and Wesley Higgins*, Case No. 8:03-cr-00494, Middle District of Florida. The third case, filed in U.S. District Court in Miami, is *United States vs. George Norris and Manuel Arias Silva*, Case No. 1:04–cr–20144, Southern District of Florida. The investigative files, obtained from the Fish and Wildlife Service via a Freedom of Information Act request, formed the basis for those three cases. The Kovach and Selby files are lumped together in one file, which the agency has designated as Investigation No. 2002503514. The Norris and Arias files are designated as Investigation No. 2002202919R008.

Epigraph

It was the founding father . . . : Berliocchi, *The Orchid in Lore and Legend*, 29.
As dead flies give . . . : Verse quoted is from the New International version of the Bible.

Prologue

If, when you finish it . . . : Stout, *Black Orchids*, 103.
The bride glided across . . . : Author's personal observations, double-checked with my wife's recollections.
But as Adam and Eve could . . . : The story of Adam and Eve in the Garden of Eden comes from Genesis 1.
That perfect Selby Gardens wedding . . . : Selby wedding figures provided by Selby staff.
The wedding is all about . . . : Interview with Selby Gardens marketing director Debby Steele.
This was not just any . . . : Attendance figures and tourism ranking from Selby staff.

Orchids have always been . . . : For more details on Selby's origin and mission, see chapter 2.

Floridians are accustomed to . . . : In 2005, the CBS News *60 Minutes* television program dubbed Florida "A Paradise of Scandals." In 2009, the *New Yorker* labeled it "The Ponzi State." Florida scandals can reach absurd levels: One Miami-Dade commissioner was indicted for bank fraud and money laundering, reelected anyway, then convicted of vote fraud, too. One of the most notorious scandals, involving both politics and sex, involved Florida congressman Mark Foley, who in 2006 resigned after being caught sending sexually explicit text messages to congressional pages.

When I began writing this book . . . : The person who told me I didn't know much was Peter Croezen. I should add that most of the time, the movie that this case reminded me of was not *Rashomon* but Humphrey Bogart's *Beat the Devil*, where adventurers and con men chasing what they think is a fortune run amok and turn on each other.

What we weren't aware of . . . : Interview with John Atwood.

But rival orchid expert . . . : Interview with Eric Christenson.

Chapter 1. The Most Beautiful Party in Town

I never before realized . . . : Lowman, Burgess, and Burgess, *It's a Jungle Up There*, 196.

As the party swirled around . . . : Interview with Meg Lowman.

The soiree Lowman was presiding . . . : Interviews with former Selby staffer Ilene Denton and now-retired *Sarasota Herald-Tribune* society columnist Marjorie North.

Since it was an outdoor event . . . : Interviews with Ilene Denton and Marjorie North; Marjorie North, "Dancing under an Asian Moon—and a Downpour," *Sarasota Herald-Tribune*, April 8, 2001.

But on the ball's twentieth . . . : North, "Dancing under an Asian Moon—and a Downpour," *Sarasota Herald-Tribune*, April 8, 2001.

In 2002, though, the ghost . . . : Marjorie North, "Orchid Ball Resplendent with Colors and Flavors of Rio de Janeiro," *Sarasota Herald-Tribune*, April 21, 2002.

More than four hundred . . . : Mary Alice Collins, "Party Perfect: A Sampling of Successful Fund-raisers Shows How It Should Be Done," *Sarasota*, November 2002, The Free Library, www.thefreelibrary.com/Party perfect: A sampling of successful fund-raisers shows how it . . . -a094162748; review of the extensive pictures of Orchid Ball guests posted on the *Sarasota* magazine website; interviews with Ilene Denton and Marjorie North; Robert Plunket, "Beyond the Beach in Sarasota," *New York Times*, January 13, 2002.

The one anomaly in this scene . . . : Interview with Meg Lowman; Lowman, Burgess, and Burgess, *It's a Jungle Up There*, xii–xiii.

At forty-eight years old . . . : Description of Lowman from author's personal observations; interview with Lowman.

Lowman was actually the biggest . . . : Gina Edwards, "Law & Orchid," *Florida Trend*, December 2004, www.floridatrend.com/article.asp?aID=44349; Thomas Becnel, "Head in the Trees," *Sarasota Herald-Tribune*, October 27, 1992; Jeff Klinkenberg,

"Lofty Accomplishments," *St. Petersburg Times*, August 18, 1999; Liesl Schillinger, "Arbor Days," *New York Times*, August 8, 1999.

As she made plain in her . . . : Lasky and Knight, *The Most Beautiful Roof in the World*, 4; Lowman, *Life in the Treetops*, 1–16.

Her biggest scientific challenge . . . : Lowman, *Life in the Treetops*, 18–21.

She was willing to make . . . : Lowman, *Life in the Treetops*, 136–43; Thomas Becnel, "Head in the Trees," *Sarasota Herald-Tribune*, October 27, 1992.

In Australia she married . . . : Lowman, *Life in the Treetops*, 2–3, 43–44, 81–86, 103.

In 1992, after she had . . . : Lowman, *Life in the Treetops*, 157, 158.

Lowman's two worlds collided . . . : Lowman, Burgess, and Burgess, *It's a Jungle Up There*, 189–90.

Lowman hesitated. She hadn't . . . : Lowman, Burgess, and Burgess, *It's a Jungle Up There*, 190–91; Jeff Klinkenberg, "Lofty Accomplishments," *St. Petersburg Times*, August 18, 1999.

Brown first encountered Lowman . . . : Lowman, Burgess, and Burgess, *It's a Jungle Up There*, 166–67.

Still, Lowman had figured . . . : Lowman, Burgess, and Burgess, *It's a Jungle Up There*, 190–91.

She explained to the search . . . : Sean Roth, "Bruised, Pruned but Budding Again," *Gulf Coast Business Review*, June 18, 2004; Lowman, Burgess, and Burgess, *It's a Jungle Up There*, 190–91.

Wooing the donors turned . . . : Sean Roth, "Bruised, Pruned but Budding Again," *Gulf Coast Business Review*, June 18, 2004.

In his five years at Selby . . . : Sean Roth, "Bruised, Pruned but Budding Again," *Gulf Coast Business Review*, June 18, 2004; Lowman, Burgess, and Burgess, *It's a Jungle Up There*, 190.

So when he left, the board . . . : Lowman, Burgess, and Burgess, *It's a Jungle Up There*, 90. The children's book is Lasky and Knight, *The Most Beautiful Roof in the World*.

She gave up swinging . . . : Lowman, Burgess, and Burgess, *It's a Jungle Up There*, 191–92.

She took a management course . . . : Sean Roth, "Bruised, Pruned but Budding Again," *Gulf Coast Business Review*, June 18, 2004; interview with Robert Rivas.

By 2002 the veteran . . . : Interviews with Meg Lowman, Marjorie North, and Ilene Denton.

Now, as she greeted all . . . : Interview with Meg Lowman; Selby financial information from its IRS Form 1099 tax forms provided by Guidestar; Sean Roth, "Bruised, Pruned but Budding Again," *Gulf Coast Business Review*, June 18, 2004.

Lowman wasn't just focused . . . : Interviews with Meg Lowman and Carl Luer.

There were other marks . . . : Sean Roth, "Bruised, Pruned but Budding Again," *Gulf Coast Business Review*, June 18, 2004; Gina Edwards, "Law & Orchid," *Florida Trend*, December 2004, www.floridatrend.com/article.asp?aID=44349.

During the Orchid Ball . . . : Marjorie North, "Orchid Ball Resplendent with Colors and Flavors of Rio de Janeiro," *Sarasota Herald-Tribune*, April 21, 2002.

Lowman felt like she . . . : Lowman, Burgess, and Burgess, *It's a Jungle Up There*, 192.

Not everything was rosy . . . : Lowman, Burgess, and Burgess, *It's a Jungle Up There*, 191–92; interviews with Wesley Higgins, John Atwood, and Stig Dalström.

The people most skeptical . . . : Interviews with Wesley Higgins, John Atwood, and Stig Dalström.

They were no happier that . . . : Interviews with Wesley Higgins and Stig Dalström; Sean Roth, "Bruised, Pruned but Budding Again," *Gulf Coast Business Review*, June 18, 2004.

Since 1992 the scientists had . . . : Interview with Wesley Higgins.

The other staffers referred . . . : Interviews with Ilene Denton and Wesley Higgins; Lowman, Burgess and Burgess, *It's a Jungle Up There*, 202. Although Larson no longer produces his *The Far Side* cartoons for newspaper syndication, his work is still available on greeting cards, calendars, and books.

Inside 711 Palm Avenue . . . : Interview with Wesley Higgins.

At the heart of 7–11 . . . : Interview with Wesley Higgins.

Higgins had a background that . . . : Interview with Wesley Higgins.

To Lowman, the guys . . . : Interview with Meg Lowman; Lowman, Burgess, and Burgess, *It's a Jungle Up There*, 196–97.

Actually Lowman didn't see . . . : Interviews with Meg Lowman, Wesley Higgins, Stig Dalström, and Bob Scully.

Scully, a tall and slender . . . : Author's observations from a three-hour in-person interview and a longer telephone interview.

With his height and his . . . : Author's impressions; interview with Scully; interview with Marjorie North; Marjorie North, "Orchid Ball Resplendent with Colors and Flavors of Rio de Janeiro," *Sarasota Herald-Tribune*, April 21, 2002.

Scully, who was closing in . . . : Interview with Scully; Belinda Brockman, "Robert Scully, Noted Orchid Grower," *Miami Herald*, October 8, 1986; Alex Finkelstein, "Dade Firm Hopes to Turn 'Average Guy' into an Orchid Grower," *South Florida Business Journal*, January 7, 1095; Deb Kollars, "Family Orchid Farm Grows Up, Out to New Site in South Florida," *Miami Herald*, November 18, 1986; William R. Levesque, "Benlate's Bitter Legacy," *St. Petersburg Times*, September 24, 2006; Craig Pittman, "Storm's Howl Fills the Ears of Survivors," *St. Petersburg Times*, August 18, 2002.

Scully and his wife, Sue . . . : Interview with Scully.

When word got around that . . . : Interviews with Scully and John Atwood.

Atwood had run Selby's . . . : Interview with John Atwood.

They're almost animal . . . : Phyllis Orrick, "Petal Pushers. Orchid collectors, watch your back: Uncle Sam knows what you're up to," *SF Weekly*, February 22, 1995.

Atwood did a superb sales . . . : Interviews with John Atwood, Bob Scully, and Meg Lowman.

But soon Scully clashed . . . : Interviews with Bob Scully and Meg Lowman.

Scully was proud of his . . . : Interview with Bob Scully.

The director, already on . . . : Letter from Selby executive director Mark Bierner to Bob Scully, March 24, 1999, provided by Meg Lowman; interview with Scully. Bierner declined to be interviewed about his tenure at Selby Gardens and his relations with the board and Scully.

The director subsequently sent . . . : Postcard and other documentation on harassment charges, provided by Bob Scully.

So after Lowman took charge . . . : Interviews with Scully and Lowman; letter from Lowman to Scully, provided by Scully.

Scully was different from . . . : Interviews with Bob Scully, Meg Lowman, Stig Dalström, Caren Lobo, Bob Richardson, and Marjorie North.

Everyone praised Scully's . . . : Interviews with Bob Scully, Meg Lowman, and Stig Dalström.

That meant he had the time . . . : Interviews with Bob Scully and Meg Lowman.

Lowman, for her part, found . . . : Interview with Meg Lowman.

Scully, she soon discovered . . . : Lowman, Burgess, and Burgess, *It's a Jungle Up There*, 197–98; interviews with Bob Scully and Wesley Higgins.

None of them—not Scully . . . : Interviews with Bob Scully, John Atwood, and Stig Dalström.

Chapter 2. The Garden of Earthly Delights

[Susan] Orlean looks at a . . . : Charlie Kaufman and Donald Kaufman, "Adaptation" script, second draft, September 24, 1999, 49, www.dailyscript.com/scripts/adaptation.pdf. There is no Donald Kaufman, but one of the conceits of the film is that Charlie Kaufman has a twin who is also a screenwriter.

Among the first visitors . . . : Grismer, *The Story of Sarasota*, 31–32.

That piscatorial abundance is . . . : Charlie Huisking, "The Selby Legacy," *Sarasota Herald-Tribune*, July 15, 1979.

The close quarters might have . . . : Mark Zaloudek, "Bill, Marie Selby Were Genuine, Down-Home," *Sarasota Herald-Tribune*, May 31, 2005; Charlie Huisking, "The Selby Legacy," *Sarasota Herald-Tribune*, July 15, 1979; "Two Very Special Residents from Our Past," *Sarasota County History Alive!* www.sarasotahistoryalive.com/people/william-g.-and-marie-selby/.

Early on, the queen of Sarasota . . . : Nolan, *Fifty Feet in Paradise*, 149–53.

In the meantime, another kind . . . : Nolan, *Fifty Feet in Paradise*, 155–56, 185–86; John and Mabel Ringling Museum of Art website, www.ringling.org/CadMansion.aspx.

But Bill and Marie Selby wanted . . . : Mark Zaloudek, "Bill, Marie Selby Were Genuine, Down-Home," *Sarasota Herald-Tribune*, May 31, 2005; Charlie Huisking, "The Selby Legacy," *Sarasota Herald-Tribune*, July 15, 1979.

While the Palmers and Ringlings strove . . . : Charlie Huisking, "The Selby Legacy," *Sarasota Herald-Tribune*, July 15, 1979.

As she grew older, Marie . . . : Interview with Carl Luer; Charlie Huisking, "The Selby Legacy," *Sarasota Herald-Tribune*, July 15, 1979.

She left the home and . . . : Interview with Carl Luer.

All she wanted was to . . . : Interview with Carl Luer; Cooper Levey-Baker, "While Some Selby Gardens Insiders Say Poor Management and Risky Finances Have Imperiled the Sarasota Institution, Current Leadership Insists the Organization Is Stronger Than Ever," *Creative Loafing*, February 10, 2010.

Luer, a dapper man with . . . : Interviews with Carl Luer and Cal Dodson; "Luers' Films on Program," *Sarasota Journal*, February 9, 1965; "Clown 'Doing Well' after Operation," *Sarasota Herald-Tribune*, July 13, 1965; "New Medical Building Planned," *Sarasota Herald-Tribune*, November 25, 1967.

I twisted his arm, . . . : Interview with Carl Luer.

What Luer wanted the new . . . : Interview with Carl Luer.

In 1957, someone showed . . . : Luer, *The Native Orchids of Florida*, 7.

Finding a ghost orchid . . . : Luer, *The Native Orchids of Florida*, 14.

At last, they spied their . . . : Luer, *The Native Orchids of Florida*, 278. This is the page quoted by Orlean in her book *The Orchid Thief*, and the one she is depicted reading in the film *Adaptation* (as quoted at the beginning of this chapter). For more on Orlean's book, see chapter 3.

Finding that first orchid . . . : Luer, *The Native Orchids of Florida*, 7.

Luer had become so enamored . . . : Interview with Carl Luer.

While most orchid fanciers . . . : Hansen, *Orchid Fever*, 11, 38.

The historian Luigi Berliocchi . . . : Berliocchi, *The Orchid in Lore and Legend*, 9.

Writers have struggled for . . . : Orchids are featured frequently in popular literature as a symbol for sensual indulgence and sublimated lust. In Raymond Chandler's 1939 novel *The Big Sleep*, detective Philip Marlowe meets his client, the decrepit General Guy Sternwood, in a steamy hothouse full of orchids. The general describes his flowers as "nasty things. Their flesh is too much like the flesh of men. And their perfume has the rotten sweetness of a prostitute." Then he talks to Marlowe about his two wild daughters, whom he describes as not having "any more moral sense than a cat."

Even the name says sex . . . : McDonald, *Wordly Wise*, 78. The Greeks even had a story about it: Originally Orchis was the handsome but libidinous son of a nymph and a satyr. He gave in to unbridled lust during the feast of Bacchus and attempted to rape a priestess. For this offense, he was torn apart by wild beasts. His remains were transformed into a beautiful flower with roots that served as a reminder of the organ that got him in trouble (Berliocchi, *The Orchid in Lore and Legend*, 16).

Because of this scrotal resemblance . . . : Berliocchi, *The Orchid in Lore and Legend*, 107, 113.

Even in the nineteenth century . . . : Berliocchi, *The Orchid in Lore and Legend*, 89; Marcel Proust, *Swann's Way* (New York: Modern Library, 1956), 336.

Although the sublimated-sex explanation . . . : I asked nearly every orchid person I interviewed what he or she found attractive about these flowers. Most cited the flowers' staggering beauty and dazzling variety. Hansen, *Orchid Fever*, 59; Koopowitz, *Orchids and Their Conservation*, 6.

The variations are tied to . . . : Koopowitz, *Orchids and Their Conservation*, 13.

The nectar in slipper orchids . . . : Transcript for "Orchid Hunter," *NOVA*, November 26, 2002, www.pbs.org/wgbh/nova/transcripts/2915_orchid.html; for a more detailed discussion, see Van der Pijl and Dodson, *Orchid Flowers: Their Pollination and Evolution*

Some people see that . . . : Roger Sanders, "Orchids: A Bouquet of Adaptations," *Answers*, November 12, 2008, www.answersingenesis.org/articles/am/v4/n1/orchids.

For Charles Darwin, on the . . . : Darwin, *On the Various Contrivances by Which British and Foreign Orchids Are Fertilised by Insects*, 1–3.

Invariably, anyone who writes . . . : Orlean, for instance, quotes from it in *The Orchid Thief* (78), and the PBS program *NOVA* quotes it in the show "Orchid Hunter" (see the transcript at: www.pbs.org/wgbh/nova/transcripts/2915_orchid.html); "Books: Travelogue," *Time*, July 24, 1939, www.time.com/time/magazine/article/0,9171,771703,00.html.

In recent years orchids . . . : V. L. Sheela, *Flowers for Trade* (New Delhi: New India Publishing House, 2008), 223; Chuck Woods, "Orchid Mania: Exotic Plant Now the Fastest Growing Segment of Nation's $13 Billion Floriculture Industry," University of Florida press release, August 26, 2004, http://news.ifas.ufl.edu/2004/08/26/orchid-mania-exotic-plant-now-the-fastest-growing-segment-of-nations-13-billion-floriculture-industry/.

That's just the legal . . . : "Orchid Show Marred by Thefts," *Virgin Islands Daily News*, October 21, 1975; "$8,750 in Plants Stolen," *Miami Herald*, November 24, 2002.

It is an extremely important . . . : David Ferrell, "Fancying Forbidden Flowers," *Los Angeles Times*, March 5, 1995.

Back in 1971, though . . . : Interview with Carl Luer.

At Luer's behest, the . . . : Interview with Carl Luer.

Actually, Dodson came from . . . : Interview with Cal Dodson.

Dodson was considered an . . . : Interviews with Cal Dodson and Carl Luer.

One day Luer took his . . . : Interview with Dodson.

Luer was not deterred . . . : Interviews with Luer and Dodson; Sally Glendenning, "Dodson to Head Gardens," *Sarasota Herald-Tribune*, March 23, 1973.

Despite his strong interest . . . : Sally Glendenning, "Dodson to Head Gardens," *Sarasota Herald-Tribune*, March 23, 1973; Calaway Dodson, "Orchids Occupy Center Stage," *Sarasota Herald-Tribune*, March 14, 1978.

Dodson, his wife, two sons . . . : Interview with Dodson; Dorothy Stockbridge Pratt, "Foremost Perennial Says Adieu to Selby," *Sarasota Herald-Tribune*, December 11, 1995.

Over the next two years . . . : Interviews with Luer and Dodson.

At Dodson's insistence they . . . : Interview with Dodson.

In those early days . . . : Interviews with Dodson and John Atwood.

Harry Luther was a shy . . . : Interviews with Dodson, Carl Luer, and Harry Luther; Craig Pittman, "Save the Planet," *St. Petersburg Times*, June 14, 1992.

Then he heard Selby . . . : Interviews with Cal Dodson and Harry Luther; Craig Pittman, "Save the Planet," *St. Petersburg Times*, June 14, 1992; Art Levy, "Man Finds Unlikely Fame as Selby Gardens' Bromeliad Giant," *Sarasota Herald-Tribune*, July 3, 2000.

He would also let his . . . : Interview with Cal Dodson; Art Levy, "Man Finds Unlikely Fame as Selby Gardens' Bromeliad Giant," *Sarasota Herald-Tribune*, July 3, 2000.

Another gifted amateur who . . . : "Besse to Be Honored," *Sarasota Herald-Tribune*, October 6, 1998; Dorothy Stockbridge, "Behind the Scenes at Selby Gardens," *Sarasota Herald-Tribune*, February 15, 1984.

However, Dodson soon found . . . : Interview with Dodson. Libby Besse did not respond to my attempts to contact her.

She had learned that she . . . : Interview with Dodson.

One such Besse field trip . . . : Interviews with Dodson and Harry Luther; "This Flower Was Not Born to Blush Unseen," *Marie Selby Botanical Gardens Bulletin*, Winter 1981, provided by Stig Dalström.

Collecting the plants was . . . : "This Flower Was Not Born to Blush Unseen," *Marie Selby Botanical Gardens Bulletin*, Winter 1981, provided by Stig Dalström.

Up until then, everyone . . . : Koopowitz, *Tropical Slipper Orchids*, 200; interviews with Carl Luer and Cal Dodson.

Dodson called in Selby's . . . : Interview with Dodson.

"Although we knew there . . ." : Interview with Dodson.

Collectors quickly stripped . . . : Interviews with Dodson, Harold Koopowitz, and Lee Moore.

When Selby auctioned off . . . : Interview with Harry Luther; "Mystery Resolved at Selby Gardens," *Sarasota Herald-Tribune*, August 11, 1982.

Selby's scientific celebrity began . . . : Interview with Stig Dalström; Cooper Levey-Baker, "While Some Selby Gardens Insiders Say Poor Management and Risky Finances Have Imperiled the Sarasota Institution, Current Leadership Insists the Organization Is Stronger Than Ever," *Creative Loafing*, February 10, 2010.

"Botanical art . . . seemed . . ." : Cooper Levey-Baker, "While Some Selby Gardens Insiders . . . ," *Creative Loafing*, Febraury 10, 2010.

He flew to Miami and . . . : Interview with Dalström.

From Dr. Luer's perspective . . . : Interview with Luer; Jack Gurney, "2 Major Figures at Selby Gardens Leaving," *Sarasota Herald-Tribune*, December 2, 1983.

His replacement, a retired army . . . : Interviews with Carl Luer and Cal Dodson.

One day in November 1983 . . . : Interview with John Atwood.

"I was dismayed to discover . . ." : Jack Gurney, "2 Major Figures at Selby Gardens Leaving," *Sarasota Herald-Tribune*, December 2, 1983.

Dodson headed back to . . . : Interview with Dodson.

Over the next twenty years . . . : Interviews with Harry Luther, John Atwood, and Stig Dalström.

"Comments were like, 'We . . .'" : Interview with Stig Dalström.

In fact, by May 2002 . . . : Interviews with Wesley Higgins and Bob Scully; Wesley Higgins e-mail to Bob Scully, May 14, 2002, provided by Scully.

"The way out of this . . ." : Interview with Stig Dalström.

Chapter 3. The Adventurer

Adventure and excitement . . . : Orlean, *The Orchid Thief*, 202.

The most popular book . . . : Orlean's website, www.susanorlean.com.

A lot of orchid people hate . . . : For a full list of why orchid people hate it, see Craig Pittman, "The Orchid's Revenge," *St. Petersburg Times*, October 10, 1999, www .sptimes.com/News/101099/Floridian/The_orchid_s_revenge_.shtml. The list of errors goes beyond orchid facts, though. For instance, Orlean says a gun-toting park ranger, Mike Owen, left her alone in the swamp with two machete-wielding convicts. Owen—who, like all Florida park rangers, is unarmed—contends that never happened. Ironically, in the movie *Adaptation,* screenwriter Charlie Kaufman depicts a fictional version of Orlean as "stoned on orchid dust, rutting in a greenhouse with a toothless nut, [and] chasing down a screenwriter with a loaded shotgun," as the *New York Times* puts it rather neatly (Sarah Boxer, "New Yorker Writer Turns Gun-Toting Floozy?: That's Showbiz," *New York Times,* December 9, 2002). None of that happened, either.

If you saw Moore . . . : Author's observations.

In The Orchid Thief, *Orlean . . .* : Orlean, *The Orchid Thief,* 193–94.

But if you call Moore . . . : Interview with Moore.

Moore was born in . . . : Interview with Moore; Marilyn Lane, "Lee's Wild Life—Stalking Jungle Plants," *Miami News,* February 14, 1965; Jack W. Roberts, "Dade Port Board Gift to U.S. Official Bared," *Miami News,* September 24, 1954.

For the young Moore . . . : Interview with Moore.

"Every weekend we were . . .": Interview with Moore.

When they got back to . . . : Marilyn Lane, "Lee's Wild Life. . . . Stalking Jungle Plants," *Miami News,* February 14, 1965.

"That is when I realized . . .": Marilyn Lane, "Lee's Wild Life . . . ," *Miami News,* February 14, 1965.

He and his wife started . . . : Interview with Moore.

But Moore stuck with his . . . : Marilyn Lane, "Lee's Wild Life . . . ," *Miami News,* February 14, 1965.

"The men follow the 2,000-mile . . . ": Marilyn Lane, "Lee's Wild Life . . . ," *Miami News,* February 14, 1965.

One of his most dramatic . . . : Interview with Moore.

One day while scouting . . . : Interview with Moore; Marty Hair, "Staghorn Ferns Have Big Fans," *Detroit Free Press,* March 17, 2000.

Soon his little nursery attracted . . . : Interviews with Lee Moore and Cal Dodson; C. H. Dodson, "Ethology of Some Bees of the Tribe Euglossini (Hymenoptera: Apidae)," *Journal of the Kansas Entomological Society* 39, no. 4 (October 1966): 607–29.

The two orchid fanciers became . . . : Interviews with Lee Moore, Cal Dodson, and John Beckner.

Initially Moore could ship . . . : Interview with Moore; Moore e-mail to Peter Croezen, August 8, 2002, from the files of Wesley Higgins. (Moore tended to send his e-mail responses on the *Phragmipedium kovachii* controversy to a long list of recipients, including people he knew at Selby Gardens.)

However, Moore then discovered . . . : Interview with Lee and Chady Moore.

Taking the artifacts out . . . : Interview with Moore.

"I was considered one of . . .": Moore e-mail to Peter Croezen, August 8, 2002, from the files of Wesley Higgins.

By this time, Moore had . . . : Interviews with Lee and Chady Moore.

"We used to fly out . . .": Interview with Lee Moore.

Their investment brought a . . . : Interview with Lee and Chady Moore; Al Volker, "Mayan Art Dealer: Practices Ethical," *Miami News,* May 23, 1973.

"As dealers we are . . .": Al Volker, "Mayan Art Dealer," *Miami News,* May 23, 1973.

However, the United States soon . . . : Interview with Lee and Chady Moore.

England ruled the seven . . . : Chadwick and Chadwick, *The Classic Cattleyas,* 9–10.

Gardners clamored for these . . . : Stuart, *The Plants That Shaped Our Gardens,* 125.

Even once they figured . . . : Chadwick and Chadwick, *The Classic Cattleyas,* 11; Koopowitz, *Tropical Slipper Orchids,* 62.

The English passion for . . . : Reinikka, *A History of the Orchid,* 23; Chadwick and Chadwick, *The Classic Cattleyas,* 10.

The orchid frenzy that . . . : Reinikka, *A History of the Orchid,* 27–28.

The best orchid hunters were . . . : Reinikka, *A History of the Orchid,* 188, 209; Stuart, *The Plants That Shaped Our Gardens,* 125; Short, *In Pursuit of Plants,* 267.

They were men who . . . : Berliocchi, *The Orchid in Lore and Legend,* 77–78; Short, *In Pursuit of Plants,* 267.

The all-time king of . . . : Berliocchi, *The Orchid in Lore and Legend,* 82–83; Stuart, *The Plants That Shaped Our Gardens,* 125–26; Reinikka, *A History of the Orchid,* 209, 219–22.

The risks faced by . . . : Jason Burke, "Garden of Good and Evil," *Guardian,* April 15, 2001, www.guardian.co.uk/education/2001/apr/15/highereducation.features.

Without the orchid hunters . . . : Darwin, *On the Various Contrivances,* 4.

Then, too, he had fallen . . . : Interviews with Lee and Chady Moore, and Stig Dalström.

Gringos had been hunting . . . : Isaias Rolando, "Fifteen Years of In-Situ Conservation at Macchu Picchu," *Selbyana* 25, no. 1, 2 (2005): 134–45.

Although some things had . . . : Conover, *The Routes of Man,* 16–17, 36; Starn, Degregori, and Kirk, *The Peru Reader,* 382–83, 385–86; Wehner and Del Gaudio, *Moon Peru,* 245.

By the 1980s the whole country . . . : Starn, Degregori, and Kirk, *The Peru Reader,* 401–9, 425–37; "Fujimori Convicted of Corruption," BBC News, July 20, 2009, http://news.bbc.co.uk/2/hi/americas/8160150.stm.

For someone like Moore . . . : Wilson, *The Diversity of Life,* 197, 218.

In the early 1990s, Moore . . . : Interview with Lee and Chady Moore; Wehner and Del Gaudio, *Moon Peru,* 242; Box and Murphy, *Footprint Peru Handbook,* 471.

Moyobamba is known as . . . : Moyobamba website, www.moyobamba.net/moyobamba/; Wehner and Del Gaudio, *Moon Peru,* 244.

It's one of the richest . . . : Interview with Lee Moore.

The Moores kept their overhead . . . : Interview with Lee and Chady Moore.

To mark their new beginning . . . : Interview with Moore.

In 1991 he attempted to . . . : Susana Barciela, "Rules Have Hurt Orchids, Says Botanist," *Miami Herald,* September 23, 1991; interview with Lee Moore.

The mislabeling of wild . . . : Interview with Lee Moore.

Moore was incensed at . . . : Susana Barciela, "Rules Have Hurt Orchids, Says Botanist," *Miami Herald,* September 23, 1991.

The outcome had a certain . . . : Interview with Lee Moore.

Despite his problems with . . . : Moore e-mail to Croezen, August 8, 2002.

In 2001, while flying . . . : Interviews with Lee Moore and Michael Kovach.

Chapter 4. The Carpenter

With some individuals it . . . : Berliocchi, *The Orchid in Lore and Legend,* 73.

The town where Michael Kovach . . . : "History of Gold Mining in Fauquier County, Virginia," from Goldvein history website, www.goldvein.com/history.html.

Kovach lived in Goldvein . . . : Description of house from U.S. Fish and Wildlife Service search warrant for Kovach's house, issued August 16, 2002; Ellison biographical information from her essay "Living with Orchids," *Digital Journalist,* August 2005, http://digitaljournalist.org/issue0508/orchids.html.

The couple had come to . . . : Interview with Michael Kovach.

Ellison particularly liked shooting . . . : Ellison essay, "Living with Orchids," *Digital Journalist,* August 2005, http://digitaljournalist.org/issue0508/orchids.html.

One day in 1991 Ellison brought . . . : Cathy Jett, "Orchids: Goldvein Couple's Idea for a Part-Time Business Has Blossomed," *Fredericksburg (Va.) Freelance-Star,* May 14, 1996.

Kovach built a greenhouse . . . : Greenhouse description from Fish and Wildlife Service search warrant for Kovach's home as well as an interview with Fish and Wildlife Service orchid expert Robert "Roddy" Gabel, who participated in the search; J. Michael Kovach, "The True Story of the Phragmipedium kovachii," Global Paphiopedilum Alliance newsletter, June 2003.

He found in their . . . : Interview with Kovach.

However, he soon learned . . . : Interview with Kovach.

Kovach began pestering orchid . . . : Kovach, Global Paphiopedilum Alliance newsletter.

He struck up an acquaintance . . . : Interview with Michael Kovach; Andrew Grossman, "The Unlikely Orchid Smuggler: A Case Study in Overcriminalization," Heritage Foundation Legal Memorandum No. 44, July 27, 2009, www.heritage.org/research/reports/2009/07/the-unlikely-orchid-smuggler-a-case-study-in-overcriminalization; Sandy Gillians, "American Justice," Pollenatrix blog, June 22, 2004, http://offpollen.typepad.com/pollenatrix/2004/06/american_justic.html. Norris, when I talked to him, said he had no recollection of ever meeting or talking to Kovach, but conceded they may have exchanged e-mails. E-mails Norris sent to Wesley Higgins at the height of the *Phragmipedium kovachii* controversy show he and Kovach had previously exchanged correspondence but Kovach had ended contact with him.

Following Norris's lead, Kovach . . . : Interview with Kovach. Copies of various import documents fleshing out Kovach's history as an orchid dealer are contained in the U.S. Fish and Wildlife Service investigative file.

For this trip, Norris helped . . . : Interviews with Michael Kovach and Lee Moore. The history of Norris and Arias's friendship comes from the case files on Arias and Norris as well as from the Heritage Foundation report on Norris's case; Manuel Arias Silva website, www.orquidaria.com/. Norris says he does not recall helping Kovach contact Arias.

Despite Arias's polite façade . . . : Interview with Kovach.

Through experience, Kovach had . . . : Interview with Kovach.

At first he phoned the . . . : Kovach's story of calling the U.S. Fish and Wildlife Service was confirmed by Roddy Gabel of that agency (see chapter 8).

Finding a way of sliding around . . . : Kovach's April 17, 1998, letter to Vietnamese orchid dealers from *U.S. vs. Kovach.* The five-page handwritten letter appears to be drafted as a form letter to be sent to a number of dealers.

Over time, he became adept . . . : Kovach's February 14, 2000, letter to Rodrigo (no last name given) from the evidence in *U.S. vs. Kovach.*

He has told his story repeatedly . . . : The three primary sources for Kovach's story about what happened in Peru and in Florida are his handwritten letter to the U.S. Department of Agriculture dated June 27, 2002; his handwritten affidavit to the U.S. Fish and Wildlife Service, dated July 16, 2002; and the first-person article he wrote titled "The True Story of the Phragmipedium kovachii," that appeared in the June 2003 issue of the Global Paphiopedilum Alliance newsletter. The USDA letter and Fish and Wildlife Service statement are both contained in the files of *U.S. vs. Kovach.* The newsletter I obtained from a source involved in the case, and Kovach verified its authenticity. Other sources, such as newspaper articles, will be cited individually.

Even Kovach calls himself . . . : Interview with Kovach.

To Lee Moore, who is . . . : Interview with Moore.

Yet despite that, they . . . : Interview with Kovach.

For instance, Kovach says . . . : Kovach's June 27, 2002, letter to the USDA, from *U.S. vs. Kovach.*

Kovach did not name his . . . : Kovach, Global Paphiopedilum Alliance newsletter, June 2003; interview with Lee Moore.

During his two-week visit . . . : Kovach, Global Paphiopedilum Alliance newsletter, June 2003.

In one account of his . . . : Kovach, Global Paphiopedilum Alliance newsletter, June 2003; description of El Progresso, the El Paraiso diner, and Faustino Medina from September 2002 video supplied by Lee and Chady Moore.

"I was unsure what it . . .": Kovach affidavit to U.S. Fish and Wildlife Service from *U.S. vs. Kovach.* This is a good example of how Kovach's stories changed. He told the USDA he went to Peru every year for eight years, including in August 2001. He told the U.S. Fish and Wildlife Service he'd gone to Peru in 1996, May 2001, and May 2002. He told the Fish and Wildlife Service he'd first seen the new species of orchid during his May 2001 trip. He told the USDA that he'd first seen it during his August 2001 trip. When I interviewed him, Kovach first said August 2002 was right, then said he couldn't remember. Further complicating matters is a September 2002 video I obtained from Lee Moore that features an interview with Faustino Medina, who says he did not begin selling plants from his roadside stand until March 2002. That would mean Kovach could not possibly have stopped off there in 2001 and seen the nonblooming slipper orchids. However, Medina admits his memory is hazy, and Lee Moore says Kovach met him on a flight from Peru to Miami in May 2001, so that's the date I'm using for that trip.

Chapter 5. The Holy Grail

On the whole, the flower . . . : Berliocchi, *The Orchid in Lore and Legend*, 149.

The biggest orchid show . . . : Eunice Sigler, "Orchid Festival Returns to Fruit & Spice Park," *Miami Herald*, May 16, 2002; Redland International Orchid Festival website, www.redlandorchidfestival.org/; interview with Bill Peters of Whimsy Orchids, one of the festival's organizers. Peters also provided me with a spreadsheet showing all of the 2002 show's vendors.

"There's no other event . . .": Eunice Sigler, "Orchid Festival Returns to Fruit & Spice Park," *Miami Herald*, May 16, 2002.

The most expensive orchids . . . : George Norris testimony to U.S. Fish and Wildlife Service, from Norris-Arias case investigative files.

Ted Green flew in . . . : Interview with Ted Green

Other people at the Redland . . . : George Norris testimony to U.S. Fish and Wildlife Service, from Norris-Arias case investigative files; interview with John Beckner.

One of the judges picking . . . : Interview with John Beckner.

Beckner's friends gave him . . . : Interview with Beckner; map of 2002 Redland show from U.S. Fish and Wildlife Service's Selby Gardens investigative file; temperature from Weather Underground's historic weather data website.

Beckner wasn't the only . . . : Interview with Bob Scully.

Beckner loved to be the . . . : Interviews with Beckner, Stig Dalström, and Wesley Higgins; Dalström letter to Meg Lowman dated September 15, 2002.

Then, on Monday, June 3 . . . : June 3, 2002, e-mail exchange between Dave Hunt and Wesley Higgins, provided by Higgins; interviews with Higgins and Dave Hunt.

The orchid boys all studied . . . : Interviews with Wesley Higgins and John Atwood.

"We were glad to see . . .": Interview with Stig Dalström.

The Selby experts feared . . . : Interviews with Wesley Higgins and Stig Dalström.

Vivero Agro-Oriente had been . . . : List of Redland vendors, provided by Bill Peters of Whimsy Orchids, one of the festival's organizers; interviews with Wesley Higgins, Stig Dalström, and John Beckner.

Agro-Oriente sent its photos . . . : September 4, 2002, e-mail from George Norris to Wesley Higgins, provided by Higgins.

With all the photos floating . . . : Interview with Wesley Higgins; Koopowitz background from his author profile from Timber Press, www.timberpress.com/author/harold_koopowitz/1011.

Lee Moore's wife, Chady . . . : Chady Moore wrote a lengthy narrative of events, which she called "Chronological History of the Discovery of Phragmipedium kovachii," as part of her attack on Renato and Karol Villena. Lee Moore e-mailed copies to dozens of people on October 7, 2002, including Wesley Higgins, who shared it with me (and later Moore e-mailed me a copy too).

Still, she knew Renato Villena . . . : Interview with Lee and Chady Moore.

Villena, a slender, hawk-faced . . . : Description from photo of the Villena family on the Agro-Oriente website, www.agroriente.com/es/; interviews with Marni Turkel and Lee Moore. I should add that Turkel does not share Moore's views expressed here. Moore's own views regarding Renato Villena have moderated somewhat from when I first interviewed him about these events.

When Renato Villena wanted . . . : Interviews with Marni Turkel, Eric Christenson, Lee Moore, and Karol Villena; George Norris's witness proffer from U.S. Fish and Wildlife Service investigative file on the Norris-Arias case.

According to Karol Villena . . . : I sent Karol Villena numerous questions via e-mail. She responded once, giving a short account of what she said had occurred, but did not reply to any of my other queries. The only orchid person who was less responsive to my requests for information was Manuel Arias Silva.

On May 2, 2002—two weeks . . . : Moore's fax to Kovach is included in the files of *U.S. vs. Kovach.*

On May 21, 2002, Kovach . . . : Kovach's timeline is part of the affidavit he wrote for the U.S. Fish and Wildlife Service, which became evidence in *U.S. vs. Kovach.*

The drive from Tarapota to . . . : Interview with Lee and Chady Moore.

"And where was Michael . . .": Interview with Lee and Chady Moore.

Kovach later told federal . . . : Kovach's itinerary and timeline from his Fish and Wildlife Service affidavit, used as evidence in *U.S. vs. Kovach.* His complaint about the tax scam is in his letter to the USDA, later used as evidence in *U.S. vs. Kovach.*

Early on the morning . . . : Kovach, Global Paphiopedilum Alliance newsletter, June 2003. Kovach's first-person story written for this slipper-collectors' newsletter is his most detailed version of what happened when he first encountered the new orchid, and the one he told me is the most accurate account. Interview with Lee Moore.

There were four people . . . : Kovach, Global Paphiopedilum Alliance newsletter, June 2003.

They pulled in and . . . : Kovach, Global Paphiopedilum Alliance newsletter, June 2003; Inca Kola product information from Amazon, www.amazon.com/Inca-Kola-2-liter/dp/B0000GIZR4.

"I was struggling not . . .": Ian Shapira, "Horticulturist in an Exotic Predicament," *Washington Post,* December 29, 2002.

"I guessed that it was . . .": Kovach, Global Paphiopedilum Alliance newsletter, June 2003.

"Now, you must consider . . ." : Kovach, Global Paphiopedilum Alliance newsletter, June 2003.

Kovach couldn't wait to . . . : Interview with Lee and Chady Moore.

In one account he gave . . . : Kovach affidavit to U.S. Fish and Wildlife Service, used as evidence in *U.S. vs. Kovach.*

They were duly impressed . . . : Interview with Lee and Chady Moore.

They snapped a few . . . : Although Kovach's wife, Barbara Ellison, was a professional photographer, she was shooting slide film, which would take some time to develop, Moore told me. That's why the Moores snapped some shots that could be developed quickly.

They were excited about . . . : Interview with Lee and Chady Moore.

Right about then, according . . . : Kovach, Global Paphiopedilum Alliance newsletter, June 2003.

"At any rate, Senor Villena . . .": Kovach, Global Paphiopedilum Alliance newsletter, June 2003.

Kovach did not define what . . . : Juan Forero, "A Swirl of Foreboding in Mahogany's Wake," *New York Times*, September 28, 2003.

However Villena achieved the . . . : Kovach, Global Paphiopedilum Alliance newsletter, June 2003.

Kovach and Moore then spent . . . : Kovach, Global Paphiopedilum Alliance newsletter, June 2003.

Her farm business included . . . : From Chady Moore's history of the *Phragmipedium kovachii*, via Lee Moore's e-mail of October 7, 2002.

"I couldn't believe the . . .": Chady Moore's history of the *Phragmipedium kovachii*, via Lee Moore's e-mail of October 7, 2002.

As she gazed around at . . . : Interview with Chady Moore.

Instead of rushing back . . . : Kovach, Global Paphiopedilum Alliance newsletter, June 2003.

Meanwhile Chady Moore told . . . : From Chady Moore's history of the *Phragmipedium kovachii*, via Lee Moore's e-mail of October 7, 2002.

Finally, on June 2, the Kovachs . . . : Kovach, Global Paphiopedilum Alliance newsletter, June 2003.

Moore says Kovach knew . . . : Interview with Lee Moore.

Moore says he told . . . : Interview with Lee Moore.

Chady Moore, too, urged . . . : Interview with Chady Moore.

Yet Kovach and his wife . . . : Kovach, Global Paphiopedilum Alliance newsletter, June 2003.

The "experience," Kovach said . . . : Interview with Michael Kovach.

Yet still they did not . . . : Kovach, Global Paphiopedilum Alliance newsletter, June 2003.

Kovach packaged his divinely . . . : Ian Shapira, "Horticulturist in an Exotic Predicament," *Washington Post*, December 29, 2002.

At the Lima airport . . . : Kovach, Global Paphiopedilum Alliance newsletter, June 2003.

Chapter 6. The Rival

The majority of these botanists . . . : Letter from Eric Christenson to Peter Croezen, July 23, 2002, provided by Christenson.

Marni Turkel didn't really like . . . : Interview with Marni Turkel.

They made an odd pair . . . : Description of Turkel based on photos from her website, http://marniturkel.com/, and interview with her; description of Christenson from author's impressions.

Turkel, who first met Christenson . . . : Interview with Turkel.

He really needed her . . . : Interviews with Turkel and Christenson.

One of the stops . . . : Interview with Turkel.

So Turkel wasn't too surprised . . . : E-mail of May 22, 2002, from Karol Villena to Marni Turkel supplied by Turkel.

"It was big and flashy . . . ": Interview with Marni Turkel.

Turkel translated the e-mail . . . : E-mail exchange among Turkel, Christenson, and Villena supplied by Turkel; interview with Turkel and Christenson.

Christenson alerted the editor . . . : Interview with Christenson.

The science of taxonomy owes . . . : Fara, *Sex, Botany, and Empire*, 19–20.

Taxonomists hold an obscure . . . : Stephanie Pain, "A Touch of Class in the Field," *New Scientist*, September 15, 1988, 55.

The American Orchid Society's list . . . : List obtained in 2002 from AOS website. The seventh taxonomist on the list who was affiliated with Selby was Robert Dressler of Micanopy, Florida.

There was an eighth . . . : Interviews with Christenson, Carl Luer, Cal Dodson, Stig Dalström, Bob Scully, and Meg Lowman.

Yet Christenson's initial interest . . . : Interview with Christenson.

In five years there, Christenson . . . : Interview with Christenson.

He contended for years . . . : Interviews with Christenson and Dalström.

Christenson regarded the gardens' . . . : Interview with Christenson. He named names but without offering any independent verification, so I have left them out.

Christenson made no secret . . . : There are several versions of what ended Christenson's career at Selby, some of them involving him being fired. However, a Selby source showed me a memo from the executive director at the time. It verifies Christenson's own story that he resigned but was not asked to stay.

Christenson's big ambition was . . . : Interviews with Christenson and Harold Koopowitz.

In between his scientific studies . . . : Interviews with Christenson, Bob Scully, Stig Dalström, Meg Lowman, and Carl Luer; quote about Carl and Jane Luer from October 30, 2001, letter from Christenson to Jane Luer, provided by Meg Lowman.

When he alerted other . . . : Interview with Christenson; Christenson summed up his attitude toward the AOS and all other botanic institutions in a July 23, 2002, letter to Peter Croezen, which was then circulated widely on orchid-collector Internet forums.

"Everyone treats it with . . ." : Interview with Christenson.

"They want to be the . . .": Interview with Roddy Gabel.

The people caught smuggling . . . : Interview with Gabel; TRAFFIC *Bulletin Seizures and Prosecutions*: 16, no. 3 (March 1997) to 22, no. 2 (June 2009): 7.

Even though post-9/11 America . . . : Craig Welch, *Shell Games: Rogues, Smugglers, and the Hunt for Nature's Bounty* (New York: HarperCollins, 2010), 12, 14.

Some of the orchid smuggling . . . : Interview with Roddy Gabel.

The mislabeling can be . . . : Interviews with Roddy Gabel; George Norris proffer to U.S. Fish and Wildlife Service, part of the agency's Norris-Arias investigative file; Marni Turkel e-mail to Karol Villena, provided by Turkel.

Still, getting such rare . . . : Interviews with Michael Kovach, Stig Dalström, and Marni Turkel.

Botanical garden employees have . . . : Interviews with Roddy Gabel and Harold Koopowitz.

To Christenson, letting a . . . : Interview with Christenson.

Without facing the prospect . . . : Interviews with Harold Koopowitz and Eric Christenson.

Christenson's frustration about these . . . : Interviews with Christenson and Meg Lowman; Christenson's October 30, 2001, letter to Jane Luer, provided by Lowman.

Now Christenson studied the . . . : Interview with Christenson.

"Anyone with half a . . .": Interview with Christenson.

Instead, Christenson e-mailed to . . . : Interviews with Christenson and Turkel.

He started off by noting . . . : Eric Christenson, "Phragmipedium peruvianum," *Orchids* 7, no. 7 (July 2002): 620–23.

Turkel, in forwarding Christenson's . . . : Turkel's June 3, 2002, e-mail to Karol Villena, provided by Turkel.

The Villenas had inquired . . . : Turkel's June 3, 2002, e-mail to Karol Villena, provided by Turkel; interview with Marni Turkel.

Instead, because this was . . . : Interview with Eric Christenson.

In early June, Christenson . . . : Interview with Harold Koopowitz.

Chapter 7. The Race

Only for some of us . . . : Stuart, *The Plants That Shaped Our Gardens*, 7.

The Kovachs landed at . . . : Kovach, Global Paphiopedilum Alliance newsletter, June 2003.

Miami's airport is the . . . : "Miami: International," *Florida Trend*, March 1, 2010.

For that reason, Miami . . . : Associated Press, "Air Baggage Handlers Held in Big Drug Bust," *Pittsburgh Press*, September 27, 1996; George Volsky, "U.S. Seizes an Airliner That Carried Cocaine," *New York Times*, October 25, 1988.

Miami is also considered . . . : Craig Pittman, "Struggling to Stop the Smuggling," *St. Petersburg Times*, September 5, 2002.

But there are plenty of . . . : Bryan Christy, "The Kingpin," *National Geographic*, January 2010, http://ngm.nationalgeographic.com/2010/01/asian-wildlife/christy-text.

Why Miami? It's not . . . : Government Accounting Office, "Wildlife Protection: Fish and Wildlife Service's Inspection Program Needs Strengthening," RCED-95–8, December 29, 1994, 24–25, 27.

On July 22, 1998, George . . . : Indictment of George Norris and Manuel Arias Silva from *U.S. vs. George Norris and Manuel Arias Silva.*

Kovach, however, carried no big . . . : Kovach, Global Paphiopedilum Alliance newsletter, June 2003. This is the one part of Kovach's story that has remained consistent in every version: He told customs officials he had live plants and they waved him through instead of sending him to USDA's "smokehouse."

The morning of Wednesday . . . : The events of this day were reconstructed using interviews with Wesley Higgins, Stig Dalström, John Atwood, John Beckner, Calaway Dodson, and Mark Jones, as well as Kovach's own writings.

When the Kovachs drove . . . : Kovach, Global Paphiopedilum Alliance newsletter, June 2003; interviews with Kovach and Lee Moore.

Kovach, afraid of missing . . . : Kovach, Global Paphiopedilum Alliance newsletter,

June 2003. Some Selby sources told me they spoke with the elderly volunteer after this publication came out, and she denied making any such comment to Kovach.

Accounts vary as to who...: Interviews with Wesley Higgins, Stig Dalström, Cal Dodson, John Atwood, John Beckner, and Mark Jones; Dalström testimony to grand jury, June 11, 2003, included as evidence in *U.S. vs. Kovach*.

Dalström viewed Kovach's orchid...: Interview with Stig Dalström.

As Kovach walked in ...: Kovach, Global Paphiopedilum Alliance newsletter, June 2003.

"To say that it created...": Dalström letter to Meg Lowman dated September 15, 2002.

This was just the reception...: Interview with Wesley Higgins.

Someone asked Kovach what he...: Kovach, Global Paphiopedilum Alliance newsletter, June 2003.

Higgins then tapped a...: Kovach, Global Paphiopedilum Alliance newsletter, June 2003. Higgins confirms showing him the photos from Dave Hunt.

"Someone is advertising them...": Kovach, Global Paphiopedilum Alliance newsletter, June 2003.

According to Dodson, Higgins...: Interview with Cal Dodson.

"Kovach assured us that...": Dalström letter to Lowman dated September 15, 2002.

Atwood, the slipper orchid expert...: Atwood letter to Meg Lowman dated August 23, 2002.

The orchid boys began...: Kovach, Global Paphiopedilum Alliance newsletter, June 2003; Kovach affidavit to U.S. Fish and Wildlife Service, used as evidence in *U.S. vs. Kovach*; interview with Dodson.

Thus the scientists set...: Interview with Wesley Higgins.

According to Kovach, Higgins...: Kovach, Global Paphiopedilum Alliance newsletter, June 2003.

Higgins recalls a different...: Interview with Wesley Higgins.

Kovach also had a brief...: Kovach letter to USDA, June 26, 2002, entered as evidence in *U.S. vs. Kovach*. For the judges' own recollections, see chapter 13.

Now he was ready to go ...: This later became a point of contention among the attorneys in *U.S. vs. Kovach*, with the prosecution arguing that the waived fee constituted evidence he had profited from his discovery.

Then Kovach ran for the...: Kovach, Global Paphiopedilum Alliance newsletter, June 2003.

While Higgins says that...: Interview with Wesley Higgins.

But then Cal Dodson ...: Higgins e-mail to Lowman and Scully, June 7, 2002, provided by Higgins.

According to Dalström, though...: Interview with Stig Dalström.

"We're an organization, we ...": Dalström testimony to grand jury, June 11, 2003, included as evidence *in U.S. vs. Selby Gardens*.

Atwood and Dalström worked...: Interviews with Atwood and Dalström; Dalström testimony to grand jury, June 11, 2003, included as evidence in *U.S. vs. Kovach*.

The ever-methodical Atwood ...: Atwood testimony to grand jury, July 9, 2002, included as evidence in *U.S. vs. Kovach*.

Meanwhile Higgins took a ...: Interview with Higgins.

Atwood's written description began . . . : John Atwood, Stig Dalström, and Ricardo Fernandez, "Phragmipedium kovachii, A New Species from Peru," *Selbyana* 23, Supplement (June 12, 2002): 1–2, included as evidence in *U.S. vs. Kovach.*

On the afternoon of . . . : Higgins e-mail to Scully and Lowman, June 6, 2002, and replies from Scully and Lowman, provided by Scully; interviews with Lowman and Scully. Lowman has repeatedly suggested Scully was in Sarasota on the day Kovach showed up at Selby, but Scully showed me date-stamped receipts from a gas purchase and his own business to show he was in South Florida.

Higgins did not attach . . . : Interview with Higgins.

But there was a problem . . . : Dalström testimony to grand jury, June 11, 2003, included as evidence in *U.S. vs. Kovach.*

But for once she wasn't . . . : Lowman, Burgess, and Burgess, *It's a Jungle Up There*, 187–98. Just as Lowman accused Scully of being in Sarasota, so Scully accused Lowman of being present. Lowman's own calendar reflects that she was on vacation all week, packed on Wednesday, June 5, 2002, and then flew to Cincinnati with her sons on Thursday, June 6, 2002. I took the additional step of checking with regatta organizers to see if a Sarasota team competed, and they verified it. No one in the OIC said anything about seeing her the day Kovach showed up, and given the hostility between Lowman and the OIC scientists, it seems unlikely they would conspire to hide her complicity.

By the next morning, Friday . . . : Interview with Lowman.

"It is great news . . .": Lowman's June 7, 2002, e-mail to Higgins, provided by Scully.

"The only way we can . . .": Higgins's June 7, 2002, e-mail to Lowman, provided by Higgins.

The news left Lowman elated . . . : Lowman, Burgess, and Burgess, *It's a Jungle Up There*, 198.

Actually, Higgins explained years . . . : Interview with Wesley Higgins.

Still, Higgins called Kovach . . . : Interviews with Higgins, Stig Dalström, John Atwood, and Cal Dodson.

The special Friday staff meeting . . . : Dalström testimony to grand jury, June 11, 2003, included as evidence in *U.S. vs. Kovach.*

Higgins outlined the issue . . . : Higgins e-mail to Lowman and Scully, June 7, 2002.

The group gathered in their . . . : Interview with Higgins.

Higgins's meeting of the 7–11 . . . : Interviews with Higgins, Dalström, Atwood, Beckner, and Dodson.

Dodson and Holst didn't like . . . : Interviews with Dodson, Dalström, Beckner, and Atwood.

"It's a grim mistake . . .": Interview with Dodson.

But the rest of the . . . : Interviews with Beckner and Dalström.

"If there's a problem . . . ": Interview with Atwood.

According to Dodson, though . . . : Interview with Dodson. Higgins confirms this story.

At last the scientists . . . : Interviews with Dalström, Atwood, and Beckner. While Dodson may not have voiced further objections, this plan did not really satisfy him either—he took his arguments to Scully.

The publication was credited . . . : Interview with Ricardo Fernandez.

Only later did Dalström realize . . . : Interview with Stig Dalström.

Higgins and Cal Dodson served . . . : Interview with Wesley Higgins.

Lowman got one more e-mail . . . : Lowman, Burgess, and Burgess, *It's a Jungle Up There*, 199.

Scully stopped by Selby . . . : Interview with Scully.

But Scully got a different . . . : Interview with Dodson.

The following Monday, June 10 . . . : Lowman's June 10, 2002, e-mail to the Selby staff, provided by Higgins.

A half hour later, Scully . . . : Scully's June 10, 2002, e-mail, provided by Higgins.

Selby's press slowly began . . . : Press run and mailing info from Bruce Rinker June 14, 2002, e-mail to Selby staff, provided by Higgins.

On Friday, June 14, Selbyana's . . . : Scully's June 14, 2002, e-mail to Lowman and Luer, provided by Higgins.

Meanwhile Beckner went to a . . . : Interview with Beckner.

Christenson was supposed to . . . : Lowman's June 14, 2002, e-mail to Scully, Carl Luer, and chief financial officer Rita Aughey, provided by Higgins.

The orchid world seemed . . . : Lowman, Burgess, and Burgess, *It's a Jungle Up There*, 200–202.

Lowman wrote later that . . . : Lowman, Burgess, and Burgess, *It's a Jungle Up There*, 198.

On June 18, Selby's marketing . . . : The Selby press release is part of the evidence in *U.S. vs. Kovach.*

The Sarasota Herald-Tribune . . . : Mark Zaloudek, "Big, New Orchid Species Creates Quite a Stir," *Sarasota Herald-Tribune,* July 8, 2002.

Christenson called up his . . . : Interview with Marni Turkel.

Kovach, back in Virginia . . . : Interview with Lee Moore.

Chapter 8. The Investigation

With most species of . . . : Michael Holzman, *James Jesus Angleton, the CIA and the Craft of Counterintelligence* (Boston: University of Massachusetts Press, 2008), 140.

The letter from Lima arrived . . . : Letter from INRENA to U.S. Fish and Wildlife Service, June 26, 2002, and its translation both included in the U.S. Fish and Wildlife Service's Kovach investigative file .

Along with the letter . . . : INRENA was not on *Selbyana's* subscription list, nor was it a recipient of Selby's press release. What prompted the agency to take action? Lee Moore contends Karol Villena tipped them off. He said she was ticked off about how Selby had rushed to print an identification that failed to credit Agro-Oriente—although given what happened to Agro-Oriente, that seems unlikely. Selby's partisans blamed either Eric Christenson, who denied being the source of the tip, or Christenson's writing partner David Bennett. Bennett is dead so I could not ask him, but Christenson said that if Bennett tipped off INRENA, he never took credit for it. Other sources—Peter Croezen, for instance—contend that Peruvian orchid growers such as Dr. Isaias Rolando heard about Selby's publication and notified INRENA. My attempts to query Peruvian officials yielded no response.

INRENA officials clearly were . . . : Conover, *The Routes of Man,* 44.

Kovach didn't know about . . . : Kovach's call to Feinstein and what the USDA agent told him are referenced in Kovach's June 27, 2002, letter to the USDA, included as evidence in *U.S. vs. Kovach.*

The next day Kovach sat . . . : Kovach, June 27, 2002, letter to the USDA, included as evidence in *U.S. vs. Kovach.*

Kovach's letter produced a . . . : Feinstein's July 1, 2002, e-mail to four USDA colleagues included as evidence in *U.S. vs. Kovach.*

Special Agent Holt worked . . . : Holt outlined her background in applying for a warrant to search Kovach's house, and it was included as evidence in *U.S. vs. Kovach.* Her description and the information about the Virginia smuggling ring she nabbed comes from a photo and caption on page 7 of the January/February issue of *Fish & Wildlife News,* the agency's internal publication, and author's observations in court.

Agent Holt called up . . . : Holt's initial contact with Kovach is described by Kovach's attorneys in their sentencing memorandum, part of *U.S. vs. Kovach.*

On July 16, 2002, Holt . . . : Holt's report of the interview with Kovach is contained in the investigative files of *U.S. vs. Kovach;* the description of how she drew him into talking about orchids came from Kovach's attorneys during his sentencing in that case, and was not disputed by the prosecution.

Even before Holt arrived . . . : Holt's report says he had already written the first page of the affidavit before she got there.

As with his letter to . . . : Kovach's affidavit is included as evidence in *U.S. vs. Kovach.*

About a week later, though . . . : Kovach's attorneys brought this up several times in motions and oral arguments, calling it "surveillance." However, the prosecution said Holt was merely making sure she had an accurate description of his house for the search warrant she was preparing.

After Agent Holt left . . . : Interview with Lee Moore.

When Agent Holt checked with . . . : Holt's report on this is included in *U.S. vs. Kovach.* Prosecutors included copies of the paperwork from those prior shipments as evidence that he was not ignorant about the laws on importing orchids.

She asked agents in Miami . . . : Holt's request is included in the Fish and Wildlife Service investigative file on the Kovach–Selby Gardens case. A copy of Kovach's customs declaration form is included as evidence in *U.S. vs. Kovach.*

Holt still had questions . . . : Holt's follow-up report included in Fish and Wildlife Service investigative file on Kovach–Selby Gardens case.

Before Holt could dispatch . . . : Interviews with Peter Croezen and Georgia Tasker.

A Canadian orchid grower . . . : Interview with Croezen.

"Faustino came up and . . ." : Croezen's story about his near-miss was posted on the "Slipper Talk" orchid forum on January 14, 2007, www.slippertalk.com/forum/showthread.php?t=2384&highlight=phragmipedium+kovachii, and confirmed by Peruvian orchid grower Alfredo Manrique.

Now Croezen was determined . . . : Interview with Croezen; Croezen's original message and subsequent e-mail exchange with Wesley Higgins, provided by Higgins.

Croezen read this and . . . : Interview with Croezen.

Higgins, believing his comments ... : Interviews with Higgins and Croezen.

Meanwhile Eric Christenson sent ... : Christenson's July 23, 2002, letter to Croezen, provided by Christenson.

Croezen, of course, posted ... : Interview with Croezen. Sadly, Croezen's website is no longer operational.

When Croezen posted Christenson's ... : Copy of Croezen's posting and Moore's August 7, 2002, response provided by Lee Moore.

Moore also faxed a scrawled ... : Moore's August 7, 2002, fax to Kovach is included as evidence in *U.S. vs. Kovach.*

Moore wasn't the only ... : Interviews with Higgins and Croezen. Higgins sent an e-mail to Bob Scully asking for advice on how far to go in defending Selby's honor, but Scully urged him to cool off.

So the flame war continued ... : Interviews with Eric Christenson, Stig Dalström, and Harold Koopowitz.

Inevitably, word of the ... : Interview with Georgia Tasker; Tasker, "Orchid Intrigue," *Miami Herald,* August 10, 2002. This may be the only time in journalism history that a newspaper's gardening writer broke a crime story on the front page.

Years later, Tasker said ... : Interview with Tasker.

She called up Kovach ... : Interview with Tasker.

The Fish and Wildlife Service ... : Interview with Tasker.

So it was up to ... : Tasker, "Orchid Intrigue," *Miami Herald,* August 10, 2002.

Years later, Tasker explained ... : Interview with Tasker.

Tasker reported that Moore ... : Tasker, "Orchid Intrigue," *Miami Herald,* August 10, 2002.

Martin Motes wasn't the ... : Interview with Harold Koopowitz.

Even Bob Scully got ... : Interview with Bob Scully.

Years later, Moore said ... : Lee Moore e-mail to author, March 20, 2011. I talked to Moore's friend Ruben Saleda, who has a doctorate from the University of South Florida. Saleda said he was convinced that what Moore wanted him to do was illegal and thus he refused to even touch the seedpod. Saleda also said he remembers it happening in 2005, not 2002, but Moore is insistent that the orchid was "something new and unnamed," which would make it 2002. He mentions taking flasks to Saleda in an August 2003 e-mail.

Three days after Tasker's ... : Carol Kaesuk Yoon, "New Orchid Species Leaves Admirers Amazed," *New York Times,* August 13, 2002.

Instead, the Times *piece* ... : Carol Kaesuk Yoon, "New Orchid Species Leaves Admirers Amazed," *New York Times,* August 13, 2002; interview with Christenson.

After that story ran, Moore ... : Moore's fax to Kovach was part of the evidence in *U.S. vs. Kovach.*

However, the relationship between ... : Interview with Kovach.

Agent Holt read the ... : Holt's report, with copies of the news reports attached, is part of the Fish and Wildlife Service investigative file on the Kovach–Selby Gardens case.

Lowman was in her office ... : Lowman, Burgess, and Burgess, *It's a Jungle Up There,* 202.

Based on what they heard . . . : The reports on the interviews with the OIC scientists and with Dave Hunt are part of the Fish and Wildlife Service investigative file on the Kovach–Selby Gardens case.

Under questioning, Hunt yielded . . . : The report on Hunt's interview part of the Fish and Wildlife Service investigative file on the Kovach–Selby Gardens case.

She told me, You . . . : Interview with Dave Hunt.

In the meantime, a University . . . : August 16–17, 2002, e-mail exchange between the University of Florida's Lorena Endara, Cal Dodson, and Wesley Higgins, provided by Higgins.

Just to be on the . . . : August 16, 2002, e-mail exchange between Bruce Holst and Ricardo Fernandez, provided by Higgins.

What he didn't say . . . : Interview with Ricardo Fernandez.

The knock on Kovach's . . . Interviews with Kovach and Roddy Gabel; Agent Holt's report on serving the search warrant is part of the evidence in *U.S. vs. Kovach.*

Gabel already knew Kovach's . . . : Interview with Roddy Gabel.

"They came in like . . .": Interview with Kovach.

Gabel, meanwhile, headed for . . . : Interview with Gabel.

Nevertheless, Gabel and his . . . : The inventory of everything seized in the raid is contained in Holt's report, which is part of the evidence in *U.S. vs. Kovach.*

"You know that show . . .": Ian Shapira, "Horticulturist in an Exotic Predicament," *Washington Post,* December 29, 2002.

On the same day Holt . . . : The subpoena and a report on how it was served are part of the evidence in *U.S. vs. Selby Gardens.*

The document they delivered . . . : Lowman, Burgess, and Burgess, *It's a Jungle Up There,* 202–3; interview with Lowman.

She called her husband . . . : Interview with Lowman.

She had already gotten . . . : Interview with Scully; Lowman, Burgess, and Burgess, *It's a Jungle Up There,* 205

After talking to her . . . : Interview with Lowman.

The next morning, she . . . : In *It's a Jungle Up There* (203), Lowman says she woke up at 4:00 a.m. and sent the e-mail to Atwood. She told me it was 5:00 a.m. But the time stamp on the e-mail (which is part of the Fish and Wildlife Service's Selby investigative file) says she sent it at 7:00 a.m.

In response to her request . . . : Interview with Lowman; Lowman, Burgess, and Burgess, *It's a Jungle Up There,* 203.

The most alarming response . . . : Interview with Lowman.

Chapter 9. The Last Condor

Part of the allure of . . . : Koopowitz, *Tropical Slipper Orchids,* 17.

Back on June 5, 2002 . . . : Interview with Atwood.

Thus, when the herbarium . . . : Atwood's August 27, 2002, letter to Lowman, included as evidence in *U.S. vs. Selby Gardens.*

Telling the story years . . . : Interview with Atwood.

Would you kill . . . : According to Jeff Tucker, the Tampa crisis management specialist whom Selby Gardens later hired to deal with the publicity fallout from the investigation, the "condor" comparison is the one that the OIC scientists themselves brought up that day.

Everything hinged on whether . . . : Dalström's August 27, 2002, letter to Lowman, included as evidence in *U.S. vs. Selby Gardens*.

Or, as he put it . . . : Interview with Atwood.

Even if Kovach's permits weren't . . . : Dalström's letter to Meg Lowman is dated September 15, 2002—after Atwood had revealed what they had done.

Who made this fateful . . . : Interview with Atwood.

He identified the colleagues . . . : Interviews with Atwood, Dalström, and Higgins.

When the orchid boys . . . : Atwood testimony to grand jury, July 9, 2002, included as evidence in *U.S. vs. Kovach*.

There was another way . . . : Interview with Atwood.

When he was younger . . . : Interview with Atwood.

When he got to . . . : Interview with Atwood.

Months later, after the . . . : Atwood testimony to grand jury, July 9, 2002, included as evidence in *U.S. vs. Kovach*.

"What I did do . . .": Atwood testimony to grand jury, July 9, 2002, included as evidence in *U.S. vs. Kovach*.

Atwood knew his slippers. . . . : Interview with Atwood.

Although Atwood had been . . . : Atwood's August 27, 2002, letter to Lowman, included as evidence in *U.S. vs. Selby Gardens*.

Atwood's argument, which would . . . : I spent four years covering criminal courts prior to becoming the paper's environmental reporter, so I contacted several of my former sources on the court beat and got this reaction.

Lowman, reading through Atwood's . . . : Interview with Lowman; Lowman, Burgess, and Burgess, *It's a Jungle Up There*, 203.

She called her husband . . . : Interview with Lowman.

"The gardens has hired . . .": Lowman August 27, 2002, e-mail to Atwood, from the Fish and Wildlife Service investigative file on the Selby case.

Chapter 10. The Law and the Loophole

Instead of protecting . . . : Koopowitz, *Tropical Slipper Orchids*, 60.

Guido Braem speaks four . . . : Interview with Braem; Braem's resume accessed at: http://faculty.ed.umuc.edu/~gbraem/about.html.

But he may be best . . . : Hansen, *Orchid Fever*, 157.

On February 12, 1973, delegates . . . : Train, *Politics, Pollution, and Pandas: An Environmental Memoir*, 144–45; *CITES World*, special edition, March 3, 2003, 3, www.cites.org/eng/news/world/30special.pdf.

Previous treaties, some with . . . : *CITES World*, special edition, March 3, 2003, 2, www.cites.org/eng/news/world/30special.pdf.

The late 1960s had . . . : John C. Whitaker, "Earth Day Recollections: What It Was Like When The Movement Took Off," EPA website, www.epa.gov/history/topics/earthday/10.htm; Andrew O'Hehir, "When We Thought We Could Save the Earth," *Salon*, August 14, 2009, http://mobile.salon.com/ent/critics_picks/2009/08/14/earth_days.

The IUCN had been the . . . : Interview with Lee Talbot.

In 1972, the United Nations . . . : *CITES World*, special edition, March 3, 2003, 3, www.cites.org/eng/news/world/30special.pdf.

Talbot convinced his White House . . . : Interview with Talbot.

The original negotiations leading . . . : Interview with Talbot; Train, *Politics, Pollution, and Pandas*, 143–45; Hansen, *Orchid Fever*, 217–18.

In the end, however . . . : Train, *Politics, Pollution, and Pandas*, 143–45; interview with Talbot; *CITES World*, special edition, March 3, 2003, 2–3, www.cites.org/eng/news/world/30special.pdf.

The treaty said the . . . : U.S. Fish and Wildlife Service Division of Management Authority website, www.fws.gov/international/dma_dsa/Permits/web_list_cites.html.

The public heard little . . . : A search of Lexis-Nexis and the Google News Archive for 1973 turned up only a few perfunctory stories about CITES, none of them fully encompassing the scope of what was going on—no surprise, since I found similarly superficial coverage of the passage by Congress of the Endangered Species Act that same year; *CITES World*, special edition, March 3, 2003, 3, www.cites.org/eng/news/world/30special.pdf.

The CITES treaty that won . . . : *CITES World*, special edition, March 3, 2003, 3, www.cites.org/eng/news/world/30special.pdf; International Fund for Animal Welfare press release, "CITES Conservation Crisis," March 25, 2010, www.ifaw.org/ifaw_canada_english/media_center/press_releases/3_25_2010_61036.php.

What marked CITES' biggest . . . : Bean and Rowland, *The Evolution of National Wildlife Law*, 495–99.

The rules about the species . . . : Valerie Cochran, "Pre-Booker CITES Enforcement: Will the Booker Decision Impact CITES' Role in Stemming the Illegal Trade in Wildlife and Plants?" University of South Carolina School of Law, April 22, 2006, 23–24, http://law.sc.edu/environmental/papers/200611/eas/cochran.pdf.

The largest single group . . . : U.S. CITES website on orchids, www.uscites.gov/species/orchid.

The attitude that most . . . : Motes, *Orchid Territory*, 3. The author is the wife of Florida orchid grower Martin Motes, and according to the jacket copy of this comic novel, she "has more awarded orchids named after her than anyone else, one of the latest being Vanda Mary Motes, Best in Show, at the World Orchid Conference, Dijon, 2005."

In 1986, Braem was . . . : Hansen, *Orchid Fever*, 156–58. Hansen tells this story in greater, and more amusing, detail. Braem confirmed its accuracy for me.

In the 1980s, an adventurer . . . : Hansen, *Orchid Fever*, 69–76, 81–86.

The newspapers ate it . . . : Hansen, *Orchid Fever*, 13, 72; Dick Donovan, "Raider of the Lost Orchids," *Weekly World News*, July 18, 1989.

Eighteen months later, in . . . : "Court Case Strengthens Plant Protection Law," *New Scientist*, June 17, 1989; Hansen, *Orchid Fever*, 85.

Eventually, though, an appeals . . . : Hansen, *Orchid Fever*, 86; "Second-Class Species," *New Scientist*, July 22, 1989.

Dealers in rare orchids . . . : Hansen, *Orchid Fever*, 86; "Second-Class Species," *New Scientist*, July 22, 1989.

However, Eric Hansen's book . . . : Hansen's book touched off a storm of debate, as well as demands by some of the scientists involved that he retract his charges. He responded with a four-page letter in which he strongly defended his evidence and challenged critics to take him to court. None has. His letter, posted online, may be accessed at www.cnyos.org/E%20Hansen-letter.pdf.

After he walked out . . . : A BBC documentary called *The Mythologist* examines his tangle of identities as "émigré, diplomat, adventurer, orchid-smuggler, crop circle researcher, UFO investigator, [and] phone pest." The film's website may be accessed at www.mythologist.co.uk/film.html.

The same year Azadehdel stood . . . : Hansen, *Orchid Fever*, 79–80. According to Hansen, Philip Cribb was not only Azadehdel's chief accuser but also one of the primary advocates of switching slipper orchids to Appendix I.

Their concerns were fueled . . . : Koopowitz, *Tropical Slipper Orchids*, 55, 57.

Although no studies had . . . : Koopowitz, *Tropical Slipper Orchids*, 55, 57; interview with Koopowitz.

However, according to Harold . . . : Koopowitz, *Orchids and Their Conservation*, 118.

Nobody at the CITES . . . : Interview with Koopowitz.

Before the new rule took . . . : Interview with Koopowitz; Koopowitz, *Orchids and Their Conservation*, 120.

How effective was this . . . : Jim Doyle, "Indonesian Pleads Guilty to Smuggling Orchids," *San Francisco Chronicle*, November 30, 1994; Jim Doyle, "Black Market Orchids," *San Francisco Chronicle*, January 8, 1995; Phyllis Orick, "Petal Pushers," *SF Weekly*, February 22, 1995; David Ferrell, "Fancying Forbidden Flowers," *Los Angeles Times*, March 5, 1995; "5-Month Prison Term for Orchid Smuggler," *San Francisco Chronicle*, April 15, 1995; TRAFFIC Bulletin 16, no. 3 (March 1997): 53.

As Dodson pointed out . . . : Interview with Dodson.

In Agent Holt's affidavit . . . : Holt search warrant affidavit included as evidence in *U.S. vs. Kovach*.

A story by New Scientist . . . : Stephanie Pain, "The Case of the Stolen Slippers," *New Scientist*, June 24, 1989, 53.

Then, in 1995, Atwood . . . : Jim Doyle, "Black Market Orchids," *San Francisco Chronicle*, January 8, 1995.

Yet, like all orchid fanciers . . . : John Beckner, Orchid Conservation Committee newsletter, August 1991.

The main flaw in CITES . . . : Interview with Harold Koopowitz; Koopowitz, *Tropical Slipper Orchids*, 63; Hansen, *Orchid Fever*, 17; David Ferrell, "Fancying Forbidden Flowers," *Los Angeles Times*, March 5, 1995.

But let some botanical . . . : Hansen, *Orchid Fever*, 17. I should add that I heard this same refrain from nearly every orchid hobbyist and expert I interviewed.

Roddy Gabel, the Fish . . . : Interview with Gabel.

Ironically, despite all of . . . : Hansen, *Orchid Fever*, 173–76.

Selby's own rules required . . . : Higgins e-mail to Peter Croezen, July 19, 2002, provided by Higgins.

"We follow the standard . . .": Chris Grier, "Flower of discord," *Sarasota Herald-Tribune*, September 1, 2002.

Lee Moore said in . . . : Interview with Lee Moore.

That was never considered . . . : Interview with Carl Luer.

The pugnacious Guido Braem . . . : Interview with Braem.

So when word of . . . : At the time I was reporting on this case for the *St. Petersburg Times*, I printed out reams of these discussions on the *Orchid Guide Digest* LIST-SERV and several others that are no longer online.

Under CITES, botanical gardens . . . : Interviews with Roddy Gabel and Guido Braem.

That was Selby's defense . . . : Interviews with Wesley Higgins, Stig Dalström, and Bob Scully.

According to Braem, the . . . : Interview with Braem.

However, the CITES rules are . . . : David L. Roberts and Andrew R. Solow, "The Effect of the Convention on International Trade in Endangered Species on scientific Collections," *Proceedings of the Royal Society B*, doi:10.1098/rspb.2007.1683.

According to Braem, the CITES . . . : Interview with Braem; Holt's search warrant affidavit included in evidence used in *U.S. vs. Kovach*.

Because botanical gardens such . . . : Interview with Braem.

"Everyone treats it with . . .": Interview with Eric Christenson.

As it turned out, though . . . : Charging documents in *U.S. vs. Selby* and *U.S. vs. Higgins*.

But Stig Dalström's assumption . . . : Dalström testimony to grand jury, June 11, 2003, included as evidence in *U.S. vs. Kovach*.

Lee Moore couldn't believe it . . . : Moore's August 15, 2002, e-mail to Higgins, provided by Higgins.

Still, some of Selby's orchid . . . : Lowman, Burgess, and Burgess, *It's a Jungle Up There*, 206.

Instead of hiding behind . . . : Transcript for "Orchid Hunter," *NOVA*, November 26, 2002, www.pbs.org/wgbh/nova/transcripts/2915_orchid.html.

That just proved how . . . : "Orchid Fracas," *Science*, September 27, 2002, 2205, www.sciencemag.org/cgi/content/short/297/5590/2205a.

And naming the orchid . . . : Interview with Christenson.

Chapter 11. The Circular Firing Squad

I don't want to . . . : Hansen, *Orchid Fever*, 232.

Agent Holt knocked on . . . : Interview with John Atwood; Holt's report of Atwood interview and orchid seizure included in U.S. Fish and Wildlife Service investigative file on Selby Gardens.

When Lowman had informed . . . : Interview with Lowman.

The mild-mannered Atwood . . . : Interview with Atwood.

He lived on a plot of . . . : Interview with Atwood.

They grilled him for three . . . : This is Atwood's estimate. Holt's report does not specify a length for the interrogation.

At one point Holt . . . : Interview with Atwood.

Given his qualms about . . . : Interview with Atwood.

Atwood sent Lowman, Higgins . . . : Atwood's September 23, 2002, e-mail to Lowman and Higgins, provided by Higgins.

Although Peru's INRENA was . . . : Agent Holt's report on the seizure of the orchid from Atwood, included in U.S. Fish and Wildlife Service's investigative files on Selby and Higgins.

On September 1, 2002, the . . . : Chris Grier, "Flower of Discord," *Sarasota Herald-Tribune*, September 1, 2002.

Selby drew its revenue from . . . : Chris Grier, "Flower of Discord," *Sarasota Herald-Tribune*, September 1, 2002; Selby Gardens' IRS Form 1099 for 2001–2, obtained via GuideStar.

That same day, Lowman . . . : Interview with Scully; Tom Bayles, "8th Selby Gardens Trustee Resigns," *Sarasota Herald-Tribune*, October 20, 2003; Dorothy Stock-bridge-Pratt, "Longboat Key Tour Has Mix of Homes," *Sarasota Herald-Tribune*, February 25, 2006; Roberta C. Nelson, "Ancient Art of Bonsai," *Bradenton Herald*, August 4, 2006.

He counted himself as . . . : Interview with Lowman; Tom Bayles, "8th Selby Gardens Trustee Resigns," *Sarasota Herald-Tribune*, October 20, 2003.

Fedder and Lowman explained . . . : Interviews with Lowman and Scully.

When Scully heard about . . . : Interview with Scully.

But he didn't blame . . . : Interview with Scully.

Then Lowman and Fedder showed . . . : Interview with Scully.

Scully had to break . . . : Interview with Scully.

Some of them also . . . : Interviews with Scully, Caren Lobo, Carl Luer, and Barbara Hansen.

They were already annoyed . . . : Interviews with Scully and Caren Lobo.

Many of the board . . . : Interviews with Lowman, Carl Luer, and Caren Lobo.

One board member, a . . . : Interview with Caren Lobo.

But Lowman, when she . . . : Interviews with Lowman and Carl Luer.

Privately, Lowman wanted to . . . : Interview with Lowman; Lowman, Burgess, and Burgess, *It's a Jungle Up There*, 204.

One board member who . . . : Interview with Carl Luer.

In the end, the board . . . : Interviews with Carl Luer, Caren Lobo, Bob Scully, and Bob Richardson.

"We were always hopeful . . ." : Interview with Bob Richardson.

Thus Selby's newly hired . . . : Interview with Bob Scully.

With Scully's approval, Lowman . . . : Interviews with Lowman and Scully.

The growing controversy over . . . : Interviews with Harold Koopowitz, Glen Decker, Peter Croezen, and Eric Christenson.

On September 2, 2002, the . . . : George Norris's September 2, 2002, e-mail to Wesley Higgins and the subsequent exchange between them provided by Higgins.

"I KNOW THAT LEE MOORE . . ." : This is one of the most tantalizing clues in the case, but one the Fish and Wildlife Service apparently did not pursue because there is no mention of it in the investigative records. On August 10, 2003, Moore

sent an e-mail to Bob Scully, Dr. Rolando, Michael Kovach, Harold Koopowitz, Stig Dalström, Wesley Higgins, and Agent Holt, among others, responding to a variety of accusations from Norris and Arias. One accusation: Moore had been smuggling in seedpods of *Phragmipedium kovachii* to grow in a "secret greenhouse" in Miami. In his e-mail, Moore wrote: "These seed pods are legally imported with proper documentation, and the 'secret greenhouse' is the laboratory of RIO Ruben in Orchids where they are flasked and returned to my nursery in Peru when ready for propagation. None are sold in the U.S. or anywhere else. I do not take orchids from Peru. I bring back orchids to Peru for propagation." The proprietor of Ruben in Orchids, Ruben Saleda, told me Moore offered him kovachii seedpods, but he refused to so much as touch them because he feared what Moore was doing might be illegal.

The uproar over Kovach's . . . : Interviews with Lee and Chady Moore, Ricardo Fernandez, and Alfredo Manrique.

Chady Moore focused on . . . : Interview with Lee and Chady Moore.

The Spanish-language broadcast . . . : Lee and Chady Moore provided me with an unedited videotape of the interviews and other footage used in this broadcast.

"From this day the media . . .": Karol Villena e-mail to author, July 10, 2010. She did not respond to e-mails I sent her containing follow-up questions.

However, the family couldn't . . . : September 26, 2002, announcement of the end of Renato Villena's candidacy, provided by both Lee Moore and Wesley Higgins.

Then Lee Moore tried . . . : Moore's October 4, 2002, e-mail to Turkel provided by Wesley Higgins, who was among the twenty or so people copied on the message.

Just as the United States . . . : Interview with Alfredo Manrique; club history from its website, www.clubperuanodeorquideas.com/nosotros.html.

But the club members were . . . : Isaias Rolando e-mail to INRENA announcing the Peruvian Orchid Club's position, September 25, 2002, provided by Higgins.

They didn't buy Kovach's . . . : Chris Grier, "Flower of Discord," *Sarasota Herald-Tribune*, September 1, 2002.

The members of the Peruvian . . . : Interview with Alfredo Manrique; *Orchid Guide Digest* website entry, July 18, 2008, headlined "Dr. Isaias Rolando passing," www.mail-archive.com/orchids@orchidguide.com/msg11466.html; Peruvian Orchid Club history page on website, www.clubperuanodeorquideas.com/nosotros.html.

Three years later, during . . . : Interviews with Alfredo Manrique, Eric Christenson, and Stig Dalström; Isaias Rolando, "Fifteen Years of In-Situ Conservation at Machu Picchu," *Selbyana* 26, no. 1, 2 (2005): 134–35.

Not everyone at Selby . . . : Interview with Stig Dalström.

Dalström was not alone . . . : Interview with George Norris.

When the Machu Picchu hotel . . . : Interviews with Alfredo Manrique and Eric Christenson.

Over the years, Rolando had . . . : *Orchid Guide Digest* website entry, July 18, 2008, "Dr. Isaias Rolando passing," www.mail-archive.com/orchids@orchidguide.com/msg11466.html.

In early October 2002 . . . : Report by Agent Santiago and Agent Holt of conversation with Dr. Isaias Rolando, included as evidence in *U.S. vs. Kovach*.

This was not the . . . : Georgia Tasker, "Orchid Intrigue," *Miami Herald*, August 10, 2002; Lee Moore's August 7, 2002, fax to Michael Kovach included in evidence used in *U.S. vs. Kovach.*

The trip was delayed . . . : Interviews with Lee and Chady Moore; Lee Moore's July 6, 2003, e-mail to Stig Dalström and Holt's report of Lee Moore's July 10, 2003, interrogation, included in U.S. Fish and Wildlife Service investigative file on Kovach.

The most important thing . . . : Its importance became clear during Kovach's sentencing hearing (see chapter 17).

Before they left, though . . . : Moore—who referred to bottles just like these in his August 10, 2003, e-mail to Holt and others—now denies telling the agent he was growing *maxillaria* in the bottles. He also denies that he was doing anything illegal with the seedpods he says he brought in from Peru and later took back there.

During their visit, Holt . . . : Holt's follow-up report and report on the August 7, 2003, interrogation of Moore, included in U.S. Fish and Wildlife Service investigative file on Kovach.

However, Moore said later . . . : Interview with Lee Moore.

Chapter 12. The Stories They Told

Without a good memory . . . : Reinekka, *A History of Orchids*, 293.

The Washington Post *finally . . .* : Ian Shapira, "Horticulturist in Exotic Predicament," *Washington Post*, December 29, 2002.

By now Selby's board . . . : Interviews with Bob Scully, Caren Lobo, and Bob Richardson.

To make matters worse . . . : U.S. Fish and Wildlife Service's March 7, 2003, letter to Selby Gardens, Selby's March 24, 2003, responses, and the Fish and Wildlife Service May 6, 2003, response, all included in Selby investigative file. Selby's attorneys attempted to meet with U.S. Department of the Interior officials to protest the suspension, but after Elinor Colbourn objected, that meeting was canceled, according to U.S. Fish and Wildlife Service e-mails in the Selby investigative file.

The investigation had also . . . : Interviews with Wesley Higgins and Stig Dalström; Lowman, Burgess, and Burgess, *It's a Jungle Up There*, 205.

The OIC staff had at . . . : Interviews with Stig Dalström and John Beckner.

Atwood complained to colleagues . . . : John Atwood's September 9, 2002, e-mail to an unidentified colleague at Missouri Botanical Gardens included as evidence in U.S. Fish and Wildlife Service Selby Gardens investigative file.

Before long, John Beckner . . . : Interviews with John Beckner and Bob Scully. Holst did not respond to a request for an interview.

Under the pressure of . . . : Interview with Stig Dalström.

The investigation into what . . . : The January 21, 2003, e-mail from Paul Tobias of the Scripps Research Institute in La Jolla, California, to Meg Lowman and Wesley Higgins, and the e-mail exchange between Higgins and Lowman on how to respond, provided by Higgins.

Beckner did not relish . . . : Interview with Beckner.

But Selby's involvement in . . . : Interview with Bob Scully.

Then, on Valentine's Day . . . : Eric Christenson's February 14, 2003, e-mail, provided by Christenson.

The grand jury investigating . . . : Description of grand jury room from Bob Scully, Stig Dalström, and Selby's attorney, A. Brian Albritton, who later served as U.S. attorney in Tampa.

Kovach, as one of the . . . : John Murawski, "Flower's Power," *Palm Beach Post,* March 9, 2003.

The first witness stood . . . : Transcript of Agent Holt's March 26, 2003, testimony before the grand jury included as an exhibit in *U.S. vs. Kovach.* Normally grand jury testimony is secret, but the attorneys in Kovach's case cited some of the testimony in their pretrial motions and then included the entire transcript as an exhibit.

Colbourn stood five foot two . . . : Author's observations of Colbourn's appearance; Colbourn's background from *Environmental Law,* a publication of the Yale Law School Career Development Office, June 2009, 17–18, www.law.yale.edu/documents/pdf/CDO_Public/cdo-10-Enviro_Guide-PUBVERSION.pdf.

Some prosecutors are pragmatists . . . : Observation based on author's four years of covering criminal courts; interviews with Scully and with defense attorneys A. Brian Albritton, Jack Fernandez, and Robert Hearn.

She lacked the vanity that . . . : A search of the Department of Justice website turned up no press releases containing her name. In 2004, when she was one of a group of people given a conservation award by the Fish and Wildlife Service, she was the only one who did not pose for a photo with the agency official handing out the plaques.

Although she was a mother . . . : Interviews with Jack Fernandez and Robert Hearn; Associated Press, "Trial Set for Four Accused of Importing Illegal Lobsters," *Tuscaloosa News,* October 29, 2000; Jim Leusner, "Smuggling Ring Suspect Sent to Miami," *Orlando Sentinel,* August 12, 1998; Linda Goldston, "Smuggling Probe Snares San Diego Zoo Curator," *San Jose Mercury News,* August 7, 1999.

What Colbourn found more . . . : *Environmental Law,* a publication of the Yale Law School Career Development Office, June 2009, 17–18, www.law.yale.edu/documents/pdf/CDO_Public/cdo-10-Enviro_Guide-PUBVERSION.pdf.

Now, in the grand jury . . . : Transcript of Agent Holt's March 26, 2003, grand jury testimony included as an exhibit in *U.S. vs. Kovach.*

As Colbourn and Holt . . . : May 7, 2003, letter from Peruvian Embassy to U.S. Fish and Wildlife Service included in Fish and Wildlife Service investigative file on Selby Gardens. The letter references a prior letter of August 9, 2002, but that letter was not provided by the agency in response to my FOIA request.

The response from the . . . : Fish and Wildlife Service's May 29, 2003, response to Peruvian embassy included in Fish and Wildlife Service investigative file on Selby Gardens.

At one point, Colbourn . . . : Agent Holt's report detailing the March 26, 2003, request sent to Interpol and the December 16, 2003, response included in Fish and Wildlife Service investigative file on Selby Gardens. The part of the report identifying the source of the tip was redacted prior to its release to me, but in court Kovach's attorneys attempted to blame Lee Moore, and Colbourn revealed that the tipster was Christenson.

Christenson's own trip to . . . : Interview with Eric Christenson.

The grand jury had subpoenaed . . . : Interviews with Bob Scully, Meg Lowman, Stig Dalström, John Atwood, John Beckner, Wesley Higgins, and A. Brian Albritton.

The board's anxiety over . . . : Interviews with Meg Lowman and Bob Scully; Tom Bayles, "Selby's Deep-Rooted Discord," *Sarasota Herald-Tribune*, September 23, 2003.

Dalström warned several board . . . : Interview with Stig Dalström.

By now the uproar . . . : "Blooming Mad," *People* 59, no. 9, March 10, 2003, www.people .com/people/archive/article/0,,20139502,00.html.

In June 2003, two months . . . : Kovach, Global Paphiopedilum Alliance newsletter, June 2003.

This was the story . . . : Interview with Lee Moore.

What Moore didn't realize . . . : Colbourn made this clear during Kovach's sentencing hearing (see chapter 17).

The blond-haired man settled . . . : Transcript of Stig Dalström's June 11, 2003, testimony to the grand jury included as an exhibit in *U.S. vs. Kovach.*

Although he didn't show it . . . : Interview with Dalström.

Despite his annoyance, he . . . : Transcript of Stig Dalström's June 11, 2003, testimony to the grand jury included as an exhibit in *U.S. vs. Kovach.*

Harry Luther, who had . . . : Interview with Luther.

As the investigation continued . . . : Interview with Bob Scully.

When Agent Holt showed . . . : Interview with Cal Dodson.

When the gardens' attorney . . . : Interview with Bob Scully.

To help deal with . . . : The crisis manager was Jeffrey Tucker of Tucker/Hall Inc. of Tampa: www.tuckerhall.com/ab_tucker.html.

For board member Bob Richardson . . . : Interview with Richardson.

Scully says he did . . . : Interviews with Richardson and Scully.

Richardson had once pledged . . . : Interview with Richardson.

Lowman had begun considering . . . : Interview with Meg Lowman.

In the negotiations with . . . : Interviews with Bob Scully, Meg Lowman, and Caren Lobo.

"I didn't want to be . . .": Gina Edwards, "Law & Orchid," *Florida Trend*, December 2004, www.floridatrend.com/article.asp?aID=44349.

So on a trip to . . . : Interviews with Meg Lowman and Robert Rivas.

The man who showed . . . : Interview with Atwood; transcript of John Atwood's July 9, 2003, testimony to the grand jury included as an exhibit in *U.S. vs. Kovach.*

By the end of July . . . : Tom Bayles, "Selby's Deep-Rooted Discord," *Sarasota Herald-Tribune*, September 23, 2003.

Farr's resignation proved to . . . : Tom Bayles, "Selby's Deep-Rooted Discord," *Sarasota Herald-Tribune*, September 23, 2003; interviews with Barbara Hansen, Caren Lobo, Carl Luer, and Bob Scully.

Normally the Selby trustees . . . : Interview with Lowman.

The July 26, 2003, special . . . : Sean Roth, "Bruised, Pruned, but Budding Again," *Gulf*

Coast Business Review, June 18, 2004; interviews with Meg Lowman, Barbara Hansen, Bob Scully, Carl Luer, and Caren Lobo.

Scully's replacement as chairman . . . : Interview with Hansen; Sean Roth, "Bruised, Pruned, but Budding Again," Gulf Coast Business Review, June 18, 2004.

Hansen tracked Lowman down . . . : Interviews with Barbara Hansen and Meg Lowman; Tom Bayles, "Selby's Deep-Rooted Discord," Sarasota Herald-Tribune, September 23, 2003.

"It's a tragedy what . . .": Tom Bayles, "Selby's Deep-Rooted Discord," Sarasota Herald-Tribune, September 23, 2003.

Farr agreed to return . . . : Tom Bayles, "Selby's Deep-Rooted Discord," Sarasota Herald-Tribune, September 23, 2003; interviews with Bob Scully and Bob Richardson; Tom Bayles, "Turmoil Grows in Gardens," Sarasota Herald-Tribune, August 22, 2003; Tom Bayles, "Donations to Selby Gardens Dwindle over Turmoil," Sarasota Herald-Tribune, August 26, 2003; Tom Bayles, "8th Selby Gardens Trustee Resigns," Sarasota Herald-Tribune, October 20, 2003.

The turmoil soon claimed . . . : Tom Bayles, "Selby's Deep-Rooted Discord," Sarasota Herald-Tribune, September 23, 2003; interview with Hansen; Sean Roth, "Bruised, Pruned, but Budding Again," Gulf Coast Business Review, June 18, 2004.

In October 2003, Bob . . . : Interview with Scully.

Scully would be the . . . : This is one of many points in the narrative that make me wish that the Department of Justice had allowed Colbourn to speak to me about the case.

Chapter 13. The Judges

The overall desire to . . . : Glen Decker, "Phragmipedium kovachii," Orchids, November 2007, 829.

The last witness turned out . . . : The transcript of Agent Holt's November 19, 2003, testimony included as an exhibit in U.S. vs. Kovach.

Jim Clarkson and Mark Jones . . . : Interviews with Mark Jones and Wesley Higgins.

Holt had phoned both . . . : Interview with Mark Jones; Holt's report on her interrogation of Clarkson was included in the U.S. Fish and Wildlife Service's investigative file on Michael Kovach. Sadly, the agency did not provide me with a copy of the tapes, and Clarkson is now dead so I could not interview him.

When Holt and Colbourn . . . : Interview with Mark Jones; Holt's report on her interrogation of Jones was included in the U.S. Fish and Wildlife Service's investigative file on Michael Kovach. The agency did not provide me with a copy of the tape, and Jones said he could not find his copy in 2010. However, the gist of what he said in the interview with me is confirmed by statements Colbourn made during Kovach's sentencing hearing (see chapter 17).

The next forty-five minutes . . . : Interview with Mark Jones.

On the morning of . . . : Interview with Mark Jones.

What of Kovach's later . . . : Interview with Mark Jones.

Clarkson had told Holt . . . : Agent Holt's report of the Clarkson interrogation is included in the U.S. Fish and Wildlife Service investigative file on Kovach, and his story was also commented on by Colbourn during Kovach's sentencing hearing.

So Holt, in testifying . . . : The transcript of Agent Holt's November 19, 2003, testimony included as an exhibit in *U.S. vs. Kovach.*

A week later, on . . . : Kovach's grand jury indictment, dated November 26, 2003, included in the files of *U.S. vs. Kovach.*

"The whole thing was . . .": Interview with Kovach.

The Justice Department was . . . : Interview with Wesley Higgins.

If Selby balked, Colbourn . . . : Interviews with Bob Scully, Wesley Higgins, Barbara Hansen, and Caren Lobo.

"At a certain point, the . . .": Interview with Caren Lobo.

The growing stack of . . . : Interview with Scully.

Not everyone wanted to . . . : Interview with Carl Luer.

Less than a month after . . . : The December 17, 2003, charging document filed by Colbourn is part of the court files in *U.S. vs. Selby Gardens and Wesley Higgins.*

Selby's attorney had discussed . . . : Interview with Wesley Higgins.

The plea agreement for . . . : Plea agreement included in court files of *U.S. vs. Selby Gardens and Wesley Higgins.*

As part of his plea . . . : Interview with Higgins.

Later, when she wrote . . . : Agent Holt's report on the questioning of Higgins is included in the U.S. Fish and Wildlife Service's investigative file on Selby Gardens.

On January 6, 2004 . . . : Interviews with Higgins, Hansen and the gardens' attorney, A. Brian Albritton; change of plea documents included in the files of *U.S. vs. Selby Gardens and Wesley Higgins.*

When it came Higgins's . . . : Interviews with A. Brian Albritton and Wesley Higgins.

Four months later, on . . . : Sentencing documents included in *U.S. vs. Selby Gardens and Wesley Higgins.*

"I suppose you'd say . . .": Interview with Barbara Hansen.

At Colbourn's insistence, Selby's . . . : Interviews with Barbara Hansen, Bob Scully, and Wesley Higgins; sentencing documents included in *U.S. vs. Selby Gardens and Wesley Higgins.*

"It's not a good . . .": Interview with Barbara Hansen.

After dealing with Selby's . . . : Higgins's sentencing documents are included in the court files of *U.S. vs. Selby Gardens and Wesley Higgins.*

On his way out of . . . : Interviews with Wesley Higgins and John Atwood.

Even after nailing Selby . . . : Interview with Robert Rivas.

Chapter 14. The Hike from Hell

We are abysmally ignorant . . . : Koopowitz, *Orchids and Their Conservation,* 21.

The first picture Glen . . . : Interview with Glen Decker.

The expedition had been . . . : Interviews with Glen Decker, Harold Koopowitz, and Angela Mirro.

As usual, his critics . . . : Isaias Rolando's January 15, 2003, e-mail to Stig Dalström, provided by Dalström.

Dalström took that as . . . : Interview with Stig Dalström.

He wanted to promote . . . : Interview with Harold Koopowitz.

At a London orchid show . . . : Interview with Harold Koopowitz.

As the trip took shape . . . : Author's observations of the pair.

They rounded out their . . . : Interviews with Harold Koopowitz, Glen Decker, and Angela Mirro.

Once the group landed . . . : Interviews with Alfredo Manrique, Harold Koopowitz, Lee Moore, Peter Croezen, and Glen Decker.

Thus, while other Peruvian . . . : Interviews with Alfredo Manrique, Harold Koopowitz, Peter Croezen, and Glen Decker.

If Manrique's plan worked . . . : Interview with Harold Koopowitz.

The tour group took . . . : Interviews with Harold Koopowitz and Glen Decker.

Outside the airport sat . . . : Interviews with Harold Koopowitz and Lee Moore.

The next day Rolando's . . . : Interviews with Harold Koopowitz and Glen Decker; Harold Koopowitz, "Phragmipedium kovachii in the wild," *Orchid Digest* 67, no. 4 (October/December 2003): 248–55.

"The footpath seemed muddy . . .": Harold Koopowitz, "Phragmipedium kovachii in the wild," *Orchid Digest* 67, no. 4 (October/December 2003): 248–55.

They came to a stream . . . : Harold Koopowitz, "Phragmipedium kovachii in the wild," *Orchid Digest* 67, no. 4 (October/December 2003): 248–55; interviews with Angela Mirro and Harold Koopowitz.

Soon the rain let up . . . : Harold Koopowitz, "Phragmipedium kovachii in the Wild," *Orchid Digest* 67, no. 4 (October/December 2003): 248–55.

By then Koopowitz had noticed . . . : Harold Koopowitz, "Phragmipedium kovachii in the Wild," *Orchid Digest* 67, no. 4 (October/December 2003): 248–55; interview with Koopowitz.

By now the hikers were . . . : Interviews with Harold Koopowitz and Glen Decker.

"There was no way . . .": Interview with Koopowitz.

There, perched on the . . . : Harold Koopowitz, "Phragmipedium kovachii in the wild," *Orchid Digest* 67, no. 4 (October/December 2003): 248–55.

Exhausted and filthy, the . . . : Interviews with Harold Koopowitz and Glen Decker.

At one point, they . . . : Harold Koopowitz, "Phragmipedium kovachii in the Wild," *Orchid Digest* 67, no. 4 (October/December 2003): 248–55.

Now Decker and Koopowitz . . . : Interviews with Glen Decker and Harold Koopowitz.

On the return trip . . . : Interviews with Glen Decker and Harold Koopowitz.

On the drive back . . . : Harold Koopowitz, "Phragmipedium kovachii in the Wild," *Orchid Digest* 67, no. 4 (October/December 2003): 248–55.

The next day, Camacho . . . : Interviews with Alfredo Manrique and Harold Koopowitz.

Instead, Decker said, he . . . : Interview with Glen Decker.

Ultimately they had to . . . : Interviews with Glen Decker, Harold Koopowitz, Alfredo Manrique, and Angelo Mirro.

"It was incredible," Mirro . . . : Interview with Angela Mirro.

Later, Mirro returned to . . . : Interview with Angela Mirro; information about Smithsonian exhibit from its website, http://asbalosingparadise.blogspot.com/2010/07/slipper-orchid-watercolor-by-angela.html.

He also brought back . . . : Interview with Harold Koopowitz.

Decker came home from . . . : Interviews with Glen Decker, Alfredo Manrique, and Peter Croezen.

Six weeks after their . . . : Interviews with Glen Decker and Harold Koopowitz.

Not long after the . . . : Interviews with Lee and Chady Moore, Glen Decker, and Harold Koopowitz.

In July 2003, Arias . . . : Manuel Arias Silva's July 17, 2003, e-mail to George Norris, and Norris's forwarding of that e-mail on the same date, provided by Wesley Higgins.

A week after passing . . . : George Norris's July 23, 2003, e-mail to his customers, and Eric Christenson's July 24, 2003, forwarding of that e-mail to Agent Holt, also went to Lee Moore and Wesley Higgins, and was provided to me by Wesley Higgins.

The tip came in April . . . : A June 2, 2003, report about how the case started and the steps taken prior to searching Norris's home (penned by an agent whose name was redacted by the agency) is included in the U.S. Fish and Wildlife Service's investigative file on the George Norris and Manuel Arias Silva case.

In October 2003, three . . . : The search warrant and report on the October 22, 2003, search of Norris's house are included in the U.S. Fish and Wildlife Service's investigative file on the George Norris and Manuel Arias Silva case.

They also had him . . . : The affidavit written by George Norris is included in the U.S. Fish and Wildlife Service's investigative file on the George Norris and Manuel Arias Silva case.

"Let me assure y'all . . ." : George Norris's October 31, 2003, posting on the *Orchid Guide Digest* Internet forum was forwarded via e-mail by Peter Croezen to Lee Moore and Wesley Higgins and provided to me by Higgins.

A sympathetic Arias sent . . . : A copy of the November 13, 2003, Arias letter to Norris about the raid is one of the exhibits in the case of *U.S. vs. Norris and Arias.*

Chapter 15. The Courtroom Drama

We have strict statutes . . . : William Shakespeare, *Measure for Measure*, act 1, scene 3.

Facing the power of . . . : Interview with Michael Kovach.

He couldn't look to . . . : Prosecution's list of expert witnesses included in the filings of *U.S. vs. Kovach.* The third expert witness listed by the prosecution was Norris Williams of the University of Florida.

When Kovach talked about . . . : Interview with Kovach.

Jack Fernandez and Robert Hearn . . . : Interviews with Kovach, Jack Fernandez, and Hearn.

Fernandez flew to Virginia . . . : Interview with Jack Fernandez.

As Hearn and Fernandez . . . : Interview with Hearn.

The attorneys decided that . . . : Interviews with Jack Fernandez and Hearn.

Stig Dalström had been . . . : Interview with Dalström.

She asked him again...: Transcript of Stig Dalström's January 22, 2004, testimony to the grand jury included as an exhibit in *U.S. vs. Kovach.*

When he left the witness...: Interview with Stig Dalström. Because I could not interview Agent Holt or the prosecutor, we have only Dalström's word on this.

The motion Kovach's attorneys...: Kovach's motion to dismiss included in the filings of *U.S. vs. Kovach.*

The magistrate overseeing Kovach's...: Wilson's biography is posted on his official website, www.flmd.uscourts.gov/judicialInfo/Tampa/JgWilson.htm.

At the hearing, Hearn...: The court clerk keeps the minutes of hearings, noting the time each attorney begins and ends, as part of the case record.

"The defendant... concedes...": Magistrate's recommended order is part of the case file of *U.S. vs. Kovach.*

On March 3, 2004...: Details of Arias's arrest at the Miami airport and his subsequent interrogation contained in agents' reports included in U.S. Fish and Wildlife Service investigative file on George Norris and Manuel Arias Silva.

Riding in the car was...: Manuel Roig-Franzia, "Undercover to Bust Wildlife Smugglers," *Washington Post*, July 19, 2004. (For a fuller account of the fake gorilla bust, see pages 163–64 in my book *Manatee Insanity*.)

Picon, only months from...: Manuel Roig-Franzia, "Undercover to Bust Wildlife Smugglers," *Washington Post*, July 19, 2004; Picon's report on his interrogation of Arias is included in the Fish and Wildlife Service's investigative file on the George Norris–Manuel Arias Silva case. I should note that while Arias apparently named names, the Fish and Wildlife Service redacted them before releasing the documents to me.

As soon as George and...: Andrew Grossman, "The Unlikely Orchid Smuggler: A Case Study in Overcriminalization," Heritage Foundation Legal Memorandum No. 44, July 27, 2009, www.heritage.org/research/reports/2009/07/the-unlikely-orchid-smuggler-a-case-study-in-overcriminalization; Kathy Norris's July 22, 2009, testimony before the U.S. House of Representatives Subcommittee on Crime, Terrorism and Homeland Security, http://judiciary.house.gov/hearings/pdf/Norris090722.pdf.

A federal grand jury...: The March 11, 2004, indictment of George Norris and Manuel Arias Silva is included in the court papers of *U.S. vs. George Norris and Manuel Arias Silva.*

In an interview with...: Bill Murphy, "Spring Man Faces Indictment over Orchid," *Houston Chronicle*, March 13, 2004.

The indictment listed all...: March 11, 2004, indictment in *U.S. vs. George Norris and Manuel Arias Silva.*

Norris flew to Miami and...: Andrew Grossman, "The Unlikely Orchid Smuggler: A Case Study in Overcriminalization," Heritage Foundation Legal Memorandum No. 44, July 27, 2009, www.heritage.org/research/reports/2009/07/the-unlikely-orchid-smuggler-a-case-study-in-overcriminalization.

Looking for a break...: Unnamed agents' report on George Norris's proffer testimony is included in the U.S. Fish and Wildlife Service's investigative file on Norris and Arias Silva. As with the report on Arias's questioning, the Norris report was provided to me with the names redacted, although I was able to identify a few people from their descriptions in the text. Ironically, when I interviewed him, Norris insisted that he was targeted for prosecution because "I wouldn't rat out my friends."

So in the days preceding . . . : Agents' reports on inspecting the Ecuadorean shipment and Karol Villena's booth at the Redland show contained in the U.S. Fish and Wildlife Service's investigative file on George Norris and Manuel Arias Silva.

At 9:30 a.m. on . . . : Temperature obtained from Weather Underground historical weather database; details of the interrogation of Alfredo Manrique from the agents' report, filed in the George Norris–Manuel Arias Silva investigative file, and from an interview with Alfredo Manrique.

"I am the only . . .": Manrique's quotes are taken from the agents' own report of the interrogation.

Manrique got another surprise . . . : Interview with Manrique.

George Norris was there . . . : Interview with George Norris.

Unlike Kovach, Arias did . . . : Manuel Arias Silva's guilty plea is contained in the court files of *U.S. vs. George Norris and Manuel Arias Silva.*

The judge set a . . . : Exactly how Arias got a new passport and fled the country is not mentioned in the investigative files that the U.S. Fish and Wildlife Service turned over to me. Lee Moore, however, says it would be easy to walk into the embassy and say he'd lost his passport and needed a replacement.

Arias sent the judge a . . . : Arias's undated letter to the judge, mailed July 17, 2004, from Peru, is included in the files of *U.S. vs. George Norris and Manuel Arias Silva.*

The plea for mercy . . . : U.S. District Judge Patricia Seitz sentence on Manuel Arias Silva is included in the files of *U.S. vs. George Norris and Manuel Arias Silva.*

In an odd bit . . . : Department of Justice press release from July 27, 2004, www.justice. gov/opa/pr/2004/July/04_enrd_515.htm. The headline on this Justice Department release always makes me chuckle, suggesting (through its mention of geography) that the judge had sent Arias to something far nicer than prison: "Peruvian Orchid Dealer Sentenced to 21 Months in Miami for Smuggling Protected Peruvian Orchids."

Reporters in Peru tracked . . . : Marco Vasquez and Enrique Flor, "The Peruvian Orchid Thief," Agency Peru, June 13, 2004, http://agenciaperu.com/investigacion/2004/jun/orquideas.htm.

Colbourn tried to extradite . . . : Reports on the extradition attempts included in the U.S. Fish and Wildlife Service investigative file on Manuel Arias Silva and George Norris; the decree of the Peruvian president and cabinet can be accessed on page 37 of this document: http://spij.minjus.gob.pe/Normas/textos/170506T.pdf. I sought access to the U.S. Marshal's Service file on the fugitive orchid dealer so I could better document the efforts to track him down, but the agency's reply to my request said I could only see Arias's file if I could get Arias's permission to look at it—a clear catch-22.

Because Arias had fled . . . : Andrew Grossman, "The Unlikely Orchid Smuggler," Heritage Foundation Legal Memorandum No. 44, July 27, 2009, www.heritage

.org/research/reports/2009/07/the-unlikely-orchid-smuggler-a-case-study-in
-overcriminalization.

Meg Lowman had avoided . . . : Interview with Lowman.

Given the acrimony over . . . : Interviews with Lowman, Bob Scully, and Robert Rivas.

Ultimately, though, Lowman hit . . . : Interview with Robert Rivas. Rivas praised Lowman's husband, Michael Brown, with guiding her defense behind the scenes and keeping Rivas's anger at the government in check.

The Fish and Wildlife Service . . . : Although Lowman's record is clean, a copy of the Notice of Violation and an internal memo noting that she had paid it are both contained in the U.S. Fish and Wildlife Service's investigative file on the Selby Gardens case.

It was considered a . . . : Interview with Robert Rivas.

However, because she was . . . : Interviews with Meg Lowman, Robert Rivas, Bob Scully, and Caren Lobo.

Kovach's attorneys tried negotiating . . . : Interviews with Jack Fernandez and Robert Hearn; transcript of Kovach's sentencing included in court papers in *U.S. vs. Kovach.*

It didn't help that . . . : Kovach's driving record and his drug test came up in the course of his sentencing hearing, which was conducted in open court.

His attorneys tried the . . . : Interviews with Jack Fernandez and Robert Hearn.

Meanwhile, Colbourn signaled that . . . : Colbourn's notice of intent to use testimony from an unindicted co-conspirator is part of the filings in *U.S. vs. Kovach.*

Kovach's attorneys flew The Adventurer . . . : Interview with Lee Moore. Neither Jack Fernandez nor Hearn would discuss this aspect of their case, and no transcript of Moore's deposition was filed with the court, so we only have Moore's word for it.

The defense next tried . . . : The defense motions for records relating to Agent Holt's personnel file and her notes from interviewing Kovach are part of the files of *U.S. vs. Kovach.*

With a trial date looming . . . : The prosecution's efforts to line up witnesses from Peru is commented on in one of Agent Holt's follow-up reports on the case, included in the U.S. Fish and Wildlife Service investigative file on the Kovach case.

Kovach's attorneys decided they . . . : Interviews with Jack Fernandez and Robert Hearn.

On June 11, 2004, two . . . : Kovach's guilty plea included in court papers in *U.S. vs. Kovach*; quotes and observations on setting from author's own coverage of the guilty plea.

Sentencing was set for . . . : U.S. Department of Justice June 10, 2004, press release, www.justice.gov/opa/pr/2004/June/04_enrd_397.htm.

Seven days after Kovach . . . : George Norris's guilty plea is part of the court papers in *U.S. vs. George Norris and Manuel Arias Silva.*

He said it was . . . : Kathy Norris's July 22, 2009, testimony before the U.S. House of Representatives Subcommittee on Crime, Terrorism and Homeland Security, http://judiciary.house.gov/hearings/pdf/Norris090722.pdf.

Norris's attorney tried to . . . : Defense motion for downward departure on sentencing, medical records, and letters of support for the defendant, included in *U.S. vs. Norris and Arias.*

The prosecutors—one of . . . : The government's response to the defense motion is included in *U.S. vs. Norris and Arias.*

George Norris, Kovach's original . . . : Norris's sentencing included in *U.S. vs. George Norris and Manuel Arias Silva.*

Chapter 16. The Scarlet Letters

There is that in . . . : John Muir, *A Thousand-Mile Walk to the Gulf* (Boston and New York: Houghton Mifflin, 1916), 108.

The congress had been planned . . . : Interviews with Bob Scully and Wesley Higgins.

And even though Wesley . . . : Interview with Wesley Higgins.

Selby's leaders hoped the . . . : Interviews with Wesley Higgins and Stig Dalström; Chris O'Donnell, "Experts Converge on Selby," *Sarasota Herald-Tribune*, May 20, 2004.

Actually, according to Higgins . . . : Interview with Wesley Higgins.

Dalström, unfazed by the . . . : Interview with Stig Dalström.

At eighteen dollars apiece, he made . . . : Interviews with Stig Dalström and Wesley Higgins.

The pressure proved to be . . . : Interview with Ricardo Fernandez; Ricardo Fernandez's March 19, 2004, e-mail to Higgins and Dalström, with the e-mails from Croezen attached, provided by Dalström.

This climactic gathering would . . . : Interviews with Bob Scully, Stig Dalström, and Wesley Higgins.

The attendees included Phillip . . . : List of attendees from Selby's published IOCC program, accessed online at www.selby.org/index.php.?src=gendocs&link=iocc&category=researc; Cribb, (2005), 511: "Phragmipedium kovachii," *Curtis's Botanical Magazine* 22 (2005), 8–11; interview with Harold Koopowitz.

Also there was Ted . . . : Interview with Ted Green.

Harold Koopowitz, who had . . . : Interviews with Koopowitz, Wesley Higgins, and Bob Scully; Isaias Rolando, "Fifteen Years of In-Situ Conservation at Macchu Picchu," *Selbyana* 25, no. 1, 2 (2005): 134–45; Fernandez's November 2, 2003, letter complaining about Rolando to Dalström, provided by Dalström; interview with Ricardo Fernandez.

Roddy Gabel, the Fish . . . : Interview with Roddy Gabel.

Even though they were . . . : Interviews with Bob Scully, Wesley Higgins, and Roddy Gabel.

Afterward, Gabel said he . . . : Interview with Roddy Gabel.

Rolando got another blast . . . : Interviews with Bob Scully and Wesley Higgins.

Despite his past complaints . . . : Interview with Wesley Higgins.

A month later, the . . . : Rolando's June 4, 2004, e-mail to Higgins, provided by Higgins.

That was, of course . . . : Interview with Wesley Higgins.

So Selby submitted a . . . : A copy of Selby's letter is included in the Fish and Wildlife Service's investigative file on Selby Gardens and Higgins; interviews with Wesley Higgins and Stig Dalström.

The change in the gardens ... : Interview with Marjorie North, society columnist for the *Sarasota Herald-Tribune*.

With Lowman out ... : Lowman, Burgess, and Burgess, *It's a Jungle Up There*, 208; interviews with Bob Scully and Carl Luer.

But the trustees struggled ... : Interview with Caren Lobo; Tom Bayles, "Selby's Deep-Rooted Discord," *Sarasota Herald-Tribune*, September 23, 2003; Chris O'Donnell, "Experts Converge on Selby," *Sarasota Herald-Tribune*, May 20, 2004.

Chapter 17. The Final Showdown

When it's all over ... : Georgia Tasker, "Orchid Intrigue," *Miami Herald*, August 10, 2002.

The big windows that line ... : Author's observations.

The bench sits beneath ... : Author's observations; court clerk's notation of the time the hearing began included in files of *U.S. vs. Kovach*.

This was U.S. District ... : Author's observations from covering Merryday in this case and others; interviews with Jack Fernandez and Robert Hearn; Carrie Weimar, "'Band-Aid Bandit' Judge Works at His Own Pace," *St. Petersburg Times*, April 3, 2007.

Around the courthouse, Merryday ... : Carrie Weimar, "'Band-Aid Bandit' Judge Works at His Own Pace," *St. Petersburg Times*, April 3, 2007; interviews with Jack Fernandez and Hearn.

Now Merryday peered through ... : All the dialogue in this chapter comes directly from the transcript of the sentencing hearing, which is part of the court file in *U.S. vs. Kovach*. All descriptions of how the parties at the hearing behaved are based on the author's observations from covering this hearing for the *St. Petersburg Times*.

Normally, when probation officers ... : Interview with Fernandez and Hearn. The probation officer's report was not part of the court file available to the public, so I was not allowed to see it. But because its contents were discussed at length in open court, we know pretty much everything it said.

Her history took the form ... : Chady Moore, "Chronological History of the Discovery of *Phragmipedium kovachii*," e-mailed on October 7, 2002.

The connection with Lee ... : Kovach's defense attorneys never did provide any evidence that Agent Holt had threatened the Moores, or that such threats had prompted the Moores to send the e-mails and faxes. Given the timing of those messages, and the Moores' own history of dealing with the law, such a scenario seems highly unlikely. Moore himself says it's "a complete lie."

Photographers are not allowed ... : The photos were shot and published by the *Sarasota Herald-Tribune* and the *St. Petersburg Times*.

"I felt relieved," Kovach ... : Interview with Michael Kovach.

Epilogue

The concentrated romance, mystery ... : Reinikka, *A History of the Orchid*, xviii.

As soon as Chuck Acker ... : Interview with Chuck Acker.

Arias had such good . . . : Interview with Chuck Acker; interviews with Lee and Chady Moore and Alfredo Manrique.

When Manrique sought permission . . . : Interview with Alfredo Manrique.

The Moores had a bigger . . . : Interviews with Lee and Chady Moore, Peter Croezen, and Chuck Acker; photos of *Phragmipedium kovachii* shown on the Moores' nursery website, www.nuevodestino-us.com/store/viewItem.asp?idProduct=709.

Still, Moore warned Acker . . . : Interview with Chuck Acker.

So in 2005—even . . . : Interview with Acker; description of Manolo Arias Silva from photos provided by Acker.

Although Harold Koopowitz had . . . : Information on Decreto Supremo No. 043–2006-AG provided by Lee and Chady Moore, Alfredo Manrique, and Peter Croezen.

"What are the exporters . . .": Chady Moore's letter to INRENA was posted on the "Slipper Orchid" Internet forum, www.slipperorchidforum.com/forum/archive/index.php/t-6865.html.

In 2006, a Dutch taxonomist . . . : Interview with Paul van Rijckevorsel; Paul van Rijckevorsel, "Proposal to add Selbyana vol. 23 Supplement to the 'opera utique oppressa,'" *Taxon* 55, no. 4 (November 2006): 1053.

Higgins—now freed from . . . : Wesley Higgins and David H. Benzing, "Response to: Proposal to add Selbyana vol. 23 Supplement to the 'opera utique oppressa' by Paul van Rijckevorsel," *Taxon* 56, no. 3 (August 2007): 968–69.

Not even Peru's top . . . : Blanca León, Betty Millán, Asunción Cano, and Joaquina Albán, "No rules violated, but . . .—A response and comments from the Herbario San Marcos (USM) to Rijckevorsel's proposal to suppress *Selbyana* vol. 23 Supplement," *Taxon* 57, no. 2 (May 2008): 664–65.

Ultimately the committee in . . . : R. K. Brummitt, "Report of the Nomenclature Committee for Vascular Plants: 60," *Taxon* 58, no. 1 (February 2009): 283–84.

While the debate about . . . : Dr. Isaias Rolando's April 2007, postings about the *Phragmipedium kovachii* and the responses that it elicited, www.slippertalk.com/forum/showthread.php?t=3278.

"It is happening already . . .": Rolando's May 10, 2007, posting and the responses it elicited were on the same "Slipper Talk" thread as his April posting, www.slippertalk.com/forum/showthread.php?t=3278.

In January 2008, a jubilant . . . : Curtis Morgan, "World Orchid Conference," *Miami Herald*, January 23, 2008.

Before long, Rolando was . . . : Interview with Alfredo Manrique.

On the night of . . . : Interview with Alfredo Manrique; "Doctor Found Dead at Club Regatas Lima," *El Comercio*, July 16, 2008, http://elcomercio.pe/ediciononline /html/2008–07–15/medico-fue-hallado-muerto-instalaciones-club-regatas-lima .html; Israel Ruiz, "Peru: Man Found Dead at Upscale Lima Country Club," *Living in Peru* website, www.livinginperu.com/news-6903-law-and-order-peru -man-found-dead-upscale-lima-country-club.

He tried to contact . . . : Interview with Alfredo Manrique.

About 8:00 p.m., a . . . : "Doctor Found Dead at Club Regatas Lima," *El Comercio*, July 16, 2008, http://elcomercio.pe/ediciononline/html/2008–07–15/medico -fue-hallado-muerto-instalaciones-club-regatas-lima.html; Israel Ruiz, "Peru:

Man Found Dead at Upscale Lima Country Club," *Living in Peru*, www.living inperu.com/news-6903-law-and-order-peru-man-found-dead-upscale-lima-country-club; "Médico se lanza de puente peatonal en club Regatas," *La Republica*, July 16, 2008, www.larepublica.pe/archive/all/larepublica/20080716/pasadas/12/160006.

Was it suicide? Initially . . . : I could not find any online mention of this TV report, but heard about it from both Alfredo Manrique and Lee Moore; interviews with Manrique and Ricardo Fernandez. I attempted to contact Rolando's widow in 2010, but got no response. Manrique, who gave me her contact information, said she was still grieving and did not want to talk about her husband's death.

"There's been a lot . . .": Interview with Wesley Higgins.

"He was always a . . .": Interview with Glen Decker.

The mystery doesn't surprise . . . : Interview with George Norris. When I spoke to Norris in 2010, he did not know until I told him that Rolando had died. His first reaction was a sarcastic quip: "It couldn't have happened to a nicer guy."

Lee Moore wondered if . . . : Interview with Lee and Chady Moore.

Moore shook his head, still . . . : The Moores' chapter 7 bankruptcy case is filed in the U.S. Southern District Court civil division.

Could Rolando's mysterious death . . . : Interview with Alfredo Manrique. *The Maltese Falcon* was originally a book by Dashiell Hammett, published in 1930, but the line about "the stuff that dreams are made of" is found in the 1941 movie adaptation written and directed by John Huston, starring Humphrey Bogart as detective Sam Spade.

In 2005, Selby sold . . . : Interviews with Wesley Higgins, Stig Dalström, and John Beckner.

Thanks to Beckner's departure . . . : Interview with Stig Dalström.

The loss of so many . . . : Cooper Levey-Baker, "While Some Selby Gardens Insiders Say Poor Management and Risky Finances Have Imperiled the Sarasota Institution, Current Leadership Insists the Organization Is Stronger Than Ever," *Creative Loafing*, February 10, 2010; Selby Gardens' IRS 1099 form obtained via GuideStar.

In February 2009, Selby's . . . : Debby Steele, "Marie Selby Botanical Gardens Announces New Chief Executive Officer," Selby Gardens press release, February 20, 2009, www.selby.org/index.php?src=news&refno=70&category=Press%20Releases&PHPSESSID=a8867e400f5ef2d9cb2ebb476f68fd92.

Buchter's mission was to . . . : Interview with Thomas Buchter. In addition to answering my questions with patience and good humor, Selby's current CEO was kind enough to give me a lengthy behind-the-scenes tour of Selby Gardens. Afterward, though, he reneged on a promise to send me a photo of himself, or to have his staff supply me with photos of Marie Selby and others connected with the gardens.

For Higgins, this was . . . : Interview with Wesley Higgins.

Still, Higgins had done . . . : Interview with Wesley Higgins; Higgins's motion for early termination of probation, the objections of the prosecutor, and the judge's order granting the motion are all contained in the files of *U.S. vs. Selby Gardens and Wesley Higgins*.

But now, thanks to . . . : Interview with Wesley Higgins.

Dalström, on the other...: Interview with Stig Dalström; *"Wild Orchid Man"* website, http://wildorchidman.com/.

With both Higgins and...: Interviews with Carl Luer and Thomas Buchter. Wesley Higgins's termination agreement included a promise he would not say anything bad about Selby, and in our interviews he scrupulously held true to those terms.

The shutdown sent a...: Cooper Levey-Baker, *Creative Loafing*, February 10, 2010.

Then the unthinkable occurred...: Interview with Harry Luther.

Buchter insists Selby is...: Interview with Buchter.

The fact that Dalström...: E-mail from Marni Turkel to the author; Anthony Cormier, "Selby Orchid Controversy Made Bradenton Botanist Famous," *Sarasota Herald-Tribune*, April 13, 2011.

His obituary in the...: Cormier, "Selby Orchid Controversy Made Bradenton Botanist Famous," *Sarasota Herald-Tribune*, April 13, 2011.

Another of the kovachii's...: Andrew Grossman, "The Unlikely Orchid Smuggler: A Case Study in Overcriminalization," Heritage Foundation Legal Memorandum No. 44, July 27, 2009, www.heritage.org/research/reports/2009/07/the-unlikely-orchid-smuggler-a-case-study-in-overcriminalization.

Two years later, though...: Andrew Grossman, "The Unlikely Orchid Smuggler," Heritage Foundation Legal Memorandum No. 44, July 27, 2009, www.heritage.org/research/reports/2009/07/the-unlikely-orchid-smuggler-a-case-study-in-overcriminalization.

That same summer, Norris's wife...: Kathy Norris's July 22, 2009, testimony before the U.S. House of Representatives Subcommittee on Crime, Terrorism and Homeland Security, http://judiciary.house.gov/hearings/pdf/Norris090722.pdf.

A year after the Heritage...: Interview with George Norris.

In September 2010, a Peruvian...: Miguel Sarria, "Los peruanos más buscados por Interpol," *Peru21*, September 12, 2010, http://peru21.pe/noticia/637992/peruanos-mas-buscados-interpol.

A few days after the...: Interview with Lee Moore.

Up in Vermont, John...: Interview with John Atwood; *A. David Moore Pipe Organs* website, www.adavidmooreorgans.com/aboutus.html.

The one kovachii he did...: E-mails from Christine Flanagan and Rob Pennington of the U.S. Botanic Garden to the author.

Ultimately, Higgins contended, what...: Interview with Wesley Higgins.

Kovach still lives in Virginia... Interview with Michael Kovach.

Agent Holt showed up...: Holt's March 2005 report on returning Kovach's property is included in the Fish and Wildlife Service investigative file on Kovach.

But that was fine with...: Interview with Kovach.

Dalström, as he was about...: Interview with Stig Dalström. The visitor, of course, was me. A picture of the statue of the *Phragmipedium kovachii* is posted on a Moyobamba tourism website, www.moyobamba.net/galeria/displayimage.php?album=lastup&cat=0&pos=0.

Selected Bibliography

Bean, Michael, and Melanie Rowland. *The Evolution of National Wildlife Law*. Westport, Conn.: Praeger, 1997.

Berliocchi, Luigi. *The Orchid in Lore and Legend*. Translated by Lenore Rosenberg and Anita Weston. Portland, Ore.: Timber Press, 1996.

Box, Ben, and Alan Murphy. *Footprint Peru Handbook*. Bath, U.K.: Footprint Handbooks, 2003.

Chadwick, A. A., and Arthur E. Chadwick. *The Classic Cattleyas*. Portland, Ore.: Timber Press, 2006.

Conover, Ted. *The Routes of Man: How Roads Are Changing the World and the Way We Live Today*. New York: Knopf, 2010.

Darwin, Charles. *On the Various Contrivances by Which British and Foreign Orchids Are Fertilised by Insects, and on the Good Effects of Intercrossing*. London: John Murray, 1862.

Fara, Patricia. *Sex, Botany, and Empire: The Story of Carl Linnaeus and Joseph Banks*. New York: Columbia University Press, 2003.

Grismer, Karl H. *The Story of Sarasota*. Sarasota, Fla.: M. E. Russell, 1946.

Hansen, Eric. *Orchid Fever: A Horticultural Tale of Love, Lust, and Lunacy*. New York: Pantheon Books, 2000.

Koopowitz, Harold. *Orchids and Their Conservation*. Portland, Ore.: Timber Press, 2001.

———. *Tropical Slipper Orchids: Paphiopedilum and Phragmipedium Species and Hybrids*. Portland, Ore.: Timber Press, 2008.

Lasky, Kathryn, and Christopher G. Knight. *The Most Beautiful Roof in the World: Exploring the Rain Forest Canopy*. New York: Harcourt Brace, 1997.

Lowman, Margaret D. *Life in the Treetops: Adventures of a Woman in Field Biology*. New Haven: Yale University Press, 1999.

Lowman, Margaret D., Edward Burgess, and James Burgess. *It's a Jungle Up There: More Tales from the Treetops*. New Haven: Yale University Press, 2006.

Luer, Carlyle A. *The Native Orchids of Florida*. New York: New York Botanical Garden, 1972.

McDonald, James. *Wordly Wise*. New York: Franklin Watts, 1985.

Motes, Mary. *Orchid Territory*. Petaluma, Calif.: Woodrunner, 2006.

Nolan, David. *Fifty Feet in Paradise: The Booming of Florida*. New York: Harcourt Brace Jovanovich, 1984.

Orlean, Susan. *The Orchid Thief.* New York: Random House, 2000.

Reinikka, Merle A. *A History of the Orchid.* Coral Gables, Fla.: University of Miami Press, 1972.

Short, Philip. *In Pursuit of Plants: Experiences of Nineteenth and Early Twentieth Century Plant Collectors.* Portland, Ore.: Timber Press, 2003.

Starn, Orin, Carlos Ivan Degregori, and Robin Kirk, eds. *The Peru Reader: History, Culture, Politics.* Durham, N.C.: Duke University Press, 2006.

Stout, Rex. *Black Orchids.* New York: Pyramid Books, 1941.

Stuart, David. *The Plants That Shaped Our Gardens.* Cambridge: Harvard University Press, 2002.

Train, Russell. *Politics, Pollution, and Pandas: An Environmental Memoir.* Washington, D.C.: Island Press, 2003.

Van der Pijl, L., and Calaway Dodson. *Orchid Flowers: Their Pollination and Evolution.* Coral Gables: University of Miami Press, 1966.

Wehner, Ross, and Renee del Gaudio. *Moon Peru.* Emeryville, Calif.: Avon Travel, 2007.

Wilson, Edward O. *The Diversity of Life.* Cambridge: Belknap Press of Harvard University Press, 1992.

Index

Moore, 102; and Meg Lowman, 15–16, 85, 89–90, 132–34, 153, 158–59, 161, 163, 197, 204; at Orchid Ball, 12; as orchid show judge, 16, 55; and publicity over case, 148; as Selby board chairman, 15, 86, 88–89, 133; and Selby plea deal, 169; spots something missing on *P. kovachii* holotype, 108–10; volulnteers at Selby, 14–15; warned by Cal Dodson, 89; and Wesley Higgins, 32, 84–85

Selby, Bill, 17–19

Selby, Marie, 4–5, 16, 18–21, 27, 196, 249, 287

Selbyana (Selby's scientific journal), 84–92, 108, 177, 188, 201, 218, 254, 263–64, 273, 284, 286

Selby Foundation, 21, 26

Selby Gardens: *See* Marie Selby Botanical Gardens

Slipper Talk internet forum, 233–34, 265

Southwind Orchids (nursery), 57, 141, 241

St. Petersburg Times, 2, 6, 172, 243, 247–48, 251–52, 271, 285, 306

Talbot, Lee, 116–17, 269

Tarapota, Peru, 29, 58–59, 176, 258

Tasker, Georgia, 100–101, 265–66, 274, 285

Turkel, Marni, 66–67, 72–74, 125, 137, 238, 257–61, 264, 273, 288

U.S. Department of Agriculture, 44, 92–93, 95–96, 165, 186, 193, 210–11, 216–17, 219, 256, 258, 261, 265

U.S. Fish and Wildlife Service, 255; investigates George Norris and Manuel Arias Silva, 183–84, 189–91, 193, 258, 260, 280–82; investigates *P. kovachii*, 94, 104, 107, 109, 130–32, 141, 143, 149, 196, 211, 256–58, 262, 265–68, 271–72, 274–75, 277–78, 283–84, 288; investigative files of, 245; news coverage, 100, 127; praised by Eric Christenson, 99, 147; pressured by Peruvian government, 152, 275; questioning of Alfredo Manrique, 193; raid on Michael Kovach's house, 106, 255; receives complaint from Peru, 91, 264; and Roddy Gabel, 71, 106, 125, 202; and smuggling, 49, 123, 256, 261

van Rijckevorsel, Paul, 231, 286

Villena, Karol, 56–57, 59, 67, 72, 74, 97, 104, 135, 137, 175, 182, 192, 257–61, 264, 273

Villena, Renato, 56–59, 62–65, 67, 73–74, 80, 88, 93, 95, 104, 137–38, 156, 183, 207, 215, 231–32, 257–61, 273

Vivero Agro-Oriente (nursery), 43–44, 56–57, 59, 62, 63–64, 67, 73, 75, 104, 137, 207, 215, 257, 264

Washington Post, 145, 258–59, 267, 274, 281

World Orchid Conference, 234, 269, 286

Craig Pittman is an award-winning environmental reporter for the *St. Petersburg Times.* He is the author of *Manatee Insanity: Inside the War over Florida's Most Famous Endangered Species,* and coauthor, with Matthew Waite, of *Paving Paradise: Florida's Vanishing Wetlands and the Failure of No Net Loss.* He lives in St. Petersburg with his wife and two children.